CONTENTS

LIST OF ILLUSTRATIONS

Color

On the jacket: A Game of Polo (detail). Painting on silk. Attributed to a Chinese artist of the late fifteenth or early sixteenth century. Victoria and Albert Museum, London.

DEFINITION OF CHINA

Chinese Isolation and Originality

Like India—even more than India—China is an entire continent. True, it is directly attached and adheres by its whole
hinterland to the enormous mass of the world of the steppes
and of Central Asia. As recent events sufficiently prove, it forms
a part of *Eurasia*. But geographically it turns its back upon
Central Asia and upon the world of the steppe, like its rivers
which flow the other way and follow the slope of its plains,
and like its shores which face an ocean that for thousands of
years remained without an opposite shore. Until the surprisingly
belated discovery of America, China was really one of the extrem-
ities of the world. But Eurasia itself—the total continent
composed of Asia with its terminal peninsula, Europe—did not
reveal itself as such before the beginning of the first century B.C.,
when the Chinese emperor Han Wu-ti, by his conquests extending to Pamir, established contact between the classic East and
the Far East. Up to that time China had always lived in a self-
contained world. Indeed, from the 'cultural' point of view, this
self-containment was really broken in upon only in the first
century A.D., with the introduction of Buddhism, and in a political sense three centuries later, with the first great Tartar invasions. If we situate the origins of China's proto-history at

about the beginning of the second millennium B.C., we thus have some twenty-three centuries of isolated and continuous civilization before the irruption of the outside world. Passively committed though it was to the Eurasian base, the 'continent of China' during this immense span of time none the less enjoyed all the advantages of insularity. For, as geographers know, high frozen plateaux and desert solitudes form far more effective barriers than the sea between civilizations that have sprung up at the opposite points of their periphery.

For the elaboration of a civilization that was in all respects original, China was thus assured an exceptional situation from the start. We have only to consider that such a privilege was accorded neither to Greece, immemorially in symbiosis with the old cultures of Near Asia, nor to India itself, which, from the pre-Aryan civilization of the Indus valley (Mohenjo-daro) to the Graeco-Buddhist, also remained more or less constantly in contact with Near Asia. To find an isolation comparable to that of China, extending over thousands of years, we should have to turn to pre-Columbian America. But the Amerindians, despite an undeniable creative power, never produced human values as universal as the Chinese world.

An isolation so prolonged, making possible so long an incubation sealed off from all contacts, inevitably endowed Chinese culture with a powerful originality. But this originality, as in the case of the pre-Columbian and Negro civilizations, might have developed only conceptions that were practically closed, untranslatable into foreign thinking. It so happened that the Chinese mind, like the Greek mind, like the Latin mind, possessed such a predisposition to general ideas that, like Greece and Rome, it 'thought universally'. Like the Graeco-Roman genius, the Chinese genius, on its side of the planet, has created a wisdom, an art, a humanism that are complete.

To eastern Indochina, to Korea and to a part at least of Central Asia, China through its scholars and its 'legionaries' has thus been both Greece and Rome. Even in a country where its arms never penetrated, and where it therefore could not assume the role of Rome (I am thinking of Japan), China has performed a work of 'Hellenization' that has endured. By virtue of this, and from the point of view of its natural satellites, it merits its title of *Middle Kingdom*, just as Greece, with its holiest of sanctuaries, was entitled to regard itself as the *omphalos* of the Mediterranean world.

The characteristic feature of Chinese civilization is, then, that it is one of the great original civilizations of humanity, a civilization having made its law prevail far and wide, civilizing and humanizing a large part of Asia. But if China's historic mission had been limited to this task—in truth, a capital one—it would nevertheless have remained for a long time in total isolation, reduced to playing a kind of 'pre-Columbian' role. What is striking about Chinese history is that after having had the time, in the course of some twenty centuries, to develop this wholly original culture within its tight confines, China should have been able to establish contacts—maintained almost continuously ever since—with some of the highest civilizations of the outside world.

These contacts began to develop in the first century of our era with the introduction of Buddhism, which brought with it the best of Indian thought, of Indian art, and through Indian art a rather close reflection of Greek art as of the arts of Iran. Later and over the same caravan trails were to come Nestorian Christianity and Manicheism, not to mention Islam. We shall see the considerable influence of such contributions—of Buddhism, of course, first and foremost. Yet the only route that the men who introduced these diverse influences had at their disposal was the double caravan trail through present-day Chinese Turkestan or Sinkiang—the Silk Road—a route stretched out across such an immensity of desert reaches, of mountain ranges and high plateaux as to prevent any wholesale invasion of foreign ideas. Through the centuries and the solitudes, external influences could thus reach the Chinese continent only in minute doses.

There was always time for them to be assimilated and, whatever their qualitative importance, they stimulated Chinese originality without ever imperilling it.

To these historic influences by way of the caravan trails should perhaps be added, for a much more remote past, immemorial contacts with the neolithic cultures of Eastern Europe. In the first half of the second millennium B.C. we shall in fact see a polychrome pottery with spiral ornamentation spreading in Northern China, which would seem to have originated in Rumania and the Ukraine. It must be borne in mind, however, that in the Far East the finest of these potteries have been found in a peripheral province (Kansu), which was then outside of China; that their designs have hardly left a trace on the subsequent evolution of Chinese ornamentation and that the remote art influences in question thus cannot have had an effect on the development of the Chinese genius.

Agrarian Foundations of Chinese Civilization

Chinese originality, as we have seen, remains entire. Does this mean that what we may call the 'miracle of China', as we speak of the 'miracle of Greece', is really inexplicable? By no means. Chinese humanism, like Mediterranean humanism, is immediately explained by human geography. The two have, it is true, different foundations. Like the pre-Hellenic civilizations before it, like Phoenician civilization alongside of it, like the Indonesian or Japanese civilizations in Eastern Asia, Greek civilization grew up under the preponderant influence of the sea. The most archaic Chinese civilization, on the other hand, like the Babylonian or the Egyptian under the Pharaohs, was pre-eminently a land civilization, based on the tilling of the soil. All three possessed an alluvial soil, annually made fertile by the river flood, by a 'gift of the River', as Herodotus says of Egypt and as we could equally well say of the Great Plain of China. But in all three cases, too, the 'Count of the River' (Ho-po)

1. *Jar, earthenware, from Pan-shan (Kansu). Second millenium B.C. Musée Cernuschi, Paris.*

was looked upon, as the Chinese admit with mingled gratitude and terror in connection with the Yellow River, as a formidable benefactor who must be attentively observed, used, appeased, curbed. The extraordinary fertility of the soil that it has created with its silt and that it continues to enrich, can be maintained only so long as the annual inundation is curbed and domesticated by a whole system of canals, and only so long as the flood is controlled by a system of carefully maintained dikes.

The essential function of the chief—whether he be Egyptian pharaoh, Sumerian *patesi* or archaic Chinese *wang*—thus consists in maintaining this system of canals and dikes.[1] The king of alluvial lands, who is both hydraulic engineer and agronomist, must forecast, watch for and determine, with the same solicitude as the moment of the life-giving inundation, the time of sowing, the time of harvest, the time of garnering; in each case he has to make the agrarian cycle coincide with the seasonal cycle or, as the ancient Chinese expressed it, 'the Earth with Heaven'. By virtue of these various functions, his 'chieftainship' is essentially 'calendrical', his powers, his 'heavenly mandate' (*t'ien ming*), being derived from the observation of the stars. The pantheons of Mesopotamia, of Egypt, and of China are in large part to be explained by this double origin—agrarian and astronomic—even as the stable, utilitarian and relatively peace-loving character of the royal institution in the three countries has its source in an agricultural priesthood so conceived. It matters but little that there can obviously have been no contact in the archaic period between the 'Fertile Crescent' of Near Asia and the stretches of loess * and alluvial soil of North China. Human geo-

---

[1] Of Yü the Great, the legendary founder of the first Chinese dynasty of the Hsia, the *Shih Chi* tells us, 'Yü spent his strength in digging canals and in building dikes. He guided the rivers'. (*Shih Chi*, 2).

* Loess, better known to us by the name 'yellow earth' (*huang t'u*), is a fine grained rock or soil covering most of China like a blanket, filling up depressions and lying deepest in the valley bottoms. Its depth varies from 300 feet, in parts of Kansu, to 50 feet or less. (See William Willetts, *Chinese Art*, London, 1958, p. 33). (Translator's note).

graphy, when it is rooted in analogous physical conditions, impresses upon human groupings, in other respects so different, a pattern that is at times rather similar.[2]

The archaic Chinese dynasty that was to enjoy the longest reign, the Chou (1027-256 B.C.) had as its ancestor 'Prince Millet' or Master of the Harvests (*Hou-chi*). And along with the 'Lord on High' (*Shang-ti*) who is *T'ien*, Heaven personified, ancient China was to worship the 'Earth-Sovereign (*Hou-tu*) who is essentially the 'god of the soil' (*she*)—of the cultivated soil, in this case.

We must, however, beware of definitions that are too schematic. Beyond any doubt the essentially agrarian bent of the primitive Chinese people was to predispose them, in the realm of the mind, to a wholly social conception of wisdom, to a utilitarian and perhaps somewhat limited philosophy, to a positivist turn of mind that was to manifest itself in a certain kind of Confucianism. The same could probably be said of Babylonian thought and of one whole aspect of Semitic wisdom, both in Mesopotamia and in Phoenicia. Yet it is Mesopotamian society, which produced the 'Gilgamesh Epic' and the poem of the 'Righteous Sufferer' as early as the period of Sumer and Accad, that reveals to us the whole anguish of metaphysical speculation. So it is in China. Despite a peasant religion whose 'matter-of-factness' can be compared only to the primitive Roman religion, despite the virtual agnosticism, as it has been called, of the wisdom of Confuceism, China is the country to which we owe

---

[2] See P. Gourou, *La Terre et l'homme en Extrême-Orient*, 2d ed. Paris (Colin), 1947. And also M. Gourou's lecture, Considérations géographiques sur la Chine, delivered March 18, 1948, at the Centre d'Etudes de Politique Etrangère, rue de Varenne, Paris. We may add that the Yellow River basin may, in the archaic period, have had a warmer and more humid climate than in our day. Cf. the study by our Chinese colleague, Hu Hou Hsüan, Climatic changes. Study of the Climatic conditions of the Yin dynasty. *Bulletin of Chinese Studies*. IV, i, Chengtu, 1944. Review by A. Rygaloff, in *Hanhiue, Bulletin du Centre d'Etudes Sinologiques de Pékin*, II, 4, 1949, p. 431.

the spirituality of philosophical Taoism, the metaphysical exalta-
tion of a Chuang-tzu.

Although Confuceism and Taoism are both related to conceptions that are undoubtedly rather similar in origin (the immemorial prescriptions of sorcerers and soothsayers), it is impossible to imagine a more total divergence. We must resign ourselves to such contradictions with which history, despite theoreticians, abounds. Confucianist society, reaching its perfect expression in the classical mandarinate, has given us the most typical
example both of intellectual positivism and of social traditionalism. And the Taoist Fathers of antiquity, the T'ang poets and
the Sung painters of the middle ages have enriched us with the
most disinterested messages of spiritual release and of cosmic
communion...

Variety and Unity of China

Such outstanding diversities, by revealing to us China's initial
richness, afford an anticipation of that capacity for recovery and
renewal that was to be manifested through the centuries and,
one might almost say, the millennia. We may add, turning to the
Chinese continent itself, the variants that provincial differences
could not fail to contribute to Chinese culture. By far the most
important of these was the broad contrast between Northern
China and Southern China, the former still in symbiosis with the
Great North of the Tartars and the world of the steppes, the
second already in harmony with the world of subtropical Indo-
china.

It may in fact be said that a good part of Chinese history can
be understood only in the light of this contrast: the China of
the loess plateaux or the alluvial Great Plain as against the China
of the Sinian folds; the kingdom of 'Prince Millet' as against
the kingdom of rice. But more than this: even within this general division, secondary subdivisions appear that would have
sufficed, in Europe, to give rise to as many separate nations.

Each Chinese province was a virtual beginning (as it later became a virtual risk) of an autonomous State—autonomous because sufficiently individualized in physical geography and in human geography; a regional particularism that, in each period of 'great crumbling', caused most of the great provinces to recover their temporary independence.

Shensi and Shansi, each on its terraces of loess overhanging the Great Plain, were capable (as history has proved on many an occasion) of barricading themselves in and defending themselves alone against attack. The same was true of Shantung, with its back against a terminal spur (a 'Brittany in reverse') and its holy mountain of T'aishan. The Peking region, transitional between the Mongolian steppe and the Great Plain, retained the character of a border region surveying the world of nomadic hordes to the north, and to the south commanding the immense sweep of ploughed land extending to the Yang-tze. Honan, that 'central flower', the Chinese Touraine, the seat of so many successive capitals, for a long time kept its primacy as an Empire State.

In contrast to this broken-up Northern expanse, where the Yellow River often constitutes an obstacle rather than a link between provinces, the course of the long-navigable Yangtze Kiang forms a link between adjoining regions, even though the valleys of its southern tributaries, distinctly separated by the watersheds, here too favour provincial particularisms. And we must not forget Szechwan, an immense province, peripheral and at the same time rich, committed by its remoteness to a quasi-independence. Finally, a China dedicated to purely maritime pursuits and nursing colonial ambitions was to emerge on the coasts of Fukien and in the region of Canton, which were to serve as stepping stones to the 'Overseas China' of Indonesia and the Pacific.

* * *

Diversity such as this could not fail to influence the mental and artistic evolution of the Chinese people. Geographic oppositions and regional contrasts, moreover, are further emphasized by the fact that the history of China is characterized by a rhythmic alternation between periods of provincial crumbling and periods of consolidation [3].

One of the factors that have periodically made possible the joining together of the Chinese lands is surely the unity of the writing—of the 'characters', which there as elsewhere began by being purely pictographic, then became ideographic. The script was finally standardized during the reign of the first emperor, Ch'in Shih Huang-ti, at the end of the third century B.C.. In the absence of dialectal unity, the 'characters' constituted the common medium of communication, which could subsequently be interpreted as one wished, in pronunciations as varied as present-day Pekingese and present-day Cantonese. It is not inconceivable that the political unity of the West, in Europe, could have been indefinitely maintained, if the Italian, Spanish, French, German and English languages had used an identical ideographic script. But this obvious initial advantage was subsequently accompanied by grave disadvantages for China. The Chinese ideograms, similar in principle to the hieroglyphs of ancient Egypt, as well as to the primitive Mesopotamian cuneiforms, never underwent the Phoenician simplification of the alphabet. Those marvellous ideograms, rich with a vast potential of intellectual developments, containing a mysterious fund of supplementary interpretations and 'explosive' with a whole dynamics of thought, are perhaps a more powerful stimulus to the mind than our poor alphabetic signs. But the practical superiority of these signs, based on the

[3] History will perhaps include among the periods of crumbling the years 1912-1949, despite the diplomatically maintained fiction of the unified states...

principle that the rest of the world owes to the Phoenicians, is
none the less obvious. Chinese culture, having in this respect
remained at the 'hieroglyphic' or 'cuneiform' stage, has thus been
deprived of precious advantages. This, and this alone, accounts
for the apparent immobility of Chinese literature. For while
pronunciation and language evolved, as in other countries, the
characters on the other hand remained practically immutable,
finally absorbing new interpretations as well as different phon-
emes. If we can imagine the Moslems of Irak having kept to the
present day the cuneiform characters of their Babylonian ancestors, and having had to adapt them through the centuries to the
evolution of ideas and techniques, we shall have some understanding of the complexity of the *phenomenon of China.*

If the maintenance of the 'characters' has entailed disadvantages that have not beset the rest of civilization, which progressively adopted alphabetic writing, we must nevertheless recognize
the 'obverse' of the question. Independently of their aesthetic
value, which is such that for 'the arts of the brush' calligraphy
achieved the level of painting (so that painting is often but a
transposition of calligraphy), the ancient Chinese ideograms
remain, as we said, extraordinarily full of ideas, rich with an
immemorial dynamism, vehicles of seminal ideas which have
become progressively accentuated through the ages. There is in
them such a store of riches that the Chinese and Japanese, rather
than abandon this timeless treasure, are willing to subject themselves to a mnemotechnical effort and to a labour of adaptation
well-nigh incredible in our day.

Chinese Continuity and Renewal

The example of the fixed nature of the Chinese characters as
well as of the variations in the Chinese language (and we here
refer the reader to Bernard Karlgren's learned phonetic recon-

structions) [4] suggests to us the complexity of a more general problem: how has the Chinese 'constant' adapted itself to an evolutionary curve, at times even to abrupt mutations, of which the history of art furnishes some startling examples? In this realm, indeed, we find asserting itself a Chinese aesthetics that remains one of the three or four great original and permanent aesthetics of universal humanism. But from period to period, within this same tradition, we witness such a renovation in technique, sensibility and philosophy of art that Chinese art has appeared again and again to become 'its own contrary'. What relation is there between the architecture of the Shang bronzes, so solidly and ruggedly constructed, and the evanescence of the Sung landscapes? Between the severe monochrome of these same Sung washes and the playful polychrome of Ming or Manchu ornamentation? Contrasts, these, as striking as those that separate the statuary of the Parthenon from Byzantine iconography.

The fact is that despite the apparent 'cultural' continuity between the Parthenon and Saint Sophia, society from Pericles to Justinian had entirely charged. Art here merely translated on the surface what was a transformation in depth. Likewise, in the Far East, the transformations of Chinese art give us, almost at first glance, a hint as to the modifications in the structure of Chinese society. And as its curve of evolution extends over nearly thirty-five centuries, we are in the presence of a human experience of fascinating interest.

The present volume (which does not, however, claim to be a history of China) aims to follow this evolutionary curve—that of Chinese society and civilization—by means of the open-sesame of the history of art. The history of art, in turn, will be considered here first and foremost in terms of 'cultural' evolution. We hope in this way to give a correct view of the entity that is China, of

---

[4] Karlgren, *Etudes sur la phonologie chinoise*, Upsala and Leiden, 1915-1926. — *Idem, Analytic Dictionary of Chinese and Sino-Japanese*, London, 1923. — *Idem., Philology and Ancient China*, Oslo, 1926.

its eternal values, of its powers of renewal. A view that concerns the future of all humanity, if we remember that we are considering an ant-hill of four to six hundred million people out of the three billion inhabitants presumed to be living on our planet, and that by the year 2000 the Chinese mass, with its irresistible numerical increase, with its immemorial conceptions, which have often remained unchanged beneath the most unexpected adaptations, will perhaps play a decisive role.

2. Left: Ko, *jade blade mounted in bronze inlaid with turquoise, probably from An-yang. Late Shang Dynasty.* Right: *Nephrite blade mounted in bronze inlaid with turquoise, probably from An-yang. Late Shang Dynasty. Freer Gallery of Art, Washington.*

CHINESE ART AND CULTURE

Chapter One

BEGINNINGS

The Neolithic Age

China experienced the equivalent of the Western paleolithic series. Skeletons have been discovered in Chou-k'ou-tien, south-west of Peking, of *Sinanthropus Pekinensis*, the contemporary of a very archaic fauna preserving Pliocene characteristics, hence ante-dating our Chellean of Europe, even though 'Peking man' already had the use of fire. Later, also in North China, it is presumed that there followed tools of quartzite, equivalents of our Mousterian implements, 'hearths' of Aurignacian aspect, and finally ornamental objects of bone or shell having Magdalenian affinities. But Teilhard de Chardin, who points out these analogies and traces them in this sequence, by no means intends thereby to imply an exact synchronism between each Occidental series and its remote Chinese equivalent. A local chronology, on the other hand, is provided by the stages in the formation of the blanket of loess that today covers a large part of North China: the Sinanthrope, at the base of the loess deposit; the successive paleolithic stages on the various 'steps' of the loess; and the Chinese neolithic on the surface.[1]

[1] See Teilhard de Chardin, Esquisse de Préhistoire Chinoise, *Bulletin catholique de Pékin*, March 1934.

According to legendary traditions Chinese civilization owes its origin to the 'Three Kings' and the 'Five Emperors', patriarchs to whom are attributed the principles of age-old wisdom as well as the labours of clearing land, building dikes and sowing crops that gave rise to agriculture. Beneath these legends we perceive the slow work of generations by which the ancestors of the Chinese people, within the confines of the loess plateaux (in the north-west) and of the alluvial Great Plain (in the north-east) passed from intermittent and semi-nomadic agriculture to sedentary agriculture. This sedentarization, by differentiating the primitive Chinese from surrounding tribes which undoubtedly belonged to the same race but remained at a more backward stage, can properly be said to have created China.[2] These legendary sovereigns, according to Chinese annals, were succeeded by the dynasty of the Hsia (approximately between the twentieth century B.C. and the first half of the sixteenth), then by the dynasty of the Shang-Yin (between the second half of the sixteenth century and the eleventh century B.C.).[3] According to the same traditions, the original seat of power of the Hsia is supposed to have been in the extreme south of the present province of Shansi; that of the Shang in the north-east of the province of Honan. This confirms the fact that Chinese agriculture—hence the Chinese nation—originated within the confines of the loess plateaux and of the Great Plain.

[2] On the originality of the Chinese language and its affinities with certain other languages of the Far East (*Thai*, for example), see Henri Maspero, La Langue Chinoise, in *Conférences de l'Institut Linguistique de l'Université de Paris*, year 1933 (1934), pp. 33-70. Also Bernard Karlgren, *Sound and Symbol in Chinese*, London, 1923 : Georges Margouliès, *La Langue et l'Ecriture Chinoises*, Paris, 1943 : Paul Demiéville, Le Chinois, *Cent cinquantenaire de l'Ecole des Langues Orientales*, Paris, 1948, p. 130.

[3] The Bamboo Annals, a chronicle dating back to the end of the fourth century B.C., gives for the Hsia dynasty, 1989-1558, and for the Shang-Yin, 1558-1051; according to Karlgren's latest revision the last date should be 1523-1028 (Karlgren, *Bulletin of the Museum of Far Eastern Antiquities*, Stockholm, no. 17, 1945, pp. 114-121).

3. *Vase, white pottery, from An-yang. Freer Gallery of Art, Washington.*

4. *Ceremonial vessel, type* ku, *bronze. Shang Dynasty, fourteenth to twelfth century B.C. Musée Guimet, Paris.*

A distinguished specialist in this field, the Swedish archaeologist J. G. Andersson, places the pottery of Ch'i-chia-p'ing, in Kansu, at the beginning of the Chinese neolithic series. We may note that in this case we have to do with a culture both external to and anteceding the true proto-historic civilization of China, since Kansu, at this period, was certainly inhabited by another race and since, if we accept Andersson's relative chronology, the pottery in question belongs to the very height of the 'legendary' period, between 2500 and 2200, and therefore even before the Hsia dynasty. The Ch'i-chia-p'ing vases, some of which have the *kuan* amphora shape, are often decorated with long parallel scores, as though drawn with a comb. The Chinese archaeologist G. D. Wu, on the other hand, relegates the Ch'i-chia-p'ing style to a much later date (about the middle of the Shang period?) [4] And he assigns the pottery found at Hou-kang, in the extreme north of Honan—very simple wares, likewise decorated with parallel streaks, as if incised, but almost without painting—to the beginning of Chinese neolithic pottery-making. In any case, we may note that 'combed' ornamentation existed in early times in the pottery of northern Russia and of Siberia.[5]

Next comes the beautiful polychrome painted pottery, with spiral designs, found particularly at Yang-shao (Honan province) and at Pan Shan (Kansu province). The Yang-shao style dates back, roughly, to the Hsia dynasty (according to Andersson it might extend from 2200 to 1700); the Pan Shan group, with its very elaborate designs, represents a phase that the same archaeologist calls 'middle Yang-shao'. These chronological

[4] Bylin Althin, putting Ch'i-chia-p'ing even later, brings this pottery down to the period of the Shang bronzes (Ch'i-chia-p'ing and Lo-han-t'ang, B.M.F.E.A., Stockholm, Bulletin no. 18, 1946, p. 467). Cf. Sidney Kaplan, Some Observations on Ch'i-chia-p'ing and Li-fan Pottery, Szechwan, *Harvard Journal of Asiatic Studies*, 1948, p. 187.

[5] Menghin placed between 2000 and 1500 the 'recent' phase of 'combed' pottery known in central Siberia, the region of Yenisei, by the tombs of Bazaicha near Krasnoyarsk (*Weltgeschichte der Steinzeit*, p. 80).

hypotheses aside, Pan Shan brings us to a great art, with a magnificent geometrical ornamentation composed of spirals, volutes, 'waves' or festoons, check patterns, lozenges and 'snakeskins', of a strikingly decorative quality. At Pan Shan, likewise, certain wares in this style have anthropomorphic or zoomorphic designs, the neck of the vase being sometimes surmounted by a human head. At Pu-chao-chai, a site close to Yang-shao, belonging to a period called by G. D. Wu 'Yang-shao II', real clay figurines have been discovered. Finally, Pu-chao-chai has yielded very crude earthenware tripods, unpainted, without any other decoration than longitudinal and parallel scores impressed upon the fresh clay, tripods that already have the ritual form of the *li* or *ting* vases and the *hsien* that we shall find again in the archaic Chinese bronzes.[6]

In addition, jade axes, ranging from green to black, have been unearthed in Yang-shao and also in the lower layer of Ch'eng-tzu-yai (in Shantung), the black pottery layer.[7] Fine jades, of a form that is already ritual (the circular *pi*, symbol of Heaven), have likewise been discovered in Pan Shan.

Despite these links with later China, it is well to recall here again that while Yang-shao and Pu-chao-chai were situated well within the proto-Chinese domain, the Pan Shan site where the finest pieces of painted pottery have been found remained definitely outside it. It may further be mentioned that this same painted pottery (in particular the ornamentation of volutes and spirals) somewhat recalls the similar spiral-form decoration of the painted pottery of the Ukraine (in Tripolye, near Kiev), of Bessarabia

---

[6] The Pu-chao-chai site has likewise yielded earthenware vases that anticipate forms of later Chinese bronzes such as the *chia, ku, kuei*, etc. See J. G. Andersson's Prehistory of the Chinese, B.M.F.E.A., Stockholm, 15, 1943, pp. 256-262. Also G. D. Wu, *Prehistoric Pottery in China*, London 1938, and Creel, Les Récents Progrès de l'Archéologie en Chine, *Revue des Arts Asiatiques*, IX, 2, 1935, p. 97.

[7] Andersson, Prehistory of the Chinese, l. c., p. 126, pl. 74.

(at Petreny) and of Rumania (at Cucuteni, near Jassy), dating from about the middle of the third millennium B.C.[8]

Next comes the painted pottery of Ma-chang, a locality likewise situated in Kansu. The Ma-chang ornamentation continues that of Pan Shan, but with special themes: frequent lozenges or circles filled with checks, zigzags, T's and L's intertwined, the whole at times recalling ornamental basket-work; or else lentoid and leaf-shaped designs, perhaps derived from cowrie shells and finally, here too, highly stylized anthropomorphic designs.[9] We may note that the imitation of basket-work and T L designs are to be found again in the bronze age, among the Shang bronzes.[10] According to Andersson, the Ma-chang pottery belongs to the late Hsia period and the beginning of the Shang period immediately anteceding the An-yang bronzes (these being presumed, as we shall see, to have been produced between 1300 and 1028). It might be placed between 1700 and 1300. Andersson, moreover, finds similarities between the Ma-chang ornamentation and that of the neolithic painted pottery recently discovered in Turfan and in Cherchen in Chinese Turkestan.[11] Already we can observe the transmission of influences along the trail of oases of the future 'Silk Road'.

It should be remarked, moreover, that most of the decorative

---

[8] Gordon Childe, *Dawn of European Civilization* (4th ed., London, 1947), places the beginning of Ukrainian civilization or the civilization of Tripolye about 1900 B.C. and situates its last flowering about 1400 B.C. (*loc. cit.*, p. 145). For the present state of the question as regards the culture of Tripolye, Cf. Tatiana Passek, *Classement Chronologique des Colonies de Tripolyé*, Moscow, 1950, and the review in *Soviet Literature*, August 1950, sec. 8, p. 202.

[9] As we know, the cowrie shell (undoubtedly because of its 'religious' meaning) served as currency among several proto-historic populations.

[10] See Max Loehr, Neue Typen grauer Shang-Keramik, in *Sinologische Arbeiten*, Peking, 1943, pl. 1, pp. 86-87, showing the transmission and the evolution of geometric motifs between (1) the painted pottery of Kansu, (2) that of Honan, (3) black pottery, (4) grey pottery, (5) white pottery, (6) the ornamentation of the Shang bronzes.

[11] Folke Bergman, *Archaeological Researches in Sinkiang (Sino-Swedish Expedition)*, 1939, and Andersson, Prehistory of the Chinese, pp. 279-280.

motifs of Yang-shao and of Pan Shan, in particular their fine
spirals, do not recur in those later products of Chinese art proper,
the Shang bronzes. On the other hand, several of the themes developed in the next neolithic phase, found at Ma-chang (check-work
and lozenge designs with angular or T L strip patterns, all equally
in imitation of basketry) were to pass over, as we have just indicated, into the ornamentation of the Shang bronzes.[12] More than
this, we may suspect in a Ma-chang motif (two arms lifted in
the gesture of prayer) the origin of a similar theme from the
Shang period that Umehara was to find both on the white pottery
of An-yang and on a bronze in the Sumitomo collection, a theme
that is in fact a very clear anthropomorphic schematization whose
filiation would thus be established.[13]

At the same time as the painted ware of Eurasian affinities
was being made, neolithic China produced a wholly different type:
the black pottery (ranging from grey to jet-black), which is found
predominantly in the province of Shantung, and may date from
the end of the Hsia dynasty. Often of an extreme fineness and
polished on the outside, this black pottery was made on the
wheel.[14] The site of Ch'eng-tzu-yai (near Tsinan, in Shantung)
where it has been found in abundance, is on the location of a
sizeable neolithic city, surrounded by a rampart of stamped earth
a mile or so in length. Black pottery is also found on the lower
level of Hsiao-t'un (An-yang), a level contemporaneous, it seems,
with Ch'eng-tzu-yai.[15]

---

[12] Loehr, Neue Typen grauer Shang-Keramik, *loc. cit.*, pl. i.

[13] Harada Yoshito, K'uei according to the definition in the Shuowen, *Bulletin
of Eastern Art*, no. 28, Institute of Art Research, Tokyo, April 1942, p. 4, fig. 2.
Compare with Andersson's Researches into the Prehistory of the Chinese, B.M.F.E.A.,
Stockholm, no. 15, 1943, pp. 190-191.

[14] A monograph by the Chinese archaeologist Li Chi (1934). Numerous
specimens of black pottery are to be seen in the museum at Toronto. Several
vases of this pottery conform to the various ritual types of the Shang bronzes that
we shall describe further on. There is also in this museum a statuette in the
round of a passant bull, likewise in black pottery.

[15] Wu, *Prehistory Pottery*, pp. 23, 36 and 59.

Other centres of prehistoric pottery have been discovered in Szechwan, near the gorges of the Yangtze, and in the tombs in the terraced slopes in the surroundings of Li-fan (north of Chengtu). This region has yielded up, successively, a corded pottery, at first very crude; a red pottery with black geometric décor recalling the painted pottery dating from the end of the neolithic period in North China; a black pottery recalling that of Shantung, and a white pottery similar to the Shang pottery of the An-yang excavations.[16] This sequence is interesting. It confirms the fact that the prehistoric and proto-historic civilization attested by the series of potteries was not peculiar to the regions inhabited by the Proto-Chinese (Honan, Shantung), but also extended over regions certainly inhabited by other races, as Szechwan then was, equally with Kansu.

The Civilization of the Shang-Yin

The Shang dynasty, which towards the end received the name of the Yin dynasty, and which according to Karlgren's rectified chronology reigned between 1523 and 1028 B.C., was for a long time nothing more than a name to us.[17] Yet Chinese traditions assure us that these rulers were established on the middle course of the Yellow River, in the north of Honan and its neighbouring districts, that is to say at the junction of the loess plateaux and the alluvial Great plain, in that 'Chinese Touraine' that in fact constitutes one of the most fertile regions of ancient China. The same traditions gave us to understand that in the midst of this wealth of nature the material civilization of the Shang reached a remarkably high level and that the royal court gave free rein

[16] Cheng Te-k'un, *Szechwan Pottery*, West China Union University Museum, Pretty Press (Nicholls and Co.), London, Apollo Annual, 1948, and *The Lithic Industries of Prehistoric Szechwan*, also W.C.U.U.M., Offprint Series no. 1, 1942.

[17] For the Shang chronology, see Karlgren, B.M.F.E.A., Stockholm, no. 17, 1945, p. 121.

to an ostentation and a luxury that could not but bring down upon it the wrath of 'Heaven'. We also know that the last capital of this dynasty (it had had several) was situated in the far north of Honan on the present site of An-yang, whither in 1300 King P'an-keng had transferred his residence and where the seat of royalty, in principle, remained established until the end of the dynasty (1300-1028).[18]

The excavations undertaken in the An-yang district (villages of Hsiao-t'un and Hou-chia-chuang and adjoining fields), at first somewhat haphazardly, but since 1943 methodically, through the instrumentality of the *Academia Sinica* (under the direction of Messrs Fu Ssu-nien, Li Chi and Liang Ssu-yung), have revealed Shang civilization during the last three centuries of its existence.[19] A very great number of secondary tombs have been brought to light, as well as four great Royal tombs, and extending over an area of approximately twenty acres, the foundations, it seems, of an ancient royal palace. The material discovered reveals to us a bronze civilization that had already reached its apogee. In order to explain the attainment of such a degree of perfection we are bound to assume for the preceding epoch (before the year 1300 B.C.) a phase of elaboration during which the technique of

[18] Karlgren, *loc. cit.*, Stockholm, 1945. p. 121.

[19] For a comprehensive view, see the lecture delivered by Pelliot in London in 1936, published under the title, The Royal Tombs of An-yang, *Studies in Chinese Art and Some Indian Influences*, India Society, pp. 51-59. The *Academia Sinica* has published in Chinese four volumes of *Preliminary Reports* on the An-yang excavations (*An-yang fa chüeh pao kao*, Peking, 1929-1933), Tung Tso-ping, *Archaelogia Sinica* II, *Hsiao-t'un*, vol. II. *Yin hsü wen tzu, Chia-pien* (Kegan Paul, London, 1947). Cf. Sueji Umehara, *Kanan anyō ihō. Selected Ancient Treasures Found at An-yang Yin Sites*, Kyoto, 1940, and *Kanan anyō ibutsu no kenkyū. Research on Relics from Anyang*, Kyoto, 1941. In the European languages, the chief work is that of Creel, *The Birth of China*, London, 1936. The most recent studies are J. Leroy Davidson's Note on some An-yang Finds, *Artibus Asiae*, XIII, 1/2, Ascona, 1950, pp. 17-24, and Umehara, Antiquities Exhumed from the Yin Tombs outside Chang te fu, *Artibus Asiae*, XIII, 3, 1950, pp. 149-165, an article supplementing a work by the same author, *On the Shapes of the Bronze Vessels of Ancient China*, Kyoto, 1940.

bronze had become acclimatised in China. Had the knowledge of bronze come to China directly (that is to say through the Turkestans) from Hither Asia, where, in Syria and Mesopotamia, it was already in general use at the end of the third millennium B.C.? [20] Had it come by the Siberian route and was it, as was at one time believed, from Siberia that China learned the technique of bronze? In Siberia, in the region of Minusinsk, there did in fact flourish, between 1200 and 700 B.C., a bronze culture, the Karasuk culture, which roughly corresponds to the An-yang period, but with, it seems, a certain chronological discrepancy. Indeed the latest Soviet research, in particular the work of Professor Kiselev, has proved (we shall come back to this) that it was not Karasuk that influenced An-yang, but on the contrary, the An-yang bronzes that influenced those of Karasuk.

Can we then assume a previous Siberian influence, which might have transmitted the art of bronze to the early Shang before the period of An-yang and of Karasuk? Here again the work of Kiselev may provide an answer.

We may leave aside the earliest of the Siberian 'cultures', that of Afanassievo which radiated to the region of Minusinsk, the upper Jenisei and the Altai in the third millennium B.C. and at the beginning of the second. This is a purely eneolithic culture in which, alongside tools of polished stone, metal appears only towards the end, in the form of copper plaques and rings.[21] There follows the Andronovo period (about 1700-1200), extending from Minusinsk and the Siberian Altai to the north of the Balkash and of the Aral.[22] Bronze makes its appearance here, but apart from a few arrow-heads, needles and awls, it is very rare.[23] The

---

[20] Cl. Schaeffer, *Stratigraphie Comparée et Chronologie de l'Asie Occidentale*, IIIe et IIe *millénaires*, Oxford, 1948.

[21] S. Kiselev, Histoire Ancienne de la Sibérie Méridionale (Drevnaya istoriya yuzhnoi Sibiri), in *Materiali i isleddovaniya po archeologii* S.S.S.R., no. 9, 1949 (chap. II, pp. 14-40 and map, p. 15).

[22] Kiselev, *loc. cit.*, pp. 30-62 and map p. 41.

[23] Id., p. 46.

few bronze daggers also found must belong to the end of the Andronovo period, if not even to the following epoch, the Karasuk. In any case, what we have here is only a very primitive metallurgy that seems hardly capable of having given rise in China to an art of bronze as developed as that of An-yang. It would be more reasonable to seek the direct origins of Chinese bronze in the area of Hither Asia through Iran and Kashgar. We must in any case recognize that no solution is to be anticipated so long as the sites of the first Shang capitals in Honan, antedating An-yang, which hide the secret of the origins of Chinese bronze, have not been excavated.[24]

But what can be done—and Granet has taken this immense task upon himself—is to rediscover the ancient legends relating to the magic powers of the metal-founder and the smith—powers associated with the notion of the *K'uei*, the demi-god dragon (a dragon with a single foot, as in its animalized representations on the Shang of 'Warring States' bronzes). Yü the Great, the legendary founder of the Hsia dynasty, is the metal-founder *par excellence*, and a good part of Chinese primitive magic, with the concordance between the Drum and Thunder, goes back as he does 'to the brotherhood of smiths, custodians of the most wondrous of magic arts and of the secret of the primal powers'.[25] Before him, Huang-ti (the last of the mythical Three Kings) had cast a tripod cauldron, 'after which he rose to Heaven, mounted on a Dragon'. Yü the Great, who in the same way cast nine tripod cauldrons, which after him were the dynastic talismans of the Hsia household, 'was aided in battle against the Fan-feng genii by Dragons and by Thunder'.[26]

Throughout these legends we see to what extent the introduction of metallurgy must have transformed Chinese society,

---

[24] Karlgren, Some Chinese Bronzes in the Museum of Far Eastern Antiquities, B.M.F.E.A., 21, Stockholm, 1949, pp. 22-23.

[25] Marcel Granet, *Danses et Légendes*, p. 611.

[26] Id., *Ibid*, p. 511.

II. *Mirror, bronze inlaid with gold and silver. Chou Dynasty.*

since it is found associated with the most ancient myths and magic practices of the following epoch.

It may be interesting to recall, moreover, that according to the Chinese tradition, if Yü the Great was able to create a dynasty by having cast the nine magic cauldrons of the Hsia, it was because 'the metal had been brought him from the Far Countries and offered in tribute by the Nine Pastors'.[27] Is this a blurred reminiscence of the importation of metallurgy to China through pastoral tribes? [28]

* * *

Although it had already achieved an amazing mastery of the art of bronze, the civilization of the Shang, as the An-yang excavations reveal it, had not wholly relinquished neolithic tools. Knives, axes, even fragments of vases in polished stone, as well as marble vases, are found in An-yang. There is a connection to be made between this industry and the working of jade, a noble material for which the Chinese have always had a special predilection because of the 'virtue' that it contains.

The Shang religion involved, in particular, the worship of ancestors and the practice of divination. The oracle was consulted by means of tortoise-shells or ox-bones, in which cracks produced by the application of heat were interpreted by soothsayers as if

[27] Id., *Ibid*., p. 489.

[28] The first Shang bronzes (those of the hitherto unknown period preceding An-yang) may have been 'translated' not only from pottery, but also from wood. The Abbé Breuil has informed us that certain *li* in the Marguerite Glotz collection seemed to suggest, in the way the motifs were carved ('as if with a knife'), an imitation of ancient sculptures in wood (Grousset and Demoulin, *Evolution des Bronzes Chinois Archaïques*, 1937, p. 34, fig. III, 2). Now Umehara has discovered, through imprints (in colours) left on the floor of An-yang tombs, the trace of ancient wooden vases with the same ornamentation painted on them as is found on the Shang bronzes and on the white pottery and the marbles of the same epoch. Cf. Umehara, Antiquities Exhumed from the Yin Tombs outside Chang Te fu, *Artibus Asiae*, XIII, 3, 1950, pp. 158-165.

they were a magic writing bearing the response of the divinity.[29] In addition to oxen, sheep, etc., sacrificial offering was also made of human victims, as is attested by the discovery of corpses decapitated and buried side by side, sometimes by the hundred.

These details are confirmed by inscriptions on bones or on tortoise-shells, exhumed by the thousands from the Shang tombs. Writing was not only known but had even reached a certain stage of generalization. The Shang characters (of which the present-day Chinese characters are but the stylization) were pictographic, and we can still discover in them the drawings (human figures, animals, plants, objects) that gave rise to them. But if pictography is the basis of these signs, it is already highly developed, stylized and at first sight often unrecognizable. The same thing holds here as for the origin of Chinese bronze: in order to know the primitive Chinese pictograms one would have to excavate beneath the first Shang capitals, and even beneath those of the Hsia, long ante-dating An-yang.

The art of An-yang is of great importance. The painted pottery of the neolithic period has been replaced by a beautiful white pottery of which the ornamentation, with slightly raised fillets (*t'ao-t'ieh* masks and geometric motifs), is identical with that of the bronzes of the same period.[30] We may, for example, compare in this respect the lozenge motifs of a *ting* vase in the Guimet Museum and the similar ornamentation of a fragment

[29] The choice of the tortoise carapace as an instrument of divination is not a haphazard one: 'The tortoise is the image of the world: its carapace is round above like the sky, square below like the earth. By virtue of this, tortoises have a stabilizing role: they support and bear certain islands of the ocean. It is because they stabilize the world that they were later represented as supporting the steles of the classic period (Han steles of Szechwan, steles of the Liang and the T'ang, etc.) In the archaic period, the tortoise-shell is therefore well qualified to assist in the knowledge of terrestrial and celestial things'. (N. Vandier-Nicolas).

[30] Umehara, Etude sur la Poterie Blanche Fouillée dans les Ruines de la Capitale des Yin, *Memoirs of the Toho Bunka Gakuin*, Kyoto, 1932, and Kanan shō anyō shutsudo haku shoku doki sairon. Once More on the White Earthenware Vessels Found at Anyang, *Shinagaku*, vol. IX, no. 4, November 1939, p. 548.

of white pottery in the Cernuschi Museum;[31] and especially, in the Freer Gallery in Washington, a certain admirable large vase of white pottery, intact and complete, and a certain bronze, also Shang, both decorated with the same themes.

The Shang bronze vases, found in great numbers in the An-yang excavations, show us a 'typology' that is already fixed: the forms of several categories of these vases were hardly to change through the centuries.[32] These are, in fact, forms consecrated by religion, ritual types, each of which had its special function in the sacrificial offerings (viands, cereals, beverages). Thus we see appear in Shang art the *li* tripod, with its mammary allusion, which really only translates into bronze the type of terra cotta tripods already met with in neolithic pottery; the round *ting*, a round pot, likewise mounted on three legs, and the square *ting*, a rectangular pot, mounted on four legs; the *li-ting*, a hybrid form of tripod, combining the *li* and the round *ting*; the *yu* and the *kuang*, covered pots, the former being characterized by a movable handle and the second by a grasp, the cover of the *kuang* often assuming, in addition, the form in high relief of a ram's, ele-phant's or other animal's head; the *tsun* and the *ku*, varieties of cups, the first wider, the second in the form of a very tall, slim chalice, wide-mouthed, of a very elegant design; the *i* or *fang* (square *i*), a vertical parallelepiped surmounted by a cover; the *chüeh* and the *chia*, tripods characterized by two small protube-rances rising from the orifice, the first type of which, the *chüeh* cup, has a remarkable elegance due to the strut of its legs and the widening out of the chalice, prolonged by two long lips.

As for the sacrificial use of these bronzes, the *ting* and *li* tripod

[31] René Grousset and Henriette Demoulin-Bernard, *L'Evolution des Bronzes Chinois Archaïques*, 1937, p. 35 and pl. III.

[32] See, as a basis for what is to follow, Karlgren, Yin and Chou Researches, B.M.F.E.A., Stockholm, 1935, and New Studies on Chinese Bronzes, ibid., 1937; also the very important study (in Chinese) by Jung Keng, *The Shang and Chou Bronzes*, summarized by Rolf Stein in the *Bulletin de l'Ecole Française d'Extrême-Orient*, 1942, pp. 394 to 405.

cauldrons were intended for the cooking of meats; the large cups or low urns with side handles, called *kuei* (or *tuei*) served for offerings of vegetables or grains: the fruits were presented in the cups mounted on legs, called *tou*; the beverages were offered to ancestors or divinities in the tall 'bronze jar' with three superimposed sections, round or square, called *tsun*, in the *chüeh* and *chia* tripod goblets, or in the *ku* chalice; liquids were also poured into the covered ovoid wine pot called *yu*.[33]

As well as establishing the typology of the forms exemplified by the sacrificial vases, Shang art also established a number of highly characteristic decorative themes: decoration in the form of nail-heads; segmented edges; simple or double, rounded or angular spirals, spirals ending in a kind of swelling, spirals whose contours are punctuated by lines in the form of commas; festoons; double or triple chevrons; cowrie-shell motifs; the whirls and windings of the *lei wen* and the *yün wen* that often move, like our Greek-Key pattern, at right angles, and that perhaps evoke the cloud from which the lightning bursts (whence the name 'lines of lightning' by which they are sometimes designated);[34] horizontal bands formed of a 'procession' of 'hooked z's'; bands of lozenges joined end to end to form a vast woven groundwork; variations, apparently confused, but in reality quite regular, on the theme of crossed T's or L's composing a motif of arabesques, etc. We may recall that some of these motifs, in particular the 'circlet of lozenges' and the intertwined T's and L's, already appeared on the neolithic painted pottery of the Ma-chang

---

[33] The covered pot with movable handle called *yu* should not be confused with the wide, deep vase with a slightly bell-mouthed edge and likewise used for wine, called *yü*. In the period with which we are concerned, the *yu* is much more frequent than the *yü*. Nor must the *i* or *fang-i*, a vertical parallelepiped, be confused with the *i* (Middle Chou), which is a 'quadruped sauce-dish'. Cf. Jean Buhot, correcting himself, *Revue des Arts Asiatiques*, XI, 3, September 1937, p. 176.

[34] The ancient character used to represent thunder was in fact identical with the old form of the *lei wen* (two spirals turning in opposite directions). We may also note the variants of the *lei wen* in hooks, breasts, waves, etc.

5. *Ceremonial vessel with cover, type* kuang, *bronze. Late Shang Dynasty. Freer Gallery of Art, Washington.*

period. But what is entirely new in the decoration of the Shang bronzes is the figures of monsters, dragons and *t'ao-t'ieh*.

The *t'ao-t'ieh* (a word of uncertain etymology) is the mask, seen full-face and spread out flat, of a monster whose horns, big eyes, ridge of forehead and nose, and powerful muzzle with lips curled back, baring the fangs, cannot fail to produce a startling impression. In the *Shan hai ching* (ch. 3), it is an anthropophagous monster, dwelling in a mountain rich in copper (Granet, *Danses et Légendes*, p. 491). As in other similar masks of Asiatic mythology (the Javanese *kâla*, for example), the lower jaw is usually absent.[35] Claws sometimes flank the lower part of the animal's head on both sides, making the animal seem to be crouching, ready to spring. For it is indeed an animal, quite realistic initially.[36] On several of our Shang bronzes, the *t'ao-t'ieh* is clearly the face of a bull, a ram, a tiger or an owl (more rarely a stag).[37]

[35] See Gilberte de Coral Remusat, Animaux Fantastiques de l'Indochine, de l'Inde et de la Chine, *Bulletin de l'Ecole Française d'Extrême-Orient*, vol. XXXVI, 2, 1937; and Gisbert Combaz, Masques et Dragons en Asie, *Mélanges Chinois et Bouddhiques*, VII, Brussels, 1945, pp. 72 ff. On what may be the equivalent of such masks in ancient Hither Asia, see Parrot's Deux Lions Gardiens, *Musées de France*, April 1948, p. 64. The absence of a lower jaw in the *t'ao-t'ieh* as in other zoomorphic monsters is perhaps due to the fact that they may have been derived from the skin of an animal used as a disguise by sorcerers in certain magic dances, a skin of which the head, in order to 'cap' the shaman, had necessarily to be reduced to the upper part.

[36] In the Shang bronzes there are also to be found human masks, which sometimes (in contrast to the *t'ao-t'ieh*) have a lower jaw. Mr Minkenhof, a keen specialist, notes that these human masks, as they break away from the influence of the *t'ao-t'ieh*, become increasingly realistic. See S. H. Minkenhof, *Bulletin der Asiatische Kunst*, Amsterdam, no. 29, April 1950. On the initial relations between the *t'ao-t'ieh* and the human mask, see also Harada, *Bulletin of Eastern Art*, no. 28, Tokyo, April 1942. Mr Harada here compares an An-yang white pottery motif and a human mask that appears on a bronze in the Sumitomo collection. We ourselves suggest a comparison between the motif on the white pottery in question (human arms raised and spread out in a gesture of supplication) and rather similar anthropomorphic designs on the Ma-chang painted pottery (reproduced by Andersson, Researches into the Prehistory of the Chinese, B.M.F.E.A., Stockholm, 15, 1943, pp. 190-191).

[37] Simply by way of an example of a clearly zoomorphic *t'ao-t'ieh* we may mention the large *li* tripod of the Michel Calmann collection, with its rough

Such is the case on the two *yu* (which are in fact nearly identical, forming a pair) one in the Cernuschi Museum and the other in the Sumitomo Collection, which represent a tiger without a lower jaw, clasping (and, according to Henri Maspero, perhaps protecting) a human being;[38] such is also the case on a number of haft-ends, one at the Cernuschi Museum, another in the David-Weill collection, and a third in the von der Heydt Collection, representing a ram surmounting a human head.[39] The elephant is more rare and is seldom to be found except on a limited number of vases; nor can it really be said to be related to a *t'ao-t'ieh*.[40]

green patina, its ornamentation composed of deeply incised hooks, its legs capped by three powerful masks of rams with coiled horns decorating the bulge (See Georges Salles, *Bronzes Chinois*, Orangerie, 1934, pl. 2). Or else the *li* tripod of the Marguerite Glotz collection, a tripod of rather squat form, with comma motifs, a heavy green patina, and above each leg a *t'ao-t'ieh* mask with buffalo *horns* (Grousset and Demoulin-Bernard, *L'évolution des Bronzes Chinois Archaïques*, Cernuschi Museum, 1937, p. 34 and pls. 3, 11). On the role of the owl, which is the bird of lightning and (by virtue of this) a metamorphosis of the magic drum and can change itself into a dragon (*k'uei*), see Granet, *Danses et Légendes*, pp. 515 ff. On the *t'ao-t'ieh* as owl and as ram, *ibid.*, p. 491 ('although the *t'ao-t'ieh*, by its name, appears to be an owl, it resembles a ram with a human head, tiger's teeth, human fingernails and eyes in its armpits').

[38] We may point out another prodigious tiger's head (but having a lower jaw) as 'front termination' of the covers of a pair of *kuang*, in the Freer Gallery (*Freer Gallery, Catalogue of Chinese Bronzes*, 1946, pl. 26-27). A head like this might be compared with the famous Shang wild beast statue in marble, from the An-yang excavations, of which we shall speak further on. The two 'tiger' *kuang* of the Freer are, however, of a later style (Middle Chou). As for the *kuang* at Harvard, with a cover in the shape of a tiger's head, it seems to be of a transitional style between the Shang and the Chou, a style that Karlgren calls 'Yin-Chou' (eleventh to ninth centuries). Cf. *Bulletin of the Fogg Museum of Art*, x, 2, November 1943.

[39] V. Griessmaier, *Sammlung von der Heydt*, Vienna, 1936, fig. 122.

[40] The elephant on a *kuang* vase lid, reproduced by W. C. White in his article on one of the An-yang tombs, the so-called 'elephant's tomb' (because of the representations of this animal, it seems), in *The Illustrated London News*, March 23, 1935, p. 482. We may note that the Chinese archaeologist Jung Keng distinguishes no less than sixteen ways of representing the *t'ao-t'ie* under the Shang and the early Western Chou (1300-950). We may call attention to an exceptional representation, in the form of an oblong pointed leaf (pseudocicada),

This realism was to disappear progressively in the course of the succeeding epochs to make way, in the *t'ao-t'ieh* masks, for a general and conventional stylization, which was to obliterate not only the characteristics of the animal represented, but finally the animal allusion itself. The Han *t'ao-t'ieh*, as we shall see, was already tending toward the 'mascaron'. At the end of its evolution, in the Ming period (sixteenth to seventeenth centuries A.D.), the *t'ao-t'ieh* was no longer anything but a purely decorative theme whose elements were decomposed, dissociated, unrecognizable. The value of Shang art, on the contrary, resides in the realism, for a long time so powerful, of these semi-bestial, semi-divine representations.

Along with the *t'ao-t'ieh*, dragons (*k'uei*) occupy an important place in Shang ornamentation (bronzes, jades, white pottery).[41]

on the *ku* and the *tsun* (Keng, Bronzes of Shang and Chou, *Yen-ching Journal of Chinese Studies*, Harvard Yen-ching Institute, Peking 1941, summarized by Rolf Stein, *Bulletin de l'Ecole Française d'Extrême-Orient*, 1941, 2, p. 402).

[41] On the various forms of *k'uei*, cf. the important article by Serge Elisseeff, Quelques Heures à l'Exposition des Bronzes Chinois de l'Orangeries, 1934 : Les Motifs des Bronzes Chinois, *Revue des Arts Asiatiques*, VIII, 4, p. 229. The *Kuo-yü* (a compilation of approximately the third century B.C.) establishes a distinction in meaning between the two terms *k'uei* and *lung* that designated the dragon. The *lung* (like the Indian *makara*) is supposedly the water dragon; the *k'uei*, the dragon of trees and rocks. But other texts represent the *k'uei* itself as an aquatic monster, while in medieval Chinese painting, the *lung* appears as the dragon of storm clouds. See also the article, quoted above, by Harada, K'uei According to the Definition in the Shuo-wen, *Bulletin of Eastern Art*, 28, Tokyo, April 1942. We may note that the *Shuo-wen* referred to here is a dictionary of the end of the Han period (about 200 A.D.), or possibly even later, which may have confused the meanings of two quite distinct Chinese characters which were roughly similar in pronunciation, the one—*k'uei*—referring to the archaic dragon, the other—*kuei*—to 'spirits' and phantoms. In the case of the *k'uei* as of the *t'ao-t'ieh*, it must be recognized that the explanations we have of them are comparatively late, dating from a time when the links had been lost with that 'primitive mentality' that might give us the key to such conceptions. Granet is the only one to have worked along this line by showing that originally '*k'uei* and *lung* are two dragons connected with the drum'. In general, he notes, our sources connect the *k'uei* with 'stone and wood', in other words, with the mountain, whereas Confucius connects it with water, and vice versa for the *lung*. According to the *Shan hai ching*, studied by Granet, the *k'uei* is 'an animal having the

They generally appear with their body seen in profile, with gaping mouth, and in a form that from the beginning is highly stylized. The bird, a similar decorative theme in Shang art, sometimes has a relatively more naturalistic form (hoopoe or phoenix), and at other times also becomes stylized, ending, like certain dragons, in a long horizontal tail rolled up at the end. A variety of winged dragon (*k'uei-feng*, or k'uei-phoenix) seems intermediary between the dragon thus conceived and the bird. Another category, the plumed dragon, has been compared to the pre-Columbian plumed serpent. Still another hybrid form is that of the dragon with a trunk that seems a composite of the dragon and the elephant. The elephant appears in profile as a design in relief in the decoration of certain bronzes, more rarely in the round.[42] Related to the dragon, too, are the more simplified motif of the serpent, and that of a reptile, likewise in the form of a serpent, covered with scales.

appearance of an ox, with a green body, no horns and only one leg. It lives in the Eastern sea. When it enters the water or emerges from it, there must be wind or rain. Its brilliance is like that of the sun or the moon. The noise that it makes is like thunder. Huang Ti, having caught it, made a drum of its hide. He struck with the bone of the Thunder Beast—the sound could be heard five hundred li—in order to inspire a respectful fear. The Thunder Beast has the body of a dragon and a human head; it plays the drum on its belly and explodes with laughter' (Granet, *Danses et Légendes*, p. 510). 'The dragon is characterized, moreover, by its mobility. Thus it reveals itself in the torrent that seethes in the depth of the valleys, in the fleeing cloud, in lightning and in thunder. By virtue of the same analogies, it lives on the edge of rivers. It also serves as a draught animal for saints. A certain sovereign of the Hsia dynasty had a team of four dragons, two from the Yellow river and two from the Han river'. (Vandier-Nicolas).

[42] W. C. White, *The Illustrated London News*, May 18, 1935, p. 888. We may note that the entire 'body' of certain *huo* bronze vases may take the form of an elephant, as in the case of the two elephant-shaped *huo* of Chou style in the Guimet Museum ('Camondo elephant') and in the Freer Gallery (*Freer Gallery, Chinese Bronzes*, 1946, p. 24), the lid of the latter being surmounted by a second and smaller elephant, likewise treated in the round. For elephants drawn in profile on the reliefs of various *Kuang* vases, see Karlgren, New Studies on Chinese Bronzes, B.M.F.E.A., 1937, pl. XXVII (Tokyo Imperial Museum); and *The Sumitomo Collection*, abridged catalogue of 1934, p. XXIX.

We have mentioned only the best-known—what we might call the classic—types of the *k'uei* theme. But the archaeologist Jung Keng, who has just made an exhaustive study of them, distinguishes no less than fifteen categories. Of these let us merely mention some of the most interesting in addition to the ones already referred to: the two-headed *k'uei*, current under the Shang; the triangular *k'uei* ('in which are placed two other *k'uei* facing each other'); the *k'uei* with two tails and four legs, and the two-tailed and legless *k'uei*; the dragon with two horns rolled up in a circle; the horned dragon (an 'umbrella-like' horn, with the nose forming a trident, or lance-shaped horn and the nose curved upward) etc.[43]

The cicada is another of the classic themes of Shang decoration, and often appears in a form that is quite naturalistic; but a distinction must be made between this and a spindle-shaped motif that at first sight looks as if it might be a cicada, but which is found to have the head of a *t'ao-t'ieh*, or to be composed of two extremely stylized facing dragons. Some of these motifs have indeed been given a geometric stylization that renders them well-nigh indecipherable, as is the case with the rectangular strips in three decorative registers, the whole of which is supposed to constitute the body of a dragon. An instance of this kind of stylization is provided by a type of *t'ao-t'ieh* mask found on certain archaic bronzes or jades (particularly in the Chou period), in which the mask is formed by the bodies of two dragons placed symmetrically face to face.[44] These stylistic tricks bear witness to a technique in full command of its medium, which makes use of

[43] Jung Keng, *Shang Chou i-ch'i t'ung-k'ao* (The Bronzes of the Shang and Chou), Ed. Harvard-Yenching Institute, 2 vols., Peking, 1941 (Yenching Journal of Chinese Studies, Monograph Series, no. 17). Important review by Rolf Stein, *Bulletin de l'Ecole Française d'Extrême-Orient*, XLI, 1941-2, p. 403.

[44] See the substantial article on this subject by Cl. Lévi-Strauss, Le Dédoublement de la Représentation dans les Arts de l'Asie et de l'Amérique, in *Renaissance*, Ecole Libre des Hautes Etudes de New-York, XL, II-III, 1945, pp. 168-186.

its virtuosity to pose for us, by an interplay of themes, a series of enigmas which lead to the unexpected and bring new life to the subject.

Karlgren, who has analysed Shang decoration found at An-yang better than anyone, discerns two tendencies, in fact, in the bronze motifs of this period: the first, still naturalistic, the second tending towards an increasing stylization that gradually destroyed the original simplicity of the motifs. It was the latter tendency that was to triumph in the following period, at the beginning of the Chou dynasty.[45]

The ritual vases of the Shang, in particular those of the first An-yang style, are all the more surprising in that they abruptly reveal to us not only, as we have seen, an already perfect technique, but also an aesthetic that has in one leap reached its apogee. The power of architectural construction of certain *yu, kuei* or *fang-i* cooking vessels, the elegance and slenderness of certain *chüeh* cups, have never been surpassed. To be sure, the following epochs, up to the approach of modern times, were indefinitely to repeat these forms, which were thenceforth traditional. But the decorative motifs were never to regain the same vigour. This is because what appears to be decoration was in reality primitive magic. Each of these motifs, whose complete meaning eludes us, held an occult power. There is, for example, in the Shang *t'ao-t'ieh* the same power of enchantment as in the pre-Columbian or negro masks.[46] The aesthetic value, the decorative splendour of these bronzes reside in the fearful powers with which they were invested and which, in the quiet of our display cases, still at moments bring them to life before our eyes. But immediately after the Shang this vigour was to lessen. Professor Karlgren, here too, distinguishes two styles in the An-yang bronzes: the first, still naturalistic, in which the monster clearly shows his animal origin;

---

[45] Karlgren, New Studies on Chinese Bronzes, B.M.F.E.A., 9, Stockholm, 1937, pp. 9-118.
[46] Cf. Georges Bureau, *Les Masques*, 1948.

the second, already in the process of stylization, in which the simplicity of the mythological mask begins to dissolve with the breaking up of the elements composing it.[47]

Very fine marble vases, having basically the same ornamentation as that of the bronze vases (*t'ao-t'ieh*, dragons, etc.), have likewise been discovered in the region of An-yang. Several American museums hold magnificent specimens of these.[48]

The same vigour as in the most archaic sacrificial vases is shown by the Shang sculptures, likewise originating in the Anyang region.[49] These are blocks of white marble or polished limestone like alabaster, blocks carved in the round in great masses, both crude and powerful, in which the planes flow into one another, neglecting contrasts as well as details and aiming solely at over-all effects, except that the whole surface is chiselled in lines of the same style as in the ornamentation of the bronzes and especially of the jades. There is a marked contrast between the simplified realism contained, as it were, within the contours, and the stylization of the linear incised décor. The animals represented in these sculptures are the same as those of the bronzes: rams, bulls, owls, felines, and a peculiar kind of tiger or bear, mouth gaping, sitting monkey-fashion;[50] there is also a fragment of a person seated, hands clasping the knees;[51] and there is the marble statuette of an elephant in the Inoué (Tsuneichi) collection in Tokyo, a reproduction of which was recently published by

---

[47] Karlgren, New Studies on Chinese Bronzes, B.M.F.E.A., Stockholm, 9, 1937, pp. 14-17.

[48] Marble vase I of Kansas City, reproduced by Umehara, in Antiquities Exhumed from the Yin Tombs outside Chang tê fu, in *Artibus Asiae*, XIII, 3, 1950, pl. II, p. 252.

[49] See O. Karlbeck, Anyang Marble Sculpture, Yin and Chou Researches, B.M.F.E.A., Stockholm, 1935, p. 61.

[50] Reproduction in H. J. Timperley, *The Illustrated London News*, April 4, 1936, p. 589, fig. 14.

[51] Creel, *Birth of China*, pl. III, p. 66.

Umehara.[52] Another piece of white marble from An-yang has a type of *t'ao-t'ieh* mask also found on the bronzes, definitely feline in character, but with curled-up horns: a combination of two distinct animal themes for the representation of this monster that was to become classic.[53] The same collection has jade figurines representing a small person standing, with arms which were apparently movable.[54]

Weapons of bronze are entitled to a special place in An-yang art. Excavations have yielded lance-heads, rectangular or trapezoidal knives and powerful axes whose edge-side is often decorated with a robust Shang theme. We may note in particular the dagger-axes (*ko*) of which the 'heel' frequently curves over and is sometimes cut out into a dragon motif, occasionally with delicate insets of turquoise and of malachite, a mosaic of precious stones of wonderful decorative effect, which makes of the *ko* a veritable jewel.[55] On the other hand, the *ch'iang* halberd or battle-axe, which is mounted like the *ko* perpendicularly to the handle, has not yet come to light among the An-yang finds.

Chariot ornaments in bronze, harness adornments, also in bronze, small bronze appliqué fittings, also sometimes with deli-

[52] Umehara, Antiquities Exhumed from the Yin Tombs outside Chang tê fu, in *Artibus Asiae*, XIII, 3, 1950, pl. 1, pp. 150-151.

[53] Creel, *Ibid.*, pl. v, p. 106.

[54] Reproduction in White, *The Illustrated London News*, May 18, 1935, p. 889, fig. 5-7.

[55] See Karlgren, Weapons and Tools of the Yin Dynasty, B.M.F.E.A., Stockholm, no. 17 (1945), pp. 101-144. Cf. Percival Yetts, *Collection Eumorfopoulos, Bronzes*, vol. I, A-148, 149. *Freer Gallery, Catalogue of Chinese Bronzes*, 1946, pp. 44-45 (in certain of these *ko* the knife-blade is not of bronze but of a jade whose brightness adds further to the dazzling multicolored effect). Andersson and the Chinese archaeologist Li Chi believe the *ko* to stem from a stone axe attached to a handle. But another Chinese archaeologist, Chiang Ta-i, is of the opinion that the *ko* developed from a stone knife which, attached to a short handle, was used in harvesting, but could become a fighting weapon if it was fastened to a longer handle (Chiang Ta-i, On the Jade Weapons of Ancient China, *Bulletin of Chinese Studies*, vol. II, Chengtu, Sept. 1942, report by A. Rygaloff in *Han-hiue, Bulletin du Centre Sinologique (Français) de Pékin*, vol. 2, section 4, 1949, p. 412).

6. *Ceremonial vessel, type* kuei, *bronze. Late Shang Dynasty, twelfth century B.C. Freer Gallery of Art.*

7. *Pole top, bronze. Shang Dynasty, fourteenth to twelfth century B.C. David - Weill Collection, Paris.*

cate turquoise details (even, on occasion, with 'turquoise mosaics'),
—all these fragmentary remains show us the refinement achieved
by the art of the late Shang period.

The An-yang tombs have likewise yielded fragments of mural
paintings, with red, white and black colours (or green, red and
yellow?) and motifs similar to those of the bronzes. Unfortunately, these paintings, attested to by Mr Creel's Chinese informants,
have never been reproduced.[56]

It seems, according to the Chinese archaelogist Li Chi, that
the An-yang site has yielded fairly numerous jades,[57] but here too
the clandestine character of the excavations and the absence of
methodical publications greatly impede our study of them. May
we note, so as not to have to revert to it, that the Chinese character
yü, which we generally translate by 'jade,' really designates several kinds of nephrite often very dark in colour, brown, black,
rust-coloured, very deep green, sometimes without any translu-
cency and then resembling marble. We know, moreover, or sur-
mise, thanks to the canonical texts, that *yü* was an essentially
'pure and noble' material, possessing and yielding a magic 'virtue'
(the quintessence, perhaps, of the *yang* principle) and that for this
reason it played a considerable role in the ceremonial life of the
sovereign or the great feudal lords, as well as in funerary ritual.[58]

Despite the absence of precise knowledge of the provenance
of the finds, Creel, White, Karlbeck and Howard Hansford believe it possible to classify as 'Shang' and to attribute to the An-
yang region various jades, already classical in form—forms that
we shall come upon again in the succeeding periods of the Chou

[56] Creel, *Birth of China*, p. 100. The An-yang tombs had also contained
wooden vases painted red and green. The wood has disappeared, but the colours
have been 'imprinted' on the walls of the tomb. (Umehara, *Artibus Asiae*, XIII,
3, 1950).

[57] Madeleine David, Ecole du Louvre thesis on *Les Jades du Musée Guimet*
(1948).

[58] Karlgren, Early History of the Chou-li, B.M.F.E.A., Stockholm, no. 3, 1931,
pp. 1-62. *Idem*, Fecundity Symbols in Ancient China, *ibid.*, no. 2, 1930, p. 39.

4.

and of the Warring States: the circular disc *pi*, symbol of Heaven, the rectangular tube *ts'ung*, symbol of Earth; weapons, ceremonial no doubt, like the dagger-axe *ko*, whether it be a *ko* entirely of jade, or the *ko* with a jade blade set in a mounting (itself often very rich) of bronze; rectangular or trapezoidal jade knives, of the same model as the bronze knives mentioned above; even the *ch'iang* halberd or battle axe, a form that has not yet been found among the Shang bronzes. There is reason, moreover, to classify as Shang art a certain number of small jades representing either animals (bears, tiger, owls, various birds, fish, etc.), or fantastic beings (*k'uei* or dragons) that are in fact identical in style with the same representations on the An-yang bronzes.[59]

* * *

When we speak of Shang art on the basis of the An-yang finds, there is one consideration that must never be lost sight of: although these are the first Chinese bronzes to have come down to us, we are confronted, as we have seen, quite suddenly with a high peak of achievement. Certain combinations of motifs already show a remarkable refinement, for example the 'double' form of the *t'ao-t'ieh*, to which we have already called attention. On the belly of a *p'o* vase aquired by the Louvre fund and now in the Guimet Museum, the three *t'ao-t'ieh* masks that adorn the

---

[59] A very subtle and circumspect analysis of the various arguments on this is found in Mlle Madeleine David's manuscript thesis, pp. 45-55. See also the recent monograph by S. Howard Hansford, *Chinese Jade Carving*, London, 1950, a very precise study both from the mineralogical point of view and in respect of the working of the jade. In this author's private collection (pls. 15-16), as well as in that of King Gustav Adolph (pls. 41-42), are found jades that can clearly be attributed to the An-yang excavations. There are also jades in existence that can be 'certified' to be Shang by their reinforcement or hafting of bronze (*Freer Gallery, Catalogue of Chinese Bronzes*).

main band are each composed of two dragons facing each other or rather of one dragon with the body, as it were, divided down the middle by a vertical line and the two halves aplied flat to the band;[60] these facing dragons, as M. Leroi-Gourhan has pointed out, juxtaposed in this way, very precisely form a *t'ao-t'ieh*.[61] On the belly of a certain *chia* of the former Loo collection, which has appeared in exhibitions at the Cernuschi Museum, the second band is decorated with four winged dragons whose bodies have likewise been split down the middle, as it were, and applied on to the vase.[62] Such tricks, of which examples could be given by the dozen, testify to a virtuosity of workmanship that obviously presupposes a rather long previous elaboration.

Even more than an amazing technical skill, the Shang bronzes often reveal an artistic mastery never since equalled. There is power and sureness of 'architectural' construction as, for example, despite its crude and almost savage character, in the great *li* tripod with the three 'ram-shaped' *t'ao-t'ieh* of the Michel Calmann collection; in the large *yu* cooking vessel ('the *yu* of Andigné') at the Cernuschi Museum;[63] in the four monumental *ho* wine vases, seventy-three centimetres tall, of the Nedzu (Kaichiro) collection that we recently admired in Tokyo, one of which was exhibited in 1935 at Burlington House.[64] There is power, no less commanding, even though the piece is of the transition period between the Shang and the Chou (Yin-Chou style), in the large animal-shaped *tsun*, forty-five centimetres tall, with green and emerald patina, of the former Eumorfopoulos collection, 'a real piece of

[60] Grousset and Demoulin-Bernard, *Evolution des Bronzes Chinois Archaïques*, Cernuschi Museum, 1937, p. 39, fig. 9.

[61] A. Leroi-Gourhan, *Bestiaire du Bronze Chinois*, Editions d'Art et d'Histoire, Van Oest, 1936.

[62] Grousset et Demoulin-Bernard, *Evolution des Bronzes*, p. 42, fig. 12.

[63] *Evolution des Bronzes*, frontispiece.

[64] These bronzes were discovered in 1933 in the Hou-chia-chuang excavations. There an splendid reproductions in *Seizansō Seishō: Illustrated Catalogue of the Nezu Collection, vol. VI, Chinese bronzes* (particularly pls. I to VIII), Tokyo, 1942, with text by Umehara,

sculpture in which the fore-quarters of two rams back to back are welded to form the body of the receptacle'.[65]

Faced with works like these (which are given only as examples), observing the building up and distribution of volumes in so many *yu* and *chih* vessels, we realize that a true 'thoroughbred' Shang vase is at once an architectural symphony and a great piece of sculpture. We are here in the presence of masterpieces that compel immediate recognition. Never, in the working of this material, has such innate strength been displayed, revealing as it does, in the very manner in which it controls and disciplines itself, an unparalleled mastery.

The quality and the placing of the ornamentation are no less surprising. We have enumerated the motifs of 'Chinese Greek,' of *lei-wen*, of *yün-wen*, of lozenges, spirals, of variations of cicada forms, which are basic to Shang ornamentation. But the sureness of taste that dictates their disposition should be emphasized; attention should be called, for example, to the sense of values shown by the bronze-caster whose design for a certain *ting* that has come down to us consists of a robust band of dragons round the edge, and below, as though suspended from it, a dozen elegant triangles with cicada designs.[66] Even when this ornamentation becomes complex, the artist always controls it and distributes it without heaviness; this is why, still today, despite the fact that the underlying mythology is closed to us, the *Shang* bronzes speak to us, whereas so many later bronzes remain mute.

Also it will be noted that none of these motifs has been treated cursorily. However reduced they may be (and some of them are composed of extraordinarily minute 'punctuations'), the bronze-founders have been careful to give each its own accent. What might seem a mere lacework of motifs while we are at a distance

---

[65] Yetts, *Catalogue of the Eumorfopoulos Collection*, Bronzes, vol, 1, pls. VIII and IXa.

[66] *Ting* vases of the Hellström and Karlbeck collections studied in Grousset and Demoulin-Bernard, *Evolution des Bronzes*, p. 36, pl. IV, figs. 5 and 6.

from the vase becomes, as we approach, a living harmony in which each theme comes alive and plays its own part. In spite of the frequent filling-in of all free spaces by the web of *lei-wens*, lozenges, spirals, curlicues and interlacings (the '*yu* of Andigné' at the Cernuschi Museum for example), there is never any over-crowding, because all the motifs are alive and eloquent with their own vitality. They either stand out in sharp relief or are hollowed out in deep grooves; for the master bronze-founder was at pains to give them the maximum force. One has only to compare a Shang bronze with a Ming bronze that aims to treat the same themes as its distant predecessor in order to grasp, in the realm of art, the difference between life and death.

The Shang bronzes, by their strength as by their elegance, represent one of the high moments of the world's art.

* * *

The latest Soviet works lead us to believe that the art of the An-yang bronze-founders may have influenced the Siberian bronzes of the Karasuk epoch (An-yang, as we have seen, dates from 1300 to 1028 B.C.; Karasuk, according to S. Kiselev, from 1200 to 700 B.C.).[67] We do in fact already find in An-yang those slightly curved bronze knives with animal heads (deer, horses, rams) that Siberian art in the 'Minusinsk depression' was to

[67] Karasuk is situated on the river of the same name, a tributary of the upper Yenisei, near the village of Bateny in the region of Bograd, on the territory of the Khakas, west of Minusinsk. The essential work on the question is now that of S. Kiselev, *Drevnaya istoria Juzhnoy Sibiri*, in *Materiali i isledovaniya po archeologi* S.S.S.R., no. 9, 1949 (*Ancient History of Southern Siberia*, in *Materials and Researches on the Archaeology of the* U.S.S.R., no. 9, 1949), pp. 62-108. We may recall the previous works of Kiselev on related subjects: Mongoliya v drevnosti (Mongolia in Antiquity), *Bulletin of the Academy of Sciences of the* U.S.S.R., 1947, vol. IV, pp. 355-372; by the same author: *Sovietskaya archeologiya Sibiri perioda metalla*, VDI, 1938, i.

popularize in its various stages.[68] We ourselves have held in our hands, through the courtesy of Mr C. T. Loo, two bronze pieces in the round, the one representing a goat, the other a hemione standing, feet together, ready to leap. The grainy roughness of the bronze and the eyes of the two animals inlaid with turquoise immediately suggested to us that their source was An-yang, whence O. Karlbeck assured us he had seen similar pieces exhumed.[69] Clearly we have here one of the animal themes that subsequently became characteristic of the art of the steppes. The latest works of Kiselev, describing the bronze battle axes of Karasuk, with animal motifs (animals still heavy, low on their feet, their noses dragging on the ground), and the sculptured stone steles of Karasuk with human faces in the manner of Chinese *t'ao-t'ieh*, do in fact show the Shang art of An-yang and, secondarily, the art of the early Chou period, to be the inspirers of the Siberian art of the Minusinsk region in the Karasuk phase. Bronzes of the Karasuk type (flat axes, etc.), likewise inspired by An-yang art, also begin to appear in Suiyuan in Inner Mongolia towards the end (according to Kiselev's estimate) of the Shang-Yin period and at the beginning of the reign of the Chou.[70]

A Regression: the Period of the Western Chou

In 1027, according to Professor Karlgren's new rectified chronology, the Shang dynasty was overthrown by a third royal house,

---

[68] See Karlgren, Weapons and Tools of the Yin Dynasty, in *Bulletin of the Museum of Far Eastern Antiquities*, Stockholm, no. 17, 1945, p. 144, pls. 28-38. Minkenhof, Some Bronze Knives from Ancient China in American Collections, in: *Phoenix*, v, 2, Amsterdam, March 1948, p. 47; also the works of Kiselev referred to in the previous note.

[69] Grousset, Nouvelles Vues sur l'Art des Steppes, in *Beaux-Arts*, May 15, 1940.

[70] Kiselev, *Histoire Ancienne de la Sibérie Méridionale*, p. 105 (and the commentary that M. Roman Ghirshman has been good enough to provide). See also, in connection with Kiselev's book, Karl Jettmar's important article, The Karasuk

that of the Chou. The Shang, as we have seen, reigned over the rich alluvial lands of northern Honan, over that garden of China—the 'Chinese Touraine'—where dynasties have since then so often reached their apogee and, through a laxity born of their wealth, caused their own downfall. The Chou, on the contrary, were the rude lords of a frontier march, that of the Wei valley, in what is today Shensi. These hardy pioneers, these land-tilling soldiers (one of their divinities, as we have seen, was Hou-chi, 'Prince Millet'), toughened by their perpetual struggles to 'make land' and defend it against the barbarians, flung themselves in 1027 on the Shang royal domain, wiped out the dynasty and replaced it. From 1027 to 771, they nevertheless kept their residence in their native Shensi. Only in 770, following a revolt of the lords, accompanied by a raid of barbarians, did they transfer their seat from this frontier march to the more central lands of Honan, where their capital, until their disappearance about 250 B.C., was the city of Lo-yang, which has since been so famous.

There can be no doubt that the victory of the Chou over the Shang in 1027 brought in its wake, if not a total regression, at least an arrest of Chinese material civilization. As far as art is concerned, there is in any case a definite slowing-up.[71] Not for a long time, to our knowledge, do we again come upon the 'great' sculpture on stone in the round that had achieved such power in the Shang marble pieces. Sculpture as such was not to reappear until much later, in the time of the Han, with the horse of Ho Ch'ü-ping (117 B.C.), not to mention the funerary terra cottas of the same epoch. As for the ritual bronze vases, they continue for some time to imitate the Shang themes, and this is what Karlgren calls the Yin-Chou transitional style that he situates

Culture and its South-Eastern Affinities, in B.M.F.E.A., Stockholm, no. 22, 1950, pp. 83-126 (including bibliography, pp. 123-126).

[71] Creel calls attention to the cessation of creative activity that is already manifest if one compares the An-yang vases with those of Hsün-hsien, centre of excavations situated in the same region, south of An-yang, and dating from the beginning of the Chou period.

between the end of the eleventh century and the middle of the
tenth; then a new style appears, which Karlgren designates as
'Middle Chou' and which would very approximately be dated as
being between 950 and 650 B.C.[72]

The Chou period appears to have had a predilection for
certain types of vases, in particular the *tsun*, a tall bronze jar
in three sections (spreading base, convex belly, calix-shaped neck)
that sometimes affects a square construction like the famous
fang-tsun of the Freer Gallery.[73] The *kuei*, low, very deep urns
supported on a round or square base and provided with side
handles, generally in the form of animals (dragon heads), a type
already favoured in Shang times, continue under the Chou with
large specimens having a simplified, powerful and crude décor.[74]
In the 'Middle Chou' style, properly speaking, new forms appear,
in particular the *i* vase, a kind of 'sauce-boat' without a cover,
in a form resembling an ox, the lip sometimes in the form of
the head of a bull lowing, while the four legs are bovine in
appearance and the handle ends in the head of a dragon or feline leaping on the animal's croup.[75]

In the same vein, but here fully worked out in the round,
may be noted the two bronzes in the Freer Gallery, deriving from
Shensi and representing two tigers.[76] These are also vases (the
animal is hollow, with an opening in the back), but entirely
zoomorphic. The two wild creatures are treated with a direct
realism, standing ready to leap, the tail whipping. In profile,
their outline has an arresting vigour. Full face, the feline head,
with its fierce snout, its open mouth revealing 'saw teeth', its
'machaerodous daggers', its flaming eyes, creates the same halluc-

[72] Karlgren, New Studies on Chinese Bronzes, B.M.F.E.A., 9, Stockholm,
1937, p. 2.
[73] *Catalogue of Chinese Bronzes*. Freer Gallery, 1946, p. 18.
[74] *Freer Gallery*, pl. 28.
[75] *I* of the Louvre, now in the Guimet Museum, studied in *L'évolution des
Bronzes Chinois Archaïques*, Cernuschi Museum, 1937, p. 53, fig. 26.
[76] *Freer Gallery, Catalogue of Chinese Bronzes*, 1946, pls. 26 and 27.

8. *Ceremonial vessel, type* huo, *bronze. Early Chou Dynasty or earlier. Freer Gallery of Art, Washington.*

9. *Wine can, type* hu, *bronze. Yin or Early Chou Dynasty. Minne-apolis Institute of Arts.*

inatory impression as the most powerful *t'ao-t'ieh*. The Middle Chou ornamentation, simple and crude also, effectively suggests the stripes of the hide. Such pieces, rare and perhaps exceptional though they be, nevertheless prove that sculpture in the round, forgotten in marble, was perpetuated by the bronze-founders.

The Middle Chou style is noteworthy also for the abundance of its bells (*chung*), which were of great ceremonial importance.[77]

A great number of Shang motifs disappear in Middle Chou, particularly among the various categories of dragons. The *t'ao-t'ieh* mask 'abandons its prominent place on the flank of vases and, now barely recognizable, appears only on their base or at the points at which their base or legs are attached. It is only on the handles that heads of monsters in the round are to be seen, and the almost total disappearance of any animal ornamentation gives to these added force and expression'. The same revolution appears in technical processes: 'a flat relief, standing out against the bare background, replaces the contrasting effects of high relief and fine engraving'.

Middle Chou ornamentation is also characterized by a number of innovations: horns in the form of spirals on the animals that decorate the handles and the covers; dragons placed back to back; strips of horizontal shells or shells hung vertically on the body or the base of the vase, or else shells turned upward and surrounding the neck of the vase; a wavy line running round the body of the vase (the replacement of the spiral by waves is indeed one of the distinctive features of this artistic revolution); parallel vertical lines or strokes standing out against an unornamented background; a wide band decorated with conventional motifs, often of dragons quite remote from any animal prototype and repeated in rather monotonous geometric patterns. On the whole, these motifs, which are in fact much more rigidly

[77] Granet has clearly shown 'the associative links that the Chinese myths make it possible to establish between bells, drums, dragons, thunder'. Cf. Granet, *Danses et Légendes*, pp. 504, 509, 527, 577.

5.

geometrical than those of the Shang, are rather heavy and poor. At best it may be noted that this rigid and dry art assumes at times a truly architectural and even monumental character, as in the large seventy-seven centimetre *hu* with a cover in the Guimet Museum.[78]

This same impression of both heaviness and impoverishment matches the 'cultural' regression that we pointed out as a consequence of the coming of the Chou. These warriors of the north-west marches were obviously backward in comparison with the rich Shang civilization that they had destroyed. Proof of this is to be found in their political behaviour. Instead of establishing themselves in the beautiful plains of Honan that they had just conquered they remained, as we have seen, for 257 years (1027-770), confined to their frontier-march of the Wei valley, retaining as their capital the ancient city of Hao, near present-day Sianfu. Only in 770, as we also saw, following a barbarian raid, did they decide to transfer their capital to Honan, choosing Lo-yang, where they quickly fell into decadence. The great feudal houses that divided Chinese territory among themselves became practically independent. From 325 B.C. the most powerful of these provincial dynasties assumed the royal title. The only superiority left to the legitimate king of the house of Chou who, for all his Lo-yang palaces, was king in name only, lay in his religious offices. Despite his political impotence, he remained the Son of Heaven (*T'ien-tzu*), recipient of the heavenly mandate, high pontiff of the agrarian religion, as of the worship of ancestors, hence the only one qualified to maintain harmony between Earth and Heaven, and by virtue of this fact relatively respected as religious chief of the Chinese Confederation.

This Confederation was torn by feudal wars, which grew

[78] Osvald Sirén, *A History of Early Chinese Art*, London, 1928, pl. LIV. Georges Salles, *Bronzes Chinois, Exposition de l'Orangerie*, 1934, no. 282, p. 168, fig. 18. Grousset and Demoulin-Bernard, *L'Evolution des Bronzes Chinois Archaïques, Exposition du Musée Cernuschi*, 1937, p. 52 and pl. IX, fig. 24.

increasingly violent and increasingly frequent, so that the period extending from 481 to 221 B.C. came to be known as the age of the Warring States (Chankuo).[79]

It should be pointed out that at this time the Chinese Confederation, beneath the theoretical sway of the Chou kings, barely extended beyond the basin of the Yellow River and the associated rivers (Pei-ho, Huai-ho). The Yangtze basin remained outside the Chinese domain, even though it was undoubtedly inhabited by tribes related to the Chinese nation, differing from the Chinese people only in the backward character of their culture. Nevertheless two of these tribes, established respectively on the northern bank of the middle Yangtze (the present province of Hupei) [80] and at the very mouth of the river,[81] spontaneously sinicized themselves under the influence and through the example of Chinese civilization. When at last (in 224 B.C.) the northern Yangtze basin was finally annexed by the Chinese of the North (that is to say by the original China), it had in practice already been sinicized for a long time.[82]

---

[79] According to Karlgren, the 'style of the Warring States' (which, as we shall see, he calls the Huai style) may be considered to extend from 650 to 200 B.C., approximately (Karlgren, New Studies on Chinese Bronzes, B.M.F.E.A., 9, Stockholm, 1937, p. 5).

[80] Kingdom of Ch'u.

[81] Kingdom of Wu.

[82] As for Szechwan, it must have followed the same evolution, but at an even slower rate. Mr Cheng Te-k'un has just published a series of objects recently discovered in T'ai-p'ing-ch'ang, to the north of Chengtu. These include tools that are still eneolithic, bearing the symbols of heaven and earth, *pi* and *tsung*, in sandstone or jade, *yüan* jade rings, knives (*yen-kuei*) of jade ranging from dark grey-green to a neutral grey (knives, as we know, were generally regarded as scepters, the symbol of sovereign power), 'pearls' of jade, turquoise or diorite (similar to the ones that Andersson had discovered in Sha-kuo-tun), *celt*-axes and 'chisels' in stone, and finally a pottery of two categories: a red one with 'corded' décor and a grey one, the latter being similar to the black pottery of Northern China in the so-called 'Ch'eng-tzu-yai II' stage, situated between 1200 and 500 B.C. Dr Cheng Te-k'un concludes that the eneolithic tool-making of Szechwan might also go back to approximately 1200-700. It is interesting to note that this culture of an outlying province is already Chinese. But it remains obviously

The Civilization of the 'Warring States': Art

Chinese historians distinguish two great periods in the time
of the Eastern Chou. The first is called the 'period of Spring
and Autumn' *Ch'un-ch'iu*), from the name of old annals thus
designated that cover the years from 722 to 481 B.C. The second
period, as we have seen, is the so called 'period of the Warring
States' (*Chan-kuo*) and extends from 481 to 221. The testimony
of archaeology during these two periods is highly important for
our knowledge of Chinese society. In the art of bronze, in particular, a wholly new style then develops, which, already in
evidence from the middle of the seventh century, becomes not-
iceable from the middle of the sixth and continues to the end
of the third century. Swedish archeologists call it the 'Huai
Style', because several of the most characteristic pieces (bronzes
with a water-green patina) have been discovered in the basin
of the Huai river, particularly in the vicinity of Shou Chou
(province of Anhwei), as well as in Ku-shih-hsien (in south-
eastern Honan) and in Hsin-cheng (south-west of Kaifeng, in
Honan).[83] 'Art of the Warring States' is more generally used,
even though this style, as we have just seen, seems to have begun
as early as the middle of the sixth century, or before the historic
period properly known as that of the 'Warring States' (481-221)
and must have continued during the brief period of the Ch'in
empire (221-207). This appellation, in our view, is all the more
appropriate as bronzes of rather similar style have been found

backward in relation to the North-Chinese civilization of the same epoch, at the
time of the Western Chou. Cheng Te-k'un, The T'ai-p'ing-ch'ang Culture, *Hsieh-
ta Journal of Chinese Studies*, vol. I, pp. 67-81, pls. 1-4, Foochow, Fukien Christian
University, 1949.
    [83] See Pelliot, A propos des Bronzes de Sin-tcheng, in *T'oung-pao*, 1924,
pp. 255-259. O. Janse, Le style du Houai et ses Affinités, *Revue des Arts Asiatiques*,
VIII, 3, 1934, pp. 159-182. Karlbeck, *Catalogue of the Collection of Chinese and
Korean Bronzes at Hallwyl House*, Stockholm, 1938, pp. 14 ff.

at great distances from the Huai, in particular in Li-yü, in north-eastern Shansi.[84]

As to the dates of the style in question, we have points of reference which seem to be fairly precise. One of the Hsin-cheng vases, found in conjunction with a circular gold plaque which is clearly 'Warring States', belongs, according to its inscription, to 575 B.C.[85] The inscribed *piao* bells, found in Chin-ts'un (within the walls of ancient Lo-yang) and reproduced, notably by White among others, can be presumed to be from 550 (in tombs that can be dated, according to Karlgren, between 450 and 230 B.C.[86]

The style of the so-called 'Warring States' bronzes, after the Middle Chou regression, marks a reawakening of the Chinese creative genius. Middle Chou ornamentation had been distinguished by its rigidity, its static appearance, its impoverishment, its heaviness. In the ornamentation of the 'Warring States' there is once again that sense of movement that imparts animation to the motifs so that they seem to dance, to be literally moving.

[84] On the Li-yü bronzes which, thanks to Mr Georges Salles, are today in the Guimet Museum, see Salles, *Revue des Arts Asiatiques*, VIII, 3, pp. 146-159; also Freer Gallery, *Catalogue of Chinese Bronzes*, 1946, p. 58, pl. 31. On Li-yü in historic geography, see the study by Shikazo Mori, appended to Umehara, *Etude des Bronzes des Royaumes Combattants*, Toho-Bunka Gakuin, Kyoto Ken-kyusho, 7, 1936. On the acquisition of an important group of Li-yü bronzes by the national museums (now in the Guimet Museum), see Vandier Nicolas, Le Trésor de Li-yü, *Bulletin des Musées de France*, March 1935, p. 37, in which Mme Vandier-Nicolas shows the affinities of Li-yü art (animals in the round, braid motif, etc.) with the animal (Hunnish) art of the steppes. We must not forget that Li-yü lies close to Tatung, in the extreme north of Shansi, then a real frontier-march in contact with the Huns who occupied Chahar, Suiyuan, and the Ordos. If 'Ordos' influence could penetrate Chinese art anywhere, it was certainly in this region.

[85] See Andersson, Goldsmiths in Ancient China, in B.M.F.E.A., Stockholm, 1935, p. 23.

[86] See Karlgren, B.M.F.E.A., Stockholm, 10, 1938, pp. 65-82. Reproductions of the *piao* bells of Chin-ts'un in White, *Tombs of Old Loyang*, pls. CLXVII-CLXIX, figs. 501-502. On the Chin-ts'un finds, likewise works by Umehara, *Die alte Gräber in An-yang und Chin-ts'un*, Shigakuzasshi (Zeitschrift für Geschichtswissenschaft), vol. 47, no. 9, Tokyo, September 1939; also, *Selections from the Ancient Tombs at Chin-ts'un*, Kyoto, 1937.

Everything dances: the volutes and the spirals, the plaits, the interlacings, cords, dots and criss-crosses—'engraved or in faint relief like a delicate embroidery' on the surfaces of the vases, where inlaid gold and silver, turquoise and malachite replace the former contrasts in relief. In harmony with this new 'grammar of motifs' the *t'ao-t'ieh* masks, decomposed into their elements, are now often no more than a festooning of hooks and spirals, producing a curious effect of swarming. The same impression of dancing is given by the small inter-crossing dragons or serpents, in some cases several times interlaced, and which seem to pivot round one upon the other, which are so frequently found in this style of ornamentation.[87] A special predilection is in fact shown not only for dragons but also for other fantastic animals (hydras, etc.) or animals deformed to the point of becoming fantastic (serpents, tigers, birds). Moreover, in many cases only the heads make it possible to guess the original animal, even though these heads themselves are often nearly unrecognizable: 'a crested bird with upcurved beak, a tiger whose snout and jaw describe a double inverted spiral, a dragon with a triangular face like a snake's'. There is, besides, frequent transference of one motif to another: winged dragons, winged tigers, crested tigers, tigers with feathered tufts, tigers with bird-claws. More fantastic still, a single body has a head at each end, one of a dragon the other of a bird'.[88]

[87] The specimen *par excellence* of this aspect of the style of the 'Warring States is, perhaps the famous chiselled gold hilt from the former Eumorfopoulos Collection, now in the British Museum, with its swarm of small interlaced dragons (Sirén, *History of Early Chinese Art*, pl. 92 b); or else the no less famous *tui* bronze vase of this same collection, with its ornamentation likewise consisting in a multitude of serpent-shaped dragons interlaced, which seem literally to writhe about upon one another, as though we were looking at an arabesque of live reptiles. (Sirén, *op. cit.*, I, pl. 55); or the circle of gold-leaf found in Hsin-cheng (Honan) with the same interlacings of serpents (Andersson, Goldsmiths in Ancient China, in *Yin and Chou Researches*, B.M.F.E.A., Stockholm, 1935, p. 22 and pl. XVII). On the Hsin-cheng discoveries, see also: Sung Hai-p'o, *Hsin chêng i ch'i* (Illustrated Catalogue of the Bronzes found in Hsin-cheng), Kaifeng, 1937; and Yetts, *The Cull Chinese Bronzes*, London, 1939, pp. 48, 50, 51, 105.

[88] David, Ecole du Louvre thesis on the jades in the Guimet Museum.

Even the motif of braiding, so regular and heavy in the middle Chou period, is carried away by the dancing rhythm of the other motifs. The dragons that rise in the round on the vases or on top of bells (the two elegant dragons face to face that surmount the famous 'Stoclet bell')[89], or those that run in a simple filiform design on the mirrors, are animated by a similar movement. 'However fantastic and unreal they may be', writes Daisy Lion-Goldschmidt, 'they have a movement, a tension, that confer upon them a quivering power of life and reality'. On a number of our mirrors (Freer Gallery, Stockholm Museum),[90] the dragons, half lizard and half imp, dance in such frenzied spinning, with such freedom, such fancifulness, that they leap into the air with a speed that the eye can barely follow. At times the elegant play of moving lines that has brought them into being is lost in a whirl of scrolls and arabesques, in a flight of spirals, in a spinning play of curves in which only the apparition, here and there, of a delicate dragon's head allows us to recognize the fantastic animal that has served as a pretext for the whole.[91] This ornamentation that the Chinese call p'an-ch'e (from p'an 'interlaced', and ch'e 'dragon without horns'), characterizes the whole style of the 'Warring States'.

The same fantasy is to be found in the very elongated dragons whose tails end in scrolls that form the most elegant of the bronze clasps of the 'Warring States'. Rarely has a decorative theme achieved such virtuosity in sheer fantasy. However, as Madeleine David observes, this fantasy which appears so untrammelled is governed by a secret law: the law of rhythm. A single rhythm animates the twists and interlacing of motifs, balances the curves by counter-curves, the volutes by counter-volutes, and

---

[89] Salles, *Bronzes Chinois*, Orangerie, 1934, p. 206, no. 396 and fig. 30. A similar bell is at the Amis de l'Orient d'Amsterdam; Otto Kummel, *Georg Trübner zum Gedächtnis*, 1930, pls. 26-29.

[90] Sirén, *History of Early Chinese Art*, pl. 84 b.

[91] *Freer Gallery, Catalogue of Chinese Bronzes*, 1946, pl. 36.

thus through the balancing of the forms and the movement of the lines maintains a permanent principle of unity.[92]

It should be noted that the theme of intertwined animals is one of the favourite motifs of the art of the steppes. Its frequency on the Chinese bronzes of the 'Warring Sates' is fresh proof of the link between the Hunnish world and the China of the fifth to the third centuries.[93]

As for the ornamentation in this art of the 'Warring States', it is primarily composed, as we said, of the most diverse variations on the theme of the spiral. A whole 'grammar of the spiral' of the 'Warring States' could be worked out, as a 'grammar of the arabesque' has been established for Moslem art. 'Rounded or angular', Madeleine David notes, 'the spirals undulate in s's, fold into T's or L's, form heart-shapes or geometrical compositions. Sometimes simply inverted, they also overlap, forming ladder-like patterns that are endlessly repeated. Or they may be accompanied by a line with a sharp angle, forming the motif of the volute and the triangle'.[94]

* * *

Special attention must be given to the bronze mirrors, the study of which has enabled Professor Karlgren to distinguish in the ornamentation of the 'Warring States' as we have roughly

[92] This was to become clear when the Ming archeologists attempted to copy the bronzes of the 'Warring States'. No matter how precisely all the archaic motifs were reproduced, they remained scattered and lifeless, for the rhythm that alone animated them was not recaptured.

[93] Cf. Anna Roes, *Tierwirbel*, Ipek II, Berlin, 1936-1937, pp. 85-105. Josef Zykan, Die verschlungenen Drachen, *Artibus Asiae*, VIII, 1937, p. 178. T. G. Frisch, Scythian Art and some Chinese Parallels, *Oriental Art*, II, London 1949, pp. 16-24 and 57-67.

[94] Excellent sketches of the various 'Warring States' (or Huai) motifs will be found in the album *Selected Chinese Antiquities from the Collection of Gustaf Adolf, Crown-Prince of Sweden*, Stockholm, 1948, pp. 27-39.

10. *Ceremonial vessel, type* li-ting, *bronze. Early Chou Dynasty.*
Museum of Fine Arts, Boston.

11. *Ceremonial vessel, type* hu, *bronze. Middle Chou Dynasty, ninth to seventh century B.C. Musée Guimet, Paris.*

described its several successive phases.[95] A first category, which
presumably had its beginning in the seventh-to-sixth centuries
(one of the specimens comes from the Lo-yang region), is still
rather heavy. The true style of the 'Warring States' is adumbrated
in category B of Karlgren's classification, the date of which, on
the basis of the Chin-ts'un finds, near Lo-yang, would be some-
where between the sixth and fifth centuries. It develops with
category C, represented above all by mirrors deriving from the
Huai basin, that can be dated between 500 and 250. The background of these is composed of a very tight pattern of 'commas';
and against this background we sometimes find four petals springing from the central button (round or square); at other times,
proceeding from the outer edge, the T motif—a T here placed
askew; a circular pattern of dragons also appears on the middle
circular band. The mirrors of style D, chiefly represented by
pieces from the region of Lo-yang, are from the fourth and third
centuries B.C. This is undoubtedly the high point for the Chinese
mirror. The background is composed either of a network of
overlapping lozenges, or of the T L type of design (at times
assuming the form of a kind of Greek key pattern), or else of
a very close lacing of tiny lozenges, spirals and granulations. As
for the ornamentation, we sometimes find dancing dragon-lizards,
with very elongated bodies of an incredible simian suppleness,
yet sinuously feline, their tails breaking into leafy branches or
hooked forks, to the elegance of which we have already called
attention;[96] at other times lozenges in zigzag show the same
movement, the same freedom, the same fantasy; the central motif

[95] Karlgren, Huai and Han, B.M.F.E.A. Stockholm, no. 13, 1941. See also
Umehara, Kan izen kokyō no kenkyū, Etude sur les Miroirs Antérieurs a la
Dynastie des Han, Kyoto, 1935.

[96] As a characteristic example, see the famous mirror of the Stockholm Museum
reproduced in Leigh Ashton's and Basil Gray's *Chinese Art*, 1935, pl. 10, p. 49,
and in the *Guide to the Exihibitions of the Museum of Far Eastern Antiquities*,
Stockholm, September 1933, p. 13. Cf. Kummel, *Georg Trübner zum Gedächtniss*,
1930, pl. 37. There is a similar mirror in the Museum of Copenhagen.

is sometimes composed of a kind of large tréflé cross or of an
octagonal festooned star. The mirrors classified by Karlgren in
category E come from the Huai basin and he dates them between
250 and 200 B.C. The background is composed of the same elements as in the preceding series, but here reduced to such a tight
network that it is often nearly indecipherable. The ornamentation that stands out against this background evokes to the practiced eye the circles of elongated dragons described a moment
ago, but here unrecognizable, having been reduced to a geometry of arabesques, spirals and scrolls that blossom forth into
beaks, hooks, tendrils, buds and 'aces of spades' or are cut by
unexpected zigzags.[97]

On several bronze mirrors of the 'Warring States' (in the
Moriya collection, of Kyoto, in particular), on several bronze
clasps of the same period (in the Coiffard collection), as on several sword guards, tubes and spear-ends, chariot studs and ornaments, the inlaid enamel, turquoise, malachite and lacquer, the
gold or silver damascening, add even further, by the richness
of the precious materials and the play of colours, to the quality
of the object, to the point of making it a real jewel.[98].

There are also, in particular in the Moriya collection, mirrors
that are both lacquered and painted in bright colours, among

[97] As an aid to deciphering a motif of this kind and discovering the continuity
of the dragon's body beneath the wild fancifulness of the scrolls, see Karlgren's
diagrams, Huai and Han, B.M.F.E.A., Stockholm, 13, 1941, pp. 82-84.

[98] See Solange Lemaitre, Les Agrafes de la Collection Coiffard, Revue des
Arts Asiatiques, September 1936, p. 132. Minkenhof, An Exihibition of Chinese
Belt Buckles in America, Oriental Art I, 4, London, 1949, p. 161. Also the
admirable reproductions in the Selected Chinese Antiquities from the Collection
of Gustav Adolf, Crown-Prince of Sweden, 1948-1949, pl. 28. On the Jacques Orcel
sword in the Cernuschi Museum, see Vandier-Nicolas, Nouvelles Acquisitions
du Musée Cernuschi, Revue des Arts Asiatiques, VIII, 3, p. 194, pl. 64. On the
weapons of the 'Warring States' or of the Han, see Janse, 'Epées Anciennes
Retrouvées en Chine', B.M.F.E.A., Stockholm, 2, 1930, p. 67. On relationships
between the sword of the 'Warring States' or the Han with the Scytho-Siberian
and Ordos swords, see Loehr, The Earliest Chinese Swords and the Akinakès, in
Oriental Art, no. 3, 1948, p. 132.

which red, blue and white predominate, which give us an idea of the refined luxury of the 'Warring States'. The late Shang period conveyed the same impression of luxury. In this respect, as in creative spontaneity, the two periods link up with each other across the colourlessness of the Middle Chou style. These apart, some of the bronzes inlaid with threads and designs of gold, silver and, secondarily, of turquoise and malachite, found in the Lo-yang region of Honan, and which W. C. White hesitated to date, rightly appear to Andersson to belong partly to the style we have just been studying.[99] This is an identification of great consequence which shows among other things that the regularity of the Han inlaid décor already appeared under the 'Warring States'. The same is true, according to Andersson, of the similar geometric ornamentation in red and black lacquer that adorns the wooden reinforcements for bronze masks found in Ku-wei-tsun, near Hui-hsien in northern Honan.[100] Thus we here already have a manifestation of the geometrical designs of the Han, as we shall find them on the Han lacquers of the Korean district of Lolang.

Finally, numerous jades reveal the style of the 'Warring States' by the very fantasy that their ornamentation exhibits. As Madeleine David observes, these jades no longer appear to be wholly dominated by ritual requirements. They are more in the nature of ornaments. The cosmic symbols *pi* (heaven) and *tsung* (earth) are henceforth frequently covered with an attractive décor of grains, spirals or checkerwork. Alongside these traditional objects, we find clasps and sword ornaments (pommel tips or sheath buckles) chiselled in jade, all of them objects imitated from similar pieces in bronze. Numerous small jades represent fantastic or fantastically treated animals (dragons, hydras, tigers,

---

[99] W. Ch. White, *Tombs of old Loyang*, Shanghai, 1934. Andersson, The Goldsmiths in Ancient China, p. 34.
[100] Andersson, *l. c.*, p. 17, pl. XVI.

birds) that we know from the 'Warring States' bronzes. Here too the ornamentation consists in infinite variations on the spiral theme.

* * *

Presenting an almost complete contrast to these stylistic or decorative inventions, we find on the lids of bronze vases of the 'Warring States' (more precisely, the vases from Li-yü, in the Guimet Museum) representations of animals in the round (tigers, bulls, etc.) of a remarkable realism. This simultaneous emergence of animal realism and of treatment in the round—appearing quite unheralded and yet already fully developed—is a combination of tendencies that appears to go against the trend towards fantastic stylization that we noted a moment ago, and announces a return to sculpture—a genre that seems to have been forgotten since the fall of the Shang.[101] But the resemblance of these same animal statuettes (which are almost entirely independent of the bronze to which they are riveted) to the small Ordos bronzes raises the question as to whether this return to the round is not due, at least in part, to the influence of the steppes.

The Han funerary terra cottas, representing various animals, are in the tradition of this animal art, so free, so spontaneous, and

[101] Prudence, however, forbids too affirmative a statement as to this. In the Pillsbury collection, at the Minneapolis Institute of Art, for example, there is a recumbent buffalo in bronze which is clearly of the Middle Chou period, even though it undoubtedly once surmounted some ritual vase; and this is practically a carving in the round. (Seen the *Exhibition of Chinese Bronzes*, Metropolitan Museum, New York, October-November 1938, fig. 146 of the catalogue). And can we not say that the three famous zoomorph bronzes of the Chou period in the Freer Gallery, one of which represents an elephant and the other two tigers, are magnificent specimens of sculpture in the round? (*Freer Gallery, Catalogue of Chinese Bronzes*, Washington, 1946, pls. 24 and 26). On the animal bronzes in the round used as lampstands under the Eastern Chou, and in the 'Warring States' or Han periods, see Maude Rex Allen, *Early Chinese Lamps*, in *Oriental Art*, II, 4, London, 1950, pp. 133-140.

becoming less and less clumsy, which is found on the 'Warring States' bronzes. In addition, the bull fighting, the hunting scenes (naked archers or hunters armed with swords, fighting stags or wild beasts) as well as the fantastic anthropomorphic or animal figures that decorate in flat relief certain bronze vases also of the 'Warring States' period, prepare the way, as we shall see later, for the Han period, in particular for similar scenes in the Han funerary reliefs of Shantung and Honan.[102] While mentioning these vases, let us note the fantastic birds that are sometimes found on them (in particular on certain *hu* vases) and the no less fantastic creatures that hunt them, from which we may infer that such hunting scenes had primarily a magic significance.

The style of the 'Warring States' (in particular in the bronzes of Li-yü, a site very close to the ancient Hunnish camps of Sui-yüan) shows, as we said, numerous analogies with the art of the steppes of the same period, and in particular with that of Inner Mongolia (Ordos district and Sui-yüan, Chahar and Jehol provinces), an art usually called 'Ordos art' and which, according to Karlgren, must have reached its height in the fourth to third centuries B.C.[103] What we have here is a branch of the animal art, more or less stylized, which was common to various Hunnish (and more generally, Altaic) tribes established not only in Inner Mongolia but also in Upper Mongolia and in Siberia as well, in particular in the Minusinsk depression. The latest Soviet ex-

---

[102] *Hu* vase of the Stoclet collection, David-Weill bronzes, etc.

[103] For dates, see Karlgren, New Studies on Chinese Bronzes, in *Bulletin of Museum of Far Eastern Antiquities*, no. 9, Stockholm, 1937 (Ordos and Huai, p. 108). Outside the Ordos 'Ordos' bronzes have chiefly been found in Hallong-hosso and in Hattin-sum in Chahar, in Hsüan-hua near Kalgan, and in Luan-p'ing in Jehol. See T. J. Arne, Die Funde von Luan-p'ing und Huan-hua, in B.M.F.E.A., Stockholm, V, 1933, p. 166. Griessmaier, Entwickelungsfragen der Ordos-Kunst, in *Arbibus Asiae*, VII, 1-4, Leipzig, 1937, p. 122. There is also a good summary in the small *Guide to the Exihibition of the Museum of Far Eastern Antiquities*, Stockholm, September 1933.

cavations, as described by Professor Kiselev, have brought to light a cultural stage around Minusinsk, succeeding that of Karasuk and continuing it: the *Tagar Culture*, which Kiselev situates between 700 and 100 B.C., with two periods, the first from 700 to 400, the second from 400 to 100—the first one of 'pure bronze', the second marked by the introduction of iron in the fifth century. In the Tagar period the Siberian, so-called Minusinsk, bronzes (knives, axes, even mirrors) reveal a continuous evolution of this animal art. The heavy, lumbering creatures of the Karasuk style are succeeded by animals (bears, lynxes, tigers, cervidae, ibexes, boars, etc.) which give an astonishing impression of rapid movement and are intensely dynamic and alive, and yet which already show a tendency towards stylization (heraldic symbolism, fitting of animals into a circular 'rose' form, animals 'welded' to one another, paws, nails, claws or hooves of animals ending in curls and spirals), and of being adapted as motifs for the open-work bronze plaques that were coming in.[104] In the second Tagar period (from approximately 400 B.C.), deer and ibex appear among our bronzes, their heads turned back over their shoulders, hooves joined (so that the animal almost appears to be lying down). Now these various motifs (deer in 'recumbent gallop', coiled animals, open-work plaques) pass, according to Kiselev, from Tagar art over to Ordos art, then to the so-called Huai art. The fierce beast flinging itself upon a member of the deer or horse family etc., presumably originates in Tagar, whence the motif would have passed over to the Ordos, then also to the China of the 'Warring States'.[105]

---

[104] On the coilings and 'whirlings of animals', see Anna Roes, Tierwirbel, in *Ipek*, vol. II, Berlin, 1936-37, p. 85.

[105] Ancient History of Southern Siberia (Drevnaya Istoriya Juzhnoy Sibiri) In *Materials and Research on the Archaeology of the* U.S.S.R. (Materiali i isledovaniya po arkheologiya S.S.S.R.), no. 9 (1949), pp. 108-176. (The reader is reminded of another work by Kiselev, *The Tagar Culture*, Publications of the Sayan Expedition, IV [Sektsii Arkheologii, R.A.N.I.D.N., IV], Moscow, 1928, pp. 257-264). For the western area of the art of the steppes, the latest Soviet discoveries are

The reports of the latest Soviet excavations in the Minusinsk region thus enable us to establish the following suppositions:

1) The 'animal' art of the Minusinsk region, still at the stammering stage in the Karasuk period (1200-700) derives from the Chinese art of An-yang.

2) By a reverse movement, the Ordos (and Sui-yüan, etc.) 'animal' art, much more highly elaborated, was influenced by the Siberian art of the Minusinsk region, in the Tagar period (700-100 B.C.), and Ordos art in turn then influenced the Chinese art of the Warring States.[106]

Comparison of the 'Warring States' bronzes and the Ordos bronzes will undoubtedly make it possible to date the latter more exactly, but meanwhile the chronology is still far from certain. For the Ordos weapons, for example, Max Loehr places some of the daggers, of the *akinakès* type, between the eighth and fifth centuries B.C., and another series (daggers with hilts 'in a circle' and 'roof-type' guards) between the eighth and seventh centuries, still other series (which would be contemporaneous with Anino in the steppes and Chin-ch'üan in China) between the sixth and the third, while T. J. Arne has the Luan-p'ing and Hsüan-hua Ordos bronzes begin only about 350 B.C.[107]

Since the dawn of history the Altaïc peoples—in particular the Huns, ancestors of the Turko-Mongolians of today—had been the neighbours and sworn enemies of China. To the agricultural Chinese they seemed to represent the very essence of barbarism. Against these nomad herdsmen, the mobility of whose

---

set forth in the following works: Rudenko, *Histoire des Scythes de l'Altaï*, Pushkin Museum, 1949; Franz Hancar, L' Elargissement de nos Perspectives Historiques par les Recherches Préhistoriques Soviétiques, in the review *Coup d'oeil à l'Est*, fasc. II, 1/2, Jan.-June 1949, pp. 37-63, (Halstatto-Cimmerian relations, Scythian origins, etc., with Soviet bibliography brought up to date). P. Schultz, New Archaeological Discoveries in the Crimea, in the review *Voks*, no. 55, Moscow, 1948, p. 59.

[106] Kiselev, *Histoire Ancienne de la Sibérie méridionale*, pp. 108-176.

[107] Loehr, Ordos Daggers and Knives, New Material, Classification and Chronology, I, Daggers, *Artibus Asiae*, XII, 1949, pp. 23-83.

mounted archers made them formidable, the Chinese armies, still equipped only with heavy chariots, were often at a disadvantage. But in 307 B.C., in order to fight them on equal terms, they in turn created a cavalry. By the same token, the Chinese directly borrowed from the Huns a part of their equipment, in particular the bronze ornaments and buckles. With these buckles and plaques (as we can verify by the pieces in the Coiffard Collection being shown in the Cernuschi Museum) we find a number of motifs spreading through China that were directly taken over from Ordos art or influenced by it.[108] The main body of several of the buckles in our collections is formed by a single wolf or hind such as those found in the art of the steppes; other buckles are composed of animals interlaced, entangled, devouring one another or issuing from one another, or of an 'animal network', a theme common to the so-called Minusinsk bronzes (Tagar period) and to those of the Ordos.

We may note, moreover, that, as Solange Lemaitre points out, it is possible that on the clasps or buckles of the 'Warring States' the animal-type or fantastic theme may vary in China itself, according to region. It is possible that on the buckles originating in the provinces of the lower Yangtze (the Huai region, properly speaking), the head of an elephant (an animal then prevalent in South China) replaces the *t'ao-t'ieh* head, the latter motif being perhaps more confined to North China, the original home of Chinese culture.[109]

We shall call attention, finally, to works having a style so local as to be positively alien, which have been revealed by the Ch'ang-sha discoveries in Hunan.[110] Hunan, in the period of the 'War-

---

[108] Lemaitre, Les Agrafes Chinoises jusqu'à la Fin de l'Epoque Han, *Revue des Arts Asiatiques*, vol. X, 1939, Cf. Tosio Nagahiro, *Die Agraffe und ihre Stellung in der altchinesischen Kunstgeschichte*, Kyoto, 1943.

[109] Lemaitre, vol. X, 3, p. 132 (evolution of the elephant motif).

[110] Cf. Yale University, *Catalogue of the Exhibition of Chinese Antiquities from Ch'ang-sha, lent by J. Hadley Cox, March-May* 1939. F. Löw-Beer, Two Lacquered Boxes from Ch'ang-sha, *Artibus Asiae*, Ascona, X, 4, 1947, p. 302, and XI, 4, 1948 p. 266.

12. *Jade disc, type* pi. *Warring States. Nelson Gallery of Art, Kansas City.*

ring States', was in fact a country that was still 'barbarian', even while it was undergoing a progressive Sinicization as a result of the fact that the Ch'u princes in Hupei—themselves former 'barbarians' spontaneously Sinicized—had extended their domination as far as Ch'ang-sha. The lacquered and painted boxes found in Ch'ang-sha and dating, it seems, from the fifth to third centuries B.C., introduce, when compared with the foliated scrolls of the 'Warring States', motifs that are patently foreign. Even more foreign are the bronze or lacquered wooden supports representing cranes, and especially the extraordinary sculpture in painted wood representing perhaps a local genie, the workmanship of which is absolutely un-Chinese, It was not until the Han period (numerous pieces of which are likewise found, particularly lacquers, in the Ch'ang-sha excavations), that the Chinese influence finally predominated.

The art of south China in the period of the 'Warring States', as the Ch'ang-sha discoveries reveal it to us, explains the fact that certain motifs of the 'Warring States' style (double S spirals, S spirals with 'regressive' volutes, circles with tangents, etc.) are to be found on the bronze drums of the so-called Dong-so'n culture in Tonkin and in Annam. Karlgren concludes from this that in Indo-China the Dongsonian stages may go back to the fourth to third centuries B.C., whereas the recent Dongsonian might date only from the Former Han onwards, as is proved by the discovery, in this layer, of Wang Mang coins (9-22 A.D.).[111]

* * *

Before leaving the art of the 'Warring States', we must return to a topic which we have already mentioned as something which points the way towards one aspect of the art of the Han period,

[111] Karlgren, The Date of the Early Dong-s'on Culture, in B.M.F.E.A., no. 14, Stockholm, 1942, pp. 1-28.

namely: the friezes that decorate several bronze vases, generally of the *hu* type, and which represent scenes of hunting, dances or magic ceremonies.

On the magnificent *hu* of the Stoclet Collection in Brussels,
naked hunters armed with pikes, knives or bows face wild beasts
in single combat. The central frieze is particularly vivid. The hunted animal, already wounded—a bull, it would seem—falls on its
knees but still faces the enemy, its head lowered to gore the
hunter. On the upper frieze, near the neck of the vase, tigers or
other felines, gathered to spring, are stopped short by the hunter
who pierces their necks with his lance.[112] On a similar *hu*, in
the former C. T. Loo Collection, the central frieze is almost
identical, but the hunted animal, wounded by an arrow and
facing its pursuer, horns lowered, is a large stag. Hunters and
animals, whether treated in simple outline, in profile, or in flat
relief, are full of a powerful and almost savage movement, and
at the same time arranged in accordance with a remarkable decorative discipline.

Even more interesting are the mythical or magical themes of
some of the friezes on these *hu* vases. On the bronze in the Loo
Collection that we have just called attention to, we see on the
lower friezes, near the foot of the vase, 'figures wearing masks
of birds or other animals and executing animal-like dances, and
other figures that are horned and wear wings of a kind and
what may be a bird's tail hung from the waist: probably sorcerers executing a magic dance'.[113] The Curtis gift has contributed
to the Guimet Museum another *hu* bronze jar decorated with
friezes which are no less remarkable. On the register encircling
the neck appears an archery scene—'the archery ceremony', it

[112] Sirén, *History of Early Chinese Art*, pl. 101. Cf. Rolf Stein, based on
the study by Jung Keng on the Shang and Chou Chinese bronzes, in *Bulletin
de l'Ecole Française d'Extrême-Orient*, 1942, 2, pl. 405.
[113] Serge Elisseeff, Quelques Heures à l'Exposition des Bronzes Chinois (de
l'Orangerie en 1934), *Revue des Arts Asiatiques*, VIII, 4, p. 239 and pl. LXXI.

would seem, of the rite described by the *I-li* and the *Chou-li*. Next, on the same register there is a scene thought to represent the gathering of mulberry leaves. On the shoulder of the vase, the lower register shows a musical scene: 'four bells and four sounding-stones are hung from a cross-piece with a dragon's head at each end and supported by two uprights in the form of phoenixes'; a performer stands in readiness to strike a bell, another plays the drum. At a little distance, figures armed with lances appear to be dancing. In another part, naked men and women pursue hares or, with lance or sword, battle against stags or boars.

'One of them, holding a dagger-axe (*ko*) in his right hand, a knife in his left, attacks a kind of rhinoceros; another is lifted on the croup of a boar that he has seized by the ear'.[114] We here again encounter the movement and the freedom displayed by dragons in the circular designs on the mirrors of the same period, but here applied to the representation of real animals; 'the supple line of the great stags leaping and galloping' is particularly amazing in its fidelity.

Turning from these creatures of the chase as it was practised in the scrub-land of archaic China, here are naked hunters and huntresses attacking creatures that are most strange, 'dragons with horns and antennae and the heads of fabulous animals, double-tailed horse-dragons. Even more curious are the beings with birds' heads on men's bodies'; a human figure with the head, it appears, of a buffalo is perhaps a masked hunter; 'his hands and forearms seem to be gloved with skin and imitate an animal's paws'. There can be no doubt that these masked sorcerers and these naked witches, these animal disguises, shaman's dances, and hunts after fabulous stags or other half-mythical crea-

---

[114] Vandier-Nicolas, Note sur un Vase Chinois du Musée du Louvre, *Revue des Arts Asiatiques*, XII, 4, December 1938, pp. 133-141.

tures, take us straight into the world of primitive magic.[115] They belong to the practices of a religion of initiates that the Confucianist 'positivism', which established itself in the Han period, attempted to abolish, but the persistence of which is vouched for by the Shantung funerary reliefs dating from this same Han period. Thus the friezes of these bronze *hu* vases of the period of the 'Warring States' are a direct transition between the circular patterns of dragons on the mirrors of that period and the Han reliefs of Shantung.

In another connection Mme Vandier-Nicolas points out the affinities between the representations of animals and of fabulous creatures on the *hu* vases and many of the animals, fabulous or real, of the Hunnish bronzes or, more generally, of the art of the steppes.

The Civilization of the 'Warring States': Ways of Thought

We have purposely dealt first with the art of this period, because it is primarily through its art that the rich complexity of the society of the time is conveyed to us, and that we get some idea of the freedom, the spontaneity, the creative power,

---

[115] Vandier-Nicolas, *op. cit.*, p. 140. In connection with the magic representation of the bird-man and of the stag-man on the *hu* in question, see also: Karlgren, B.M.F.E.A,. no. 14, Stockholm, 1942, p. 18 and pl. 17. Granet likewise shows us the mythical hero Yü the Great wearing feathers to dance 'the Dance of the Pheasant' or a bear's skin to dance 'the Dance of the Bear'. 'Yü had become the master of thunder by dancing in the appropriate seasons the dances needed to provide Nature with a regular course, which he did either by dancing the dance of the bear, holding a drum, or, like a pheasant, by leaping and beating the drum with his wings' (Granet, 'Le Pas de Yu' in *Danses et Légendes de la Chine Ancienne*, II, 1926, pp. 575-576). Perhaps, as we have seen, and as both Serge Elisseeff and Madeleine David suggest, it might be wondered if the *t'ao-t'ieh* mask, originally the mask of a ram, a bull, a tiger, a bear or a stag—but always without a lower jaw—does not represent the animal skin that the masked sorcerer wore to dance the appropriate totemic dance, from which (as today in the case of so many of our 'tiger skins' and other hunting trophies) the lower jaw had been removed in the process of skinning the animal.

III. *Procession of Dignitaries, wall painting. Han Dynasty. Tomb at Liao-yang, Manchuria.*

and the diversity of tendencies which characterized it. Never, perhaps, has Chinese society contained within itself such a tumult of unleashed forces, such a clash of potentialities.

The same impression emerges from the texts. For this is the great age of Chinese literature, the age when literature was diversified by a lively variety of trends, in contrast to the repetitive and often impoverished literary tradition of later centuries.

Among the various 'schools' into which learning in ancient China was divided, was that of the soothsayers; and this was the source for one of the earliest works of Chinese literature. Divination, as we have seen, was practiced either by means of the carapaces of turtles (to which heat was applied, the resulting cracks being 'read' by the soothsayers), or by yarrow stalks (which, according to their arrangement in curved or broken lines, were 'read' by the soothsayers and foretold the future). There was a table of sixty-four hexagrams, which provided a code for reading the omens. These were figures formed of six superimposed lines, some unbroken (—), some broken (- -). The symbol, or rather, the essence, of everything that existed was thought to be contained in these hexagrams, the first of which was the symbol of heaven (six unbroken superimposed lines), and the second the symbol of earth (six broken superimposed lines). The broken line represents shadow, cold, passivity, the feminine element, even numbers, and was what the Chinese called the *yin* element; the unbroken line represents light, heat, activity, the male element, odd numbers, and was what the Chinese called the *yang* element.[116] With the exception of Heaven and Earth, the first of which is purely *yang*, and the second purely *yin*, all things are composed of both *yang* and *yin* in unequal proportions. It is the balance between these complementary forces which constitutes the order of the universe; or more exactly, not so much the balance between them as the 'changes' that take place between

---

[116] Translation of the Chinese texts on the *yin* and the *yang* in Alfred Forke, *World-Conception of the Chinese*, London, 1925, pp. 12-223.

them, since each periodically changes into the other (which accounts for the alternation of the seasons, of day and night, and for such phenomena as the metamorphoses of animals, etc.). As can at once be seen, here were the elements of a philosophy of the universe and of life, and of a logical classification of things. But more than this: it was a coherent system of 'Platonic ideas' translated into geometric formulae, by means of which, it was believed, the essence of things could be apprehended; the hexagrams revealed the ideal and permanent archetypes upon which concrete things had been modelled and of which they were but the temporary reflection. Whoever possessed these diagrams which were the archetypal ideas of all creatures and all things, possessed also the secret of all things and all creatures, and could not only predict their behaviour, but even to a certain extent control it. This theory provided a metaphysical justification for the powers, deriving directly from primitive magic, to which the school of soothsayers laid claim.

The theory of the eight trigrams (*pa-kua*) and of the sixty-four hexagrams (*ch'ung-kua*) on which these conceptions rest, was elaborated in the manual of divination called *I-ching* or 'Book of Changes', a work, according to Maspero, that may go back either to the beginning of the eighth century or the beginning of the seventh.[117] Later the 'philosophy' that was derived from it and that we have just sketched (the theory of the *yin* and the *yang*) was added to the *I-ching* in the appendix known as the *Hsi-tz'u*, a treatise whose elements, according to Maspero, must have been already fixed by the end of the fifth century B.C.[118] Another archaic philosophic text is the *Hung-fan*, 'the Great Rule' (or 'Great Plan')[119], which establishes the concordance (so

[117] Maspero, *Chine Antique*, p. 448, note 1. On the *I-ching*, see also Arthur Waley, The Book of Changes, B.M.F.E.A., no. 5, Stockholm, 1933, p. 121.

[118] Maspero, *op. cit.*, p. 480.

[119] Subsequently joined to the *Shu-ching* of which we shall speak, which in the main goes bach to the ninth to eighth centuries B.C.

often invoked since) between the Universe and man through the
'Five Primordial Elements', to each of which corresponds one of
the 'five cardinal points', a cosmological conception harmonizing,
like that of the *yin* and the *yang*, with a theory of the qualitative
components of the universe.[120]

We are confronted here with the immemorial data of primitive geomancy in association with ancient secret lore pertaining
to the 'virtue' of the elements—conceptions which, we may note,
were never to be disavowed by later Chinese thought. Among
the various concordances laid down by these principles, that of
Earth with Heaven, of the human with the cosmic order, was
also manifested by the doubling of each other by the Sovereign
on High, who crowned the celestial order, and the Chinese king
(at this time, of the dynasty of Chou), who crowned the human
order. The theory of royal power derived from the conception.
The earthly monarch, whose throne, the 'August Supreme', is
the keystone of the human order, exercises his power only because
it corresponds to that of the Lord on High, who has his seat in
the Great Bear, and because he holds the 'heavenly mandate',
which invests him with cosmic 'virtue'. In fact, the Chinese king
in the time of the Chou was above all the high priest of the
primitive agricultural and calendrical religion, who alone is qualified to 'open the seasons' or to close them by performing the

[120] To *North* correspond Water and the colour black (symbol: the Black
Turtle). To *East* correspond Wood and the colour green (symbol: the Green
Dragon). To *West*, metal and the colour white (symbol: the White Tiger). To
South, Five and the colour red (symbol: the Red Bird). To *Centre* (which in China
is the fifth of the Cardinal Points) correspond the Earth and the colour yellow (the
Earth on which the Yellow Emperor reigns). We may add that the theory of the
Five Elements and the Five Cardinal Points appears to antedate the dualism of
the *yin* and the *yang*, with which we dealt first in the interest of clarity. See
Maspero, *Les Religions Chinoises*, Musée Guimet, 1950, pp. 89-90. Translation
of Chinese texts pertaining to the 'Five Elements', with tables of concordance. in
Forke, *World Conception of the Chinese*, pp. 227-300. Cf. Granet, *La Pensée
Chinoise*, p. 228, on the application of these categories to Chinese music. On the
animals of the 'North', see in particular L. de Saussure, La Tortue et le Serpent, in
T'oung pao, XIX, 1920, p. 247.

suitable sacrifices, and who thereby makes the agrarian cycle accord with the seasonal cycle, so that the work of agriculture can be carried out; in other words, here, too, Earth is brought into concordance with Heaven.

* * *

Another important text of archaic Chinese literature is the *Chou-li* ('Rites of the Chou'), an administrative collection of the fourth century B.C., which underwent various alterations and interpolations in the time of the Han. Composed at a time when the Chou dynasty no longer exercised any power, the *Chou-li* tends to describe for us not so much the governmental system that must previously have functioned when the authority of that house was effective, as a kind of ideal government in line with the theories of the learned men of the fourth century—an ideal, which, in reaction and protest against the brutality and the tumult of the 'Warring States', provided the solacing picture of a majestically ordered patriarchal society.[121] We may mention also, in this connection, the *I-li*, on the ritual practices of the nobles, of great importance for a period in which it was only the nobility that engaged in political activity; and the *Li-chi*, another commentary on the rites, covering a period from the fourth to the first centuries B.C., which enlightens us as to religious ceremonies, feasts and sacrifices, mourning rites, filial piety and the religious role of music as a harmonizing moral influence etc.

Another text that was to become canonical is the *Shih-ching*, or 'Book of Odes', a collection that includes on the one hand popular songs, and on the other religious hymns. The most ancient of the hymns appears to go back to the ninth century B.C., the apogee of the Chou dynasty; it was probably sung to a dance

[121] Cf. Karlgren, The Early History of the Chou-li and Tso-chuan texts, in B.M.F.E.A., Stockholm, III, 1931.

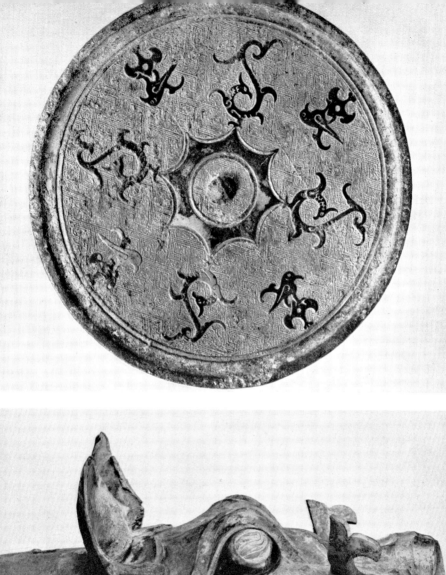

13. Above: *Mirror, bronze. Warring States. Ramet Collection, Paris.*
Below: *Dragon head, terminal ornament of a chariot pole, bronze.*
State of Han, Late Chou Dynasty, fifth to third century B.C.
Freer Gallery of Art, Washington.

rhythm at the time of the sacrifices in honour of the ancestors of the dynasty.[122] The latest are presumed to be of the sixth century. As for the popular songs, they evoke, according to the view of Granet, the 'courts of love' of the young peasant youths and maids when they meet in the countryside in early spring.[123] They are often, despite their archaism, very direct and of great freshness.[124] Maspero held the view, however, that many of these pieces (which he dated as being of the eighth to seventh centuries) are poems in the style of folksongs, composed in princely courts on themes of peasant idylls.

The period of the 'Warring States', is marked by one outstanding poetic figure, that of Ch'ü Yüan (approximately between 350 or 343 and 295 or 285 B.C.). His principal poem, the *Li-sao*, is a kind of elegy or complaint in which the author, after bemoaning the misfortunes of his existence (he had been unjustly banished and exiled, like Ovid, whose *Tristia* come to mind), finds himself swept up into the sky in a mystic flight during which he disports himself in mid-air in the home of the gods. We shall come upon the latter theme again in Taoist mystic writings of the same period.

History is represented for the period of the 'Warring States' by the *Shu-ching*, by the book known as the 'Spring and Autumn Annals'. (*Ch'un-ch'iu*) and by the *Tso-chuan*.

The *Shu-ching* ('Book of Documents') is a collection of texts, the most ancient of which may date back to the ninth century B.C., when the Chou dynasty was at its height; the latest events referred to in this collection occurred in 625 B.C. Maspero discerns in it fragments of more or less euphemerized mythological legends,[125]

---

[122] A poem of the same collection (a satire against bad government) is exactly 'dated' by the eclipse of 775 B.C.

[123] As still today among the Tai of Upper Tonking (Maspero, *Les Religions Chinoises*, Musée Guimet, 1950, p. 160).

[124] Granet, *Fêtes et Chansons Anciennes de la Chine*, 1919.

[125] See Maspero, Légendes Mythologiques dans le Chou-king, *Journal Asiatique*, CCIV, 1924, pp. 1-100.

8.

moral speeches put into the mouths of the 'sage kings' of that supposedly patriarchal epoch with which the Chinese furnished their proto-history (as for example in the legendary account of the hero Yü the Great, founder of the Hsia dynasty), and passages that are probably echoes of actual royal edicts and proclamations of the Chou dynasty.

The 'Spring and Autumn Annals' are the local chronicle, for the years 722 to 481 B.C., of the principality of Lu—where Confucius was born—in the present-day province of Shantung. Another chronicle is linked with it, that of the *Tso-chuan*, which is a general history of China from 722 to 450, undoubtedly written toward the end of the fourth century B.C. These annals are the work of moralists, who select suitable anecdotes in order to point a lesson for princes and their advisers. This kind of moralizing was for long to be a feature of Chinese historical writing, despite its precision with regard to facts and dates.

During the period of the 'Warring States' that follows that of the 'Spring and Autumn Annals' (from 481 B.C.), the Chinese world offers us the contradictory spectacle of social foundations based on eternal values and of political organizations in perpetual upheaval. From the political point of view, war raged permanently among the provincial kingdoms, a fierce and merciless war in which, amid torrents of blood, each State sought to exterminate the others in order to achieve the unification of the empire and imperial power for itself. It was to take two and a half centuries of carnage before the best organized among them, the state of Ch'in, in the present-day province of Shensi, was able to bring about this kind of unification by violence.

And yet, as we have said, never was a social religion more securely established than the Chinese religion of that time, founded on the solidarity binding the generations together and expressed in the worship of ancestors and in the practices of filial piety. It was a religion based on pacts, as was the agrarian religion of which the Chinese king, as 'first tiller', remained the supreme pontiff. In the agrarian worship there was, as we have seen, a pact of concordance between Earth and Heaven, between the earthly king and the Sovereign on High, for the greater benefit of sowings and harvests. In ancestral worship the pact was one concluded between the ancestor and his descendants. The descendants, by the sacrificial offerings with which they fed the ancestor's soul, indefinitely prolonged its survival, and the ancestor, by way of recompense, would then protect them from on high. Not to nourish the ancestor's soul was to condemn it to the wretched fate of a roaming phantom (*kuei*), of a ghost avid for vengeance. This steadfastness in the worship of the ancestor would begin even in the latter's lifetime, in the form of a filial piety that constitutes one of the most constant of the social dogmas that help to account for the continuity of Chinese culture.[126]

* * *

It was not only in social life (and, as we have seen, in the field of art as well), that the period of the 'Warring States' can be seen to be full of contradictory trends: the same was true in the field of speculative thought. This was the time when Chinese thought, having set out, as we have also seen, from the notions common to all 'primitive mentality', now proceeded to rationalize these notions following two different directions so opposed as to lead, on the one hand, to Taoism, and on the other, to Confucianism.

Taoism is expounded in three fundamental works: (1) the *Tao Te Ching*, attributed to a more or less legendary sage,[127] a

[126] On the Chinese family traditionally constituted on these foundations, see in particular Olga Lang, *Chinese Family and Society*, New Haven, 1946.

[127] In favour of a certain historicity of Lao-tzu see, however, Fung Yu-Lan, *History of Chinese Philosophy*, Trans. Derk Bodde, Peking, 1937, p. 171. Cf. Hu Shih, Criticism of Recent Methods Used in Dating Lao-tzu, *Harvard Journal of Asiatic Studies*, 1938, p. 373.

text probably written in the fourth century or perhaps not until the third century B.C. (2) the book of *Chuang-tzu*, the author of which, bearing the same name, and who in this case was a historical personage, lived towards the end of the fourth century B.C. (3) the *Lieh-tzu*, a compilation probably dating from the end of the third century B.C.

We have seen above that in the *Hsi-tz'u* there already appears the double notion of *yin* and *yang*, that is to say of the two modalities between which all things are distributed, the alternation of which accounts for the rhythm of the universe and for the way in which things appear and disappear again. To this double notion had been added that of the *tao*, a term usually translated by 'way', which, however, does not adequately convey its meaning because what is implied is a kind of Universal Energy, an *élan* both cosmic and vital, which constitutes the essential unity of the *yin* and the *yang*, since it is the *tao* that is alternatively transformed into the one or the other modality. The aim of the Taoist school, as taught in the books of Lao-tzu, Chuang-tzu and Lieh-tzu, is to achieve an identification through ecstasy with the *tao*. Through this participation in the cosmic power, the sage becomes master of the universe.[128] The powers that he acquires in this way and that enlarge his personality to the dimensions of the cosmos obviously derive from those that the ancient sorcerers immemorially sought in primitive magic. But whereas primitive magic had recourse to a holy frenzy that was meant to produce the states of trance and of possession, in

---

[128] As in the Indian *yoga*, in order to seize Being in its entirety, as it reveals itself below the level of our thinking, it is necessary to think beyond the categories (in the Kantian sense of the word). 'The bow-net', says Chuang-tzu, 'is for catching fish; but when one holds the fish it is no longer necessary to think of the basket. The trap is for catching hares; but when one holds the hare it is no longer necessary to think of the trap. Words are for catching ideas; but when one holds the idea it is no longer necessary to think of words'. (Arthur Waley, *Three Ways of Chinese Thought*, London, 1939. See Waley also with regard to the *Tao Tê Ching. The Way and Its Power, a study of the Tao Tê Ching and Its Place in Chinese Thought*, London, 1934.

which the divine would invest the initiate, it was in motionless contemplation, in isolation in nature, in a mountain retreat, that the Taoist achieved the mystic union. It should be added, however, that subsequently Taoism was to advocate a whole mechanism of ascesis, a 'hygiene' of diet, breathing or sexuality, which appear rather trivial when we compare them to the flights of a Chuang-tzu. The evolution of Taoism is thus from primitive magic to the wonderful spirituality of Chuang-tzu, whence it soon returns to the spiritism and the utterly unintellectual recipes of thaumaturgy.[129]

The fact remains that with 'the Fathers of the Taoist system', or rather with their three books—*Tao Te Ching, Chuang-tzu* and *Lieh-tzu*—Chinese thought reached a metaphysical height that was never to be surpassed. It was largely from the great Taoist dream of communion with the universe that in the centuries to come the Chinese feeling for nature arose in the form in which it was to triumph in the T'ang poets and the Sung landscapists. In literary expression itself, the lyrical flights of a Chuang-tzu have accustomed the Chinese mind to dwell on the heights. In Chuang-tzu, we find the same spontaneous upsurge, the same creative freedom as in the art of the same period.

* * *

The contradiction that we called attention to above in the political and social field for the whole era of the 'Warring States' is to be found likewise (and nothing better shows the richness of the epoch) in the realm of speculative thought: in contrast to Taoism, Confuceism.

[129] See Maspero, *Mélanges Posthumes*, Musée Guimet, 1950, vol. I: Les Religions Chinoises (in particular, p. 49); vol. II, Le Taoisme; vol. III, Etudes Historiques (in particular pp. 225-132): Le Saint et la Vie Mystique chez Lao-tseu et Tchouang-tseu. Also Maspero, Le Taoisme, in *Hommes et Mondes*, April 1950, p. 567.

Confucius (*K'ung Ch'iu*) who—if we accept the traditional dates—lived between 551 and 479, is a definite historical personage who was born and died in the ancient principality of Lu, in Shantung. He made no other claim for his eminently traditionalist teaching than that it transmitted the lessons of the earlier sages, among whom were included the half-mythical sovereigns of the patriarchal epoch; and inversely, the entire official élite of scholars of later times claimed to stem from Confucius, attributing to him the body of books that by this consecration had become 'classical' or 'canonical'.[130]

In reality the 'classics' in which the teachings of Confucius had been collected appeared considerably after his life-time. The *Lun-yü* (*The Analects of Confucius*), which claims to transmit to us the sage's discourses, his maxims, his aphorisms, was compiled about the beginning of the fourth century B.C. The *Chung-yung* (*The Doctrine of the Mean*) and the *Ta-hsüeh* (*The Great Learning*) both dealing with the virtues of the 'Superior Man', that is to say the sovereign according to the Confucian ideal, are attributed to a descendant of Confucius, who is presumed to have lived about 400 B.C.

The teaching of Confucius would be incomprehensible if we were to forget the principles unanimously accepted by the scholars of his time and which he merely codified: the harmony between Heaven and Earth, guaranteed by the virtue of the sovereign and his counsellors; the efficacy of the rites by which this same harmony is ensured. As for Confucius's personal contribution, it seems that the supreme sage stressed above all two concepts on which the whole Chinese ethic effectively rests: the concept of equity (in Chinese *i*), and that of altruism (*jen*). The Confucian equity is based on a principle similar to our social 'contract', that of reciprocity among men. Altruism, in the broad sense of the

---

[130] For the present state of criticism, see the excellent little book by Alexis Rygaloff, *Vie de Confucius*, Presses Universitaires, 1946.

term, and as the school teaches it, involves a sense of human dignity, respect for oneself and others, and a concern for mutual welfare upon which statesmen like Wang Mang, at the time of Christ, or like Wang An-shih, at the end of the eleventh century of our era, were to base social legislation and social service measures that were highly advanced for their time.

It is appropriate to observe that Confucian philosophy was above all an ethic and that this ethic remained essentially a civic and social ethic. The perfecting of the individual here has no other aim than the perfecting of society.[131] We see the gap that separates the Confucian school and the Taoists, the latter remaining (at least for this period) the advocates of an almost anarchic individualism, to whom any civic or social preoccupation remained foreign.

A school of wisdom rivalling that of Confucius was that of Mo-tzu, or Mo-ti, who also came from the principality of Lu, and who lived between 480 and 400 B.C. Mo-tzu broadened the Confucian altruism into a doctrine of universal love, preached pacificism (an advocacy not without merit in the early period of the 'Warring States') and placed a special emphasis on piety towards Heaven, more precisely towards the Lord On High, considered as a personal god.

Confucian humanitarianism, preached by the School of the Scholars and flowering through them into a true humanism, produced in the second half of the fourth century B.C. a moralist of talent, Mencius (Meng-tzu), who like Confucius originated in the country of Lu, in Shantung, and whose traditional dates are 372-288. The work that bears the name of Mencius is the fourth—the other three being *The Analects of Confucius, The*

---

[131] It should be added, however, that in the time of Confucius, this referred only to the nobility, which alone was regarded as capable of counselling the prince and of participating in government, for the people had no part in public affairs. But Confucian humanitarianism had such a sound foundation in general ideas that it was able progressively to broaden until it embraced all people in its solicitude.

Doctrine of the Mean and *The Great Learning,*—of the canonical 'Four Books'. He too develops the two great principles of
humanity and of equity (*jen* and *i*). He dwells on the innate
goodness in the heart of man and on the role of education,
the aim of which is to make this seed germinate. Because of the
role thus assigned to education, Mencius was to be for centuries
the favourite author of the School of the Scholars.[132]

To the optimism of these theoreticians who placed their ideal
in the golden age of an archaic patriarchal monarchy, the reality
of the 'Warring States' each day brought a bloody refutation.
A few of these provincial States—that of Ch'in in Shensi, that
of Ch'i in Shantung, that of Ch'u in Hupei, to mention the most
important—were in the process of destroying the lesser principalities around them. In their service, to justify their conquests,
a special school, that of the Jurists, elevated political expediency
into a doctrine. A pessimism devoid of any illusions as to human
nature had already been taught by the philosopher Hsün-tzu
(about 300-230),[133] and the jurists cynically made practical ap-
plications of this outlook in order to crush the individual for
the benefit of the prince. The interest of the Prince—a *Prince*
according to Macchiavelli's ideal—became the supreme law.
The most remarkable representative of this theory was Wei Yang
(also called Kung-sun Yang) who, from 361 to his death in 338,
as minister of the kingdom of Ch'in, helped to establish in this
State, through ruthless legislation, a centralized and absolute—to-
talitarian—monarchy, in contrast to the feudal system of government still in force in the other principalities. Thus, by fire and
sword, with unmitigated harshness, was forged the Empire State,
which was to create the Chinese Empire.[134]

[132] On Mencius, see Waley, *Three Ways of Thought* (*op. cit.*), p. 118.
[133] About 315-235, according to the *History of Chinese Philosophy* by Hu Shih.
[134] On the School of Jurists (better called 'School of Laws', *Fa-chia*), see Waley,
op. cit., p. 143.

14. *Bell, bronze. Warring States. Stoclet Collection, Brussels.*

15. *Ceremonial vessel, type* ting, *bronze inlaid with gold and silver, from Chin-ts'un. Warring States. Art Institute, Chicago.*

* * *

The Kingdom of Ch'in Forms the Empire of China

We have shown the importance, in terms of physical and human geography, of the province of Shensi. The bleak plateaux of loess that compose it overhang, survey and dominate the 'imperial' plain of Honan toward which Shensi 'descends' in a continuous slope, following the orientation of the river Wei whose junction with the Yellow River, at the T'ung-kuan Pass, is of great strategic importance. The furrow of the Wei that cuts the plateau from west to east is bordered, especially at the approach to the junction, by fertile alluvial lands, 'the smile on this morose face'. The lords of this bellicose frontier-march had once before, in 1027, in the person of the Chou dynasty, descended into the plain of Honan for the conquest of the Chinese throne. Then, when the Chou in 770 had abandoned their native march and let themselves grow soft amid the delights of Honan, their role as barons of the marches had been taken over in the very same valley of the Wei by their vassals, the lords of Ch'in.

And history repeated itself, the princes of Ch'in completing—but this time for good—the work only begun and then abandoned by the preceding dynasty. Subordinating all affairs of state to the perfecting of their army, the princes of Ch'in made it into a first-class war machine with no other objective but conquest. Alone among the Chinese feudal lords of their time, they were able to rise above the feudal failings, to avoid the creation of fiefs on their territory and, thanks to a series of ministers like Wei Yang, already mentioned, to create for themselves a theory of the state wholly new in China. Without doubt the school of jurists, a school of realism and even of political cynicism of which Wei Yang was only one representative, propounded its maxims to many a provincial ruler. Only the princes of Ch'in proved able to put the theory into practice, because the theory

9.

merely expressed their hereditary behaviour. The unitary, centralized, absolutist, already 'modern' state that they established in
their Shensi domain was singularly 'in advance' of all the other
Chinese principalities. In less than a century, between 316 and
221, it was to conquer and unify all the rest of the territory which
then constituted China. It is true that in order to bring this
great task to completion the long lineage of the Ch'in kings was
to culminate in an exceptional personality—exceptional even in
world history—that of Ch'in Shih Huang-ti.

The task of Ch'in Shih Huang-ti had, to be sure, been prepared by his forebears. Between 256 and 249, at Lo-yang, in
Honan, they had blotted out the dynasty of the only legitimate
and pan-Chinese sovereign, the merely nominal kings of the
house of Chou. But it was Ch'in Shih Huang-ti who, in nine
blazing years, from 230 to 221, put an end to the other 'Warring
States'. In 221, disdaining the royal title that had been so long
discredited, he assumed the wholly new title of Sovereign Emperor (*huang-ti*).[135]

The Chinese empire was founded at the same time that Chinese unity was achieved.

Chinese imperial unity was beyond question the product of
the destruction, by Ch'in Shih Huang-ti, of all the 'Warring
States' except the Ch'in. It resulted above all from the fact that
the Chinese Caesar made this destruction irrevocable by extending to all China the principles of centralization and of absolutism
that had ensured all the triumphs of the north-west march for
more than a century. The Ch'in empire—that is to say the Chinese
empire that lasted for twenty-one centuries—was the state and
the organization of the Ch'in realm raised to dimensions com-
mensurable with Chinese continuity and with the scale of the
Chinese continent.

---

[135] Ch'in Shih Huang-ti properly signifies: Sovereign-Emperor the First (of
the) Ch'in (dynasty). Cf. D. Bodde, *China's First Unifier, a Study of the Ch'in
Dynasty, as seen in the Life of Li Ssu*, Leyden 1938.

For Ch'in Shih Huang-ti was not content merely to reign over the China that he had unified, that is to say over the original Chinese territories of the Yellow River basin and the countries, already Sinicized by an imperceptible osmosis, situated to the north of the Yangtze. Once he became emperor he subdued by force of arms the lands, until then peopled by other races, of the present South China as far as and including the Cantonese region. Add that by the completion of the Great Wall he put the provinces of the North in a position to defend themselves against the Huns, and it will then be understood that his reign, first as king of Ch'in (246-221), then as emperor (221-210), placed an ineradicable stamp on the whole history of China.

Like the former Ch'in kings, his ancestors, Ch'in Shih Huang-ti had been raised in the hard political realism of the School of Jurists.[136] He had no sympathy, on the other hand, for the scholars of the Confucianist school, whose humanitarian ideal, pacificism and conservatism were a hindrance to his policy. In order to have done with the past that they represented, he ordered the wholesale destruction of their works—a measure that it was doubtless impossible to carry out completely, but the effect of which was such that when later attempts were made to reconstruct the texts of the former 'Confucian canon', they were encumbered with a number of interpolations and spurious texts from which, despite an increasingly searching criticism of sources, the Chinese 'Classics' still suffer.

Ch'in Shih Huang-ti ordered that on his tomb, near the present city of Sianfu, in Shensi, an enormous tumulus should be erected, which rises more than 150 feet above its base, and 250 feet above the forward limit of the embankment, a mound of half a million cubic metres that dominates the Wei plain from afar, as the First Emperor dominates the centuries.[137] But while his work—the

---

[136] See Waley, *op. cit.*, p. 180 (Realism in Action).
[137] See Chavannes, *Mémoires Historiques de Sseu-ma Ts'ien*, vol. II, p. 193. J. Lartigue, Résultats Archéologiques, *Journal Asiatique*, May-June 1916, p. 407.

unitary Chinese Empire—was to last more than two thousand years, his dynasty did not survive him, as he died in 210 and his incapable son disappeared in 207 in the midst of a general revolt.

Until a few years ago, the name 'Ch'in art' was given to the art (in particular to the style of the bronzes) that we have described under the name of: style of the 'Warring States' (or Huai style). In point of fact, the imperial period of the Ch'in (221-207) is much too brief to make it possible to fit into it all the bronzes belonging to the style in question. The imperial art of the Ch'in is but the last phase of the art of the 'Warring States'.

CHAPTER TWO

THE SONS OF HAN

Han Rule in China and in Upper Asia: The Western Han

The structure erected, however hastily, by Ch'in Shih Huang-ti must have been built of indestructible materials, since after the civil war and the anarchy that followed the death of the Founder, Chinese unity and imperial centralization remained intact. The saviour as well as the beneficiary of the imperial idea was a soldier of fortune, Liu Pang, whom nothing—excepting perhaps his peasant cunning—seemed to designate for such a role. And while Ch'in Shih Huang-ti, the heir of a line of more than thirty princes, was able to ensure the throne for his house only for three years, Liu Pang, the upstart peasant, founded an imperial dynasty destined to reign for four centuries (206 B.C. to 200 A.D.), a dynasty whose very name was to become, as it were, the symbol of all legitimacy.

It is significant that the Han dynasty, which originated in what is today the Nanking region, should at once have transferred its capital to Ch'ang-an, or Sianfu, in the province of Shensi, the former patrimony of the Ch'in. This north-western march was retained as the core of the Empire, the territory from which the rest of the Chinese soil could be dominated. By setting up his capital in Ch'ang-an, close to the former capital of the Ch'in, Liu Pang declared himself to be their direct successor.

Liu Pang had become the emperor Han Kao-tsu (206-195), but he was nevertheless unable to prevent his lieutenants from reassuming the former feudal titles abolished by Ch'in Shih Huang-ti; yet with his customary cunning he saw to it (as did his heirs after him) that these titles coresponded to no reality of power. His work along this line was continued by one of his descendants, the Emperor Han Wu-ti (140-87 B.C.), the most powerful personality of the dynasty who, in this respect, can be compared only to Ch'in Shih Huang-ti himself. In order to complete the establishment of an absolute monarchy and put an end, once and for all, to attempts at feudal restoration, Han Wu-ti withdrew administration from the hands of the nobles who had held it from time immemorial, and entrusted it to the Confucianist scholars. Since the founding of the Empire, these had remained in opposition. Han Wu-ti reconciled himself with them in order finally to eliminate the nobility, and this union of Chinese Caesarism and of the Confucianist 'mandarinate' was to last as long as the Empire itself.[1]

The reign of Han Wu-ti was in fact accompanied by a real rebirth of Confucianism. The texts of the Confucian canon, destroyed in 213 B.C. on the order of Ch'in Shih Huang-ti, were, from 191 on, enthusiastically restored. In 175 the Five Classics, now reconstituted, were engraved on stone, like our Biblical 'tablets of the law'. The work of restitution, as we have seen, was not accomplished without alterations, interpolations and tendentious interpretations. The prime concern was to reduce the various sources to uniformity at all costs, in order to achieve a rigorous conformity. Thus it was that Confucianism became an official, syncretistic and apparently coherent doctrine, the ideological framework of the Chinese State. In 136 B.C. a college was accordingly established, to provide the orthodox interpretation of the 'Classics'. In 125 the Emperor Han Wu-ti decided that in

[1] Cf. Edouard Biot, *Essai sur l'Histoire de l'Instruction Publique en Chine et de la Corporation des lettrés*, Paris, 1847.

order to enter the administrative service a candidate would henceforth have to pass a competitive examination based on these
same texts. Such was the origin of the system of examinations,
which remained in effect from that time on until 1912. Tung
Chung-shou (who died about 105 B.C.), the theoretician of this
conception of Confucianism, who had inspired these measures,
gave the formula of the new orthodoxy by professing that the
Confucian canon 'teaches the submission of the people to the
sovereign and the submission of the sovereign to Heaven': Confucius restored gave legal sanction to, and legitimized, the authority of the Han dynasty.[2] While thus placing their ideology at
the service of the imperial government, the scholars did not
by-pass the opportunity afforded them of exerting their restrain-
ing criticism upon Chinese Caesarism. It was Tung Chung-shou
who worked out the system of 'censors', whereby these same
scholars were to serve, up to a certain point, as moderators.

The Confucianist restoration was carried into the following
generation by Liu Hsiang (77-6 B.C.) who, at the Court's request,
made an edition of the 'Five Classics'.[3]

Externally, Han Wu-ti founded Chinese imperialism in Asia.

To the north, beyond the Great Wall, in present-day Inner
and Outer Mongolia, the Chinese found themselves at grips with
the Huns, nomadic herdsmen of Turko-Mongol race, formidable
because of their squadrons of archers who made lightning raids
on the frontiers of the Empire. Han Wu-ti, using their own
tactics against them by way of retaliation, organized counter-
raids that crossed the Gobi from south to north, and fell without
warning upon the Hunnish encampments in the steppes of Upper

[2] An autocracy based on a bureaucracy, writes Wang Yü-Ch'uan, in An
Outline of the Central Government of the Former Han Dynasty, *Harvard Journal
of Asiatic Studies*, June 1949, p. 181.

[3] It should be noted that certain writers in the same circles of official
scholars showed signs of Taoist leanings which more or less harmonized with
the reigning Confucianist orthodoxy; among them may be mentioned Chia I (198-
166) and Liu An (died 122 B.C.).

Mongolia. When one of the Chinese generals who led these
expeditions, Ho Ch'ü-ping, died in the full flower of manhood,
Wu-ti had erected to the memory of the great horseman, near
Hsien-yang (Shensi), a tumulus with a great stone statue in the
round at its base, representing a Chinese horse with its feet
trampling a fallen barbarian archer, or perhaps a Tartar horse
between whose feet its mortally wounded rider has slumped.[4]
Ségalen rightly considers that 'this massive block is a splendid
piece of tragic sculpture'. Yet there is a certain crudeness about
the work as a whole which, taken in conjunction with its incised
details, is not without analogy with the marble sculptures of
the Shang period. From the Shang to the Han, with the exception of the work in the round found on the bronzes of the
Chou or the 'Warring States', sculpture—at least as far as we
know—had practically disappeared. When it reappears, after an
interruption of nine centuries, its general aspect is still the same.
Among the most ancient Han funerary terra cottas, more than
one preserves this same crude, squat character, as though the
original matter from which it was meant to emerge were still
clinging to it. And it was by a return to the same heavy masses
(but, alas, without the epic power of the Ho Ch'ü-ping horse)
that Chinese sculpture, after the 'liberation of forms' in the
Wei and T'ang periods, was to close its cycle under the Ming.

From the campaigns conducted by his squadrons against the
Huns in the two Mongolias, emperor Han Wu-ti was to achieve
one permanent conquest: the present-day province of Kansu; an
annexation that was all the more valuable since the string of
oases that continues thence from east to west, between the Gobi

---

[4] See Ségalen, De Voisins and Lartigue, *L'Art Funéraire à l'Epoque des Han*
(1935), p. 33. Seiichi Mizuno, Zeakan-dai ni okeru Boshoku Sekichō no Ichigun
ni tsuite (The Stone Sculpture of the Tomb of Ho Ch'ü-ping). *Tōhō Gakuhō*,
no. 3, Kyoto, 1933. But Jean Buhot wonders if the Ho Ch'ü-ping horse, as it
has come down to us, and which bears so little resemblance to the Han steeds
that we know, is not a late restoration of the T'ang period (or even later)
(*Revue des Arts Asiatiques*, X, 2, June 1936, p. 114).

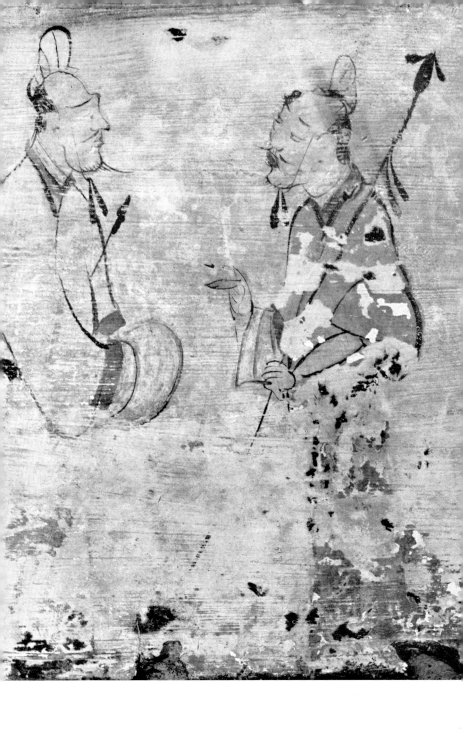

16. *Painted tiles (detail). Han Dynasty. Museum of Fine Arts, Boston.*

17. *Incense burner, type* po-shan-hsiang-lu, *inlaid bronze. Han Dynasty. Freer Gallery of Art, Washington.*

to the north and the chain of the Nanshan to the south, is the point of departure for the caravan trail—the famous 'Silk Road'—that somewhat later was to link China with the Indo-Iranian and the Graeco-Roman worlds.

The caravan oases of the Silk Road itself, in present-day Sin-kiang, our Chinese Turkestan, were then inhabited by popula-tions that we know to have been Indo-European, populations that spoke east-Iranian dialects in Kashgar, Yarkand and Khotan, and other Indo-European dialects—closer, these, to our languages of Europe (to Latin and Celtic, for example)—in Kucha, Karashar and Turfan. Over most of these small kingdoms the Emperor Han Wu-ti extended the suzerainty of China. His squadrons even reached the province of Ferghana, in present-day Soviet Turke-stan, whence they brought back, as remounts for their cavalry, stallions of the great tran-Oxianic race, and it is possibly as a result of this that we find represented in the funerary terra cottas, alongside the small indigenous Chinese horses, those great Ira-nian steeds, those 'Anglo-Arabs' with elegant 'Parthenonian' heads, well known to archaeologists.[5]

To the north-east, the Emperor Han Wu-ti subdued a part of Korea; to the south-east he likewise annexed the Vietnamese do-main, then composed of the Tonkin delta and the coastal plain of northern Annam, between Than-hoa and Hué. Korea and Vietnam undoubtedly preserved their racial and linguistic indi-viduality even under Chinese domination. But the work of Chi-nese civilization was here decisive. Everywhere the Han 'legion-aries' brough with them a knowledge of the Chinese script and the texts of their classic literature, in short the whole of Chinese humanism. In the same way, in the West, the Roman legionaries were to carry with them the whole heritage of Graeco-Latin civi-lization. Most important of all, the Chinese conquerors brought with them, to the very great benefit of the Korea and the Viet-

---

[5] Yetts, The Horse, a Factor in Early Chinese History, *Eurasia Septentrio-nalis Antiqua*, IX, Helsinki, 1934, p. 231.

nam of the future, the Confucianist conception of the State, of centralized power, of regular administration, in place of the indigenous forms of chieftainship. They also brought immense material progress, as exemplified by the introduction of the metal plough—a technical revolution which was brought to light by Henri Maspero—in place of the stone or wooden hoe. And when, later, Vietnam and Korea became independent countries, it was to be on the Chinese model, with princes who had been enlightened as to their duties by a study of Confucius and by the example of the Chinese Son of Heaven, and who had themselves become true Sons of Heaven.

In the same way—to make this legitimate comparison once again—after the fall of Rome, the German or Slav chieftain was to become, on the model of the vanished Caesars, a 'Kaiser' or a 'Czar'.

By book and by sword, the China of the Han, that Rome of the Far East, performed a Roman task.

It may be added (we shall revert to this later) that under the influence of Han China regional schools in the arts of pottery, funerary statuettes and bronze sprang up—notably those of Than-hoa (northern Annam) and of the Lo-lang and Rakuro districts (north-western Korea)—which are of great archeological interest.[6]

* * *

The events of the reign of Han Wu-ti and the whole course of Chinese history previous to it have been related by a very great historian, Ssu-ma Ch'ien, 'the Herodotus of China' (145-86 B.C.).[7]

---

[6] See O. Janse, *Archaeological Researches in Indo-China*, I, Harvard, 1947; and, for Korea, the Japanese publications (Umehara) on the Lo-lang district, and on Rakuro, *Archaeological Reasearches of the Chōsen kozeki kenkyū kai*, I, Seoul and Tokyo, 1934.

[7] Biography of Ssu-ma Ch'ien by Chavannes, *Mémoires Historiques*, vol. I, Introduction, p. XXIII.

Already close to inner government circles, his appointment as official annalist brought him into the personal service of Han Wu-ti; but through his independence of spirit (for having defended an unjustly accused general) he drew down upon himself the wrath of the emperor, who meted out a cruel punishment.[8] His 'Historical Records' (*Shih-chi*), a true monument of historical writing that for us is beyond price, is a work of the highest merit, solidly documented, and often positively scientific in its regard for accuracy in the parts dealing with the period in which the author could check his facts from his personal knowledge of them.[9]

Another famous writer, Ssu-ma Hsiang-ju, was also a protégé of the Emperor Han Wu-ti, from 138 to his death in 117. A poet of merit, he had the whims of a poet, to the point of abandoning the Court from time to time and running off with some light-o'love to lead a Bohemian life in a wayside inn. He has celebrated in his verse the picturesque landscape of the present-day province of Hupei, a region that had already produced, in the period of the 'Warring States', the author of the *Li-sao*. He has likewise described the savage beauty of the imperial hunts, in the course of which Han Wu-ti would pursue his ferocious prey with a temerity that earned him the reproaches of Ssu-ma Hsiang-ju.[10]

---

[8] This powerful personality, Han Wu-ti, caused the misfortune of several other eminent men at court. For instance, he ordered the massacre of the whole family of General Li Ling who, long victorious, had at last had the bad luck to be made prisoner by the Huns; he also had executed the high official Yang Yün, guilty of independence. See in Margouliès, *The Ku-wen*, pp. 93, 101, the letters of Li Ling and of Yang Yün, two of the most eloquent pieces of Chinese prose in this period.

[9] The translation of the *Shih-chi* by Chavannes (*Mémoires Historiques*) includes the first forty-seven chapters of the text in addition, as indicated above, to a very important introduction on the life of Ssu-ma Ch'ien, the reign of Han Wu-ti, etc. In addition to Chavanne's study, see the observations by C. S. Gardner, *Chinese Traditional Historiography*, Harvard, 1938, p. 16.

[10] See Margouliès, *Le Kou-wen*, p. 74.

The first dynasty of the Han was overthrown in the year 8 A.D. by one of their ministers, a scholar named Wang Mang who usurped the throne from the year 9 to the year 22 and who, as a theoretician, carried Confucianist altruism much further than the philosopher Motzu himself. Accordingly, Wang Mang, once he ascended the throne, undertook to modify the property system.[11] In the Confucian Canon, the golden age of the mythical sovereigns, with its supposedly patriarchal organization, was ceaselessly praised as a vanished ideal. Wang Mang took it into his head to revive it. For centuries the great estates had grown, the *latifundia*, that periodic scourge of the Chinese economy, had multiplied; the class of small property-owners, of free men, had correspondingly diminished, increasing the number of 'clients' and slaves. Wang Mang fought to put an end to this enslavement. 'The rich', said this contemporary of Christ, 'have acquired immense properties, whereas the poor do not even have a patch of land big enough to stand a needle on. People are sold like cattle and horses, which is an outrage to the dignity of man, as conceived by Heaven and Earth'.[12]

Wang Mang thus derived from Confucianism an agrarian socialism in accordance with which he proceeded to an equitable sharing-out of the cultivated lands. At the same time he promulgated the principles of a controlled economy, regulating transactions and establishing 'price equalizers', in order to build reserve granaries in the years of good harvest and provide public aid during periods of high prices or of famine.

---

[11] Hans Stange, *Leben, Persönlichkeit und Werk Wang Mangs (Kapitel der Han-Annalen)*, Berlin, 1934; Also, *Monographie über Wang Mang, Ts'ien Han chu, Kapitel 99*, Leipzig, 1939. H. Dubs, Wang Mang and his Economic Reforms, *T'oung pao*, 1940, p. 219.

[12] Cf. Martin Wilbur, *Slavery in China during the Former Han Dynasty*, Publications of Field Museum of Natural History, Anthropological Series, Vol. XXXIV, Chicago, 1943. Hans Wist, Sklaverei in China, *Artibus Asiae*, 1940, p. 238.

Han Rule in China and in Central Asia: The Eastern Han

Wang Mang succumbed before the combined resistance of conservative Confucianism and Han legitimism; also by reason of the peasant rising of the 'Red Eyebrows' (*Che-mei*), who had taken advantage of the social disturbances created by the repercussions of his reforms to break loose in the province of Shantung. (Note should be made of peasant uprisings such as this. All too explicable in themselves, they were often deflected from their social objective to mystic ends by Taoist magicians. They were to recur in the same form throughout Chinese history). Legitimacy was finally re-established in the person of the representative of a junior branch of the Han family, who thus became emperor Kuang Wu-ti (25 to 57 A.D.). This second branch of the Han, which was to reign from 25 to 220, had its capital in the city of Lo-yang (Honan-fu) in Honan.

These 'Later Han' completed the conquest of Central Asia begun by the preceding branch. From 72 to 102 of our era, a bold Chinese captain, Pan Ch'ao, who proved to be both a remarkable administrator and a great 'colonizer', re-established the imperial protectorate over the oases (which were then, as we have seen, Indo-European) of present-day Eastern Turkestan (Sinkiang)—Turfan, Karashar, Kucha, Kashgar to the north, the Lob-nor, Khotan, Yarkand to the south.[13] These oases, admirably cultivated at the time, 'vegetable-garden' oases in the heart of the Gobi desert, were also caravan oases, halting places on the northern or southern trails of the 'Silk Road' that linked the Chinese world, over the passes of the Pamirs, to the Indo-Iranian world, and beyond Iran, to the Roman world.[14] Having reached

[13] The life of *Pan Ch'ao*, translated from the *Hou-Han Shu*, was published by Chavannes, *T'oung pao*, 1906, p. 216.

[14] The exchange of goods between Levantine caravaneers and caravaneers bringing silk from China took place in a valley to the east of the Pamirs, in the spot known as 'the stone tower' (*Lithinos Pyrgos*), the present Tach Kurgan, near Yarkand.

the Pamirs, the Chinese conqueror Pan Ch'ao conceived the idea of establishing commercial and political relations with Rome, then governed by the emperors of the house of the Antonines. His plan failed, but, as we know through the Chinese annalists of the *Hou-Han shu* as well as through the Alexandrian geographers, such as Ptolemy (about 170 A.D.), traffic between the West and China over the 'Silk Road' continued to prosper.[15]

We shall see that over this road Graeco-Buddhist art brought Roman influences right to the heart of Chinese Turkestan: the mural paintings of Miran, in the Lob-nor (third century), could —apart from any religious consideration—have come from Dura-Europos or even from Pompeii. It was in fact above all the Buddhistic religion (which, incidentally, inspired the Miran frescoes) that benefited, as we shall see, by this great line of communication. Here we shall merely mention that about 60-70 A.D. we already find a Buddhistic community, organized by Indian missionaries, establishing itself on the lower Yangtze.[16] This trade in ideas, intimately linked to the trade in goods, was made possible only because the Chinese generals of the Han dynasty had extended the 'Chinese Peace' to within approach of the Graeco-Buddhistic Afghanistan and Punjab and because this *Pax Sinica* extended its hand across Parthian Iran, to the Roman Peace.

It should not be forgotten that, as well as the double trail of caravans that linked the Roman empire to the Chinese empire, from Antioch to Sianfu, across Graeco-Buddhistic Bactria, there was also a maritime route in this same period of the Antonines and the later Han. The Chinese annals mention, for the year 166 A.D., the arrival in China of a Roman merchant who claimed to have come at the behest of 'An-tun'—this, according to the date, would be Marcus Aurelius Antoninus—and who, by way

---

[15] See Albert Herrmann, *Das Land der Seide im Lichte der Antike*, summarizing previous works, Leipzig, 1938, and his *Historical and Commercial Atlas of China*, Harvard, 1935, maps 24, 27, 35, 37, 39.

[16] Maspero, *Journal Asiatique*, 1934, vol. II, pp. 87-107.

of tribute, brought curiosities obtained on the coast of Indo-China. In confirmation of this the French archaeologist Malleret has just discovered in Oc-éo, on the Cochin-Chinese coast, near the frontier of Cochin-China and Cambodia, an ancient port frequented by Roman merchants, and has found there coins of Antoninus the Pious and of Marcus Aurelius.[17] On this maritime trade the information provided, on the Graeco-Roman side, by the Alexandrian geographer Ptolemy, coincides, as it does for the Central-Asiatic 'Silk Road', with the data obtained from the Chinese annalists.[18] We may note, moreover, that it is precisely during this period that Han moralists point (in disapproval, it must be added) to the extension of trade as well as to the love of exotic products.[19]

* * *

To the long peace of the Han, Etienne Balazs notes, corresponds a stagnant period in Chinese thought: 'With Confucian pragmatism the enquiring mind rested content'. After the text of the Classics had been restored along conformist and conservative lines, official exegesis completed the work of dissimulating the discrepancies in their sources (their origins and tendencies, as we have seen, were in fact quite diverse) in order to present the whole as a homogeneous canon, the unshakeable foundation of all political and social truth. 'The key-words remain *li* and *i*;

[17] See Louis Malleret, L'Art et la Métallurgie de l'Etain dans la Culture d'Oc'éo, *Artibus Asiae*, XI, 4, 1948, p. 274; Also, Les Activités de l'Ecole Française d'Extrême-Orient, *Bibliography of Indian Archaeology*, Kern Institute, XV, Leyden, 1950, p. 46. Grousset, Traces des Romains en Indochine, *La Revue française*, no. 20, December 1949, p. 8.

[18] See Rolf Stein, Le Lin-yi, *Han-hiue, Bulletin du Centre d'Etudes sinologiques de Pékin*, II, 1/3, Péking, 1947, p. 115.

[19] In particular, the moralist Wang Fu (about 90-165). See Etienne Balazs, La Crise Sociale et la Philosopie Politique à la Fin des Han, *T'oung pao*, XXXIV, 1-3, Leyden, 1949, p. 99.

li, the proprieties, usages, rites, etiquette, and *i*, signifying impartiality, equity on the part of superiors, the duty of obedience on the part of inferiors. The whole proffered in a tone both sugary and stiff'.[20] 'Only the strict observance of the traditional social relations, the putting of everyone in the place where he is to live according to his lot, in obedience to the moral law, will put the world back on the right path'. A period of moralism and of conformity that was to be followed, as we shall see, by a harsh awakening.

At the peak of this later Han dynasty we come upon two annalists of talent: Pan Ku (32-92) and his sister Pan Chao (who died after 102). Pan Ku wrote the history of the Former Han dynasty (*Ch'ien han shu*) a history that covers the years from 206 B.C. to 8 A.D., which his sister, after him, completed.[21]

Art in the Han Period

After the work done by Chavannes in Shantung and Honan, by Ségalen and Lartigue in Szechwan and the Japanese archaeologists in Korea, our knowledge of Han art is beginning to be fairly well defined. In any case, a great number of bronzes that were considered to be Han twenty years ago, in particular among the inlaid bronzes and the mirrors, are now recognized to be earlier and are classed as 'Warring States', conforming to the description that we have given of this style. In reality, however, as the Korean finds show, it is often difficult to draw a distinction between 'Warring States' motifs and Han motifs.

Korea, or more exactly the northwest part of the peninsula, did not become a part of Chinese civilization until 194 B.C. at

[20] Balazs, La Crise Sociale à la Fin des Han, *l. c.*, p. 93.
[21] See Lo Chen-Ying, Une Famille d'Historiens et son Oeuvre, *Institut franco-chinois de Lyon*, IX, 1931. The older brother of Pan Ku and of the lady Pan Chao was general Pan Ch'ao (32-102), the conqueror of Central Asia. A famous piece is the petition by dame Pan Chao asking that the illustrious warrior, who had been governor of the Tarim basin for nearly thirty years, be at last allowed to retire (see Margouliès, *Le Kou-wen*, p. 106).

18. *Carved stone. Han Dynasty. Rietberg Museum, Zurich, Von der Heydt Collection.*

19. *Dog, earthenware. Han Dynasty. Musée Cernuschi, Paris.*

the earliest, at which date a Chinese adventurer carved out a principality for himself there, in Lo-lang (near present-day Pyong-yang); a more definitive date is that of the year 108, when the Emperor Han Wu-ti annexed this same region. The works of art discovered in 1931 in the Lo-lang district by the Japanese archaelogists Koizumi and Sawa can therefore not antecede the early Han. A bowl from the so-called Wang Hsü tomb is in fact dated 52 A.D., and the tomb of Wang Kuang (with its tray on which the goddess Hsi-wang-mu is depicted) is of the year 69 of our era.[22] As for the most interesting tomb, the so-called 'painted basket' tomb, it seems to belong to the second-to-third centuries A.D. And here, on boxes of lacquered wood, with designs in yellow and red (or occasionally dark blue) on a black back-ground, we find spirals and volutes of dragons, very elongated, of which the style is still 'Warring States'.[23]

Such comparisons show the close continuity between the 'Warring States' style and the Han style. All that can be said about the Lo-lang finds is, that despite the astonishing freedom and the soaring fantasy of linear design that they show, there is hidden within this a regularity of arrangement that is already Han. There is also an individualization that is typically Han in the elegant dragons that hurtle at a flying gallop—an equine or a leonine gallop—on the registers of the lacquer found at Lo-lang. Further, there are, also in the 'painted basket' tomb, a lacquered cylinder, which must have served as a scroll-case, and a lacquered table, both with designs in gold, silver, yellow, black and green on a red background, which have as their main

[22] Chōsen-koseki-kenkyū-kai (Society of the study of Korean antiquities) Vol. ii, *The Tomb of Wang Kuang of Lo-lang*, Keijo, Seoul, 1935.
[23] Id., Vol. I, *The Tomb of Painted Basket of Lo-lang*, 1934, pl. LI. Hague-nauer, Les Fouilles de Corée. La tombe du panier peint. *Revue des Arts Asiatiques*, X, 3, 1936, p. 143. On the pre-Han and Han lacquers in general, see O. Mänchen-Helfen, Zur Geschichte der Lackkunst in China, *Wiener Beiträge zur Kunst und Kulturgeschichte Asiens*, XI, 1937, pp. 32-65, and Löw-Beer, Zum Dekor der Han-Lacke, same number, pp. 65-73.

theme small clouds that still dance in the 'Warring States' manner, but which already have that fleecy appearance which does
not seem to occur until Han times.[24] Finally, on the second of
these lacquer pieces are depicted, along with bird-dragons that
still show the 'Warring States' influence, recumbent deer that are
quite in the Han style, as well as human figures running, which
immediately recall the little imps and sorcerers of the rubbings
of the Shantung bas-reliefs published by Chavannes.[25] Altogether, as we look through the plates of the Korean finds, we realize how the passage from the style of the 'Warring States' to that
of the Han was marked by imperceptible transitions, the final
stage of which is shown by the design of the human figures on
the registers of the 'basket' itself, which is characterized by that
slackening of tension, that restraint, that standardization, which,
in our opinion, are the typical characteristics of the Han style,
or at least of the style pertaining to the stagnant Later Han
period.[26]

Perhaps this enables us to perceive a law of evolution in Han
art: that it took over themes from the style of the 'Warring
States', with all its impulsive vigour and unbridled fancy, and
proceeded to standardize them and impose upon them an ever-
increasing symmetry of arrangement.

Han mirrors are classified by Karlgren into several catego-

---

[24] *Tomb of painted basket*, pl. LVII and LXIX.

[25] *Ibid.*, pl. LXIX.

[26] *Ibid.*, pls. XLIII-XLVI. Similarly, on one of the pieces of silk found in Upper
Mongolia, in Noin-Ula, the two pairs of fantastic horned and bearded birds joined
at their base and facing each other, still belong to the 'Warring States' in the
fancifulness of their lines, but already show the Han influence in the regularity
of their symmetry (C. Trever, *Excavations in Northern Mongolia*, Leningrad,
1932, pl. 13). It so happens that the find is exactly dated as Han by a Chinese
lacquer of 2 B.C. (Minns, *The Art of Northern Nomads*, British Academy, 1942,
p. 27). Other precise chronological references will be found in an article by
Umehara on the Han discoveries in the Pyong-yang region of Korea, *Revue des
Arts Asiatiques*, 1926, p. 28; (a lid painted in red lacquer of 4 B.C., a mirror of
5 B.C., etc.).

ries.[27] He assigns his 'Category F', consisting of pieces from the Huai-ho basin, to the early Han period, between 200 and 100 B.C. In this category, the background is reduced to zebra lines, straight lines, or scrolls, so minute that the pattern often becomes virtually indecipherable. In the ornamentation, the old 'Warring States' theme, the circle of stylized dragons, has been reduced to an interlacing of foliated scrolls and transformed into a purely ornamental motif, now submitted to a strict symmetry of design which is already somewhat heavy and, despite its regularity, at times somewhat cluttered, and even confused. On several of these mirrors we find the T L V motif prevailing (with, in the centre, a 'magic square'; they are probably connected with divination).[28] On others (and this is an important innovation) an inscription in Chinese characters is placed in a circular band that runs either round the central knob or round the outside edge. At times, too, there appears, between the two circular bands in the centre and at the circumference, a large star with 6, 7 or 8 points, which effectively balances the design.

Karlgren next distinguishes among the Han mirrors a series G, with more simplified ornamentation (a background of tiny spirals ornamented with star patterns); a series H of the second century B.C., with sketchier and at the same time heavier versions of the same motifs; a series J, likewise of the second century, with the same tendencies aggravated; and a series K, also of the same period, characterized by an inscribed square surrounding the central knob, and, on the circumference, a border of stars, usually with sixteen points (or eight arcs); a motif consisting of

[27] Karlgren, Huai and Han, B.M.F.E.A., Stockholm, 13, 1941, pp. 89 ff. See also Umehara, *Kan sangoku rikuchō kenenkyō shūroku, Repertory of dated mirrors of the Han, Three Kingdoms and Six Dynasties*. Tokyo, 1931.

[28] Cf. Kaplan, On the origin of the T L V mirror, *Revue des Arts Asiatiques*, XI, 1937, pp, 21-24. Another opinion is that of Perceval Yetts, who compares these T L V mirrors to an object represented on the Shantung stone carvings, which he takes to be a sundial (Yetts, *The Cull Chinese Bronzes*, London, 1939, no. 28, pp. 116-165, pl. XXI).

various kinds of winged figures also occurs on mirrors of this category. Finally, an L category, ascribed to the period from 100 B.C. to 100 A.D. (a few specimens bearing inscriptions from the time of Wang Mang the usurper, between 9 and 23 of our era), contains mirrors on which the design is very crowded, but at the same time disciplined: an inscribed square surrounds the knob, the ornamentation is in bosses and T's frequently combined with tigers rather similar to those of the Han reliefs of Shantung, and a second inscription in very 'square' calligraphy fills a band placed between the centre and the circumference. On the mirrors of late Han times Taoist figures appear more and more, sometimes accompanied by dragons, all of them—dragons and human figures as well—somewhat crowded and cumbersome in design; there is a voluminous central knob and an inscription round the circumference.[29]

The same preoccupation with symmetry is to be observed in the large bronze basins, such as the famous one in the Hosokawa collection, in Kyoto.[30] In this characteristic piece, the freedom of line of the central dragon as well as of the animals (tigers, bears, phoenixes) decorating the band around the periphery, might seem still to belong to the 'Warring States' style. But all these various elements, with their sharpness of outline, their subtle delicacy, are balanced and ordered with such discipline that we clearly see exemplified here the order imposed by Han rule.

[29] The Japanese archaeologists, for their part, ascribe to the middle or the end of the Former Han dynasty (first century B.C.) the mirrors with boss or star designs (the latter being the ones with the 'eight arc' star and inscription round the circumference) discovered in Pei-sha-ch'eng and in Hui-an, near Kalgan, north of Peking, on the Great Wall. See *Archaeologia Orientalis*, series B, vol. V, Pei-sha-ch'eng, in *Tōa-kōko-gaku-kai* (Société de l'Asie Orientale), 1946, plates XVII-XXII, LI-LXI, LXXI-LXXII, etc. In the same excavations there have been discovered lacquer boxes, painted with elegant foliated scrolls or filiform arabesques with cloud scrolls, fantastic birds, members of the deer or goat tribe in flying gallop, powerful and supple tigers, etc. These objects testify to the quality of the best Han style.
[30] Good reproduction in Sirén, *History of Early Chinese Art*, pl. 50-51.

Can we really say, at any rate of the masterpieces among them, that the Han bronzes are lacking in elegance? The Hoso-kawa basin proves the contrary, as does also the famous under side of the lid of a cosmetic box (*lien*) of gilded bronze, with décor of painted engraving, in the former Eumorfopoulos Collection (now in the Victoria and Albert Museum) with its back-ground of coral-pink spirals and in the centre the dazzling and delicate phoenix in pale green and bluish green touches, which is so well known to all lovers of Chinese art.[31] Han art, here achieves a true classicism, without losing any of the creative spon-taneity of the 'Warring States'. The same may be said of various mirrors painted in bright colours[32] belonging to the Moriya col-lection in Kyoto, or to the Fogg Museum in Cambridge, Massa-chussetts. The same classic order is to be observed in the large Han bronze clasps inlaid with precious metals, malachite and turquoise, and, generally speaking, in the other bronzes dama-scened with gold and silver of the same period[33]—vases, tubes, rings or ornaments—whether they bear rigidly geometric designs or foliated scrolls and spirals, waves and flames with springing curves at times blossoming into wings or beaks of birds, or else dancing clouds, this cloud theme being, it would seem, charac-teristic of Han. At times, as in the case of a certain bronze tube inlaid with gold and silver wire that we admired in the Hoso-kawa Collection in Tokyo, the foliated scrolls rise to form abrupt mountains on whose slopes deer, boars, hunting dogs or felines leap and cavort. Here, despite the dancing fancifulness of the design, we have real hunting scenes, similar to those that we shall later come upon in the reliefs of the Shantung funerary cham-bers.[34]

[31] See Yetts, *Catalogue of the Eumorfopoulos Collection, Bronzes*, vol. I, 1929, pls. LIV-A, LXXVIII. Ashton and Gray, *Chinese Art*, 1935, pp. 82-83.

[32] Blue, red, white, etc.

[33] See *Selected Chinese Antiquities from the Collection of Gustav Adolf, Crown Prince of Sweden* (1948), pls. 22 and 28.

[34] Reproductions in Sirén, *History of Early Chinese Art*, pl. 49.

On several Han bronze vases, in particular those of the *hu* and *ting* type, we find on the contrary a simplification of design amounting to a total disappearance of motifs. The vase becomes naked of all ornamentation except that on the handle rings, in the form of a small *t'ao-t'ieh*, which itself has lost the crowded detail of the 'Warring States' representations and is simplified to an extreme degree. We may pause to note, in this connection, the evolution of the *t'ao-t'ieh*. This semi-bestial, semi-divine mask, emanating directly from primitive magic, which on the Shang bronzes had been invested with great occult powers, has become under the Han a mere decorative mascaron.

* * *

The best introduction to Han art, however, is that provided by the bas-relief stone carvings of the offering chambers and funerary cells of Shantung and Honan, which were studied by Chavannes. In Shantung, the earliest series of reliefs is that at Hsiao-t'ang-shan, which today is dated by Chinese archaelogists —no doubt correctly—as of the first century B.C.[35] If these really belong, as we also are inclined to believe, to the end of the Former Han period, we may say that at that time stone relief is still in its infancy, with a contour that is precise but bald, almost mathematical, having no other object than to circumscribe objects and beings correctly. The second Shantung series is the so-called Wu-liang-tz'u series, near Chia-hsiang, this one quite precisely dated as being of 147 to 167 A.D. The style is already much more

---

[35] Hsiao-t'ang-shan is in any case earlier than 129 A.D. (Chavannes, *Mission Archéologique*, text, I, p. 62). In Honan, the Teng-feng-hsien pillars where other Han reliefs are to be found, likewise studied by Chavannes, are dated between 118 and 123 A.D. We may point out that the French Institute of Peking (Centre for Advanced Chinese Studies, under the aegis of the Sorbonne), on the initiative of its director Louis Hambis, has begun the publication in six albums of a *Corpus des Pierres Sculptées Han*. Volume 1, devoted to the Shantung reliefs, was published in Peking in 1950,

evolved, with compositions that are freer, and also more complex and more studied. 'An art of harmonious and at times dramatic grouping', notes Otto Fischer, 'is manifested in these processions of chariots and horsemen, these palace receptions, these gods and demons of Taoist mythology, in the battle around a bridge, or in the grandiose vision of the voyage of the soul to the gateway of the kingdom of supernatural beings'.

These bas-reliefs are obviously governed by the law of two dimensions, arranged as they are in registers, the stiff rows of which are in contrast to the feeling of intense movement that compares with that of the contemporaneous inlaid bronzes.[36] As for the technique of these reliefs, the contours of the figures are in some cases simply line-engraved, in the usual linear style of Han draughtsmanship, and in other cases (as in the Wu-liang-tz'u group) they have been, as we sometimes say, 'reserved' by hollowing out the stone around the figure which thus remains on the plane of the surface.

The Shantung and Honan funerary reliefs have for us the signal merit of informing us as to ancient Chinese mythology of a much earlier period—of one which antedates all canalization of thought into official Taoism or Confucianism. Sorcerers, the magic tree, fabulous beings all play important rôles. Here are the goddess Hsi-wang-mu, Queen-Mother of the West, with or without her Tong-wang-kung and accompanied by her familiar retinue of animals, the three-footed solar raven, the lunar hare grinding the drug of immortality, the nine-tailed fox, etc., or else the Seven Stars of the Great Bear, with the personages of their court. Also the first mythical civilizers, Fu-Hsi holding the square, and his sister Nü-kua holding the compass, their bodies

---

[36] See the important study by Wilma Fairbank, Structural Key to Han Mural Art, *Harvard Journal of Asiatic Studies*, April 1942, p. 52, a sequel to the article by the same author, 'The Offering Shrines of Wu Liang tz'u', in the same review, 1941.

ending in intertwined serpents' tails;[37] and the whole series of the legendary 'Three Kings' and 'Five Emperors'. In addition we find fabulous monsters: a kind of centaur with two human torsos, wild beasts bearing eight human heads issuant from the neck on as many serpents' bodies, like the hydras of our classical mythology. But the most extraordinary of all the creatures in the Chinese mythology are the winged genii (their appearance is at times reminiscent of the sprites and goblins in our own folk traditions), genii whose bodies seem to end in serpents' tails.

These fantastic beings give a prodigious sense of movement. In Wu-liang-tz'u, around a seated divinity, we see a whole crowd of genii with outspread wings, approaching, flying away or plunging to the ground; a kind of winged sprite holds out a branch of the Tree of the Three Pearls; another, kneeling, offers him a goblet; a third seems to be dancing; a certain number of them flutter in and out among the monsters that surround the divinity, monsters that are a kind of female sphinx whose animal body bears a double human torso, or human figures with bird's or horse's heads, or inversely, enormous birds with human heads. An amazing freedom, the legacy of the 'Warring States' style, pervades all these scenes.

A number of large compositions, in Wu-Liang-tz'u, represent mythological kingdoms, 'Kingdom of the Waters', 'Kingdom of the Air', etc. The Kingdom of the Waters carries us away to a strange world.[38] The water divinity, 'the Count of the River', that is to say the Huang-ho made into a divinity, advances on a chariot drawn by fish; around him swarms 'a procession of frogs, turtles, water rats, fish equipped with lances, halberds, swords or shields, men astride fish, beings with frogs' heads or

---

[37] This interlacing we shall find again on the Buddhistic frescoes of Central Asia. But we also find it in Indian art. See Taichirô Kobayashi, Nü-kua and Kuan-yin, *Buddhist Art*, II, Tokyo, 1948.

[38] Chavannes, *Mission Archéologique dans la Chine Septentrionale*, I, pl. LXVI, no. 130.

20. *Dancer, earthenware. Han Dynasty. Musée Cernuschi, Paris.*

human heads with fish bodies'. Elsewhere we see the Kingdom of the Air, Wind and Storm, with wild galloping in which strange Chinese pegasuses, winged dragons having a certain resemblance to horses,[39] fantastic quadrupeds with serpents' tails, fly past, some of them straddled by the usual winged genii, the whole enveloped in the headlong flight of squadrons of clouds. The clouds themselves are often represented in an almost animalized or humanized form: a bird or dragon head or else the torso of a winged genius dominate a 'body' and a 'wing' likewise formed of coiled volutes (snail coils that in later Chinese painting were to remain the schematic representation of clouds); the various clouds thus individualized nevertheless remain connected to one another by a maze of incidental spirals. The dragons and genii themselves seem in some cases to emerge from the cloud maze, and in others to vanish and blend into it, with their serpents' tails which, like the rest of the cloud, wave in the air. In the middle of the aerial tumult the thunder god, with mallet blows, beats his drums.[40] Goddesses, joining in the chase, brandish the 'ropes of rain'. One of the genii of thunder, leaping on the back of his prostrate victim, strikes him with lightning, sinking a chisel into the back of his neck with a hammer.[41]

We may note in this connection that the conception of the clouds as the dwelling place and substance of the dragon—who can always manifest himself there in blinding flashes—will recur throughout Chinese art right up to the painting of the Sung.

These various scenes, as we have said, are all the more precious to us since the myths of archaic China are for the most part lost. From another point of view, the fancifulness of inven-

[39] The *dragon-horse*, in Chinese mythology, lives on the approaches of the Yellow River. The legendary founder of the Hsia dynasty, Yü the Great, had dealings with him.
[40] We know the importance of drums and tomtoms in primitive magic, in negro civilizations, etc. On the connections between the Drum and Thunder in archaic China, see Granet, *Danses et Légendes*, II, pp. 440, 509-510.
[41] See Chavannes, *Mission Archéologique*, pls. LXVII to LXX, nos. 131-134.

12.

tion and the extraordinary movement that sweeps the themes and figures along are very close to the art of the 'Warring States'. On the other hand, the realistic animals and the *genre* scenes, on these same reliefs, are specifically Han. In Hsiao-t'ang-shan, in Wu-liang-tz'u, in Chiao-ch'eng-ts'un (all in Shantung province), and elsewhere as well, Chavannes has taken rubbings of hunting scenes in which the stags, does, bucks, hares, breathlessly pursued by greyhounds and archers on horseback, are rendered in all their sheer grace and speed, caught in the lightning moment of expressive action.[42] No less precise in the art of animal representation is the return from the hunt, in Wu-liang-tz'u, with the attendants carrying home the trophies on their backs: a tiger, an enormous boar, etc.[43] We are here given a glimpse of the prodigious chases for which the poet Ssu-ma Hsiang-ju reproached the Emperor Han Wu-ti.

In the same vein— a vein that at times achieves an epic quality—are the cavalcades and processions of chariots. The horses of the Han reliefs, robust animals with powerful rumps and chests, heads held high, prance nobly or carry their riders at a flying gallop. Light and graceful in Hsiao-t'ang-shan, they are heavier in Wu-liang-tz'u, with necks like a bull's, in contrast with their slender legs. The details of chariot and harness are no less precisely observed. And there are also battles. In Hsiao-t'ang-shan, a battle against the 'Hu', the Barbarians from the North (perhaps the ancestors of the Huns), showing the charge of the mounted archers, the mêlée and the final victory, evokes for us the great Hunnish wars, the epic of the Han in Upper Asia.[44] The battle on a bridge, occurring twice in Wu-liang-tz'u, with its intensity of movement, also shows that Pan Ch'ao's contemporaries had an epic strain.[45]

[42] Chavannes, pl. XXVIII, fig. 50; pl. LXXXVII, fig. 162.
[43] *Ibid.*, pl. LXVIII, fig. 132.
[44] *Ibid.*, pl. XXVI, fig. 47.
[45] *Ibid.*, pls. LIII and LXXI, figs. 109 and 136. On the *genre* scenes in the

There is a long-standing hypothesis that many of these reliefs of the funerary chambers were craftsmen's copies, for the use of the dead, of paintings for the palaces of the living. This seems particularly likely in the case of the reliefs in the chamber of offerings of Chou Wei's burial place, at Chin-hsiang, in Shantung, dating from about 50 A.D. and representing 'the meals offered to the Ancestors'.[46] Otto Fischer, who has made a searching study of the subject, discerns in these line-engraved designs all the characteristics of true painting, beginning with authentic portraits, and including the laws, already formulated, of Chinese perspective as it was to continue through the centuries.[47] There are also the elements of a Chinese landscape in the 'twin trees' of the Li Hsi stele, in Kansu, of which Chavannes has taken a rubbing (171 A.D.).[48]

But there are, in addition, some authentic Han paintings still surviving: a few painted bricks found in Lo-yang, today at the Boston Museum, which undoubtedly date from the end of the Later Han.[49] They show human figures drawn in outline with a swift, sure brush, already displaying remarkable mastery. The faces, attitudes and personalities of each of these noblemen are sketched with lightning speed and with humour. The slender grace of the women is rendered—in the long flowing robes with

Shantung reliefs, see Maspero, La Vie Privée en Chine à l'Epoque des Han, *Revue des Arts Asiatiques*, VII, 4, 1931, p. 185.

[46] Otto Fischer, La Peinture Chinoise au Temps des Han, *Gazette des Beaux Arts*, 1932, p. 20.

[47] 'The Chinese system', Otto Fischer notes in this connection, 'recognizes neither horizon nor central viewpoint, nor the convergence of the orthogonals toward the background. It treats the planes almost abstractly, from a bird's eye view. Thus the eye looks down from above on ground and floor. The lines running off into the distance are conceived and represented as parallels, as they are in reality (and not as our eye sees them), and can be seen rising obliquely toward the background'. The application of these fundamental principles will be found again in the landscape of Sung times.

[48] Chavannes, *Mission Archéologique*, pl. LXXXIX, no. 167.

[49] The essential work on Han painting is that by Otto Fischer, *Die chinesische Malerei der Han Dynastie*, Berlin, 1931.

their wide sleeves—in a single stroke. The shades of colour, red, rose-tinged beige, or dark brown, are very delicate.[50] Apart from these, a Han fresco on wood from the so-called 'basket' tomb in the Lo-lang district in Korea, shows us the elements of a cavalcade in black with some touches of red and occasionally of yellow in the elegant, swift style of the best equestrian represent-ations of Hsiao-t'ang-shan.[51] Here again we see how closely con-nected are painting and bas-relief.

* * *

There is also a good school of Han sculpture: that of Sze-chwan, studied by the Ségalen, Lartigue and de Voisins Mission. The Shantung and Honan reliefs were in most cases, it seems, but craftsmen's copies. Those of Szechwan are frequently the work of artists. The funerary pillar of Feng-huan (121 A.D.) and the Shen funerary pillars (likewise of the second century A.D.), both in Ch'ü-hsien, are certainly exceptionally fine monuments.

But it is the reliefs of these pillars that are particularly re-markable. One might mention, for instance, 'the funeral cortège' at the top of the Shen pillars, in entablature motifs, which gives an impression of unrestrained romanticism, and 'the stag ridden by an amazon', no less strange in its evocation of lost myths, ac-companied as it is by the moon hare grinding its drug of immor-tality;[52] also a 'barbarian archer', split from left to right by the line of his great diagonal gesture, the left arm holding out the bow, the right pulling the string full stretch, a technical feat wor-thy of the finest sculptors of all time.[53] Also on the capitals of

[50] Reproductions in Sirén, *History of Early Chinese Painting*, I, pls. 4-7. Fischer, *loc. cit.*, figs. 4, 5, 7. On the Chinese costume in general in late antiquity, see Harada, *Costumes of the Han and Six Dynasties*, Tokyo, *Toyo Bunko*, 1937.

[51] Chōsen-koseki-kenkyū-kai, *The Tomb of Painted Basket of Lolang*, vol. I, Seoul, 1934, pl. XXXII.

[52] Ségalen, de Voisins, Lartigue, *Mission Archéologique, Atlas*, 1, pls. XX, XXII.

[53] *Ibid.*, pl. XXV.

V. *Han Huang: Four Scholars in a Garden Collating Old Writings.*
Painting on silk. T'ang Dynasty. Hui-hua kuan, Peking.

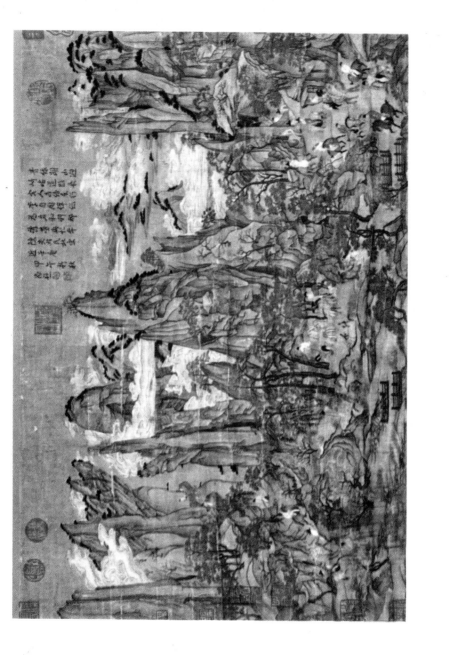

VI. *School of Li Ssu-hsüh: Travellers in a Mountain Landscape. Painting on paper. Collection of the Chinese Nationalist Government, Formosa.*

the Shen pillars, two *t'ao-t'ieh* masks, treated here as heads of burrowing animals, which are realistic despite their strangeness; on the inner front side of the right-hand pillar, the relief representing the Red Bird (in Chinese geomancy, the animal symbolizing the South), a superb piece of decorative carving, having an imperious elegance in the spread of its wings and in its strutting gait.[54] Finally, on the inner sides of the two Shen pillars, the White Tiger and the Green Dragon, the respective symbols of West and East, whose supple grace and slenderness (that of the tiger in particular) are a response to the challenge of the space —that of the length of the pillar—to be filled, are reminiscent of work in jade. What we have here is, in fact, a Han jade—a jade of the dimensions of a free-standing column.[55] The restraint, the refined simplicity of the theme, the classicism of inspiration (in the western sense of the term) invest these reliefs of the Shen pillar with the quality of the very best style of the Han.[56]

* * *

The objects of Han art most familiar in the West are the terra cotta statuettes (*ming-ch'i*) representing animals or human figures, and the terra cottas that are models of houses, household utensils, etc.[57] Undoubtedly, as in the tombs of the pharaohs, what we have here are 'substitutes' intended to enable the dead to continue his familiar existence and prevent him from feeling too much out of his element. It is true, of course, that among our funerary statuettes there are some that represent fantastic beings whose very character excludes this explanation. But their

[54] *Ibid.*, pls. XVII, XVIII; also Lartigue, *L'Art Funéraire à l'Epoque-des Han*, p. 57.

[55] *Ibid.*, pl. XXIII.

[56] See Vadime Eliseeff, Les dix-huit Piliers Funéraires, in the collective volume: *Victor Ségalen*, 1947, p. 72.

[57] On the statuettes judged to be pre-Han, cf. Loehr, Clay Figurines and Facsimiles from the 'Warring States' Period, *Monumenta Serica*, X, 1946, p. 326.

presence may be linked to other magical considerations. And above all else, the discovery in the Shang tombs of An-yang of series of skeletons pointing to animal sacrifices and even to whole-sale human sacrifices forces us to come back to the idea of the 'substitute'.[58] With the humanization of customs and the triumph of Confucianist moralism, the human or animal victims were simply replaced by representations, resembling their originals as closely as possible, by which the dead as well as the divinity would be hoodwinked. Haguenauer is of the view that in particular the figurines of horses, so numerous in the time of the Han, suggest the former sacrificial use of the horse, 'who used to be considered an animal peculiarly fitted to lead the soul of the defunct into the beyond'. He recalls that the sacrifice of the horse at funeral rites still had this significance among the Buriats and the Yakuts of Siberia.[59]

Of the smaller pieces of Han sculpture there survive, apart from the terra cottas, some statuettes in bronze. All lovers of Chinese art are familiar with the gilded bronze bears, standing or crouching, which are to be found in many of our collections (that of the Stoclet collection, for example) and which are so accurately observed, and show such 'psychological' perceptive-ness in the modelling of a body that is both heavy and supple, with its little blinking eyes and quivering muzzle, which, beneath an apparent good-nature, betray a cunning alertness. Several of these were used as supports or feet for furniture. Good specimens, having served as ends of table-feet (bears of gilded copper adorn-

[58] The reservation expressed by Sirén (*History of Early Chinese Art*, II, p. 52), based on the most virtuously orthodox Confucian texts, was made before the discovery of the An-yang sacrificial ossuaries.

[59] Haguenauer, La Tombe du Panier Peint, *Revue des Arts Asiatiques*, X, 3, 1936, p. 147. We also know that under the Han the living, like the dead, were fond of statuettes of this kind and that the moralists disapproved of them for this. Wang Fu (about 90-165) spoke out against the frivolity revealed by the love of 'clay carts, pottery dogs, horsemen, figurines of singers and dancers' (transl. Balasz, *T'oung pao*, XXXIX, 1-3, 1949, p. 101).

ed with turquoise, shown seated, the forepaws resting on the knees), have been discovered by the Japanese around the village of Tae-tong-kang, near Pyong-yang, in tombs dating from the end of the Former Han or the beginning of the Later Han (objects dated between 85 B.C. and 52 A.D.).[60]

The same sympathetic and amused understanding of animals, the same humour, so characteristic of the spirit of Chinese crowds, can be observed in a number of the Han terra cottas, particularly those dogs of various kinds (the 'bulldog' of the Cernuschi Museum), hogs, roosters, ducks, owls.[61] Similar qualities of observation are still to be found, it is true, in animal representation under the Six Dynasties and the T'ang, but what is interesting about the Han modellers is the swiftness of their 'sketches', their skill in bringing out the essence of the forms with a few deft touches, in communicating the character of the species in a curve or two. In the period of the 'Warring States', despite the animals in recumbent posture (of small dimensions, always) on the lids of certain Li-yü bronze vases, form in the round was not yet liberated. Completely liberated it becomes under the Han, with a swiftness of line equal to that of the paintings now in Boston or the best of the Shantung reliefs or the still finer reliefs of Szechwan. And at the same time, faithful as they are in observation, the realism of the Han sculptors prevents them from indulging (in the way T'ang sculptors often did) in showy effects and exaggeration of the muscle structure. Their realism remains sober, lean, wedded to simplicity, revealing in a few lines the spirit of the forms rather than dwelling on their detail; or one might say

[60] Umehara, Deux Grandes Découvertes Archéologiques en Corée, *Revue des Arts Asiatiques*, III, 1, March 1926, p. 28, pl. xi. See in the same style a white marble crouching bear, Han period, but with the incised treatment of the Shang sculptures (or the jades), reproduced by S. Mizuno, *Chinese Stone Sculpture*, Tokyo, 1950 (Mayuyama editions), pl. ii, fig. 4.

[61] A recent book redolent with the age-old subtlety of Chinese humour ever present behind the gravest acts or reflections, is that of Lin Yutang, *The Importance of Living*, with its racy philosophy.

that it considers form only in terms of movement, because it is in fact in movement that, in the case of animals, the character of the species is best revealed, and with man, the psychology of the individual (as in the Boston painted bricks). The whole art of the Han is *an art of linear movement*. The restrained and, one might be tempted to say, crude character of the Han terra cottas derives from this linear swiftness translated into the round.[62]

The same observations apply to the statuettes of horses. The general style of the modelling is sober, but we can discern several types, which perhaps correspond to different breeds of horses. On several terra cottas the horse presents the same squat appearance—massive neck, chest and rump—as on the Wu-liang-tz'u bas reliefs.[63] This is undoubtedly the typical native breed as it was before subsequent cross-breeding. (There are some good specimens at the Cernuschi Museum). Many small equestrian bronzes, likewise Han, show us, if not another breed, at least a more elongated treatment of equine forms. Finally, several large-scale terra cottas[64] and, in the Korean excavations, wooden statues[65] present us with a wholly new type—relatively slender neck, long head, sensitive and lean—that are reminiscent of the well-known outline of the Parthenon horses. It is possible that this represents a breed imported from the West, and that these

---

[62] This character is no less striking in the small bronzes found at Lo-yang, dogs, rams, boars, and particularly in the wonderful little seated monkey (like a Japanese *netsuké*), reproduced by White, *Tombs of Old Lo-yang*, pl. LXXXV). More than one of the Han clasps of the Coiffard collection, shown in the Cernuschi Museum, are in the same vein.

[63] So, too, does the recumbent horse, a stone statue from the tomb of Ho Ch'ü-ping (Sirén, *History of Early Chinese Art*, pl. 5).

[64] Characterized in our collections by the absence of legs. What the Han modeller did was to fit wooden legs to the terra cotta bodies. The wood, in the Chinese climate, perished from damp in the tombs in which these horses were buried. On the other hand, the Korean excavations have yielded up Han wooden horses with legs (Haguenauer, *Revue des Arts Asiatiques*, x, 3, 1936, pl. 50).

[65] Chōsen-koseki-kenkyū-kai, *The Tomb of the Painted Basket of Lo-lang*, pls. LXXX-LXXXII, text by Harada.

21. *Chimera, stone. Third to fourth century A. D. Nelson Gallery of Art, Kansas City.*

are no longer the native Sino-Mongolian horses but belong to the great race of Arab-Persian horses. The history of the Former Han, in fact, reveals that in 102 B.C. the Chinese made an expedition to that part of Western Turkestan now known as Ferghana to bring back steeds of the great trans-Oxianic or Bactrian race for the remounting of their cavalry, which would undoubtedly afford the imperial squadrons a certain superiority over the Hunnish archers mounted on the small Tartar horse.[66] Crossbreeding with the horses from Ferghana would thus explain the western appearance of a whole category of our Han horses, without its being necessary to assume that they were made in direct imitation of the Pegasuses and other steeds featured on the Graeco-Bactrian or Indo-Greek coins in circulation on the Silk Road.[67] It must, however, be admitted that there are certain winged horses: those on the Wu-liang-tz'u reliefs in Shantung, the one on the left pillar at P'ing-yang in Szechwan, with its bold workmanship, and, at a later date, and more striking still considering the time-lapse, those on the best of the T'ang mirrors, which do seem to hark back to Graeco-Roman models....[68]

Human representations in the round, as we have seen, antedate the Han dynasty. The bronze statues found in Lo-yang which represent a man kneeling and holding a tube (perhaps the shaft of a standard) in each hand, are generally attributed to the 'Warring States' period.[69] The Japanese archaeologist Sueji Umehara

---

[66] See Chavannes, *Mémoires Historiques*, vol. I, pp. LXXI-LXXVII; and Yetts, The Horse, a Factor in Early Chinese History, *Eurasia Septentrionalis Antiqua*, vol. IX, Helsinki, 1934, pp. 231-255.

[67] Chavannes, *Mission Archéologique*, I, pl. LXVII, fig. 131.

[68] On the other hand, the tomb guardian lions, sculptured in the round, found by the Chavannes mission (in Wu-liang-tz'u, for example) or the passant lion on the P'ing-yang pillar in Szechwan, a relief photographed by the Ségalen mission, can only be of Graeco-Iranian inspiration (since the lion exists neither in China nor in the Ganges region of India) (Ségalen, de Voisins, Lartigue, *Mission Archéologique, Atlas*, pls. XLI, XLII).

[69] White, *Tombs of Old Lo-yang*, pls. LXXVI-LXXXIII, now in the Toronto Museum. Similar bronze statuettes, found by O. Janse in Thanh-hoa, but of the Han

likewise attributes to the 'Warring States' terra cottas with a
black lustre finish presumably originating in Hui-hsien, in the
extreme north of Honan, a few specimens of which (human
figurines with rather crudely executed faces, a recumbent hog, a
seated wild beast) have come to the Boston Museum.[70] But what
chiefly survives from the Han period are the numerous and characteristic terra cotta figurines. One of the most widespread types
is that of the standing figure of a man wearing the long costume
known as p'ao: the collar facings crossing in a triangle over the
chest, the sleeves widening 'dewlap-wise', hands joined but hidden under the ample sleeves, the waist belted tight, the robe
spreading from knees to feet.[71] Another type is that of a personage wearing the *chung-tan-i* robe, which falls straight from
the waist to the feet. As for the women they also wear the long
costume and affect—as a refinement of fashion—a 'wasp waist'.
These statuettes are generally very simple in design, without much
attention to detail or indication of muscular play. It is the same
linear art as on the personages of the painted bricks in the Boston
Museum. Like these, the figurines are remarkable for their movement, whether their subjects be musicians and dancers of the
princely courts or the humblest workers at their tasks (the cook
scaling a fish, in the Cernuschi Museum).

* * *

The little pottery figurines of the Han period thus provide
us with information (as do the Shantung funerary reliefs) about
the private life of the time. In addition to human or animal

period and intended for lamp-stands; Janse, *Archaeological Researches in Indo-
China*, Harvard, 1947, pl. 9.

[70] Umehara and K. Tomita, Mortuary Figurines and Miniature Vessels of the
Epoch of the Warring States, *Far Eastern Ceramic Bulletin*, 8, 1949, p. 34, and
pl. VIII.

[71] See Maspero, La Vie Privée à l'Epoque des Han, *Revue des Arts Asiatiques*,
VII, 1932, p. 195, pl. LIX, g.

representations, we also find quite detailed models of various hab-
itations—houses of one or several storeys, pleasure-towers surrounded by stretches of water, farm houses with out-buildings
(pigsties, fish-ponds, aviaries, etc.) as well as miniature copies of
furniture, farm tools, instruments and utensils of all sorts, etc.[72]
To these must be added, as contributions to our knowledge of
the ornamental side of life in the Han period, the luxurious pieces
found in the excavations of northwestern Korea (in the ancient district of Lo-lang or of Rakurô): the painted and lacquered
basket found in the tomb known as the 'tomb of the painted
basket' which accounts for the name given to this burial site,
besides other lacquered objects from the same tomb: scroll cases,
chests, jewel cases and various boxes, toilet cases, cups and bowls,
spoons, trays, tables, the top part of various pieces of furniture
—all of them lacquered with designs generally in gold and red
on a black background, or with touches of green or yellow on
a red background, and most of them brilliantly colourful. The
many exquisite motifs decorating some of these pieces should
be noted—dragons and foliated scrolls, and, on most of the
Lo-lang lacquer pieces, those specifically Han clouds to which
we have already called attention.[73]

One cannot grasp the splendour of the Han period, its richness, its luxury, the refiniment of its taste, unless one has become
acquainted with the Korean finds belonging to this period.

[72] Maspero, *Op. cit.*, pl. LVII. *Idem*, Sur Quelques Objets de l'Epoque des Han,
Etudes d'Orientalisme, publiées par le Musée Guimet à la Mémoire de Raymonde
Linossier, 1932, p. 403. Consult further for the architecture, the models of houses
discovered by the Japanese mission in Thanh-hoa excavations, Janse, *Op. cit.*,
pls. 5, 45, 74, etc.

[73] See the plates, often in colour, of the publications of the *Chōsen koseki-
kenkyū-kai*, I, *The tomb of painted basket of Lo-lang*, II, *The tomb of Wang
Kuang of Lo-lang* (text by Harada) Keijo (Seoul) 1934 and 1935. Compare the
under-side of the lid of the cosmetic box in the Eumorfopoulos Collection mentioned earlier and reproduced in the Yetts catalogue, pls. LIV-A, LXXVIII; and also
certain lacquered boxes found in Ch'ang-sha (in South China) and undoubtedly
dating from the Former Han (Löw-Beer, Two lacquered boxes from Ch'ang-sha,
Artibus Asiae, XI, 1948, p. 266).

Among the luxurious products of Han times must be included a number of bronze clasps and many jades.

Han belt buckles seem to offer a larger variety of forms than those from other periods, and to be particularly rich in appearance. The hook seems to be more carefully treated than in the period of the 'Warring States', and it sometimes terminates in a bird's head that is in itself as large as the rest of the buckle. On the other hand, the boss is smaller (and generally placed in the centre). The decoration has a more concise and naturalistic elegance than in the time of the 'Warring States'. Here as elsewhere fancy gives way to 'a calmer and more classic pattern'.[74] But the art of the 'Ordos' bronzes, the art of animal representation of the steppes, continues to inspire interlacings of dragons, each of which bites the tail of the other, the whole forming a scroll. Several of the simple buckles, representing tigers (in the collection of the King of Sweden or in the Coiffard Collection), are likewise definitely 'Ordos'. We also find anthropomorphic motifs decorating buckles. As for the buckles that are inlaid (with turquoise, malachite, rock crystal, gold and silver), these already existed, as we have seen, in the time of the 'Warring States', but they become increasingly numerous and important under the Han. We may mention in particular a number of Han buckles, princely beyond a doubt, of large size, very sumptuous —in some cases of solid gold—inlaid with jade and secondarily with ivory and lacquered wood.[75] Of the same order is the solid gold belt buckle, enriched with turquoises and with the ornamentation of two dragons, which was found in the Nak-nang district (North Korea).[76]

[74] Lemaitre, Les Agrafes Chinoises, *Revue des Arts Asiatiques*, 1939, p. 48. Cf. Minkenhof, An Exhibition of Chinese Belt-Buckles in America, *Oriental Art*, I, 4, 1949, pp. 161-165.

[75] Lemaitre, Loc. cit., pl. IX.

[76] Umehara, Découvertes en Corée, *Revue des Arts Asiatiques*, III, 2, 1926, p. 28, pl. XI.

To conclude, we may note that under the Han, buckles are more substantial, more solid, more 'monumental' than in the time of the 'Warring States', but that as they become increasingly symmetrical (and subsequently, more and more clumsy) they lose a good deal of their former fancifulness. And here again we encounter the whole characteristic tendency of Han art.[77]

The Korean excavations at Lo-lang furnish us with a reliable chronology for the Han style in the jades.[78] We here find the small funerary jades for the sealing of the 'nine orifices' (the purity of the jade was supposed to prevent the putrefaction of the corpse), notably the cicada placed on the mouth of the dead. Other Han jades have been found in Noin-Ula, in Mongolia (chronology established, as we have seen, by a lacquer of the year 2 B.C.). Whether they be plaques, the cosmic symbols *pi* and *tsung*, or ceremonial sword ornaments, the fantasy of 'Warring States' ornamentation gives way, here too, to a more regular and simpler geometry: the same evolution, in other words, as for the ornamentation of the bronze mirrors. Moreover, on several jade plaques we see the influence of the Han sculptures or reliefs manifesting itself, as for example on the stylized recumbent hogs of the Cernuschi Museum or on the 'white tiger' (Gieseler tiger) of the Guimet Museum.[79]

* * *

It will be seen later that, towards the end of the dynasty of the Later Han, the Graeco-Buddhist influence was first to make itself felt (third century A.D.) in the south of Kashgar with the

[77] As may be seen from the proposed dates (either 'Warring States' or Han), accompanying plates 25-32 (pp. 31-62) of the *Selected Chinese Antiquities from the Collection of Gustaf-Adolf*.

[78] *Report of the Service of Antiquities, Archaeological Researches in the Ancient Lo-lang District*, 1925-1927, vol. V, pls. 17 and 29.

[79] See for the discrimination between Warring States jades and Han jades, the *Selected Chinese Antiquities from the Collection of Gustav Adolf*, pp. 81-100, pls. 40-54.

'Gandharian' stuccos of Rawak near Khotan and the 'Pompeian' mural paintings of Miran, near Lop-nor. It should also be recalled that in the Altaic world the period of the Early Han had been contemporaneous, in central Siberia, around Minusinsk, with the last phaze of the civilization of 'Tagar II' (third to first centuries B.C.), a civilization whose animal-style bronzes have a close chronological relation to a given phase of Ordos art, in Inner Mongolia.[80] In Upper Mongolia, south-east of Lake Baikal, in the lower basin of the Selenga, we know that the Troitskosavsk pieces are of a later date than 118 B.C. The Ordos country and the Selenga basin were then both inhabited by Hunnish tribes. On the other hand it seems probable that present-day Soviet Altai remained in the power of Indo-European tribes, related to the Scytho-Sarmatians of southern Russia, to the north of the Black Sea. But the animal-style art of the steppes, common to the Scytho-Sarmatians and to the Huns, likewise prevailed in the Altai.[81] In this last region Soviet archaeologists discern first of all in the fifth-to-fourth centuries B.C. a culture that they label 'pre-Pasyryk', which is succeeded by that of Pasyryk and of Shibé, characterized by undeniable Graeco-Scythian influences springing from the Crimea, or Graeco-Iranian, springing from the Seleucid, Parthian and Bactrian world. The Pasyryk and Shibé culture appears to have begun about the third century B.C., but it must have continued throughout the whole period of the Former Han dynasty, since a Han lacquer of the years 86-48 B.C. has been found in the Shibé kurgan.[82]

---

[80] Chronology of Kiselev, *Histoire de la Sibérie Méridionale*, pp. 144 ff.

[81] Cf. Otto Mänchen-Helfen, Die Träger des Tierstils im Osten, *Wiener Beiträge zur Kunst und Kultur Asiens*, IX, 1935, p. 61.

[82] Cf. Griaznov, *Le Kourgane de Pasyryk*, Leningrad, 1937; Laure Morgenstern, *Esthétiques d'Orient et d'Occident*, Paris, 1937, p. 177 (on Pasyryk). Umehara, *Northern Region Art Investigation*, Tokyo, 1938, § 178, 61. H. Kühn, Chronologie der Sino-Siberisschen Bronzen, *Ipek*, 1938, p. 62. Minns, *Art of Northern Nomads*, London, 1942, p. 19. A. Salmony, Sarmation Gold Collected by Peter the Great, *Gazette des Beaux-Arts*, 1949.

* * *

The four centuries of the Han *Pax Sinica*, like the four centuries of the Mediterranean *Pax Romana*, and for the same reasons, encouraged the development of a rich material civilization. In both cases the period of creative spontaneity—in the Mediterranean world the apogee of Athens and of Alexandria, in China the 'Warring States'—had ended. Civilization passed through a stagnant and apparently happy period in which the luxury arts, on both sides, played a considerable role. The richness of the Han inlaid bronzes—inlaid with gold, silver, turquoise, malachite or rock crystal—reminds us of the love of precious substances in Roman art at about the same period. It is curious to observe in this connection that the Han revealed their love of the polychrome not only in the inlaid bronzes but also in the coloured 'glass beads' that had their origin in the Roman East.[83] The western origin of these 'marbles', so engagingly multi-colored, has been made even more evident by the discovery of specimens of these by the Aurel Stein Mission along the 'Silk Road', in Eastern Turkestan, in particular in Lou-lan, near Lop-nor. The chronology here, incidentally, is established by discoveries of similar glass beads in the Han excavations of the Lo-lang district, in Korea. Mr. Malleret, finally, has found specimens of these also in Cochin-China, in the Oc-éo excavations, where coins of the Antonines and a Chinese lacquer were simultaneously found.

---

[83] C. G. Seligman and H. C. Beck, Far Eastern Glass: Some Western Origins, B.M.F.E.A., Stockholm, no. 10, 1938. But this study seems to prove that, as the Chin-ts'un finds show, the introduction of glass in China and even its manufacture appears to go back to the period of the 'Warring States'. We must not forget, moreover, that Hellenistic expansion in Upper Asia began in the period of the Warring States. As a result of Alexander's conquests, the Greeks kept Bactria and Sogdiana (Balkh and Samarkand) for two centuries, from 329 to about 130 b.c. See also Dorothy Blair, An Exhibition of East Asiatic Glass, *Artibus Asiae*, XI, 1948, p. 195.

* * *

Han pottery is known to us through an abundance of specimens that have come down to us. 'The vases imitate the forms
of the bronzes of the same period, the *hu*, or the *ting*; and there
are tripods, and cylindrical 'boxes' whose humped lids are adorned with waves and rocks on which animals cavort (a theme, as
we have seen, that represents 'the Isle of the Blessed' of
Taoism), etc. The ornamentation is incised, moulded, or applied in
relief. Handles (again as in the bronzes) in the form of *t'ao-t'ieh*,
a frieze (also as in the Han bronzes) surrounding the belly show
animals running and hunting scenes'.[84] The glazes often have a
greenish tinge that also imitates the bronze. The appearance in
China, in the period of the Former Han dynasty, under Han
Wu-ti (140-87), of these lead glazes, fired at low heat, giving
these green tints, is attributed to an Occidental influence. The
process is presumed to have been imported from the West at the
same time as the making of glass. Nevertheless 'the Chin-ts'un
finds have revealed the use of glass in China and its manufacture in the country itself, from the time of the 'Warring States'.[85]

The period of the Han also witnessed the appearance in
China (especially in South China) of pottery with a feldspathic
glaze, baked at high temperature, which Berthold Laufer has
named 'proto-porcelain'.[86] The pieces in question are 'a kind of
stone ware, containing kaolin in an impure state and covered
with an olive-green glaze derived from plant ash. Their forms
differ from those traditionally attributed to the Han: globular

[84] David, La Céramique Chinoise, *Guide abrégé du Museé Guimet*, III, p. 122
(1950).
[85] David, *Loc. cit.*, A lead enamel vase, of the Nelson Rockhill Collection,
of Kansas City, is presented as 'Warring States' by Honey, *Far Eastern Ceramics*,
London, 1945.
[86] The Chinese use the character *tz'u* for this 'proto-porcelain' as for true
porcelain, while the character *t'ao* is kept for common pottery.

22. *Attributed to Ku K'ai-chih (fourth to fifth century A. D.): The Admonitions of the Instructress (detail). Ink and color on silk. Undoubtedly a copy of the T'ang Dynasty. British Museum, London.*

23. *Horse, earthenware. Wei Dynasty. Art Institute, Chicago, Nick-
erson Collection.*

vases with splayed-out necks, having plaited handles or handles
formed of bastardized *t'ao-t'ieh* masks; the ornamentation, of
wavy lines and stylized birds, is engraved under the glaze, which
ends at mid-height'.[87] These Han proto-porcelains, which are
chiefly found south of the Yang-tze, have a connection with the
pottery produced by a non-Chinese people (likewise a porcellaneous stone-ware) found in 1929 in the Lamma Islands, near
Hong Kong, as well as at Hai-fèng in eastern Kwangtung, along
with 'late eneolithic' tools. The pottery of the Lamma Islands,
which has moulded ornamentation akin to the style of the 'Warring States', and which must be due to cultural influences spreading from Chekiang to Annam, has been assigned to the Han
period by Koyama and other Japanese experts.[88]

Mention should be made, finally, of other series of local pottery, found in Szechwan and studied by Cheng Te-k'un, namely,
in the tombs of Li-fan, a grey pottery dating from the 'Warring
States' and the Former Han, and in the tombs of Hsin-chin, vases,
models of houses, and statuettes of animals dating from the
Later Han or the following period, that of the Six Dynasties.[89]

As for the decoration of the Han terra cotta vases, in particular of the large *hu* with dark green glaze, it should be pointed
out that on the *hu* the decoration, slightly raised in relief, is concentrated on a wide band running round the belly of the vase.
We see a chase, at times against a curious 'landscape' of cliffs

---

[87] David, *Loc. cit.*, p. 123. On the dating of the Yüeh proto-celadons, in
Chekiang, which according to Brankston and Plumer go back to the Han, see
Brankston, Yüeh Ware of the Nine Rocks, *Burlington Magazine*, LXXVII, 1938,
no. 429, pp. 257-262. O. Karlbeck even wonders whether the proto-celadons of
Yüeh might not be 'Warring States' (Karlbeck, Early Yüeh Ware, *Oriental Art*,
II, 1, 1949, pp. 3-7).

[88] A link attested by the Matsumoto excavations of the cemeteries in the
vicinity of Hangchow (Chekiang). On the discovery by Father Finn of a pottery
of the Lamma type at Hai-feng (Kwangtung), see R. Maglioni, *Archaeological Finds
in Hoifung*, I, fasc. VIII, 3-4, Hong-Kong, 1938. Cf. C. G. Seligman, Early Pottery
from Southern China, *Oriental Ceramic Society*, 1935.

[89] Cheng Te-k'un, *Szechwan Pottery*, London, 1948.

14.

or hills, of leaping animals—tigers, boars, goats, antelopes, etc.—
or fantastic animals, both categories often pursued by mounted
archers at a flying gallop, all of them, beasts and men, being
treated with the same vigour, swept by the same impetus as on
the inlaid bronzes or on the funerary bas-reliefs of Shantung.

The same style inspires the 'hill-jars' symbolizing, in Taoist
conceptions, the 'Isles of the Blessed'. The lid of the jar
is raised in the form of a conical mountain (*po-shan-lu*)—the
mountain of the Taoist paradises, the Isle of the Blessed, the
peak of which, rising above the waves, is composed of a whirl
of spirals, while its slopes are animated by a whole crowd of
beasts and hunters. On the belly of the jar, a circular band reproduces other similar scenes.[90] We may also note, on the bellies
of the hill-jars as on those of the *hu*, highly simplified *t'ao-t'ieh*
masks, bearing a ring, which are characteristic of the Han style.
This, as we have already pointed out, is the culmination of the
t'ao-t'ieh motif, so powerfully invested with magical powers in
the period of the Shang, then decomposed into serpentiform
motifs in the time of the 'Warring States' and finally, under
the Han, becoming nothing more than a purely ornamental, very
sketchily drawn, mascaron.

---

[90] It should be recalled that the Han period has also left us hill-jars
of bronze. The Freer Gallery, in Washington, in particular has a bronze of this
type, inlaid with gold, silver, turquoise and cornelian, with the usual combats
of animals or fantastic creatures.

Chapter Three

REVOLUTIONS, INVASIONS, NEW RELIGIONS

The Fall of the Han and the Reversal of Values

The dynasty of the Han collapsed in 220 A.D. and China found itself divided among three competing native houses—whence the name of 'Period of the Three Kingdoms' (San Kuo) applied to this age (220-280). One of these kingdoms was founded in North China by the family of the dictator Ts'ao Ts'ao; the second in South China, in Nanking, by another military chief; the third in Szechwan by the last representatives of the legitimate dynasty of the Han, whose power had collapsed in all other areas. The struggles among these Three Kingdoms furnished abundant matter for the epic romances of later epochs. In 280 they were united by a family of mayors of the palace become monarchs, the Ssu-ma, which founded the imperial dynasty of the Chin, for a brief moment (280-316) ruling the whole Chinese territory once more unified. This unification did not last. By 316 the Great Invasions began; the Tartars—Huns (ancestors of the Turks) and Proto-Mongols—seized all North China (the Yellow River basin), while the Chinese national empire was thrown back on Nanking, in South China. It was to require more than two centuries and a half for North China to assimilate and Sinicize its Tartar occupants and for Chinese unity to be re-established (589).

* * *

The fall of the Han empire cannot, any more than that of the Roman empire, be explained by solely political reasons. In both cases the prevailing moral order and the approved intellectual conformity were first to be challenged. Under the Later Han dynasty (25-220) material wealth had remarkably increased. During those two centuries, in the enjoyment of the *Pax Sinica*, the population had nearly doubled. If we invoke the testimony of art we find, as in the Roman empire of the same period, that creative spontaneity has been replaced by love of luxury, as is shown by the use of jewel inlays, by the love of precious materials, by the heavy style of its riches. And yet, despite this material wealth, despite the reigning moral order and Confucianist conformity that officially prevailed, everything was being challenged.

We also have concerning this period—or rather, *against* it—acid satires, worthy of a Juvenal, entitled 'Criticisms of a hermit', the misanthropist in question being none other than Wang Fu, an embittered former official who has drawn up the indictment of his contemporaries. He inveighs against the neglect of agriculture, the flight from the land, the rush of the uprooted to the tentacular cities, the mercantilism, the frenzied luxury, all tendencies contrary to the Confucianist tradition.[1] We find the same satire in Chung-ch'ang T'ung whose *Sincere Words* were written in 206: dissipation and luxury, the harem life led by the emperors, the omnipotence of the *camarilla*, the reckless luxury of courtiers and nobles—such, the author tells us, were the reasons for the rapid senescence of the Chinese imperial dynasties, today the Han, the house of Ts'ao Ts'ao tomorrow.[2]

---

[1] Etienne Balazs, La crise sociale et la philosophie politique à la fin des Han, *T'oung pao*, XXXIX, 1-3, 1949, pp. 95-105.

[2] *Ibid.*, p. 126 (protests of moralist Chung-ch'ang Tung, about 210).

In reality it was becoming increasingly difficult to justify the traditional social order. The growth of the large domains to the detriment of small property was leaving the peasantry with no other alternative but to abandon the land or to accept servitude. The great lords, who were the beneficiaries of this extension of the *latifundia*, nonetheless deserted their estates to go and reside most of the year at the imperial court, in Lo-yang, unconcerned by the poverty of the country people. In this same court of Lo-yang and in the other large cities, the scholars, removed from power by the *camarilla*, became an opposition *intelligentsia*, even forming 'leagues' of protest. Their remonstrances, disseminated by campaigns of pamphlets, took their cue from the agitation of the students. 'Often extremely poor, numbering as many as 30,000, these students were forced to earn their living as craftsmen, farm workers or minor employees. Living among the people, they were familiar with their problems and their sufferings. They made their agitation felt throughout the empire'.[3] 'Thus', Etienne Balazs concludes, 'the scholar class (in other words the Confucianist circle), an offshoot of the dominant and owning class of the great landed proprietors, differentiated itself from it and opposed the revolting luxury of the great lords or of the newly rich as well as the corruption of the Court'.

At Court, the camarilla represented by the eunuchs brought about the dissolution, in 166 A.D., of the association corresponding to the 'League for the Rights of Man' created by the 'Intellectuals'. But the social agitation continued. 'The people of the countrysides were ready to rise up against the intolerable exploitation of the great land-owners and against the vexatory exactions of the mandarins. The farming population lived in indescribable wretchedness. The free peasant was rapidly disappearing, reduced to joining the ranks of the agricultural proletariat'. This mass of tied serfs or of uprooted people was worked on by the Taoist brotherhoods. And this is where the course of Taoism which,

[3] *Ibid.*, p. 87.

since its historic or legendary founders some six centuries before, had pursued underground channels, appears in broad daylight.

These founders, as we have seen in connection with Chuang-tzu (died about 320 B.C.), had been men of pure speculation, indifferent to all social concerns and even at odds with society, dreamers who, in their sylvan retreats, were concerned only with achieving on a strictly individual level a mystic union with the Universal Force or *tao*. But through an unexpected combination of circumstances (as happens frequently enough with the founding of the great religions) this mystical theology that seemed to be addressed to the individual or at most to a few brotherhoods of initiates, spread to the point of assuming the scope of a broad popular movement. The ancient agrarian religion, on which the archaic Chinese society was founded, no longer satisfied the needs of the new age. Responding to the general anxiety, Taoism henceforth presented itself as a religion of salvation, 'setting itself the goal', says Henri Maspero, 'of leading its faithful to Eternal Life', a goal that no previous Chinese doctrine had even conceived of.[4] The achieving of immortality was subordinated to corporal techniques (control of breathing, fasting, etc.) or spiritual ones, even to spiritistic prescriptions. The secrets of these practices conferred unlimited occult powers, and an immense prestige as well, on the initiates to whom they were transmitted.

A true Church grew up on these foundations, a whole hierarchy of pontiffs, of initiates and of members of a 'third order', with rustic communities and phalansteries, meals taken in common, religious offices and collective prayers, public confession of sins, purifications, penitences, charities. From the parish councils, directed by simple exorcists, to the highest dignitaries, thaumaturges and reputed magicians, this Church finally became, toward the end of the Han, a State within the State. It was a singularly active community, moreover, whose activities ranged from the worst sexual aberrations to the practice of the most disinterested

---

[4] Henri Maspero, *Le Taoïsme*, Musée Guimet, 1950, p. 16.

charity. In the face of the corruption and the growing slackness of the imperial administration under the last Han, the Taoist church, substituting itself for the official authorities, spontaneously and gratuitously took upon itself the works of public utility, maintenance of bridges and highways, embankments and canals, social welfare, etc., all practices that soon won the Taoists great popularity among the masses.

In short, neo-Taoism thus conceived appeared as a religion of salvation, in certain respects somewhat similar to the doctrines that were then transforming the Mediterranean world.

In 184 the Taoist communities passed over into action by announcing the coming of the 'Great Peace', that is to say the coming of the *Millennium*, the golden age, with equality among all men. The movement was led by the members of the Chang family, high dignitaries in the Taoist hierarchy, in particular by Chang Chiao, chief of the brotherhoods of the Great Plain as well as of the region of the Huai river, and by Chang Lu, chief of the communities of the West.[5] The insurgents were known as the 'Yellow Turbans' (*Huang-chin*) from the headgear that they had adopted as a rallying sign (yellow being the symbolic colour of the earth-element). At once the movement assumed the proportions of a peasant revolt—a mass uprising of the people on the land reduced to famine by the ruin of agriculture as well as by the oppression that both landlords and imperial tax-collectors exerted on them.[6] It was quelled only by dint of a ruthless repression. But the mystical agitation that had accompanied it, the outbreak that it had given rise to, the destructions that it had caused, at many points irreparable, had thrown the governmental machine out of gear. The revolution had been put down only by calling upon the soldiery, that is to say, as so often in China in similar circumstances, only through the coming upon the scene of bold adventurers turned *condottieri* and having in

[5] *Ibid.*, p. 150 (*Organisation des communautés à l'époque des Turbans Jaunes*).
[6] A. A. Petrov, Wang Pi, *Harvard Journal of Asiatic Studies*, 1947, p. 77.

fact brought together, for the service of their sole personal ambition, some band made up of unscrupulous mercenaries, dispossessed peasants, vagabonds and intellectuals without employment.

Typical of these Chinese *condottieri*, swept to the peak by the convulsions of the year 184, was the famous Ts'ao Ts'ao, who was destined to become the chief beneficiary of these events.

The revolt, and perhaps even more the necessities of the repression, for a long time destroyed the fiction of conformity, the belief in the sovereign virtue of the Confucianist moral order. In face of the terrible necessities of the moment there was a return to political realism, indeed to the politician's cynicism that had flourished some five or six centuries earlier with the School of Jurists, in the era of the Warring States. The theory, as it happened, had shortly before been refurbished by Ts'ui Shih (about 110-170) whose treatise *On Politics* was but a protest against the supporters of Confucianist routine.[7]

* * *

The typical product of this troubled age was, as we have said, Ts'ao Ts'ao (155-220), an outstanding figure whom a contemporary thus defined: 'A vile bandit in a period of calm, a heroic leader in a world in upheaval'.[8] Having distinguished himself in the repression of the Yellow Turbans, he became prominent at the Court of the last Han. Soon he assumed the role of a kind of omnipotent mayor of the palace, murdering the members of the imperial family who stood in his way and leaving the last phantom emperor (whom he had made his son-in-law) only with a shadow of power. It was left to his eldest son Ts'ao P'ei to eliminate the Han dynasty outright and to make himself emperor

---

[7] Balazs, *La crise sociale*, p. 109.

[8] On Ts'ao Ts'ao, see the article by Balazs in *Monumenta Serica*, 2, 1937, p. 410.

24. *Buddha, stone relief, style of Yun-kang. Northern Wei Dynasty, fifth century A. D. Musée Guimet, Paris, David-Weill Collection.*

25. *The Empress and Donor with Attendants, stone relief, from the Pin-yang cave at Lung-men, Honan (detail). Sixth century A. D. Nelson Gallery of Art, Kansas City.*

of China (at least, as we shall see, of North China) as founder
of the Wei dynasty (220 A.D.).

Ts'ao Ts'ao is one of the great figures of Chinese history.
A man of action, a war-lord, an unscrupulous adventurer, fearless
and fiery, with the aspirations of a superman, he was at the
same time a great poet, full of creative power and of imagination. With his two sons, the future emperor Ts'ao P'ei (187-226)
and Ts'ao Chih (192-232), poets like himself, he blazed a new
trail for Chinese lyricism. 'In his poems and in those of his
sons', Odile Kaltenmark writes, 'new themes appear that were
to remain the favorite subjects of the finest Chinese poetry:
descriptions of landscapes, swift anecdotes, laments on the evils
of war. This poetry is incomparably more personal than that
which preceded it'.[9] The impression produced by this lyricism
of action, masculine to the point of appearing Nietzschean, is
the more penetrating as we discern in this strong man, like an
accompaniment to all his thoughts, a poignant sense of the passage of time, of ever-present death and of the world's vanity.

Ts'ao Ts'ao and his two sons were remarkable not only for
the quality of their poetry but also, in respect to the other contemporary poets, for the splendour of their patronage. The literature of the time, known as 'Chien-an literature' (196-219), has
remained famous in Chinese tradition. Apart from the 'three
Ts'ao', the most highly reputed of the 'seven poets of the Chien-
an period' (and who held high office under Ts'ao Ts'ao himself)
is Wang Ts'an (177-217). Wang Ts'an 'expressed the sufferings
of this troubled period with a true dramatic sense'.[10] One of his
most famous works, the 'poem of the seven sorrows', describes

---

[9] On Ts'ao Ts'ao as poet, see the article by Balazs, Zwei Lieder, *loc. cit.*,
and Steinen, Poems of Ts'ao Ts'ao, *Monumenta Serica*, 1939-1940, pp. 125-181.
Ts'ao Ts'ao's famous poem, the *Tuan ke hsing* or 'Over wine in the presence of
song', is translated both by Wieger, *La Chine à travers les âges*, p. 128, English
ed. *China throughout the ages*, Hsien-hsien Press, 1928, p. 126, and by Sung-nien
Hsü, *Anthologie de la Littérature chinoise*, p. 119.

[10] O. Kaltenmark-Ghequier, *La littérature chinoise*, Paris, 1948, p. 54.

15.

for us in particular the desolation of the imperial capital, Sianfu (or Ch'ang-an), after the ravages of the Yellow Turbans and the terror of the population fleeing before the marauding bands.

Ts'ao Ts'ao also protected a poetess of great talent, Ts'ai Yen. As a young woman she had been carried off by a foray of Huns. One of the Hun chiefs married her. She had children by him. Then Ts'ao Ts'ao intervened to have her returned to China. After her return to her homeland, after such a long absence, she wrote a poignant 'song of distress' in which she describes for us the attacking Hun horsemen, her ravishment, her homesickness in the heart of the Mongolian steppe, among the barbarians whose life she shared, then her return, her sadness at finding men and things so changed in China, and above all her grief at having had to leave in Mongolia the children she had had by the savage chieftain: 'I dearly loved my two little Huns'![11]

Another writer of this time, the moralist Chung-ch'ang T'ung, was called, at the age of thirty, about 210, to the side of Ts'ao Ts'ao to join, says Balazs, 'the *brain trust* that the great adventurer had the cleverness to gather around him'. The *Sincere Words* that he has left us is a searing denunciation which discloses the underlying reasons for the fall of the Han—the degradation of power, the degeneration of the dynasty in the artificial 'harem' life—causes of decadence that, after consummating the ruin of the Han, were shortly to consummate that of Ts'ao Ts'ao's heirs as well: 'Everything collapses and falls apart, and one fine day the dynasty is no more'. After surveying the disasters caused by the uprising of the Yellow Turbans—cities reduced to ruins, whole regions depopulated—Chung-ch'ang T'ung, realistic sociologist though he was, and belonging to the school of innovators, concludes on a note of anguish: 'I know not whither we are going'.[12]

China was heading for four centuries of anarchy, of civil

[11] Sung-Nien Hsü translation, *op. cit.*, p. 111.
[12] See Balazs, *La crise sociale*, p. 125.

wars, of invasions and foreign occupation.—Civil war first of all. While the house of Ts'ao Ts'ao was consolidating its sway over North China, another military chief, Sun Ch'üan, was establishing himself in Nanking and in the rest of South China, Szechwan excepted. In Szechwan a last member of the Han imperial family, Liu Pei, had assembled those who remained faithful to the fallen dynasty. Legally the sole legitimate sovereign, he found all the loyalists, all the 'noble hearts' of his time, gathering round him, from the great statesman Chu-ko Liang (181-234) to the paladins Kuan Yü (died 219) and Chang Fei (died 221).[13] The last two were truly valiant knights, devoted to the death to the cause of the legitimate dynasty, who did in fact perish as victims of their fidelity. The fiction and drama that have immortalized their memory have done no more than develop the theme of the prowesses that history attributes to them. So venerated was their memory that Kuan Yü was subsequently canonized as god of war—as god of just wars, be it understood, a kind of Far Eastern Bayard, having assumed in the popular pantheon something of the role of a Saint George, the mainstay of widows and orphans, the redressor of wrongs, whose flaming sword makes justice prevail on earth.

The period of the 'Three Kingdoms' (San-kuo) (from 220 to either 265 or, better, 280) thus saw China divided between the house of Ts'ao Ts'ao in the North, the house of Sun Ch'üan in Nanking and the last Han emperors in Szechwan. It is a period, as we have said, that has left an extraordinarily vivid memory in the Chinese epic novel and heroic drama, with its well-defined characters: Kuan Yü and Chang Fei, the fearless and irreproachable heroes, wholly dedicated to honour and the defense of the law, and in opposition to them Ts'ao Ts'ao, the

[13] See in Margouliès, *Le Kou-wen Chinois*, Paris, 1926, p. 112, the text of two 'recommendations to the emperor' attributed to Chu-ko Liang, which give an idea of the personality of this great man. Chu-ko Liang, from 208 to his death in 234, was the most zealous—and after 222 the *only*—supporter of the cause of legitimacy.

typical usurper, who has become the traitor of melodrama and the genius of evil.[14]

This rattle of swords must not make us lose sight of the economic evolution in progress that was definitively to undermine the foundations of the old Chinese society. The insurrection of the Yellow Turbans, beneath its Taoist ideology, had been an immense peasant revolt. Abandoned by the central government to the caprices of the great landlords, the peasants had attempted to overthrow society. They had been vanquished. The Wei kings, of the house of Ts'ao Ts'ao, hastened to reestablish and strengthen the seigniorial system, the whole system of tenures that the peasant revolt had tried to abolish. Enormous 'fiefs' were conceded to the landlords with absolute power over their peasants.[15]

This marked reaction coincided with a general impoverishment. As a result of the revolt of the Yellow Turbans that had amounted to a social war, then as a result of the civil war that had continued uninterruptedly during the whole period of the Three Kingdoms, the population had diminished to incredible proportions. The censuses for the Empire give 56,486,856 inhabitants for the year 157, and 16,163,863 for 280. Even allowing for the fact that, through fear of the imperial taxation or seigniorial oppression, a part of the population liable to taxes or forced labour may have eluded the census-takers, the demographic drop is none the less certain.[16]

The Great Crumbling. Period of the Six Dynasties

While the last pro-Han legitimists were to preserve the admiration of posterity, through history and legend, their efforts had by no means succeeded in arresting the course of events. The

---

[14] See Ou Itai, *Le roman chinois*, Paris, 1933, p. 59. Mien Tcheng, *Répertoire du théâtre chinois moderne*, Paris, 1929, pp. 35-58.

[15] A. A. Petrov, 'Wang Pi', *Harvard Journal of Asiatic Studies*, 1947.

[16] Lien-Sheng Yang, Notes on the Economic History of the Chin Dynasty, *Harvard Journal of Asiatic Studies*, IX, 1945-47, p. 113.

strong man, the signal destiny that dominated and moulded his century, remains Ts'ao Ts'ao. Nevertheless the astounding 'romantic' poet who, setting all scruple aside, placed himself upon the throne, founded nothing that was to endure. It is true that immediately after his death his son was to occupy the throne itself, but only North China was to recognize the authority of his house. Then, under the influence of court life that caused the downfull of the Han, Ts'ao Ts'ao's descendants were to be the victims of an even more rapid degeneration. And immediately history was to repeat itself *against* them. Their mayors of the palace, great officers of the Ssu-ma family, arrogated to themselves the heredity of their office, then seized the throne (265). Since the Ssu-ma had previously conquered the legitimist Han kingdom of Szechwan (263) and likewise, shortly after, conquered the southern kingdom of Nanking (280), they found themselves at the head of a reunified China. There were grounds for believing that their house—which assumed the imperial title of the Chin dynasty and was to last from 265 to 420—would restore the *Pax Sinica* of the Han period. Such was not the case. No family, under the influence of the court life, degenerated more rapidly than did the Ssu-ma, once they became Chin emperors. This 'Byzantine Empire', by its feebleness, provoked the Far Eastern Great Invasions. Beginning in 316, the Turko-Mongolian hordes seized North China where they succeeded one another in a chaos of ephemeral barbarian royalties that mutually destroyed one another and the country with them. Before the invasion, the emperors of the Ssu-ma or Chin house sought refuge in Nanking, whence they continued to govern South China.

The fact to remember is that the true China, North China, that is to say the Yellow River basin, had fallen into the hands of the Barbarians, in this case the Turko-Mongolians. These, indeed, were never to be expelled. While, as we have said, their numerous hordes mutually destroyed one another, that of the T'o-pa (or Tabghatch), whose kings assumed the Chinese name of Wei, was able to maintain itself until its extinction (398-

557).[17] True enough, it became so thoroughly assimilated in the end, so completely Chinese that later annalists quite legitimately granted it letters of naturalization.

During this time Chinese independence, as we have also seen, had taken refuge in South China, with Nanking as its capital. Now South China, as has been pointed out, was a new China, a 'colonial' China, a territory of another race that had only since the Han been Sinicized. 'Chinese imperiality', by taking refuge there, incidentally contributed to completing its Sinization. However, the dynasties that succeeded one another on the Nanking throne after the Chin, and that were in effect national, fell one after another, like the Chin, into an incredibly rapid degeneration. Imperial adolescents rotten with wholesale vices, turpitudes and crimes blooming in the artificial 'seraglio' life, mutual family massacres that in a few years extinguished the successive dynasties—such is the spectacle afforded us by this Chinese national survival, miraculously preserved behind the Yangtze barrier, sheltered from the invasions, in the provinces recently colonized.

Moreover, the Great Invasions had caused an immense disturbance throughout the whole of society. At the time of the occupation of North China by the Huns, in 316, a tumultuous exodus had swept enormous numbers into the provinces of the Yangtze.

---

[17] The language of these Tʻo-pa was essentially Turkish with a certain admixture of Mongol elements (Peter Boodberg, 'The Language of the Tʻo-pa Weiʼ, *Harvard Journal of Asiatic Studies*, 1936, p. 185). From the recent study undertaken by Louis Bazin it appears that in the titles and names of offices among the Tʻo-pa are to be found 73 % of proto-Turkish words and 15 % of proto-Mongol words. For the names of the Tʻo-pa tribes, 56 % of proto-Turkish names, 42 % of proto-Mongol names and 2 % of proto-Tungus names. The terms of civilization and administrative language are essentially proto-Turkish. In short the framework and majority of words proto-Turkish, with a minority of proto-Mongol ones and insignificant proto-Tungus elements. The whole disappeared before the Sinization ordered by king Tʻo-pa Hung (471-479) who forbade all his household to speak Tʻo-pa and enjoined them to speak nothing but Chinese (Louis Bazin, 'Recherches sur les parlers Tʻo-pa', *Tʻoung Pao*, XXXIX, 1950, p. 320). On the Tʻo-pa in general, W. Eberhard, *Das Toba-Reich Nord Chinas: eine soziologische Untersuchung*, Leiden, 1949.

Among the ruling classes there were between 60 and 70 percent of émigrés. It may be estimated that one million Northerners thus came and sought refuge on the Yangtze.[18] Such a congestion of 'displaced persons' produced terrible eddies, and to begin with gave rise to anguishing economic problems. All these émigrés had to be housed. For some time they were inclined to consider their situation to be temporary, continuing to hope that the court of Nanking would reconquer the North and restore to them their former domains. This attitude, besides, enabled them to evade many a tax obligation. It was only from the years 364-412 onward that the Nanking government, by finalizing their status, succeeded in imposing full civic obligations upon them. But it had previously been necessary to distribute new *latifundia* to these émigré nobles. More than ever, the great families had at their beck and call a whole population of hereditary 'clients' (*k'o*).[19]

In North China—original China—the Hunnish occupation had produced a cultural regression of which the annalists have left us horror-stricken descriptions. A few Hun princes with a veneer of Chinese culture tried to give a false impression. The first of these, Liu Ts'ung, the chief of the victorious invasions of 316, had not long before, as a federated Barbarian, attended the imperial Court.[20] Another Hun king, Shin Lo (319-333), who set himself up after him in the Yellow River provinces, was not averse, on occasion, to listening to the Scholars. In reality the government of these Barbarian chiefs remained purely military. A chaos, an indescribable wretchedness prevailed throughout North China. Everywhere the 'racial' incompatibility between the Chinese population and the Hun occupants made itself felt.[21]

[18] Lien-Sheng Yang, *Op. cit.*, p. 115.
[19] Lien-Sheng Yang, *Op. cit.*, p. 116.
[20] W. Eberhard, *Liu Yüan und Liu Ts'ung*, Ankara, 1942.
[21] Arthur Frederick Wright, Fo-t'u-têng, *Harvard Journal of Asiatic Studies*, 1948, p. 322.

Only the Buddhist missionaries attempted to tame these Barbarians. One of them, Fo-t'u teng, or Fo-t'u-ch'en (undoubtedly
from Kucha), had arrived in China on the very eve of the invasion, in 310. He remained there and managed to win the respect
of the Hun king Shih Lo, and even of that prince's successor,
the savage Shih Hu. Shih Hu (334-349)—in other respects a
monster of cruelty—allowed Fo-t'u teng to extract from him an
edict in favor of the Buddhist missions.[22] We shall come back
later to the civilizing work thus undertaken by Buddhism among
the Barbarians.

* * *

At the same time that the political order of the Han had
collapsed, Confucianism to which it was so closely linked had
experienced a sharp setback. From the time of emperor Han
Wu-ti (140-87 B.C.) to the convulsions of the third century A.D.,
the Confucianist scholars had held the public offices and been
in charge of administration. From the last years of the second
century A.D. we again witness the rise of a very powerful landed
nobility that seized all the key posts. 'The overwhelming majority of scholars, no longer having access to public office—at least
to the most important offices—found itself reduced to a sometimes wretched life. Confucianism, an essentially official doctrine,
fell into discredit, for it no longer had any *raison d'être* for
people who had been shorn of public responsibilities'.[23]

From this discredit the 'religions of salvation' were to benefit—neo-Taoism first, and then Buddhism.

During those troubled times, Taoism did exert a considerable
influence. But by this very token it underwent a curious transformation. The Supreme Principle, the *Tao* of the ancient sages,
the cosmic Urge or Vital Urge, previously conceived as a pure

[22] *Idem*, p. 325.
[23] O. Kaltenmark, *Littérature chinoise*, p. 57.

26. *Buddhist stele, black stone. Wei Dynasty, c. 535-540 A. D. Nelson Gallery of Art, Kansas City.*

27. *Prabhūtaratna and Sākyamuni, gilt-bronze shrine. 518 A. D.*
Musée Guimet, Paris.

Unknowable, now became a kind of personal god, assuming a human form, the 'Lord of Tao', *Tao-chün*. Lao-tzu, the legendary founder of Taoism, was now presented as an incarnation of the 'Lord of Tao', descended on earth to enlighten men.[24] Other incarnations, other descents from Heaven to Earth, followed or were to follow, soon creating a whole pantheon of genii and of Immortals (*Hsien*), beginning with the canonical 'Eight Immortals'.[25] These Immortals could be directly invoked and their intercession might obtain for the faithful his own accession to blissful immortality. In the face of the disappearance of the ancient religion, the neo-Taoism of the Six Dynasties thus appears as a personal religion, a religion of salvation, responding to the needs of the new times.

* * *

The literature of the end of the Three Kingdoms and of the beginning of the Six Dynasties is deeply impregnated with neo-Taoism.[26] One of the most famous poets of the period, Hsi K'ang (223-262), composed a *Dissertation on the Nourishment of the Vital Principle*, a treatise on dietetics and control of breathing for the achievement of Taoist immortality. His songs in praise of nature and of wine also show a markedly Taoist inspiration. Hsi K'ang, together with six other poet-friends, had founded the 'Bamboo Forest Club'. 'They would walk while conversing in the grove, would stop for refreshment, would then resume their walk and, having drunk, conversed, composed verses, they would go to the tavern and become thoroughly intoxicated'.[27] Despite his

[24] Henri Maspero, *Le taoïsme*, p. 28.

[25] See Henri Maspero, Les ivoires chinois et l'iconographie populaire, *Les Religions Chinoises*, p. 229.

[26] On the intellectual 'climate' of this period, see in particular A. A. Petrov, 'Wang Pi', *Harvard Journal of Asiatic Studies*, 1947, p. 77. Also T'ang Yung-T'ung, Wang Pi's New Interpretation of the I-ching and Lun-yü, *Ibid.*, p. 124,

[27] Maspero, *Le taoïsme*, p. 65.

detachment from public affairs, Hsi K'ang was put to death for
having borne witness, at a trial, in favour of a friend unjustly
accused. 'Even as he was being led to his execution he still played
the lute as he gazed at a ray of sunlight'.

Among the 'Sages of the Bamboo Forest' we find other true
poets, like Shan T'ao (205-283) who, less faithful than his friend
Hsi K'ang to a life of independence, became caught up in a career
bringing official honors; Yüan Chi (210-263) who, long before
the T'ang poets, developed the theme of man lost in the world's
immensity; Liu Ling (about 265) who composed songs 'in praise
of wine': 'Wine is a noble master for whom Heaven and Earth
are but a morning, for whom eternity is but a moment'.

In the following generation, under the reign of the Chin emperors of the Ssu-ma house and while these princes still held
sway over all China (Northern or Western Chin, 265-316), we
find great poets of similar inspiration flourishing at their court
of Lo-yang. 'When two poets, the brothers Lu Chi (261-303) and
Lu Yün (262-303), presented themselves at the court of Lo-yang,
the minister Chang Hua (232-300), himself a great scholar and
poet, welcomed them saying that the arrival of such learned men
was a greater boon for the State than the conquest of Nanking'.
Lu Chi was a great lyric poet who contrasted the beauty of the
outer world with the melancholy of the human heart.

Once North China had fallen into the hands of the Turko-
Mongolian hordes, the scholars took refuge, with the Chin emperors, in the latter's new residence, in Nanking (316). And
here again it was Taoism that predominated, as may be seen
from the themes that inspired the poet T'ao Yüan-ming, also
called T'ao Ch'ien (from 365 or 372 to 427), the greatest lyric
poet between the Han and the T'ang. As a figure he is particularly
interesting, besides, as representing this 'period of fusion', for
he was a scholar of completely Confucianist culture, a Taoist in
temperament as in inspiration, and at the same time, even at
this early date, immersed in Buddhist religiosity. But the Confucianist official in him was no match for the Taoist, full of inde-

pendence, humour and imagination. Thus he resigned from his post as sub-prefect rather than comply with the formalities of protocol before an inspecting governor. In the Taoist manner he wrote about his country house, the fallow fields, the momentary escape that intoxication provides. In a few lines he has sketched landscapes suffused with poetic feeling, glimpses of distances in a countryside blurred by mist, with scattered hamlets from which an occasional spiral of smoke rises. An anticipation of T'ang poetry, of the Sung landscapists....

We find the same landscapes, with more delicate or more studied touches, in Hsieh Ling-yün (385-433). All the classical themes of descriptive lyricism are here represented: 'The monkey-cries in the forest announce that dawn is at hand; the first rays have not yet pierced through; on the hilltop the cloud forms and the dew moistens the blossoms. I follow the sinuous line of the hill. I cross the cascading torrent. I climb over the wooden foot-bridge'. And in the midst of this delicate and romantic landscape, Hsieh Ling-yün imagines that he perceives some Taoist Immortal, draped in grasses and vines. We may conclude that Taoist revery has in large part inspired the Chinese feeling for nature and, subsequently, the Chinese landscape.

We may note, moreover, that neo-Taoism did not spurn the great spiritual flights of earlier thinkers. One of the best prose-writers of the Six Dynasties, an author of tales, Ko Hung (born about 250, died between 325 and 336) was both a metaphysician, still in the tradition of Chuang-tzu, and the author of a treatise on alchemy, in quest of a drinkable gold that confers immortality. Ko Hung also concerned himself with magic recipes for exorcizing demons. He had a great deal to do with establishing the Taoist pantheon that was to influence, as we shall see, the art of the Six Dynasties. To complete his quest for immortality, he went to live as a hermit in the mountains of the Canton region.

Apart from these religious concerns, the period of the Six Dynasties is marked by 'its almost exclusive interest in literary beauty, its aesthetic tendency'.[28] Among the sources of inspiration of the Six Dynasties pretty women hold an important place —a new phenomenon in Chinese poetry, for the Confucianist scholars of the previous period were disposed to celebrate only conjugal love or friendship among philosophers. In contrast, 'in the palaces of the Nanking emperors, under the dynasty of the Liang (502-557) and especially under the Ch'en (557-589), the beauty and the sentiments of the women of the Court began to be depicted in elegant verses. This is what is called the *style of the palaces (kung-t'i)*. Several of the Liang or Ch'en sovereigns liked to compose poems of this type, which were probably accompanied by music'.[29]

The founder of the Liang dynasty, emperor Liang Wu-ti who reigned in Nanking from 502 to 549, has left us some charming and fragile poems in this manner, 'clay medals' that prefigure the feminine statuettes of the T'ang period:

'Sure of the love of her well-beloved, she wishes to advance, but timidity holds back her steps. Her ruby lips murmur passionate songs and her fingers, smooth as jade, strum on the strings airs that charm the ear. The fragrance of the blossoms rises from the steps and steals into her garments. How beautiful is spring! How can we moderate the love that stirs our heart?'[30]

It was Liang Wu-ti himself who declared, 'If I had to go three days without reading Hsieh T'iao's poems, I should lose my taste for food'. Hsieh T'iao's verses, it is true, are of very great beauty:[31] 'The chain of mountains stretches for a hundred *li*. Its peaks pierce the clouds. There the hermits have found shelter, there the spirits of the Immortals hide. Below the winding river coils. The trees hold out their twisted branches. Immense banks of mist and rain obscure the sky. I seek the desert-

[28] O. Kaltenmark, *Littérature chinoise*, p. 57.

[29] *Ibid.*, p. 57.

[30] Sung-Nien Hsü (trans.), *Anthologie de la Littérature chinoise*, p. 131.

[31] Hsieh T'iao, date uncertain (464-499?).

ed paths. I walk along a river whose source I cannot reach. The road by which I must return vanishes in the distance'.[32] All the elements of the Sung landscape are already here present. We can see how much Chinese sensibility owes to the period of the Six Dynasties.

One of Liang Wu-ti's sons, the imperial prince Hsiao T'ung (501-531), is the author of a famous anthology, the *Wen-Hsüan*, in which he has collected texts 'chosen solely by reason of their beauty, to the exclusion of canonical literature'. Such a state of mind clearly reveals the tendencies of the period: poems expressing the soul of landscapes and the melancholy of distances or court poems celebrating the elegance of pretty women—in these we have a prefiguration of the whole literature of the T'ang.

Along with this court poetry that flourished in the Nanking palaces in the sixth century, there was an outcropping of popular songs, or rather of little poems imitating the popular songs and designated as 'Songs of Tzu-yeh', because the most ancient of these quatrains were attributed to a girl so named.[33] To the Six Dynasties is also attached an oft-quoted poem, a kind of 'epic ballad', the *poem of Mu-lan*, a young heroine who took part, disguised as a man, in the great Tartar wars on the northern frontiers. An epic vein that here again announces a whole aspect of the great T'ang poetry.

* * *

The art of the Six Dynasties, to the extent to which it was not (and, as we shall see, it *was*) renewed by the inrush of Buddhist concepts, continues the Han art of the last phase with a special influence of neo-Taoist mythology. This is seen in particular in the mirrors of this period, on which we observe, in series that

---

[32] Sung-Nien Hsü, *loc. cit.*, p. 132.
[33] Tzu-yeh's dates are uncertain, and range between 265 and 486...

already appeared at the end of the Han, seated little Taoist figures—genii, Immortals or thaumaturges—either in a horizontal row or, more often, forming a circle, frequently with series of dragons interspersed.[34] These mirrors are frequently inscribed, one of the peripheral registers being adorned with scrolls framing Chinese characters in square graph. In these mirrors may be noted the accentuation of the late Han style, with a rigid arrangement of the various elements, a heaviness in the motifs and, when Taoist figures are represented, great crowding. By a curious coincidence (from which, however, it would not be legitimate to conclude that there was penetration of influences), we here find the same degeneration with multiplicity, crowding, sketchy treatment of the figures as in the art of the Roman Lower Empire of the fourth and fifth centuries.

In non-Buddhist statuary, the period of the Six Dynasties produced chimeras or winged lions, in the round, of monumental dimensions, which adorn the sepulchres of the Nanking emperors (Sung, Ch'in, Liang and Ch'en dynasties), those in particular of emperor Sung Wen-ti (died in 453), of emperor Ch'i Wu-ti (died in 493), of duke Hsiao Hsiu (died in 518), of prince Hsiao Tan (died in 522), of marquess Hsiao Ching (died in 528), and of emperor Liang Wu-ti (died in 549), the last four sepulchres belonging to the Liang dynasty (502-556).[35] As we know, the lion was unknown to the Chinese fauna, as well as to the Gangetic and Deccan fauna. The image of the lion came from Western Asia, specifically from Iran. It is found, as we have seen, as early as in the Han period, in Wu-liang-tz'u (147 A.D.) where a tomb-guardian lion, in the round, already shows all the move-

[34] Series of mirrors of the Six Dynasties in the large catalogue of the Sumitomo collection, *Senoku-seisho*, Additional Volumes. II, *Ancient Mirrors*, figs. 110-124.

[35] See Mathias Tchang, *Tombeaux des Leang*, Shanghai, 1912. Ségalen, Lartigue, De Voisins, *Mission Archéologique en Chine*, Atlas, Vol. II, 1924. Vadime Elisseeff, in the collective volume, *Victor Ségalen*, 1937, p. 81.

ment of the Liang winged lions or chimeras.[36] But it was the Nanking dynasties, in the fifth and sixth centuries, that gave to this theme its full splendor. With their formidable mouths from which protrudes an outstretched tongue, with their heads held high or slightly turned to the side, with their swelling chests, their front paws ready to spring, and the towering menace of their whole fore-quarters, these majestic beasts, both realistic and fantastic, truly belong to great art.

Chinese sculpture in the round has here sloughed off its matrix; it has liberated itself from the trammels that had subjected it to the marble or limestone block through the Shang and Han periods. This is all the more remarkable in view of the fact that this type of winged lion or chimera, springing forth in an attitude of menace for the guarding of tombs, quickly deteriorated in quality after a trial period at the beginning of the T'ang, when the quality was still high. We are here at an apogee of non-Buddhist Chinese sculpture. It is particularly interesting to note that the most powerful of these sculptures date from emperor Liang Wu-ti (502-549), an appealing personality, a noble character, a brooding spirit, who successively explored all the intellectual positions of his time, from Confucianism and Taoism to Buddhism, in the search for truth.

* * *

The period of the Six Dynasties is no less interesting from the point of view of the history of ceramics. The province of Chekiang that had been since the beginning a centre of original productions, witnessed at this time the development of the proto-celadons in porcellaneous stoneware, known as Yüeh, which form the transition between the Han proto-porcelains of the

[36] Reproduction in Sirén, *A History of Early Chinese Art*, London, 1928. Vol. III, pl. 6.

same region and the celadons properly so called of the Sung period. In 1937, Brankston unearthed the vestiges of a proto-celadon kiln in Chü-yen-chen, near Yang-chou (mouth of the Yangtze).[37] The Japanese professor Manzo Nakao had discovered other similar kilns between Shao-hsing and Ning-po, in Chekiang, and Koyama mentions another in the district of Te-ching.[38] Brankston and Plumer put the origin of these proto-celadons of Chekiang as far back as the Han period. Karlbeck even wonders if the first proto-celadons of Yüeh do not go back to the 'Warring States'.[39] In any case, it is in the period of the Six Dynasties that these proto-celadons seem to have had their full development.

* * *

The terra cotta funerary statuettes (*ming-ch'i*) of this period clearly mark the transition between the similar figurines of the Han period and those of the T'ang. In the absence of methodical excavations, we are often not in a position to say which (like the great funerary sculptures of the Nanking region) derive from the imperial and Chinese national dynasties of the South, and which are those that should be assigned to North China, occupied since 316 by the Turko-Mongolian hordes in the process of becoming Sinicized.

The terra cottas of the Six Dynasties seem to have added to the representations of the usual animals (horses, dogs, swine) certain new creatures, certain new monsters: small chimera (which, like the giant chimera of the imperial tombs of Nanking, were to guard the tomb), rhinoceros, camels. Osvald Sirén

[37] Brankston, Yüeh ware in the Nine Rocks, *Burlington Magazine*, LXXIII, no. 429, 1938, pp. 257-262.
[38] Y. Matsudaira, *Oriental Ceramics*, 1936. Site visited by Plumer in 1937 (*Illustrated London News*, March 15 and 20 1937).
[39] O. Karlbeck, Early Yüeh Ware, *Oriental Art*, II, 1, pp. 3-7.

28. *Maitreya, stone. Northern Wei Dynasty, sixth century A. D. Museum of Fine Arts, Boston.*

has aptly remarked that the camels of the Six Dynasties, heavy, squat, unprepossessing, with knotty legs, show a realism and picturesqueness that form a marked contrast, in our show-cases, with the fine camels of the following period, that of the T'ang, which are so decorative. As for the horses of the Six Dynasties, we must remember as we look at them that in this period (from 316 on) all North China—that is to say the entire Yellow River basin—was, as we have just seen, occupied by hordes of Tartar horsemen, Huns and other Turko-Mongolians who followed one upon another for two centuries. When one of these Altaic tribes, that of the T'o-pa (or Tabghatch), between 396 and 439, had absorbed the other hordes and imposed unity on North China under its own domination, it continued for a long time and in spite of its rapid Sinization to be a great military power.[40] Try as they might, until their extinction in 557, to appear as Chinese monarchs, under the Chinese name of Wei, they could not help remembering the great horsemen who had been their ancestors, in the period when the steppe had submerged China. Hence the fine statuettes of horses yielded up by the tombs of North China of the period of these 'Wei' kings.

The Wei horses are easily recognizable. On necks that are often curved they lift a long, slender head and (like so many horses of our own seventeenth century) are higher in the withers than in the rump. Rich leather trappings, covers dragging almost to the ground, add to the steeds' nobility. As for the horsemen who straddle them, they are sometimes still pure barbarians, their bodies wrapped in a vast mantle, their heads covered by a cape or a felt bonnet—some Hun scout at standstill on a high point of the Great Wall—, in other cases personages perhaps of Tartar origin but wearing clothes that are partly Chinese, often in spite of their leather jerkins; again they may be horsewomen, striking for the long draping of their sleeves or dresses and their some-what severe elegance. We are not yet far removed from the

[40] Cf. Eberhard, *Das Toba-Reich Nord Chinas*, Leiden, 1949.

17.

famous ballad on the heroine Mu-lan, half-way between the
latter and the 'Pompadours on horseback' of the T'ang period.

A little later, in the second phase of the Wei dynasty, when
the emperors had become almost entirely Sinicized,[41] they were
to retain a predilection for fine steeds, richly caparisoned, with
a trailing cloth, which they were to feature even on the lower
registers of their Buddhist steles.[42]

Aside from the horsewomen, the terra cotta figurines representing the ladies of the Six Dynasties (they can be recognized
by their affinities with the feminine figures of the Buddhist steles
or high reliefs that are authentically dated and of which we
shall speak again) are distinguished by their costume,—which,
Sirén observes, is 'close-fitting with light sleeves, but in some
cases it is so long that the train can be drawn up and hung
over the arm, otherwise a large cloth is worn over the crossed
arms. The figures are in general extraordinarily slim and slender,
reminding us by their high waists and elongated proportions of
the *Premier Empire* ladies, though with the difference that their
hair is dressed high and surrounded by a kind of large spade-
like cap, which also covers the ears and part of the back of the
head. They are perhaps not so refined and graceful as the true
ladies of the Han period,[43] but they have a peculiar charm in
their roguish smile and their spirited, sometimes stiff carriage'.
With their hair done up in a knot, sometimes even in two knots
like horns, with their long, straight and simple forms, these feminine statuettes of the Six Dynasties [44] (in all probability mainly

[41] As we have seen, it was from the time of the T'o-pa king Hung (471-
479) that the Wei finally abandoned their Turkish dialect to speak only Chinese.
  [42] A stele of 554, at the Boston Museum, Sirén, *Chinese Sculpture*, London,
1925, pl. 172.
  [43] Painted bricks of the Boston Museum, reproduced in Sirén, *History of Early
Chinese Painting*, London, 1933, I, pl. 4-7. Otto Fischer, La peinture chinoise
au temps des Han, *Gazette des Beaux-Arts*, 1932, fig. 4, 5, 7.
  [44] Sirén, *A History of Early Chinese Art*, London, 1928, vol. III, pp. 17-18.
For good specimens, see the feminine statuettes of the Collection of Gustav-Adolph
of Sweden, pl. 67.

Wei) produce somewhat the same effect upon us (though this wholly fortuitous) as some of our Gothic statues.[45]

In the course of the long period of the Six Dynasties, costume evolves. 'It assumes the character of a long cape with ornamental borders. The hair takes the form of two large wings and on the feet are broad pointed shoes'. As Sirén observes, in the latter style we have come to the second half of the sixth century, a period when the Great Wei or Northern Wei, in North China, have split into two branches, the Eastern Wei (534-550), continued by the Pei-Ch'i (550-577), and the Western Wei (534-557), continued by the Pei-Chou (557-581).

* * *

The painting of the Six Dynasties is known to us through the work of an artist famous in Chinese annals, Ku K'ai-chih (344-406). His career was spent in and around Nanking, the then capital of the Chin emperors. We have, by him, a famous handscroll, today in the British Museum. It is not certain that this is the original painting. We are inclined to consider it to be a good copy dating perhaps from the T'ang period. It depicts scenes of court life, or more precisely of the women's quarters, with slender, delicate figures of women wearing long scarves, full of grace and refinement. The general theme of the scroll is the 'Admonitions of the Monitress to the Court Ladies'. We see a young woman 'reprimanded by her husband'—a charming alcove scene (the emperor seated on the edge of a tester bed in which we catch a glimpse of his beloved, in conversation)— a toilet scene (a pretty lady-in-waiting, slim-waisted, standing, combing the hair of her mistress seated on a mat)—a famous favorite of Han times, saving her master the emperor from the

[45] As 'verifications' for certain of these statuettes, see in Lung-men the procession of women, high relief of the P'in-yang grotto, of which we shall speak later.

fury of a bear—the monitress writing before two ladies of the Court, etc.[46].

Whether this be the original or a faithful copy, such scenes evoke for our eyes the refinements of the Nanking Court—that Byzantium of Far Asia—in the period of the southern empire (between 316 and 589). T'ang painting was undoubtedly to show greater power but, at least in its beginnings, less subtle grace, perhaps because North China, where T'ang art was to develop, had in the interval absorbed the Turko-Mongolian hordes established on its soil for more than two centuries.

We also find in the 'Ku K'ai-chih scroll' of the British Museum a representation of a landscape (an archer aiming at some birds in a mountain setting). It is a rather sketchy landscape, but it reminds us of the conical peaks, with foot-hills like wave-crests, of the hill-jars of the Han glazed pottery. On the other hand, Ku K'ai-chih's mountain is a direct anticipation of the ridges and peaks of the T'ang landscape backgrounds, in Tun-huang particularly. For this theme the Chinese pattern is here already set; Chinese perspective already formulated.[47]

The most authentic specimens of the pictorial style of the Six Dynasties are furnished us by the Korean tombs; not that Korean art, even at its beginnings, does not have its own originality, but it is so closely related to Chinese art that we can judge the one by the other. These mural paintings are to be found in the northwest of Korea, either near the Yalu or near Pyong-yang. In this region, in the Shinchi-do, the mural paintings of the fifth and sixth centuries offer us 'charming little figures of donors, men and women, quickly sketched, in reddish, yellow, green, black and white shades', which aside from the garments (here finely pleated skirts and tunics with wide fur-edged sleeves),

[46] Part of the text by the poet Chang Hua (232-300), which inspired the subjects of this scroll, has been translated by A. Waley, *Introduction to the Study of Chinese Painting*, pp. 50-52.

[47] Cf. Wilfrid H. Wells, *Perspective in Early Chinese Painting*, London, 1935.

VII. *Yen Li-pên: Portraits of the Emperors (detail). Painting on silk.*
T'ang Dynasty. Museum of Fine Arts, Boston.

VIII. *Covered jar. T'ang Dynasty. British Museum, London.*

remind us, by the freshness of their attitudes, of the terra cotta figurines of the Six Dynasties that we mentioned above.[48] A horseman setting out for the hunt, with two feathers in his cap, with his bow, his quiver, his richly caparisoned horse, has the slender elegance (barbarian though he undoubtedly is) of Ku K'ai-chih's male figures.[49]

Finally, in a somewhat late tomb, in Guken-ri (the so-called Kosaï or Yang-wen tomb, dating from the years 545-559) the mural frescoes show us the animals of the Four Directions (green dragon, white tiger, black tortoise, red bird). These are true masterpieces. 'All of them', Sirén notes, 'tigers and dragons, are alike in having very elongated bodies, supported on limbs that are like springs, winged shoulders, slender necks curved in an S shape, holding out a large horned head. There is something light and fleeting about all these beasts'. The interlacings of the black tortoise and the snake (a tortoise high on its legs, a gazelle-tortoise, in some respects as serpentlike as the serpent itself), all these patterns of deft, wavy lines, twisting and untwisting before our eyes, constitute a precious specimen of the terminal style of the Six Dynasties.[50] As in the fluttering of the scarves of Ku K'ai-chih's scroll, we here discern a refined elegance that marks the peak of southern Chinese art, the art of the Nanking court radiating even to the Korean kingdom of Ko-ku-rye.

But the Buddhist influence was already invading China, particularly in the provinces of the North, and all values were to become transformed.[51]

---

[48] A. Eckardt, *History of Korean Art*, London, 1929, Coloured pl. no. 1.

[49] Cernuschi Museum (Madeleine David), *Catalogue de l'Exposition d'art coréen*, 1946, frontispiece. A. Eckardt, *Op. cit.*, pl. 82, p. 253.

[50] *Idem, Ibid.*, pl. 32, fig. 69. On the symbol represented by the *serpent and the tortoise*, see the article (by that name) by Saussure, *T'oung Pao*, XIX, 1920, p. 247.

[51] Cf. Hu Shih, The Indianization of China, in *Independence, Convergence and Borrowing*, Cambridge (Mass.), 1937. P. C. Bagchi, *India and China*, Bombay, 1950.

* * *

Invasion of China by Indian Culture. Propagation of Buddhism

We have dealt, in another work,[52] with the origins of Buddhism in India. We shall not dwell here on the personality of
its founder, nor on the 'golden legend' that the Hellenistic art
in the region of present-day Afghanistan and present-day Pakistan, around the beginning of our era, translated into images,
thus giving birth to the whole iconography of later Buddhism.
It is merely necessary to recall the concordance, the simultaneity,
around the beginning of our era, of three facts of outstanding
importance: the creation of the images of Buddhist iconography;
the transformation of ancient Buddhism into a new religion,
better adapted to a broad international dissemination; the establishment of a common frontier between the Chinese empire and
the Indo-Buddhistic empires.

Buddhist art, which up to this time had refused to represent
in pictorial form either the historic Buddha or the *Bodhisattvas*
(or Buddhas of the future), had, as we have just said, taken
the step of replacing the symbolic representation of these divine
figures by their anthropomorphic images. The worship of 'images', dear to the whole Hellenistic civilization, was replacing
'aniconic' devotion. We must note that this is a truly pan-Hel-
lenic phenomenon. The recourse to the anthropomorphic representations of the Greek pantheon for translating into 'pictorial
language' the suprahuman personages of the new Buddhistic
pantheon, reminds us of the adaptation of the same kind made
by the Christian Primitive Church and even by Roman-Syrian
Judaism. The artists of the catacombs borrowed the image of
Hermes Criophorus to represent the Good Shepherd; [53] their suc-

---

[52] *L' Inde*, pp. 11 ff.
[53] May I be permitted to refer here to the study by my father, Louis-Xavier-
René Grousset, Le Bon Pasteur et les scènes pastorales dans la sculpture funéraires

cessors, that of Zeus to represent the Eternal Father. Likewise the Judeo-Greek painters of the large synagogue of Dura-Europos in Syrian Mesopotamia (245-256 A.D.) clothed the prophets of Israel in the costumes of Graeco-Roman personages.[54] The establishing, in the sphere of art, of the forms of Buddhist iconography by the Hellenistic or Hellenizing sculptors of Afghanistan and of Punjab in the first four centuries of our era, consolidated the theological establishment of these supernatural figures of Buddhas and of Budhisattvas which were destined to play such a considerable role in the propagation of Buddhism in the Far East. At the moment when the Buddhist missionaries were about to undertake the 'evangelizing' of the Chinese world, they thus had available a whole pantheon of pious images, which soon became stereotyped, and which were an indispensable aid for preaching and for mass-conversion.

This development of a Buddhist pantheon with more and more markedly individualized divinities coincided with the transformation of the old Buddhism through the elaboration both of a new Buddhology and of a new metaphysics. The historic Buddha Sākyamuni, without losing anything of his human role, became associated with a certain number of 'future Buddhas'—the *Bodhisattvas*, who in principle constitute as many 'messiahs' whose coming would occur at intervals through the myriads of *kalpa* of the future, so that the new Buddhology, thus conceived, was going to benefit in the Far East by all the 'contagion' of a messianic ingredient.

Among these *Bodhisattvas* awaiting reincarnation in their blissful paradises we may mention *Maitreya* (in Chinese: *Mi-lo fo*), who will be the first 'messiah', represented by the Greeks with the Brahmanic headdress and the 'water jug' of the Brah-

---

des chrétiens, in *Mélanges d'archéologie et d'histoire publiés par l'Ecole Française de Rome*, 1885, p. 161.

[54] Du Mesnil Du Buisson, *Les peintures de la synagogue de Doura-Europos*, Rome, 1939.

mans; [55] *Avalokiteśvara* (in Chinese: *Kuan-yin*), who plays the role of a kind of Buddhist Providence, and much later, in the China of the Five Dynasties and the Sung, assumes the appearance of a kind of madonna; [56] *Mañjuśrī* (Chinese: *Wen-shu-shih-li*), bearing the Book, the Sword, the Blue Lotus and mounted on a lion; *Kṣitigarbha* (Chinese: *Ti-tsang*), bearing the ringed stick of the mendicant monk and the Jewel-that-fulfills-desires, who is the good judge of souls on the threshold of reincarnations; *Vajrapāṇi* (in Chinese: *Chin-kang-shou*), Buddha's companion and body-guard, first represented, in Graeco-Buddhist iconography, with the features of a lightning-bearing Zeus (lightning, in Sanskrit: *vajra*), who later in China became a divinity similar to the Bodhisattvas, but always featured with lightning in hand; *Samantabhadra* (in Chinese: *P'u-hsien*), recognizable by the white elephant that he uses as a mount; *Amitābha* (in Chinese: *A-mi-t'o*), a metaphysical or transcendant Buddha (*dhyāni-Buddha*), 'spiritual father' of Avalokiteśvara-Kuan-yin, and who as such is featured in the latter's head-dress (above the forehead); lastly, *Vairocana* (Chinese: *P'i-lu-che-na*), also a transcendant Buddha (*dhyāni-Buddha*), destined to play in certain esoteric sects of the Far East an almost theistic rôle.

The various divinities of this pantheon, in passing from Northern India to Central Asia, to China, to Japan, to Tibet, were in fact to evolve in isolation. In Central Asia, in the early Middle Ages, the faithful were presumed first to await the coming of 'the nearest messiah', Maitreya. [57] As the latter was slow in

---

[55] See Sylvain Levi, Maitreya, le Consolateur, in *Etudes d'orientalisme publiées par le Musée Guimet à la memoire de Raymonde Linossier*, Vol. II, 1932, pp. 355-402.

[56] See Marie-Thérèse de Mallmann, *Introduction à l'étude d'Avalokiteçvara*, Musée Guimet, Bibliothèque d'Etude, Vol. 57, 1948.

[57] We may note that it is Maitreya, too, who was invoked by the famous monk Hsüan-tsang on his death-bed (in 664). The latter had studied, in Central Asia as well as in India, all the doctrines on the various Bodhisattvas (*Vie de Hiuan-tsang*, trans. Stanislas Julien, p. 345).

29. *Head of Bodhisattva, stone. Sui Dynasty. Stoclet Collection, Brussels.*

appearing, their fervour had to be transferred to Avalokiteśvara, the Bodhisattva of mercy, who was subsequently to become a madonna of compassion; later, finally, piety was to attach itself to Vairocana in the esoteric and metaphysical sects, or more generally to Amitābha in the pietistic and fideist sects, preaching belief in a personal divinity, in other words, more than ever a 'religion of salvation'.

This pantheon (which, to be sure, the historic Buddha could not have foreseen) shows us that the general conception of Buddhism, on the eve of its propagation in the Far East, was evolving. For *nirvāṇa* (Chinese: *nieh-p'an*), that is to say the final extinction of the soul, at last delivered of the 'forced labours' of reincarnation, the new Buddhism as it was being elaborated in Northern India in the first centuries A.D., substituted the hope of a blissful rebirth in wonderful paradises, at the feet of the various Bodhisattvas. The paradise of Avalokiteśvara, and that of his mystically correspondent Buddha, Amitābha, were those that in the long run became, in China in particular, the most popular. The beatific vision thus took the place of the former desire for extinction; the wisdom—a little arid perhaps—of primitive Buddhism gave way either to a powerful esotericism, in the last analysis fairly close to Chinese neo-Taoism, or to a religion of the heart, full of tenderness and forgiveness, likely to appeal to the loftiest souls as well as to console the afflictions of the masses. In both cases Buddhism, with its religiosity, with its charity, with its faith, brought to China a spirituality that it still lacked.

By a curious coincidence China, like the West at the same period, was waiting for a religion of salvation. Neo-Taoism had, to be sure, attempted to respond to this need. But the complications of Taoism, its dietetics, its innumerable purifications, its exhausting control of breathing, indeed of all human behaviour, its minute prescriptions, the excesses of its magic that took its adepts back to the practices of primitive witchcraft, all this increasingly strict formalism discouraged the best-intentioned.

18.

What the contemporaries of the Six Dynasties were laboriously seeking in Taoism, Buddhism was to offer them with infinitely greater facility.[58]

* * *

At the time when neo-Buddism thus conceived—'the Great Vehicle (of Salvation)',[59] as it was called—was being developed in India, the conquests of the Han in Central Asia were bringing China into direct contact with it. We have already spoken of the expeditions of the Chinese general Pan Ch'ao (between 73 and 102 A.D.) bringing the frontiers of China as far as to the 'Roof of the World'. The Chinese empire thus made contact with the Indo-Scythian empire of the Kuchans, masters of Afghanistan and of the Punjab and one of whose sovereigns, the famous Kaniṣka (approx. 144-172 A.D.), having become the protector of Buddhism, could not fail to become interested in the dissemination of this religion in Central Asia.[60] The propaganda in question naturally followed the Silk Road, with its double trail of caravans that brought the silk merchants as far as the Pamir, that great crossroads of Eurasiatic relations. As so often happens, the trade route had in effect favoured the trade in ideas. Since the beginnings of the Christian era, the Buddhist missionaries, using these traffic lanes, had thus undertaken the methodical conversion of the caravan oases of the Tarim.

The oases in question, Kashgar, Kucha and Karashar to the north (with Turfan somewhat removed, to the northeast), and in the south, Yarkand, Khotan, Niya and Miran, thus played the same role, for the dissemination of arts and religions, as the

---

[58] Henri Maspero, *Le Taoisme*, p. 57.

[59] Sanscrit: *Mahāyāna*. Chinese: *Ta-sheng*.

[60] A new chronology of Kaniṣka, by R. Ghirshman, *Begram, Recherches sur les Kouchans*, Paris-Cairo, 1946, p. 141.

oases of the Syrian desert, as Palmyra and Dura.[61] As has been said above, these Central-Asiatic oases were then inhabited by Indo-European populations: East-Iranians (former Sakas or 'Saces') in Kashgar and Khotan, and 'Tokharian', likewise of Indo-European language, in Kucha, Karashar and Turfan. Among these peoples, racial brothers of the Indo-Iranians, the Indian culture brought by the Buddhist missionaries must have propagated without effort. It brought with it the Graeco-Buddhist sculpture from the region of present-day Afghanistan and present-day Punjab, the art of Gandhāra, as it is commonly called. The Aurel Stein Mission, in fact, found in Rawak, in the region of Khotan, around various stūpas going back to the first centuries of our era, purely Graeco-Buddhist reliefs,[62] and in Niya, on a site abandoned about the end of the third century A.D., intaglios of Roman workmanship, as well as coins from the Kuchan dynasty that reigned between 30 and 244 A.D. over Afghanistan and Punjab.[63] In Miran, finally, south of Lop-Nor, Aurel Stein has discovered third century Buddhist mural paintings of purely Graeco-Roman workmanship.[64]

Over the trails of the Silk Road, through the Tarim basin, the Buddhist missionaries, from the second half of the first century of our era onward, arrived in China. We know that in the year 65 a Han imperial prince, the prince of Ch'u, whose apanage was situated in P'eng-ch'eng, at the mouth of the Yangtze, favoured a small Buddhist community established on his terri-

[61] Compare on the one hand Rostovzeff, Les cités caravanières, Pétra et Palmyre, Tableaux de la vie antique, Paris, 1936, p. 115, and by the same, Dura-Europos and its Art, Oxford, 1936; on the other hand Aurel Stein, On Ancient Central-Asian Tracks, London, 1933, and Von Le Coq, Buried Treasures of Chinese Turkestan, London, 1928. The caravan as vehicle of new religions. Likewise today the railroad a vehicle of revolutionary propaganda.

[62] Aurel Stein, Ancient Khotan, II, pls. XIV ff.

[63] New chronology by R. Ghirshman. On Niya, see Aurel Stein, Op. cit., Oxford, 1907, pls. XLIX, LXXI, LXXXIX.

[64] Aurel Stein, Serindia, Oxford, 1921, vol. I, fig. 134 ff, p. 517 ff; vol. IV, pls. XL, XLII.

tory.⁶⁵ After his death (in 73) one of his nephews sheltered this Buddhist community in his palace, in the imperial capital of Lo-yang. The Lo-yang community prospered and in 166 a Han sovereign, emperor Huan-ti, favoured it with his benevolence.

The first translations of the Buddhist holy Scriptures, from Sanskrit into Chinese, were the work of a missionary of Iranian (Parthian) origin, called by the Chinese An Shih-kao, who is presumed to have translated, between 148 and 170, the *Amitāyus-sūtra* (in Chinese: *Wu-liang-shou-ching*), a text of which the choice is significant, for it deals with the transcendant Buddha *Amitāyus* ('Infinite Life'), the doublet of *Amitābha* ('Infinite Light'); in other words, we are here in the presence of the 'Ami-dic' beliefs, that is to say of a kind of neo-Buddhism, undoub-tedly influenced in the beginning by the 'religions of Light' of Iran, which was to develop into a true fideism, with devotion to a personal divinity, full of tenderness and compassion. Here was a note that China, even in the neo-Taoist devotions, had never before heard.

The Buddhist community of Lo-yang a little later, about 170, heard the sermons of two other missionaries, one of whom had come from India proper, the other from the old Indo-Scythian empire (Afghanistan and Punjab). Between 223 and 253 we find the son of an Indo-Scythian ambassador translating a new 'Ami-dist' work, the famous *Amitābha-sūtra* (*A-mi-t'o ching*). It is of interest to note that the Buddhist preachers did not arrive in China solely by the continental route, the Silk Road. Some also came by the sea route, the Spice Route, like K'ang Seng-hui, a Sogdian merchant, that is, originating from the region of Sa-markand, who had come via India and Indochina and landed, in 247, in Nanking where he preached Buddhism to a local prince, in the time of the Three Kingdoms.

About 270 we observe the importance that Buddhism has

---

⁶⁵ See Henri Maspero, *Les religions chinoises*, p. 205, and *Le Taoïsme*, p. 186.

assumed in the oasis of Lou-lan (northeast of Lop-Nor) where Buddhist statuettes have been found, with angular folds inspired by woodcarving technique, which were markedly to influence the 'Chinese Saint-Sulpice' of the following period.[66] Between 284 and 313 we find an Indo-Scythian resident and an Indian resident working in Ch'ang-an (Sianfu), named respectively Chih Fa-hu and Chu Shu-lan, who translated from the Sanskrit the famous *Lotus of the True Law* (Sanskrit: *Saddharma-puṇḍarīka*; in Chinese: *P'u-yao-ching*), a text that two centuries later was to play, as we shall see, such a great role in the training of the Chinese Buddhist sect (with monist tendencies) of the T'ien-t'ai.[67]

* * *

These translators found themselves faced with a difficult problem: how were they to find equivalents in Chinese for the Buddhist concepts? The genius of the Sanskrit language, an Indo-European language that basically obeys the same laws as our Greek and our Latin, has hardly anything in common with Chinese. Every Chinese character is charged with an age-old dynamism that is almost bound to produce strange distortions when it is used to interpret notions that are foreign. It is the same difficulty that the Catholic missionaries were later to encounter when they had to translate Christian dogma into characters; we know that in the sixteenth century the Catholic missions resolved the question by borrowing a certain number of terms from Confucianist philosophy.

The Buddhist propagandists and translators, for their part, borrowed the Taoist vocabulary. To translate the Sanskrit notion of *bodhi* ('Illumination') that makes a true Buddha of the *Bodhisattva* or candidate to Buddha-hood), the pious translators bor-

[66] See Folke Bergman, *Archaeological Researches in Sin-kiang*, Stockholm, 1939.
[67] The sect of Mount T'ien-t'ai (Japanese: *Tendai*) was founded by the Chinese monk Chih-i (531-597).

rowed the characteristic vocable *tao* (the 'Way'), a term by which the 'Taoists' designated their Absolute, cosmic force and vital urge. The Sanskrit notion of 'Extinction' (the extinction of the personality) or nirvāṇa was rendered by the characters *mieh-tu*, terms that designate the Taoist 'Deliverance', or else by the words *wu-wei*, the 'Non-Acting' of the Taoist Immortals, all terms having a meaning far removed from the Sanskrit concept. To designate the saints of Buddhism (Sanskrit: *arhat*), the Taoist expression *chen-jen* ('true man') was used, a term also charged with a quite different previous meaning.

It was thanks to this disguise that the first Buddhist communities were able to gain admittance in China. Their faithful passed themselves off, or allowed themselves to be regarded, as a new Taoist sect. The P'eng-ch'eng community had been, as we said, favoured by a Han imperial prince, precisely because this prince was greatly addicted to Taoism. In fact this community, as well as that of Lo-yang that derived from it, were, to borrow Henri Maspero's formula, brotherhoods of Buddhicized Taoism'.[68] The first in date of the translators, the Parthian An Shih-kao of whom we have spoken, puts into the mouth of the Buddha Śākyamuni the statement that man can achieve immortality, an astonishing assertion if we reflect that all Śākyamuni's teaching tended toward *nirvāṇa*, that is to say toward the extinction of the personality; an explicable assertion, on the other hand, if we recall that it was proffered for the use of Taoist circles in which the wise man aspired only to become an Immortal. In order to circumvent the difficulty Buddhist apologetics, as voiced in particular by Chih Ch'ien, between 223 and 253, in the first life of Śākyamuni translated (by him) into Chinese, let it be understood that Lao-tzu, and Confucius as well, had themselves been but incarnations of the Buddha.

[68] Maspero, Introduction du Bouddhisme, *Les religions chinoises*, pp. 207 ff, and Le Taoïsme et les débuts du bouddhisme en Chine, *Le Taoïsme*, pp. 185 ff.

We may note in passing the nationality of the 'Kuchan' (that is originating from present-day Afghanistan) or Parthian, or in any case Iranian missionaries, whom we find to be so numerous among the first apostles of Buddhism in China. In fact, one of the aspects of Buddhism that they were to preach, the *Mahāyāna* or 'Great Vehicle of Salvation' (and, in the *Mahāyāna* most particularly *Amidism*), seems to have been strongly influenced by the Iranian 'religions of light', a tendency that was still further to favour the propagation of Buddhism in the Far East.[69]

Amidism or devotion to the *dyāni-Buddha* Amitābha (in Chinese: A-mi-t'o) also developed in Taoistically-inclined circles. It was a Taoist converted to Buddhism, the monk Hui-yüan, also called Yüan-kun (334-416), who founded on Mount Lu-shan, in Kiangsi, the famous sect of the White Lotus (*Pai-lien shih*, or *Pai-lien tsung*), an Amidist sect in every sense of the word, all love and piety, whose faithful were to be reborn in the paradise of 'the Pure Land' (*Sukhāvatī, Hsü-mo-ti* or *Ching-t'u*), in the mystic lotus, at the feet of Amitābha. Now, Hui-yüan stated that his Taoist experience had helped him more than once to elucidate Buddhist problems.

But such accomodations could not go very far. Despite superficial analogies, there was an absolute opposition of principle between the two religions. Taoism sets out in conquest of the Vital Urge, or more exactly of the Cosmic Urge, a conquest that will make the sage into an Immortal. Buddhism has no other aim than to eliminate the Vital Urge in us so as to free us from the immortality of rebirths. No more complete divergence can be imagined.

At the end of the second century of our era, a former Taoist converted to Buddhism, Mou-tzu, ended by rejecting the principles of Lao-tzu completely. His apologetics makes curious advances, on the other hand, to Confucianism, recognized by him

---

[69] Cf. Alexander Soper, Aspects of Light Symbolism in Gandharan Sculpture. Buddha and Mithra, *Artibus Asiae*, XII, 1949, p. 252.

as the State doctrine, legitimate as such, and which Buddhism, far from combating, must complete and crown. Mou-tzu seeks to disarm the prejudices of scholars against the 'foreign religion' by proving to them that Buddhism is in no way opposed to the official national tradition.[70] But while Buddhism and Confucianism, developing in different social climates and virtually on two distinct planets, could scarcely respond to Mou-tzu's proffers of conciliation, the Taoists and the Buddhists, meanwhile, occupying adjoining grounds, but divided by bitter monkish quarrels, by terrible rivalries for customers, were soon hounding each other with an implacable hatred.

In annexing Lao-tzu the Buddhists had meant to take Taoism under their wing. The Taoists, not to be outdone, were to repay them in kind. Early in the fourth century the Taoist Wang Fu, in his *Book on the Conversion of the Barbarians*, tells how Lao-tzu had gone to the Indies and had there promoted the birth of Buddhism: Śākyamuni was but a Taoist 'Immortal', entrusted with placing the doctrine of Lao-tzu, as best he could, within the grasp of the Indian 'Barbarians'. Another polemicist of the same school, Ku Huan (died about 483), in a *Dissertation on the Barbarians and the Chinese (I-Hsia lun)*, also demonstrates that Buddhism is nothing but a reflection of Taoism, a reflection that is good enough for Barbarians, whereas the Chinese, with the school of Lao-tzu, have kept the original doctrine in all its purity.[71]

We shall witness these discussions and polemics throughout Chinese religious history, in the course of which Buddhist monks and Taoist monks ceaselessly fought for imperial favor in order, charitably, to have the opposing Church condemned. The same hostility existed, despite Mou-tzu's endeavor at conciliation, between Buddhist monks and Confucianist scholars. More than one Chinese monarch, wavering from one to another, was a

[70] Pelliot, Meou-tseu ou les doutes levés, *T'oung pao*, 1918-19, p. 255.
[71] Maspero, *Religions chinoises*, pp. 75-76.

30. *Avalokiteśvara, stone, from Ch'ang-an. Northern Chou Dynasty, c. 570 A. D. Museum of Fine Arts, Boston.*

31. *Head of Bodhisattva, stone, T'ang Dynasty. Rietberg Museum, Zurich, Von der Heydt Collection.*

living testimony to the uncertainty of minds. Such was already the case of the Nanking emperor Liang Wu-ti (502-549). This brilliant representative of a younger imperial branch, having reached the throne solely through his own merit, first showed himself to be a model sovereign according to the Confucianist ideal, a firm and generous statesman, energetic, humane and skilful, a successful captain and valiant soldier. But having subsequently been converted to Buddhism, he embraced its ideas with such zeal that he became a monk and, by dint of practicing Indian 'non-violence' (*ahimsā*), finally allowed his dynasty to crumble.

Sinization of Buddhism

Whatever the progress of Buddhism in 'Chinese China', in the southern Empire of Nanking, may have been, it was infinitely greater in North China, then in the power of the Turko-Mongolian, Hun and other invaders. These Barbarians, having become, as we have seen, masters of the whole Yellow River basin after 316, were never finally expelled from there. Their hordes, as often happens in such cases, mutually destroyed one another, but the last of them, that of the *T"o-pa* or *Tabghatch*, remained to become entirely Sinicized, and was finally absorbed, without the exercise of any compulsion, by the Chinese environment.

Now these Barbarians, who did not have the prejudices against Buddhism that the native Confucianist circles had, were soon won over by the Indian preaching. On this clean slate Buddhism could write its message without difficulty. In 335 a Hun chief who reigned in Shansi formally authorized Buddhist preaching. Another Barbarian chief, king Fu Chien, who reigned in Shensi (358-385), protected the famous missionary Kumārajīva, the son of an Indian father and of a mother originating from Kucha, in Kashgaria, and who, once established in Ch'ang-an, translated from the Sanskrit into Chinese a great number of Buddhist texts, in particular the delightful *Sūtrālamkāra* by the

19.

Indian poet Asvaghesa,[72] the *Lotus of the True Law*, the Amidist manual of the Paradises of Purity (*Sukhāvatī*), the monastic rule of the so-called 'realist' school (*vinaya* of the *Sarvāstivādin*), the treatise of the so-called *Mādhyamika* criticist school, etc.[73]

The very eclecticism of such choices proves that works of the most opposing tendencies on the most diverse subjects were being translated haphazardly, as long as they were part of Buddhist literature.[74] In the following generation, about 420, another Indian religious, Buddhabhadra, established in Ch'ang-an, then in Nanking, likewise translated the 'Garland of Flowers' (*Avatamsaka-sūtra*), a monist and mystical treatise that was to serve as a bible for the Chinese esoteric sect of the *Hua-yen* (in Japanese: *Kegon*).

Tradition has it, finally, that under the reign of the southern emperor Liang Wu-ti, about 520-525, there came to Nanking by the sea route the Indian monk Bodhidharma (in Chinese: Ta-mo), chief of the contemplative sect of the *Dhyāna* (in Chinese: *Ch'an*, in Japanese: *Zen*). If the historical details of the chronology of Bodhidharma are a matter of dispute (some claim that he arrived in Canton from India by sea as early as 470 and left Nanking in 520 to go to North China), it is none the less interesting to note to what extent the motionless ecstasy, 'the mural contemplation' of the Ch'an sect, coincided with the soulstates and the similar practices of Taoism.[75] The notion of *dyāna* (a term that should perhaps be rendered here by 'intuition' rather than by

<hr/>

[72] It may be recalled that there is an excellent French translation (By Edouard Huber, Paris 1908) of the Chinese version of the *Sūtrālamkāra*.

[73] On the translation by Kumārajīva of Amidic texts, in particular, see the English version of *Buddha bhāṣita* by Nishu Utsuki, Kyoto, 1941.

[74] See Bunyn Nanjio, *Catalogue of the Chinese Tripitaka*, II, 59, p. 407.

[75] On the legendary character of Bodhidharma's preaching, see Pelliot, *T'oung pao*, 1923, p. 253. It is well, however, to bear in mind Lionello Lanciotti, New Historic Contribution to the Person of Bodhidharma, *Artibus Asiae*, XII, 1949, p. 141 (agreeing with Hu Shih). Present position in P. C. Bagchi, *India and China*, p. 103.

'meditation') could not fail to please minds conditioned by the reading of Lao-tzu. As for Bodhidharma, after having sojourned in Nanking, in the States of emperor Liang Wu-ti, he presumably went to reside for some time in North China, with the Wei.[76]

But the Ch'an was soon to become Sinicized. The immediate successor to Bodhidharma as head of the sect, the monk Hui-k'o (died in 593), was a Chinese. With the sixth patriarch, the famous Hui-neng, head of the Ch'an church from 675 to 712 and undoubtedly the most remarkable personality in this spiritual family, the sect completed the transformation into Chinese thought of the fundamental ideas brought from India, thus achieving a Buddhist equivalent of the highest Taoism. So tumultuous was the Chinese dhyanist movement from that point on that it divided into several branches. Hui-neng and, after him, Shen-hui and T'an-lun, recommended, for the attainment of illumination, the 'abrupt' or 'instantaneous' method (Sanskrit: *yugapad*; Chinese: *tun-chiao*), conforming, it seems, to the principles attributed to Bodhidharma. Typical of these masters of the instantaneist doctrine was T'an-lun, 'an uncompromising quietist who practiced deep concentration without ever leaving his cell, without engaging in any form of worship, without ever studying in books'.[77] But in opposition to Hui-neng an antipatriarch, Shen-hsiu, founded another school, known as 'School of the North' (in opposition to that of Hui-neng, which remained the 'School of the South'). This new sect sought dhyanic Illumination by the 'gradual' way (Sanskrit: *krama-vrittya*; Chinese: *chien-chiao*).[78] Finally, upon the death of Hui-neng (712), the School of the South in turn divided into two sects, on the one hand the Ts'ao-tung sect (in Japanese: Sōtō), founded by Hsing-ssu (died in 740), on the other hand the Lin-chi sect (in Japanese: Rinzai),

[76] In the monastery of Chao-lin-ssu, in Sung-shan.
[77] Cf. Paul Demieville, Le Miroir spirituel, Sinologica I, 2, p. 113.
[78] Cf. Daisetz Teitaro Suzuki, *Essays in Zen Buddhism*, First Series, in the Collected Series, London, 1950, p. 213.

founded by Huai-jang (died in 744).[79] We shall see the influence of these diverse doctrines on later Chinese art, in particular on the painting of the Sung age.

Shortly after Bodhidharma, and without a doubt more authentically, there arrived in Nanking by the sea route, in 548, the Indian monk Paramārtha who translated from the Sanskrit into Chinese the philosophic 'Summa' of the Buddhist 'Small Vehicle', known by the name of *Abhidharma-kośa-śāstra*.[80]

Chinese Buddhism was soon to be able to fly with its own wings.[81] Independently of the Ch'an sect, so quickly penetrated by Taoist influences, the Chinese monk Chih-i (531-597), propagator of the famous text known as *Lotus of the True Law*,[82] in 575 founded on Mount T'ien-t'ai, in Chekiang, a Buddhist sect called by the same name (T'ien-t'ai sect in Chinese, Tendai in Japanese), which reached a kind of monism and pantheism, transforming the totality of the phenomena of which the Buddhistic universe is composed into the equivalent of an Absolute, 'Absolute Nature', the soul of the Buddhas and of worlds.[83]

While the Indian missionaries had come to 'evangelize' China, Chinese monks, trained in their school, had set out on pilgrimages to India, to visit the Buddhist Holy Places. Such was the case of the monk Fa-hsien. Leaving Ch'ang-an in 399, Fa-hsien

[79] Sylvain Levi, *Matériaux japonais pour l'étude du bouddhisme*, Tokyo, 1927, pp. 36-40.

[80] The *Abhidharma-kośa-śāstra* (in Chinese: *A-p'i-t'a-mo chü-she shih luen*), attributed to the Indian philosopher Vasubandhu (fourth to fifth centuries A.D.), has been remarkably well translated into French by Louis de La Vallée-Poussin.

[81] One of the most recent general studies of Sino-Japanese Buddhist thought (with nomenclature of the schools and sects) is that of Takakusu, *The Essentials of Buddhist Philosophy*, Honolulu, 1947.

[82] In Sanskrit: *Saddharma-puṇḍarīka*. It is believed of have been composed, in India, in the early third century A.D.

[83] The notion of 'Absolute Nature' (*bhūta tathatā* in Sanskrit, *chenju* in Chinese) announces the reintroduction of metaphysics into the original Buddhistic panphenomenism. An undoubted manifestation of the inner evolution of the Indian Mahayana. A proof also of the Taoist osmosis in Chinese Buddhism.

passed through Lop-Nor, Khotan, Gandhara, visited India and Ceylon and returned by sea (via Sumatra). He was back in China in 414.

Wei Sculpture

The barbarian kings, of Turkish race, known in Turkish by the name of Tabghatch kings (Chinese transcription: T'o-pa) and in Chinese by the name of kings of Wei, who from 400 on gradually extended their domination over all North China, initially reacted against the Buddhist propaganda.[84] In 444, one of them, the energetic T'o-pa T'ao, went so far as to prohibit Buddhism, a prohibition that entailed highly regrettable iconoclastic measures from the point of view of our archeological knowledge. But by 453 his successor, T'o-pa Hsün, put an end to the persecution. So great did the fervor of this dynasty presently become that in 471 king T'o-pa Hung became a monk.

The conversion of the T'o-pa or Wei kings was to have a considerable influence on the development of Chinese art. The Buddhist sculpture from the middle of the fifth century to the middle of the sixth is rightly known as 'Wei sculpture'. The first residence of the Wei kings had been, from 398 to 494, in P'ing-ch'eng, two and a half kilometres west of Ta-t'ung, in the extreme north of present-day Shansi, on the fringe of the steppe. In 414-415 the Buddhists began to build rock shrines (sculptured caves and niches) in the cliffs of Yünkang, 15 kilometres to the west of Ta-t'ung.[85] Of the first sculptures of this

[84] Cf. W. Eberhard, Das Toba-Reich Nord-Chinas, eine soziologische Untersuchung, Leiden. 1949 Peter Boodberg, The Language of the T'o-pa Wei, Harvard Journal of Asiatic Studies, 1936, pp. 167-185. Louis Bazin, 'Recherches sur les parlers T'o-pa', T'oung pao, XXXIX, 1950, p. 320.

[85] The example for the Buddhist sanctuaries dug in cliff walls came, through Tarim (Kysil and Turfan), from Buddhist Afghanistan: the imitation of the Bamiyan caves is perceptible in Yün-kang. The relay is furnished by the caves of Tun-huang (a frontier post between China and the Tarim), the first of which probably date from 366. See Hackin, The Colossal Buddhas at Bâmiyân, Their Influence on Buddhist Sculpture, Eastern Art, Vol. I, 2,

period nothing remains, most likely as a result of the persecutions of the years 446-447. The work was resumed in 453. The moving spirit in the undertaking was the Chinese monk T'an-yao, whose doctrine was based on the *Lotus of the True Law* and on the teachings of the Indian *arhat* Vimalakīrti.[86] Between 460 and 465, under the reign of the Wei king T'o-pa Hsün, it was he who directed the work on caves 14 to 20 at Yün-kang, including the colossal Buddha, seated Indian-fashion, of cave 20, whose rather rough, sketchy character is reminiscent of the Buddhas, likewise both colossal and simplified, of Bamiyan.[87] This was followed, about 480-485, by the fitting out of caves 5 to 13. The 'first' caves in the traditional numbering that has been kept since Chavannes, in particular cave 3, are in fact later, dating from the Sui period (581-617).[88]

In 494, the kings of Wei, already almost entirely Sinicized, moved their capital from P'ing-ch'eng to Lo-yang, the ancient metropolis of Honan. From the years 508-515, they had dug out and fitted as Buddhist rock shrines the black limestone cliff wall of the Lung-men pass, some eight miles south of Lo-yang. The work began with the Ku-yang-tung cave (years 508-515). Then came the caves of Lien-hua-tung, of the same period, of Wei-tzu-tung, as well as of Yüeh-fang-tung (about 530) and of Pin-yang-tung, this last until recently regarded as being of the T'ang period but which a better interpretation by our Japanese colleague Sekino enables us to bring back to about 535-536.[89]

[86] See Demiéville, 'L'Inscription de Yun-kang', B.E.F.E.O., 1925, p. 449.

[87] For the dating of the Yün-kang caves, reference should henceforth be made to Tokiwa and Sekino, *Buddhist Monuments in China*, II, Tokyo, 1926. On the colossal Buddha of Yün-kang, see Seiichi Mizuno, *Chinese Stone Sculpture*, Tokyo, 1950, p. 16, pl. III, no. 6.

[88] Until the eagerly-awaited publication of the complete series of photographs of Yün-kang, prepared by the University of Kyoto, becomes available, see Yukio Yashiro, The Present State of the Yün-kang Caves, *Bulletin of Eastern Art*, 15, Tokyo, 1941.

[89] We may note that Sekino's case in favor of pushing back the date of fitting out the Pin-yang-tung to the years 535-536 is corroborated by the fact that the

To the end, the Wei sovereigns had contributed to the em-
bellishment of the sanctuaries of Lung-men, situated so close
to their new capital (as those of Yün-kang had been dug in the
proximity of their preceding capital). One of these had been
the formidable but very pious dowager Hu, regent of the Wei
kingdom from 515 to 528. It was during the regency of this
princess also that the elegant pagoda of Sung-yüeh-ssu was built,
about 523, on a terrace of the Sung-shan, in Honan, which is
the most ancient known pagoda in China.[90] To the pious works
of this dynasty must be added the sculptures (in gray-blue limestone) of She-ku-ssu in Kung-hsien near Lung-men, sculptures
begun around the end of the Wei of the North and continued
after the division of their empire (after 534), as can be seen
by the mention of donors under the heading of the years 595-600,
in the period of the Sui.[91]

* * *

Buddhist art, we know, reached China by way of Central
Asia. We may recall in this connection that in 'Eurasiatic' relations two kinds of quite separate transcontinental trails must be
distinguished:

1. *The route across the steppes* that has its starting-point
in Inner and Outer Mongolia (between which the Gobi has never
been a barrier), negotiates the Siberian 'centres' through the

dress of the personages featured on the high reliefs of this cave is also to
be found on an engraved stone of 529, now in Boston. See *Bulletin of the Museum
of Fine Arts*, Boston, 1942, no. 242. The latest general studies on the sculpture
of Yün-kang are those of Seiichi Mizuno, *Unkō Sekkutsu to sono Jidai*, Tokyo,
1939, and *Unk Sekibutsu-gun*, Osaka, 1944. And on Lung-men, Seiichi Mizuno
and Nagahiro Toshio, *A Study of the Buddhist Cave-temples at Lung-men*,
Tokyo, 1941.

[90] Sirén, *History of Early Chinese Art*, IV, *Architecture*, pl. 105.

[91] See Seiichi Mizuno, *Chinese Stone Sculpture*, Tokyo, 1950, pls. VII and VIII.

Baïkal basin, then, across the 'Dzungarian Pass', reaches the Balkhash basin, and north of the Aral Sea the Urals, the mouth of the Volga and the South-Russian steppe north of the Black Sea. This is the great 'Barbary Road', the one followed, over the ages, going from East to West, by Scythians and Sarmatians, Huns, Avars and Turko-Mongols; the one that was also followed, in their dissemination from east to west, by the 'nomad arts', spread over long stretches of time, from the Great Wall of China as far as Hungary. Over this route, if we are to believe Kiselev and the other Soviet scientists, the stylized art of animal representation—the art of the steppes—evolved by the Siberian bronze-casters in the Karasuk period (1200-700 B.C.) was carried to southern Russia and Kuban by the Scythians, who emerged from the steppes of the Siberian Southwest—present-day Kazakistan—about the middle of the eighth century B.C.

2. *The silk road* that we have already spoken of. By its double trail, north of the Tarim (via Kucha and Karashar) and south of the Tarim (via Khotan), this road linked Kashgar to Lop Nor, in other words (back of Kashgar) Iran and India to (beyond Lop Nor) the Chinese outpost of Tun-huang.

This second route, with its double trail, is the route of civilization in contrast to the other, which is the road of Barbary. It never served as a passage for invasions, for invasions in the Eurasiatic sphere are represented by hordes of horsemen, and the caravan and truck-garden oases of the Tarim basin, linked to one another by a slender thread of cultures through the immensity of the desert, could give passage only to processions of merchants, carrying in their bundles luxury products and new ideas. A trade route, appropriate to trade in ideas. It was over this route that the Graeco-Buddhist art of Afghanistan and of Punjab, as well as the Indo-Buddhist art of Mathurā, had made their way toward the frontiers of China. The Graeco-Buddhist influences—Gandharian was the term only recently—predominated in Rawak, near Khotan (first centuries A.D.), with stucco bas-reliefs, with altogether Hellenistic drapings, in accordance

32. *Bodhisattva, polychromed clay, from Tun-huang. T'ang Dynasty. Fogg Art Museum, Cambridge, Mass.*

33. *Buddhist procession, stone relief. T'ang Dynasty, eighth century. Freer Gallery of Art, Washington.*

with the well known models of Hadda, in Afghanistan [92]; but at the same time, in Ak-terek, likewise near Khotan, a certain statuette of a seated Buddha, in terra cotta, remains properly Mathuran, following the style of the Kushan Mathurā, with its somewhat harsh *yaksha* face and the folds of its mantle drawn as if with a comb.[93]

There was also, finally, even for North China, the sea route. Five years before the fitting out of the Yün-kang caves five monks arrived on the site, from Ceylon, with Buddhist works of art.[94]

We may mention at once by way of anticipation that a certain number of Graeco-Buddhist themes, having reached China via the Silk Road, were to be repeated on the rock reliefs of Yün-kang. In Yün-kang, in Shih-fo-ssu, in cave 6 (hence about 480), we shall see scrolls of acanthuses, of vine-leaves or grape-clusters, decorations of honeysuckle or rose-patterns, suggestions of Ionic capitals, all themes deriving from the Mediterranean world via Gandhara. A little further on, in cave 8, we find the specifically Indian influence triumphing, with a *garudarāja* having five heads and six arms at whose side is ensconced a three-headed Siva-Mahēsvara, mounted on the bull Nandi.[95] Finally, the albums of photographs of Yün-kang, prepared by the University of Kyoto and unfortunately not yet published, make clear the consistently close link between the Wei art of the fifth century and the Indian-Gupta art of the same period.

[92] Aurel Stein, *Ancient Khotan*, II, pl. XIV ff. See at the Metropolitan of New York a large and very fine head of Buddha from Rawak, in the Hellenistic style of Hadda, estimated to be of the seventh century.

[93] *Idem, Serindia*, pl. VIII. Also reproduced by Sirén in the collective volume, *Studies on Chinese Art and some Indian Influences*, India Society, 1938, pl. VI, fig. 25.

[94] Cf. Yashiro, *Bulletin of Eastern Art*, no. 15, March 1941, p. 7.

[95] Sirén, *Chinese Sculpture*, London, 1925, pls. 33-34.

* * *

These different sources were already to manifest themselves
in varying proportions, these various types were already to recur
in diverse ways on the first Chinese bronze statues of Buddhas.
But we must remember also, as having possibly influenced the
first Chinese Buddhas, the small figures of the Taoist mirrors,
with squat bodies, in the 'rounded' style, wearing wholly native
dress, such as we have already described; imitation of them would
be only logical, since, as we have seen, the first Buddhist communities in China modelled themselves on the example of the
'Church of Lao-tzu'.

The specimen of specifically Buddhist Chinese statuette sculpture in bronze (or gilded bronze) that so far is regarded as the
most ancient is the seated Śākyamuni, of 338, imported by Mr. C.
T. Loo, with robe having rather simple folds, but very geome-
trically graded and symmetrical, and with scarves passing over
the forearms and falling over the knees.[96] Next come the seated
statuette of 429, in the K. Yamaguchi collection, in Kobe, a
bronze of the same type [97]; the standing Śākyamuni of 444, in
the former Ito collection, in Tokyo, with 'wet' draping as in
Mathurā and outlined against an immense leaf-shaped halo ending in a point and edged by a fringe of flames [98]; the Śākyamuni
of 451, in the Freer Gallery, in Washington, a statuette seated
Indian-fashion, with a tight-pleated garment (as in the 'Mathurā-
type' stuccos of Khotan), and here also backed by a great leaf-

[96] H. Munsterberg, Buddhist Bronzes of the Six Dynasties, *Artibus Asiae*,
IX, 4, 1946, p. 277, pl. I. Another good reproduction of the Buddha of 338 in
Harvard Journal of Asiatic Studies, 1948, pp. 320-321.

[97] Sirén, Indian and Other Influences in Chinese Sculpture, *Studies in Chinese Art*, India Society, pl. VI, fig. 24. Similar in draping, but backed by an
aureole surrounded by flames, a statuette of 437 (of the Nan-Sung of Nanking),
reproduced in Seigai Omura, 'Shina bijutsushi, Chōso-hen', (*'Histoire de l'Art
chinois*. Sculpture'), Tokyo, 1915, pl. 155, fig. 430.

[98] Sirén, *loc. cit.*, pl. VI, fig. 26.

shaped halo adorned, along with a whole gamut of specifically Chinese scrolls, with three small Bodhisattvas similar to the principal Buddha [99]; the Padmapāni of 453, standing against a large halo in cut-out flames, with a draping remarkable both for the scarves flying about the arms and for the twisted chain forming an X across his torso at the height of the navel (Freer Gallery) [100]; the two twin standing statuettes of Śākyamuni and of Prabhūtaratna of 473, in the Freer Gallery, whose sketchy, tightly pleated draping reminds us somewhat of the 'Kanishka reliquary' in Indian art [101]; the standing Maitreya of 477 (and not 486) in the Metropolitan, and the seated Śākyamuni, in *abhaya-mudrā* (hand making gesture of 'freedom from fear'), of 484, in the Fogg Museum in Cambridge, Massachusetts, to which we shall refer again in connection with its classically 'gandharan' draping [102]; the Buddha seated in *abhaya-mudrā*, of 482, formerly in the Masuda collection, now in the Umehara collection (Ryūzaburo), in Tokyo, with seven small *mānuṣi-Buddhas* in the nimbus, a Buddha who, were it not for the flames bordering the periphery of the nimbus, would be purely Graeco-Buddhist by the serenity of the modelling and the persistent classicism of the mantle-draping.[103] But what is particularly remarkable is that the decoration of the reverse of the nimbus of this last piece has an absolutely different character, for it depicts eight episodes of the life of Śākyamuni, treated with the characteristically Chinese crowding of the Taoist mirrors of the Han or Six Dynasties.[104]

We may note that artistic considerations must, in this case, have had little weight. What mattered, as far as the Buddhist missionaries were concerned, was converting the masses, 'evan-

[99] *Ibid., idem.*, pl. VI, fig. 27.

[100] Munsterberg, *Op. cit.*, p. 291, pl. 5.

[101] *Idem.*, p. 294, pl. 6.

[102] Sirén, *Op. cit.*, pl. VII, fig. 28. Munsterberg, p. 298, pl. 8 and p. 295, pl. 7.

[103] Omura, pl. 174, fig. 463. Sherman Lee, Five Early Gilt Bronzes, *Artibus Asiae*, XII, 1949, p. 5, figs. 1 and 2.

[104] *Idem*, p. 7.

gelizing'. And to this end the Buddhist imagery, with its expressive representations, whether it had to do with the human life of the Buddha Śākyamuni, with its moving episodes, or with the paradise of the coming Buddhist 'messiahs' and 'saviors', Maitreya, Avalokiteśvara or Amitābha, was as effective as any preaching.[105] We may be sure that, moved by these pious considerations, the Buddhist missionaries borrowed their imagery from every source, especially as some came from the valley of Kabul and Punjab, with all their Gandharan 'Saint-Sulpice', while others stemmed from the 'seminaries' of Kashgaria where the most curious amalgam of images from every source was being developed, and in addition these last preachers were simple Chinese neophytes who naturally introduced into Buddhism the whole tradition of the popular religious images of Taoism.

These statuettes of an art that might be called 'primitive' Sino-Buddhist art will help us to understand the origins of the great sculpture that was to follow. Indeed we see developing in statuary during the whole Wei period two styles deriving from the same diverse influences. On the one hand a *rounded style*, having rather simple forms, which via the stuccos of Khotan may stem from the characteristically Indo-Buddhist art (that is to say, not Graeco-Buddhist) of Mathurā in the Kushan and Gupta periods, a style that may, aside from this, have been likewise influenced on the spot by the small figures of the Taoist mirrors. On the other hand, making its appearance about 440, an *angular style*, in which the treatment of the draperies obviously imitates the earlier Graeco-Buddhist style, but is now conventionalized, with the folds falling stiffly and ending in sharp points, producing a 'swallow-tail' effect, and often with a floating 'shawl' likewise ending in points.[106] A variation has the scarf falling from

[105] Cf. Le Roy Davidson, Traces of Buddhist Evangelism in Early Chinese Arts, *Artibus Asiae*, XI, 1948, p. 251.

[106] Statuettes dated 484, 492, 498, 501, reproduced by Omura, plates 159, 177, 191, 192. We may note that here, too, the inspiration is a double one. We find

the shoulders and crossing over the belly where is forms a loop
before continuing down to the feet, finally being brought up
again at the back of the body.[107]

These two styles, as we said, coexisted, according to the workshops, throughout the whole Wei period. On a number of statues
and stone reliefs of Yün-kang or steles of the same dates, the
rounded forms prevail, with an 'assuaging' quality, a sheer gentleness, to which a Westerner is particularly sensitive,[108] But in
Lung-men, in the Ku-yang-tung niches (of which the dates are
509, 511 and 521 A.D.), it is the angular styke that was to prevail,
with elegant seated Bodhisattvas, slim and slender of figure.[109]
This style was to become accentuated to the point of arriving at
curious formulae which combine the elongation of some of our
Romanesque figures (Vézelay, Autun, Moissac) with ornamentation that is the equivalent of a kind of 'flamboyant' Gothic.
We may mention in this connection the 'conversation of Śākyamuni and Prabhtaratna', a gilt bronze of 518 in the Guimet
Museum, with the angular fall of the folds of the finely-pleated
mantles Steb form a geometric pattern.[110] Even more flam-

the model of the floating scarves again both in China, on the handscroll of Ku
K'ai-chih, and on the Indo-Buddhist frescoes of Central Asia (in Kysil), as well
as on the Indo-Wei frescoes of Tun-huang (particularly in the case of the *apsaras*
who here correspond to our flying angels).

[107] Typical of this crossing of the scarf to form an X through a ring at belly-
height is the fine standing Bodhisattva of the Buddhist trinity in Yün-kang (end
of fifth century), a relief reproduced by Langdon Warner, in *Studies in Chinese
Art*, India Society, 1938, pl. v, fig. 7. See also the famous statue (in grey
limestone) of a seated Bodhisattva, in *abhaya-mudrā*, in the Boston Museum, a long
hieratic figure found at Pai-ma-ssu of Lo-yang, which Sirén (*Chinese Sculpture*,
pl. 112) also dates from the Northern Wei.

[108] Cave 24 of Yün-kang, reproduction in Sirén, *Chinese Sculpture*, pls. 60
and 66, and standing Buddha in *abhaya-mudrā* and *vara-mudrā* (hand gesture of
'giving'—left arm pendent, hand turned palm outwards) in the Guimet Museum,
probably from cave 26 of Yün-kang (Sirén, pl. 69). And also the limestone stele of
543, in the Gardner collection in Boston (Sirén, pl. 180).

[109] Sirén, pls. 77-80.

[110] Georges Salles, *Arts de la Chine Ancienne*, pl. IV, fig. 6. Also in Leigh
Ashton and Basil Gray, *Chinese Art*, London, 1935, pl. 34.

boyant are the immense aureoles of the 'Berenson altar' in Florence, a gilt bronze having the date of 529,[111] and of the 'John Rockefeller altar' in New York, likewise in gilt bronze and of approximately the same date,[112] or of two other small altars in gilt bronze of the former Yamanaka collection, reproduced by Sirén,[113] all altars in which the aureole has its outside border edged either by a number of projecting bursts of flame, or by several *apsaras* (flying figures of feminine 'angels'), surrounded in turn by an outline of wisps having the appearance of flames (although these are really 'tails of flying clouds' in the manner of the Han bas-reliefs of Shantung, which shows the fusion here of native Chinese themes and Indian or 'Ser-Indian' themes).[114] As we shall see, the angular style often prevailed in Lung-men, the drapery of the earlier Buddhist statues becoming stylized into long pleats with hems which form squares or lozenges, as in the reliefs of the Ku-yang-tung cave, as well as in so many fragmentary pieces from the same source which have gone into various collections.[115]

We may observe with one of the Japanese archaeologists who have specialized in the subject, Mr. Seiichi Mizuno, that in Yün-kang as in Lung-men the Buddhas are more often to be found in the 'rounded style', while the Bodhisattvas have a tendency to evolve toward the 'angular style'.[116] It should of

[111] *Ausstellung Chinesischer Kunst*, Berlin, 1929, fig. 249.

[112] *Exhibition of Chinese Art*, London, 1935, fig. 752.

[113] Sirén, *Op. cit.*, pls. 154 and 156.

[114] See in Lung-men also the concentric circles patterned with Buddhas or *apsaras*, and with aureoles of flames, that often serve as background for the Bodhisattva statue (for example plate 208 of Omura's album-repertory). For the *apsaras* gliding through the air with their whirling scarves, see at the Lien-hua-tung of Lung-men the attractive high relief reproduced by Omura, pl. 213.

[115] For example the small reliefs representing Bodhisattvas, in the Guimet Museum and the Michel Calmann collection (Georges Salles, *Arts de la Chine Ancienne*, pl. V, fig. 8). — We may recall that one of the niches of the Ku-yang-tung cave of Lung-men is of 509, another of 529.

[116] Mizuno, *Chinese Stone Sculpture*,

course be recalled that such a differentiation is already to be noted in Central Asia, in the Buddhist stuccos and frescoes of the Tarim basin, the reason being that the Buddhas remained for a longer time canonically faithful to the Gandharan or Mathuran stereotypes, whereas for the Bodhisattvas the aesthetics of a later day could give itself free rein.[117]

A special feature in the evolution of styles is the way in which the folds fall. We have seen that in Wei drapery the folds of the garment often end in sharp breaks, with a final 'squared', or even more frequently 'lozenged' hem, and at times even, as on the Gardner stele of 543, with a hem that forms an 'ace of spades' pattern. The way in which the mantle falls and spreads on the pedestal comes to affect a rather curious 'tubular' form, the folds assuming the 'piped' appearance of so many rigidly parallel cylinders. This is true, in particular, of the charming Maitreya in meditation, a stone of around 500, in the Hayasaki collection[118] and, more generally, of a great number of Bodhisattvas of angular style, of the Ku-yang-tung cave, in Lung-men, in the niches dated, as we have seen, 509, 511, 521.[119] The same tube-effect persists on the Buddha of the grey limestone stele in the Philadelphia Museum, dated 546, thus already belonging to the period of the Western Wei.[120] Charles Vignier described them as 'corrugated iron' mantles.

Under the Eastern and the Western Wei however, after the separation of 534, new tendencies appear. The former pattern of zig-zag folds and the flamboyant character of the decoration often gives way to a 'wavy pattern', at times very harmonious, as in the stele of 534, in the Metropolitan.[121] Or else the cylindrical treat-

---

[117] See, for example, the Buddha and the Bodhisattva of cave 23, in Yün-kang, reproduced by Sirén, *Chinese Sculpture*, pl. 57.

[118] For the Gardner stele, see Sirén, *ibid.*, pl. 180. For the Hayasaki Maitreya, *ibid.*, pl. 135.

[119] *Ibid.*, pls. 77-80.

[120] *Ibid.*, pl. 184.

[121] *Ibid.*, pl. 143.

ment of the folds is replaced by a 'frothy' treatment, as in the drapery spread on the pedestal in a grey limestone stele, which dates back to the Eastern Wei, of the von der Heydt Collection.[122] The evolution continues with the standing Padmapáni, in marble, which is of the year 570 (hence of the period of the Pei-Ch'i), with the mantle spread over the pedestal in the form of wings, and having a rhythmical treatment of the draperies which is much less rigid, the folds billowing and falling more freely than in the earlier pieces.[123]

The sculpture of the Wei—whether it be that of the Wei of the North up to 534 or of their successors, the Eastern and Western Wei, after this date—represents one of the peaks of religious art of all time. It has a character to which we Europeans are particularly responsive, because in the elongation and simplicity of certain Wei reliefs, especially in the early Lung-men examples, we find fortuitous analogies with our own Romanesque sculpture, just as the assuagement, the simple delight of certain Yün-kang statues might suggest to us the expansiveness and humanity of our Gothic.[124] In reality these are no more than crude analogies and 'first impressions', since the evolution here is in the other direction and Yün-kang preceded Lung-men. Moreover, as Vadime Elisseeff points out, the elongation of forms may have been induced by the Chinese habit of writing vertically, this being the form of the inscriptions that are often found on these sculptures, in virtue of their being votive offerings.

Aside from this, as Vadime Elisseeff has also noted, the contribution of China in the field of Buddhist art in the period of the Six Dynasties, and in particular under the Wei, lies essen-

---

[122] *Ibid.*, pl. 176. This frothy treatment is markedly apparent also on a stele of the Western Wei, of 556, reproduced by Omura, pl. 235, fig. 579.

[123] Former Getty collection (Sirén, *ibid.*, pl. 204-B).

[124] Salmony, *Europa-Ostasien, Religiöse Skulpturen*, Potsdam, 1922. — Michael Grünwald, Geistige und stylistische Konvergenzen zwischen frühbuddhistischen Skulpturen und religiöser Plastik des frühen Mittelalters in Europa, *Artibus Asiae*, IX, 1946, p. 34.

34. *Horse, pottery. T'ang Dynasty. Museum of Fine Arts, Boston.*

35. *Relief on a false pillar in* Ai-ko 4, *Mai-chi-shan caves.* T'ang
Dynasty.

tially in the expression of the face. Here again a double source of inspiration can doubtless be discerned: there are on the one hand faces that have Chinese features, and these are inherited from Han art; and on the other those with 'Gandharan' features that come from the Graeco-Buddhist source. In the second, we find a very late persistence, in the Buddhas or Bodhisattvas of the sixth century and even into the beginning of the seventh, of the Apollonian profile of the early Gandhāra statues, as in the two famous heads of Bodhisattvas in limestone, of Sui style, in the Stoclet and Jean de Polignac (ex-Doucet) collections.[125] But with the exception of a few rare Hadda figures, the faces of Graeco-Buddhist Buddhas have a purely formal beauty, an inexpressive coldness.[126] The same holds for the Buddha heads of the Tarim Basin, in Central Asia, which for that matter are in general Graeco-Buddhist. The facial expression of Chinese Buddhas and Bodhisattvas, on the contrary, is a properly Chinese creation. 'The Chinese sculptor has, by his own resources, successfully given life to the religious value of the heads that he has carved'.[127]

We shall mention in this connection only a certain Buddha seated in his niche, legs crossed, in *abhaya mudrā*, in cave 24 in Yün-kang, which we reproduce after Sirén,[128] or the head of the 'Worch Bodhisattva', now in the Los Angeles Museum, a

---

[125] Sirén, pl. 304, C and D. And in larger size, the two Bodhisattva heads of grey limestone at the Philadelphia Museum, reproduced by Sirén, pl. 113.

[126] I am leaving aside, to be sure, the small Hadda stuccos, representing episodic or secondary figures, which on the contrary have faces that are often marvellously expressive. But the large Buddha heads, as such, remain very cold, even in Hadda. Only in two or three of them can one glimpse the adumbration of what was to become the 'inner smile' of Buddhism. And the anticipation of the Buddhist smile that thus appeared in Afghanistan influenced the Tarim basin hardly at all. I find a suggestion of the 'inner expression', however, in the Buddha head from Rawak (near Khotan), in the Metropolitan Museum.

[127] Vadime Elisseeff, Course at the Ecole du Louvre.

[128] Sirén, pl. 60.

21.

reproduction of which is to be seen on the ground floor of the Cernuschi Museum.[129]

It is only necessary to evoke such examples to understand that Buddhist spirituality found its expression at last in China. Like the face itself, the meditative attitude of the bodies also often evokes a spirituality of form that was unknown to Gandhāra and that is likewise a specifically Chinese creation.[130]

* * *

There can be no doubt that the variety in the modes of expression of the religious art of the Six Dynasties was due to the influences exercised by the different Buddhist sects then in favour. The *Ch'an* sect (in Sanskrit: *dhyāna*, 'meditation, or religious contemplation'), founded at the beginning of the sixth century, and in which the cult of the individual absorbed the whole of religion, certainly played a part in the evolution of the meditative smile on the Wei Buddhas.[131] On the other hand, the Mount T'ien-t'ai sect founded about 575 by the monk Chih-i, which tried to derive from the *Lotus of the True Law* a kind of syncretism with monist tendencies, had its share in imparting to the Buddhist heads an expression of intellectual austerity that was to mark some of the Sui and the T'ang sculpture.[132]

Another sect that was later to exert a considerable influence

[129] Otto Kümmel, *Georg Trübner zum Gedächtnis*, Berlin, 1930, pl. 59.

[130] See, for example, the charming little Bodhisattva in meditation, from Lung-men, of the mid-sixth century, in the Michel Calmann collection (Georges Salles, *Arts de la Chine ancienne*, pl. v, fig. 8). And in large scale stone sculpture, in Yün-kang itself, the famous seated Bodhisattva in meditation, left hand raised, one finger supporting the chin, of cave 30 (Sirén, pl. 66).

[131] We have seen that according to tradition the dhyanic doctrine was introduced by the Indian patriarch Bodhidharma (in Chinese: Ta-mo), who is supposed to have arrived by sea about 520 in Nanking, whence he went to settle among the Wei, in Lo-yang. See Suzuki, *Essays in Zen Buddhism*, First Series, London, 1924, p. 106.

[132] For the T'ien-t'ai monks, the Absolute (more precisely, 'Absolute Nature', in Sanskrit *bhūta tathatā*, in Chinese *Chen-ju*) is inherent in the world of pheno-

on art was the Amidist sect. We have seen that from the end of
the Han right into the period of the Six Dynasties a galaxy of
Indian, Indo-Scythian and even Iranian missionaries had introduced to China the cult of the 'metaphysical Buddha' Amitābha
(in Chinese: A-mi-t'o) and of the corresponding Bodhisattva,
Avalokiteśvara (in Chinese: Kuan-yin), compassionate saviours,
who having explored the depths of suffering that creatures
endured were dedicated to their rebirth in wonderful paradises.
Amidism, beyond doubt influenced in its beginnings, in Northwest India, by the Iranian 'religions of light', was to give rise in
China to a religion of the heart, to a personal devotion to Amitābha and Kuan-yin, full of trust and tenderness. This doctrine,
before long, influenced the art of Tun-huang, a far outpost of
the Chinese frontier toward Tarim—Tun-huang, where the first
Buddhist caves go back to 366 and where, in the period of the
Wei, we see shrines set up in conjunction with Yün-kang (cave
3-A). However, even though the Amidistic sect (having Taoist
influences to boot) of the *White Lotus* boasted of having been
founded as early as 381, it must be recognized that within China
Amidism was really to make its influence felt on art only under
the Pei-Ch'i, and more enduringly from the seventh century
forward, under the Sui and the T'ang.[133]

* * *

Before leaving the art of the Wei, it should be recalled that
their influence was not solely exerted by their Buddhist zeal.
Tartar princes, horsemen of the steppe who had become masters

mena, which theologically amounts to saying that the Buddhist *nirvāna* is already
inherent in transmigrating beings. An identity of contraries that has enabled
certain Far-Eastern philosophers to consider the T'ien-t'ai doctrine to be a kind
of Buddhist Hegelianism.

[133] An important stage in the development of Chinese Amidism is marked
by the coming of the Indian missionary Kalayasas who, in about 424, translated
the text of the *Amitāyus dhyāna sūtra* from Sanskrit into Chinese.

of all North China, they made their epic tastes felt in their worship, and even in their votive offerings. Thus several of their steles (the stele of the Boston Museum, of 529, for example) develop on several registers cavalcades of donors on their galloping or rearing steeds, all magnificently caparisoned and advancing in triumphal procession. [134] We way observe also how lovingly, among the scenes of Buddha's life, they dwell in their representations on the farewell that the Blessed takes of his horse Kanthaka.[135]

It is to be noted further that in Lung-men we have the equivalent of Wei frescoes of a truly lay character in the processions of donors, men and women, of the Pin-yang-tung cave, if this cave does indeed belong, as Sekino claims, to the years 535-536.[136] Masculine costume and feminine dress here have a style and elegance that enable us to establish the link between Ku K'ai-chih's handscroll and T'ang lay painting, as revealed to us by Tun-huang or the Shōsō-in.

* * *

The brief dynasty of the Pei-Ch'i (550-577) is of considerable importance in the evolution of Chinese Buddhist sculpture. It was then that it began to free itself from the preponderance of monastic clothing as from the rigidity of the draping. It is undoubtedly true that, as Vadime Elisseeff observes, such a renewal had been under way since the crumbling of the Wei dynasty (534). The stiffness and the hieraticism of early Lung-men disappeared gradually. The tubularity of rigidly parallel folds increas-

---

[134] Sirén, *Chinese Sculpture*, pl. 109-111.

[135] It was the Wei, it seems, who introduced the stirrup into China, as it was the Avar, likewise originating from Upper Asia, who introduced it at about the same period into Hungary (Zoltan Takacs, L'art des grandes migrations en Hongrie et en Extrême-Orient, *Revue des Arts Asiatiques*, VII, 1931-32, p. 71).

[136] Omura, pl. 202. There are rubbings at the Cernuschi Museum. Fragments of the procession of donors are now in the Metropolitan Museum.

ingly gave way to asymmetrical, undulating effects whereby the body sought to reveal itself beneath the garment. This revolt of living forms against the 'Byzantine' hieraticism of early Lung-men became accentuated under the Pei-Ch'i. *It was a rebirth of form.* Sirén sees here the influence of the Indian sculpture of the Gupta period, a sculpture in which the 'wet' and fluid garment was but a pretext for more effectively revealing, within the limitations imposed by Buddhist chastity, the soft lines of the Indian nude.[137] Without denying this external influence (which we shall find also in T'ien-lung-shan), Vadim Elisseeff calls attention to the fact that the internal evolution of Chinese sculpture since the dividing of the kingdom of the Wei was in the same direction.

To the art of the Pei-Ch'i, characterized by this 'return to earth', by the reappearance of form in the Indo-Gupta sense of the word, we owe the sculptures in white sandstone on the cliffs of T'ien-lung-shan, of caves 1, 2, 3 and in part of caves 8, 9, 10 and 16 that were continued under the Sui. In the seated Buddhas the former rounded style reappears, but with a graded modelling that does in fact have direct or indirect links with the aesthetics of Gupta India.[138] The fall and spread of the folds of the mantle on the pedestal, to be sure, still preserved for a time the appearance of 'tubularity' to which attention has been called; but even this convention was to relax. The faces, too, lost the mystical, severe expression of Lung-men. They became more serene, softer, rounded 'in a modelling of fullness', and, without abandon-

[137] Sirén, Indian and Other Influences in Chinese Sculpture, *Studies in Chinese Art*, India Society, London, 1938, pp. 29-30. Also *Idem*, Chinese Marble Sculptures of the Transition Period. B.M.F.E.A., Stockholm, 10, 1940, p. 484, studying various marble statues from the confines of Hopei and Honan, of the Pei-Ch'i period (years 570 to 575), which are related by their Indianizing (Gupta-Indian) style to the style of T'ien-lung-shan of the same period. On this last group, see Lartigue, Le sanctuaire bouddhique du T'ien-long-shan, *Revue des Arts Asiatiques*, 1924, p. 3.

[138] See, for example, in cave 16 of T'ien-lung-shan, the seated Buddha reproduced by Sirén in *Studies in Chinese Art*, p. 31 and pl. XI, fig. 42.

ing their Buddhist detachment, sometimes allowed an expression of purely human serenity to be revealed. This whole art was, in fact, becoming humanized.

As our Japanese colleague Seiichi Mizuno observes, we can discern here the influence of Mahāyānic 'neo-Buddhism', of the various forms of worship that had sprung from its doctrines of salvation, with their infinitely providential, infinitely compassionate divinities such as Amitābha and Maitreya. The Amidic and Maitreyan pietism and quietism led to a sculpture of gentleness of which T'ien-lung-shan gives us the best examples.[139] As for the Buddhist saints (*arhat*, in Chinese *lo-han*), or the protective and lightning-bearing genie Vajrapāṇi, or the guardian kings of the Four Directions (the four *lokapāla*; in Chinese: *t'ien-wang*), without relinquishing their harmony of proportion, they were beginning, by the expression of the eyes, of the nose, of the lips, gradually to reveal a distinct personality and a complexity of feeling that leads to the realism, fifty years later, of the T'ang.

To the period of the Pei-Ch'i and to the same style as the early T'ien-lung-shan belong the first limestone sculptures of Hsiang-t'ang-shan, on the boundary of Hopei and Honan, which were still being produced under the T'ang.[140]

Among the masterpieces of Pei-Ch'i sculpture must be mentioned the small votive stele of white marble, from Hopei, formerly in the Museum belonging to Prince Li in Seoul.[141] The chief figure, a slender Bodhisattva seated in meditation between two tall trees, the right foot crossed over the left leg, has a purity of line, a sweetness and a grace that beggar description.

[139] Mizuno, *Chinese Stone Sculpture*, p. 19.

[140] Mizuno and Nagahiro, *Kyōdō-zan Sekkustsu (Les grottes bouddhiques du Hiung-t'ang-sseu)*, Kyoto, 1937. — Mizuno, *Chinese Stone Sculpture*, p. 18 (*ibid.*, pl. x, and map, p. 34).

[141] Sirén, *A History of Early Chinese Art*, III, pl. 65, A. A very similar stele, of 559 and coming from Ting-hsien, in Hopei, reproduced by Mizuno, *op. cit.*, pl. IX, fig. 19.

The other two Bodhisattvas that flank him convey the same happy mood. Gone are the heavy drapings that replaced the body for the Wei sculptors of Lung-men. Here the body, especially in the case of the central figure, is restored in its smooth softness, making a link with the chaste, sweet nakedness of Gupta Indian art without dissipating (quite the contrary) the impression of spirituality—of spiritual bliss and at the same time of self-communion—of the whole. The two trees mingle their foliage in a harmonious 'rounding-off' that forms a background for the flight of charming *apsaras*, not unlike our angels on a Christmas tree. On the trunks of the two trees two elegant dragons, in the style of the Han dragons of the Shen pillar, show us that the Sino-Indian symbiosis created by Buddhism has achieved a harmonious synthesis. On the base, two robust Vajrapāṇi, in a posture of defense appropriate to genii whose role it is to protect the faith, already foreshadow the war-like realism of the T'ang. We may mention another stele of white micaceous marble, from Hopei, of similar composition (the Bodhisattva meditating in the same pose between two trees that mingle their foliage above him and between whose branches *apsaras* flutter), a stele exhibited in the Metropolitan Museum in which the smooth torso of the chief figure again proclaims the influence of the 'wet garment' of Gupta India.[142]

Among the Pei-Ch'i fragments may be mentioned in particular two micaceous white marbles in the Philadelphia Museum, both from Hopei artists' workshops. First an admirable Bodhisattva bust in which 'the modelling is extremely sensitive, suggesting rather than defining, and yet quite sufficient to convey an atmosphere, a veil of light and shade, or a reflection of that inward harmony that is also revealed in their smile'.[143] We here have, six hundred years ahead of time, the Chinese equivalent of the Khmer inner smile, of the 'Bayon smile'. The other

[142] Sirén, *Chinese Sculpture,* pl. 243-B.
[143] *Idem, History of Early Chinese Art,* III, pp. 38-39 and pl. 66-B.

Pei-Ch'i marble in Philadelphia is the statuette of a *dvarapala* (a temple-garden genie), head thrown back, in an appropriately menacing attitude, with realistic features and great muscular power, but without the exaggerations of the future war-like realism of the T'ang. [144] In strength as in grace, plastic beauty is thus restored to us. Chinese Buddhist art, even while it remains deeply religious, has become wholly human. For these diverse reasons, the brief period of the Pei-Ch'i marks the peak of Buddhist sculpture in China, and indeed more generally, of all Chinese sculpture. 'The workmanship', Vadim Elisseeff observes, 'shows a restraint and a compelling emotion that T'ang sculpture was never to equal'.

In some of the Pei-Ch'i works the spontaneous humanization of Chinese sculpture is further strengthened by a direct Indian (Gupta-Indian) influence. Osvald Sirén has called attention to this in the case of certain Buddhas of cave 16 of T'ien-lung-shan, obviously inspired by models from Mathurā and Sarnath. The evidence is even clearer in the case of limestone reliefs from the Nan-hsien-t'ang-shan caves near Chang-te, in the far north of Honan, and now in the Freer Gallery in Washington. [145] The scene represents a paradise, the paradise of the Bodhisattva Maitreya or heaven of the *tusita*. In the center, the chief Bodhisattva, seated in *abhaya-mudrā* and surrounded by rows of Bodhisattvas with the lotus-pond of paradise before him; above him an elegant canopy amid foliage amongst which other Bodhisattvas sit in state on their lotus petals and *apsaras* fly about. On both sides, circular buildings, of which the upper story is occupied by other blessed ones. A paradisiac vision, expressed through a harmonious grouping of figures, arranged without any crowding or heaviness, along several lines of perspective, in a 'unified space' that shows that we here have a translation in stone of some

[144] *Idem, Ibid.*, pl. 66-A.
[145] *Idem. Studies in Chinese Art*, India Society, London, 1938, pls. XI-XII, figs. 43-45.

36. *Figure of a lady, pottery. T'ang Dynasty. British Museum, London.*

painting, in the manner of the 'paradises' of Tun-huang. Slight though the relief given to the forms may be, they have in fact been caressed by so gentle a chisel that they stand out delicately. Sirén is right to connect it with similar examples of 'chisel painting' that Gupta or post-Gupta art offers us in Java (in Borobudur for example): the Freer Gallery relief is *Indo-Peich'i* painting.

After Two Hundred and Seventy Years of Tartar Invasions and of Dismemberment, China Is Again Unified

As we have seen, the Turkish house of the Tabghach (*T'o-pa* in Chinese transcription), which soon became known by the Sinicized name of the Wei dynasty (Northern Wei), had by 423 (to use a conventional date, marked by the occupation of Lo-yang) unified all the rest of North China, that is to say Tartar China, which had been occupied since 318 by the other Turko-Mongolian hordes. We have also seen that in 534 this Turko-Mongolian dynasty, by now wholly Sinicized, had divided into two branches, the Eastern Wei (in Honan, Shansi, Shantung and Hopei) and the Western Wei (in Shensi and Kansu).[146] Then each of these two dynasties was replaced by its palace mayors; the Eastern Wei in 550 by the Pei-Ch'i, the Western Wei in 557 by the Pei-Chou. We have just seen what a considerable role, despite the briefness of their rule (550-577), was played by the Pei-Ch'i as protectors of Buddhist art: in Buddhist sculpture (in T'ien-lung-shan and in Hsiang-t'ang-shan for example) the 're-birth' of form, following upon the 'medievalism' of Lung-men, dates from their reign. This liberation of form will be better understood if we consider the personality of one of them, king Wen-kung (565-577). This monarch, as devout as he was whimsical, had gathered together all the beggars of his capital in the grounds of his palace and made a 'village for the poor'; he

---

[146] On the Wei court some years before this partition, see Peter Boodberg, Coronation of T'o-pa Hsiu, 531, *Harvard Journal of Asiatic Studies*, 1940, p. 240.

would amuse himself by soliciting alms on their behalf, in a transparent disguise, among the lovely ladies of his court.

In 577 this amiable sovereign was overthrown and put to death by the neighbouring and rival dynasty of the Pei-Chou. The victor happened to be a rigid Confucianist who by 574 had had all the Buddhist temples in his State, and the Taoist ones as well, closed down. Fortunately for Buddhist art, the Pei-Chou were dethroned and replaced in 581 by their palace mayor, Yang Chien, the founder of the Sui dynasty.

Yang Chien was to reign not only over the provinces of the North like the former Wei sovereigns whose throne he occupied, but over all China, since in 589 he subjugated the provinces of the South—the Nanking empire—, thus bringing to an end the 'great schism' between the North and the South that had lasted two hundred and seventy years. Thus he reestablished Chinese unity at last, with Sianfu (Ch'ang-an), the ancient metropolis of the Han, as his capital.[147] Now Yang Chien was personally favourably disposed towards Buddhism. He revoked Pei-Chou's edicts against the sanctuaries of this religion, had a quantity of statues replaced or restored and a great number of new ones made.[148] No less pious in respect to the Taoist creeds (or those assimilated to Taoism), he undertook in 596 the pilgrimage of the holy mountain of T'ai-shan. This man of action showed hostility only toward Confucianist rhetoric. Thus he was moved, in 601, to close down numerous schools and thereby brought upon himself the lasting reprobation of future scholars.

The son and successor of Yang Chien, emperor Yang-ti (605-618), also protected Buddhist sculpture. In his fondness for display and for a life of pleasure, however, he devoted himself

---

[147] See Sirén, Tch'ang-ngan au temps des Souei et des T'ang, *Revue des Arts Asiatiques*, IV, 1922, 98-104, pp. 40-46.

[148] Two famous Indian missionaries, Narendrayasas and Dinagupta, who had had to flee the persecution of 574, returned to Ch'ang-an after the accession to the throne of the Sui who protected them (Bagchi, pp. 270, 276; Chavannes, *T'oung pao*, 1905, p. 256).

particularly to embellishing Lo-yang (after moving there from Sianfu) and to establishing (or re-establishing) a network of river communications between this city and the mouth of the Yangtze. This was the first 'Grand Canal' (Yün-ho), the course of which stretched from Chiang-tu (present-day Yang-chou), on the estuary of the river, to Lo-yang. On the great Canal, escorted by a pleasure flotilla—the famous 'dragon barks'—Yang-ti with his court led an 'inimitable life', a 'Venetian feast' existence that has in fact left an enchanted memory in the Chinese poetic imagination. Unfortunately the digging of the Canal and the fitting out of the palaces and parks of Lo-yang entailed terrible requisitions, a frightful abuse of the system of forced labor that soon ruined the popularity of the Sui dynasty. When military disasters in Korea further aggravated the general discontent, revolt broke out on all sides and Yang-ti perished by assassination (618).[149]

* * *

Brief though the Sui dynasty was (589-618), it was, nevertheless, of great historical importance, because by reestablishing the territorial unity of China it stimulated a new ferment of ideas. In particular, we see an interesting tendency toward syncretism manifesting itself at this time, both among Confucianist scholars and Buddhist metaphysicians. Thus the Confucianist Yen Chih-t'ui, in the moral instructions that he published about 580, does not hesitate, in order to support his theses, to use Buddhist anecdotes or Taoist formulae. So too the monk Chih-i (died in 597) who had founded a famous Buddhist sect in 575 on Mount T'ien-t'ai (in Chekiang) not only introduced into his monism, as we have seen, the most varied doctrines of Indian Buddhism, but also implicitly accepted points of view that we guess to be secretly Taoist. The *Ma-ha-chih-kuan*, a comprehensive elucidation

[149] Peter Boodberg, Rise and Fall of the House of Yang, *Harvard Journal of Asiatic Studies*, 1940, p. 255.

of his system, which he published in 594, is evidence of this curious state of mind. His epitaph is presumed to have been composed by the future emperor Yang-ti.

Meanwhile the Amidic doctrines, although they are at the opposite pole of Buddhist thought, were also progressing. In the last years of the sixth century the Indian missionary Bodhisri, who had come to preach in Honan, converted the Taoist monk T'an-luan (died about 600), who became the founder of a native Amidist school represented after him by Tao-ch'ao (died in 645) and Shan-tao (about 660).

During the two and a half centuries of invasions and of civil wars that had preceded the accession to the throne of the Sui, many works had been lost. Once order had been restored and unity again consolidated, the Sui turned their minds to drawing up a catalogue of all surviving books. This repertory, the *Sui Ching-chi-chih*, completed about 610, shows the effort made by Chinese erudition to link up with the past. After so many catastrophes in which traditional culture had undergone such dangers, the period of the Sui thus appears to us as marking the dawn of a conscious and methodical rebirth of humanism.

Sui art is represented chiefly by Buddhist sculpture. To this period belong caves 2 and 4 in Lung-men, and in T'ien-lung-shan a good part of caves 8, 9, 10 and 16.[150] The rock sculptures (gray limestone) of T'o-shan, Yün-men-shan (near I-tu) and Yü-han-shan (near Chi-nan), in Shantung, are also Sui.[151] We find here a marked reaction against the gentleness of the Pei-Ch'i style. Perhaps, as suggested above, this may be accounted for by the influence of the dogmatic severity of the Buddhist sect of the T'ien-t'ai. Sui sculpture is indeed characterized by squat, rigid bodies, at times slightly ovoid, yet always exuding energy, but rough, modelled without delicacy and hewn, as it were, out of

---

[150] Sirén, *Chinese Sculpture*, pls. 293-299.
[151] Mizuno, *Chinese Stone Sculpture*, p. 22.

IX. *Vaiśravana with Attendants. Painting on silk. Sung Dynasty. Musée Guimet, Paris.*

X. *Cup. Sung Dynasty. Musée Guimet. Paris.*

XI. *Cup, celadon. Sung Dynasty. Musée Guimet. Paris.*

a single block.[152] The robes, while rather light, cover the whole body, but without clinging to the flesh as was the case with the Pei-Ch'i or Gupta 'wet draping'. The eyes are lively, but the lips have a severe expression. As Seiichi Mizuno remarks, the rigidity of these Sui statues is quite different from the mystical hieraticism of early Lung-men, in the time of the Wei, just as their roundness no longer has anything of the mellowness of the rounded style of the time of the Pei-Ch'i.[153] The faces, surmounting rigid necks of a tubular appearance ('in high starched collars'), faces having a somewhat self-satisfied expression, but full of dignity and distinction, are crowned with tiaras and set off by pendants, which Seiichi Mizuno regards as an expression of the luxury of Yang-ti's court.[154] The figures are usually adorned with a heavy chain, often looped, falling from the shoulders and crossing in front, at the waist, where it is fastened by a round buckle, from which it continues to halfway down the leg and is finally brought up again to the waist behind; at the same time the mantlet or scarf that covers the shoulders extends into long falls that descend from the forearm to the feet.[155]

A special place in Sui art must be assigned to the altar centrepiece, in bronze, in the Boston Museum, dated 593, with a Buddha crowned by a halo of flowers and flames. This Buddha is in *abhaya mudrā*, seated on lotus pedestal, with the apostles Ananda and Kāśyapa at his sides, followed by two monks. Forming a canopy above the group are the branches and elaborately cut-out leaves of a large tree, which are adorned with garlands and draperies and peopled by Buddhas of times past or *apsaras* in des-

---

[152] Statues of Ananda and Kāśyapa, micaceous marbles, colored with green and brown insets, former Vignier- Densmore collection, now in the Guimet Museum (Sirén, pl. 327. Georges Salles, *Arts de la Chine Ancienne,* Musée de l'Orangerie, 1937, pl. VIII, figs. 14-15).

[153] Mizuno, *Op. cit.*, p. 22.

[154] See the famous heads of the Stoclet and Jean de Polignac (former Doucet) collections, reproduced in Sirén, *Chinese Sculpture*, pl. 304.

[155] *Ibid.*, pls. 300, 307, 308.

cending flight. At the foot of the stand are two independent
statues of standing Bodhisattvas, with tall tiaras, their heads
surrounded by pointed halos, one of them holding the Fruit, the
other with hands joined.[156] The group is interesting less for the
statuary that composes it than for its 'astonishingly rich and florid'
ornamentation and for the revelation that this example of Sui
religious art, of the vulgarized variety, affords us of the devo-
tional life.

Among many lesser works, it is possible that the Sui period
may also have produced real masterpieces if we attribute to it,
as according to Sirén we should, the two statues of Bodhisattvas,
standing 'in an upright pose'. They are carved in grey limestone,
1.86 metres and 1.90 metres respectively, and were found in Nan-
hsien-t'ang, in the extreme north of Honan. They are now in
the Philadelphia Museum.[157] The somewhat haughty dignity,
the regal majesty, the solemnity of these tall figures in which the
plastic values, which have by now triumphed, are entriely subordinated to the theological sentiments expressed; the richness
—still sober—of their necklaces with pendants and of the chain
of jewels brought together in front, in an 'X', and set in a buckle
in the middle of the torso—all this combines to make the two
'adorned Boddhisattvas' of Philadelphia the equivalent of our
noblest episcopal figures in Gothic statuary at its apogee. The
Philadelphia Museum also has a statue of a monk standing, in
a strictly frontal pose, holding in both hands, as though it were
a jewel, a lotus bud. The statue, 1.65 metres tall, is of grey limestone. The head is realistic, and the expression calm. It has
all the qualities of a portrait, and the whole figure, with its sober
drapery falling in long diagonal folds, has a Roman majesty. We
shall have cause to remember this figure and its treatment when
we study Japanese art in the Kamakura period and come, for

---

[156] *Ibid.*, pls. 319, 320, 321.
[157] *Ibid.*, pls. 469 and 471.

example, upon the wooden statue of Asanga in the Kōfukuji in Nara, dated 1208.[158]

To the Sui period is usually attributed a whole category of terra cottas, in particular some statuettes of women wearing a characteristic costume. 'Still more slender than those of the Northern Wei dynasty', Sirén writes, 'their bodies are squeezed into stiff diminutive corsets placed high under the bosom, so that the torso is like a narrow tube'. Their elegance is further heightened by sleeves that flare at the wrist, and from which long falls descend to knee-height at either side. The skirts flare slightly towards the hem, the lower part being adorned with flame-like pennants that project from the sides. Elaborate head-dresses, in the form of high crowns or double crescents, and curious shoes with turned-up toes, complete the whole. [159] The attribution of these elegant 'mannequins' to the Sui period is due to analogies of dress with certain dated Bodhisattvas (in particular the arrangement of the falls of the sleeve).[160]

[158] Ibid., pl. 470. Otto Kummel, L'art de l'Extrême-Orient, pl. 108-109. While we recognize in the monk of Philadelphia a happy rhythm close to Greek classicism as also to our 'full Gothic', there is perhaps more true religious sentiment in the Ānanda and the Kāśyapa acquired by Mr. Georges Salles and now in the Guimet Museum.

[159] Sirén, History of Early Chinese Art, pl. 91-92.

[160] See the grey limestone stele from the David Weill collection, Sirén, Chinese Sculpture, pl. 364. In point of fact, the Buddhist monk Tao-hsüan (died 667) the author of the Hsü Kao-ch'uan, 'complained that the sculptors made their religious images look like dancing girls, so that every court wanton imagined that she looked like a Bodhisattva'. Ibid., Vol. I, p. XCII.

37. *Guardian lion, white marble. T'ang Dynasty. Nelson Gallery of Art, Kansas City.*

CHAPTER FOUR

THE T'ANG PERIOD

Accession of the T'ang

The T'ang dynasty (618-907) corresponds to one of the greatest periods in China's history—in the first period (618-755) both
from the 'cultural' point of view and by virtue of Chinese expansion in Upper Asia, in the second phase (755-907) because China,
while in principle thrown back upon its traditional frontiers,
nevertheless continued to be a powerful radiating centre for all
East Asia.

The T'ang dynasty had been founded, with the placing of
the old general Li Yüan on the throne, through the exceptional
valour of the latter's son, young Li Shih-min, who triumphed over
all the competitors who had arisen amid the collapse of the Sui
dynasty.[1] Li Shih-min, who soon became Emperor T'ai-tsung
('T'ai-tsung the Great'), in the course of one of the most
triumphant reigns in Chinese history (627-649), vanquished the
Turks of Mongolia and imposed his suzerainty upon the small
Indo-European kingdoms of Central Asia (Turfan, Karashar,
Kucha to the north, Khotan and Yarkand to the south, Kashgar

---

[1] See Woodbridge Bingham, *The Founding of the T'ang Dynasty*, Baltimore,
1942. C. P. Fitzgerald, *Son of Heaven. A biography of Li Shih-min, founder of
the T'ang dynasty*, Cambridge, 1933. Bingham, The Rise of Li in a Ballad
Prophecy, *Journal of the American Oriental Society*, Vol. 61, No. 4, pp. 272-280.

to the west). His influence made itself felt beyond the Pamirs, as far as the Indo-Iranian confines. Under his son Kao-tsung (650-683), though he conquered Korea, Chinese hegemony in Upper Asia was challenged anew by the incursions of the Tibetans and the revolt of the Turks of Mongolia. Kao-tsung's widow, the formidable empress Wu Hou, better known by the name of Wu Tse-t'ien, successfully repelled the enemy onslaughts (684-705). Chinese hegemony in Central Asia was re-established in the reign of Emperor Hsüan-tsung, also named Ming-huang (712-756), whose armies reached present-day Soviet Turkestan and were even called upon to fight as far afield as certain frontier-districts of present-day Afghanistan and Pakistan. In other respects, too, the reign of Hsüan-tsung, because of its splendour in all do-mains, and because of the galaxy of great poets who flocked to this prince's court, in Ch'ang-an, was one of the 'great reigns' of Chinese history.

In the end, from 751 and especially from 755 on, the great reign terminated in great disasters—defeats in Turkestan and in Yunnan, internal revolts. The T'ang dynasty was finally saved, the court of Ch'ang-an was again to enjoy bright days, but the Chinese protectorate could not be reestablished in Upper Asia. In 907 the house of the T'ang, shaken by the ravages of a fearful peasant uprising, was overthrown by a rebel general and China, for fifty-three years (907-960), fell back into anarchy.

* * *

The reconstituting of Chinese unity, the bringing together of North and South after more than two and a half centuries of separate life, had created grave problems. The Sui dynasty had reigned too short a time to solve them. The T'ang dynasty had ample leisure to devote itself to them.[2] For the study of the 'clas-

---

[2] See Robert des Rotours, *Le Traité des Examens* (translated from the *Hsin T'ang Shu*, The New History of the T'ang), Bibliothèque de l'Institut des Hautes

sical' books, that is to say of the Confucian canon which, as we know, is so important in Chinese social morality, there were now two traditions and two methods, the version and tradition of the North, and the southern version and tradition. The T'ang, after having reestablished the institution of regular literary competitions for the recruiting of officials, undertook to establish a uniform interpretation of the canonical 'Confucian' texts. They took as the basis of their recension the critical work undertaken in this field by Lu Te-ming (or Lu Yüan-lang), a Confucianist scholar strongly opposed to Buddhism and to Taoism, who after having been the imperial librarian under the Sui lived long enough (he died only in 625) to collaborate with the new dynasty. Emperor T'ai-tsung instructed the Confucianist scholar K'ung Ying-ta (died in 648) and other learned men of the same training to draft an official commentary of the canonical books. The text of the Confucian 'Classics' thus established was engraved on stone during the K'ai-ch'eng period (836-840).[3]

The engraving on stone of the Confucian Classics was to lead, through the impressions that were taken of these, to the discovery of printing—a discovery that in fact dates from the T'ang period. Actually the 'impression' principle went back even further, to the talisman-seals, both Buddhist and Taoist, and to the 'little edifying tracts' on xylographic plates, which the propagandists of both Churches, from the time of the Six Dynasties, turned out in great number and distributed. In this way Buddhists and Taoists reached the point, under the T'ang, of being able to print actual works of literature, such as *The Million of Dharani* (Buddhist magic formulae), printed in Japan between 764 and

Etudes Chinoises, Vol. II, Paris, 1932. Idem, *Traité des Fonctionnaires et Traité de l'Armée* (translated from the same source), Bibliothèque de l'Institut des Hautes Etudes Chinoises, Vol. VI, 2 vols., Leiden, 1947, 1948. K. Bünger, Quellen zur Rechtsgeschichte der T'ang-Zeit, *Monumenta Serica*, IX, 1946.

[3] We may recall that this in no way constitutes an innovation. The Chinese classics had already been engraved on stone at the end of the Han period, between 175 and 183 A.D.

770. By the beginning of the ninth century astrological calendars for popular use were also printed, in China. The oldest printed book deserving the designation is the scroll of the *Diamond Sūtra (Chin-kang-ching)*, a Buddhist treatise published in 868 and now in the British Museum. It is curious to note that, through a conservative prejudice, the Confucianist scholars were at first hostile to this invention. They frowned upon it as being a Buddhist and Taoist innovation, which moreover was tainted with superstition. Thus it was only at the end of the T'ang period that properly literary texts began to be printed. And it was in fact only after the fall of the T'ang, in the period of the Five Dynasties (907-960) and especially in the Sung period (960-1276), that printing came into general use. The Confucian Classics were at last engraved on wood—that is to say, printed—in 932.[4]

The First T'ang Emperors and the Influence of Buddhism

The first T'ang sovereign, Li Yüan, emperor Kao-tsu, had supported the Confucianist reaction against Buddhism, which was openly acknowledged as having enjoyed too great favour under the Sui dynasty.[5] Among the grievances that the old Confucianist scholar Fu I (died 639) held against the Buddhists and to which the new court lent a favourable ear, we note a protest against the too great number of Buddhist statues made under the Sui. In 626 an edict was promulgated that sought to limit the number of Buddhist or Taoist temples. In reality the Buddhist foundations, from 636 on, soon resumed their activity. In 639 we find a high imperial official, Ma Chou, a minister of Emperor T'ai-tsung, ordering a statue for a monastery in Ch'ang-an, the T'ang capital—the powerful grey limestone statue representing

[4] See summary by Mme Vandier-Nicolas, in Georges Salles, *Arts de la Chine ancienne*, p. 70, based on Pelliot's course on the origins of printing in China.
[5] The Confucianist Han Yü, in his famous pamphlet of 819, even assures us that Emperor Kao-tsu sought to eradicate Buddhism (Margouliès, trans. *Le Kou-wen*, p. 200).

Śākyamuni seated, now in the Takahashi collection in Tokyo. This is the first dated T'ang statue.[6] A stele of 641 mentions the hollowing out or the restoration of several rock sanctuaries.[7] An inscription of 644 enables us to date a part of the rock sculptures of the Sheng-t'ung-ssu, in Shantung, sculptures that were begun under the Sui and, as we see, continued under emperor T'ai-tsung. But the decisive event that put an end to the imperial prejudices against Buddhism was the triumphal return of the pilgrim Hsüan-tsang.[8]

Hsüan-tsang, who was born in Lo-yang about 602, had been raised in the Confucianist tradition. At the age of thirteen he was converted to Buddhism and became a monk. In 629 he set out for India, both in order to visit the Buddhist holy places in that country and to study the Sanskrit canonical texts on the spot. For this great traveller was at the same time, as we shall see, a remarkable philosopher. Permission to leave was refused him, incidentally, by the T'ang court, either because the voyage that he was about to undertake was considered too dangerous or, more probably, because the young Emperor T'ai-tsung at this time had little sympathy for Buddhism.

In order to reach India Hsüan-tsang followed the northern trail of the ancient Silk Road, through the principalities of Turfan, Karashar and Kucha. These three centres, as we know today, were inhabited by populations of Indo-European language, having an economy that was based both on agriculture and on the caravan trade, and profoundly Buddhist in religion. It was really like an 'Outer India', so completely had Buddism introduced Sanskrit culture, with its holy writings, at the same time as the schools of art that the Buddhist missionaries brought everywhere

[6] Sirén, *Chinese Sculpture*, pl. 365.

[7] So-called *I-ch'üeh-fo-kan-pei* stele, referred to by Mizuno, *Chinese Stone Sculpture*, p. 23.

[8] May I be allowed to refer, for the detail and bibliography of the subject, to my book *Sur les traces du Bouddha*, 1948 edition.

with them. The Buddhist caves of Karashar have yielded up Graeco-Buddhist heads in stucco, absolutely similar to those of Hadda (Afganistan) that we can admire at the Kabul Museum or at the Guimet Museum; a little further to the west, the caves of Kysil, near Kucha, have revealed to us mural paintings whose first flowering Hackin situates approximately between 450 and 650 and in which the influences that we find side by side include the Graeço-Buddhist (in the Buddhas), the Indo-Gupta (in the Bodhisattvas, the apsaras and many feminine figures) and the Sassanid Iranian (in the lay noblemen and ladies of the court).[9]

These details are to be remembered, for Hsüan-tsang was certainly not the only Chinese pilgrim or traveller to have come upon the highly interesting artistic complex of this region. We shall have to bear them in mind when we come to examine a T'ang bas-relief at the Guimet Museum representing a prince and his court with markedly Kuchean costumes.[10]

Hsüan-tsang, after having visited the then deeply Buddhist provinces of Kapisa (region north of Kabul) and of Gandhāra (region of Peshawar), in present-day Afghanistan and present-day Pakistan, sojourned for nearly fourteen years in India, particularly around Benares and in the Magadha (South-Bihar), in which countries were to be found not only the most venerated sanctuaries of the Buddhist 'Holy Places', and the doctors most reputed for their mastery of Sanskrit philosophy, but also the most active centres of Gupta and post-Gupta Indian sculpture. We must not forget such relations when we study Gupta influen-

[9] Hackin, in Réau, *Histoire Universelle des arts*, vol. IV, 1939, p. 267. Without referring here to the great English and German albums mentioned later, we may note here a few useful summaries: Von Le Coq, *Bilderatlas zur Kunst und Kulturgeschichte Mittelasiens*, Berlin, 1925. Idem, *Buried Treasures of Chinese Turkestan*, 1928. Aurel Stein, *On Ancient Central-Asian Tracks*, London, 1933. E. Waldschmidt, *Gandhāra, Kutscha, Turfan*, Leipzig, 1925. F. H. Andrews, Central-Asian Wall Paintings, in *Indian Art and Letters*, VIII, 1, London, 1934. Harada, *Costumes Observed in the Paintings of Chinese Turkestan*, Tokyo, 1925.

[10] Sirén, *Chinese Sculpture*, pl. 448.

ces on T'ang statuary, for example at T'ien-lung-shan. Hsüan-tsang returned from India in 644, this time by the southern trail of the Silk Road, via Kashgar, Yarkand, Khotan, Lop Nor and Tun-huang. He brought back with him numerous texts of what is perhaps the most interesting philosophic system of Mahayanist Buddhism, the system of absolute idealism, which is in fact called, in Sanskrit, idealist system (*vijñanavāda*) or mystical system (*yogācāra*),[11] and in Chinese *fa-hsiang* school.[12] This mystical idealism that Hsüan-tsang was to disseminate throughout China with admirable philosophic genius and zeal can indubitably be found to have left traces on more than one T'ang work of art. We may add, moreover, that on his return to China in 645 Hsüan-tsang also brought back with him several Indian statues, which at that date must have been of Gupta or immediately post-Gupta style.[13] India had already witnessed a preestablished harmony between this fluid idealism, preached there not long before by the two metaphysicians Asanga and Vasubandhu whom Hsüan-tsang now professed to be following, and the gen-

---

[11] See *Vijñaptimātratā siddhi*, Hsüang-tsang's treatise of metaphysics, translated by La Vallée-Poussin, which I have myself summarized in my *Philosophies indiennes*, vol. II, pp. 80-130 and 404-414.

[12] *Fa-hsiang* (in Japanese *hossō*) translates the Sanskrit term of *dharma-lakṣaṇa* literally 'examination of the (Buddhist) Law'. The School is also called in Chinese *Wei-shih* School, a translation of the Sanskrit *vijñanamātra* or absolute idealism, and likewise *Yü-ch'ieh-shih School*, a transcription of *yogācāra* (mystical school).

[13] The list of seven pieces of sculpture brought back from India to China by Hsüan-tsang was completely and correctly translated by Pelliot for the first time and used by Sirén (Sirén, *Chinese Sculpture, Introduction*, pp. lxxxvii-lxxxviii). It is even possible, as the Japanese archaeologist Seiichi Mizuno believes, that the influence of Hsüan-tsang's voyage and of the two voyages (in 643 and 647) by the Chinese ambassador Wang-Hsüan-ts'e to India is to be found belatedly in the *t'ai* or 'heavenly terraces' in the manner of Indian *stūpa*, of the K'uang-chai-ssu temple, in Ch'ang-an, one of which terraces was erected under the reign of the empress Wu Tse-t'ien (684-705), the other under the reign of Hsüan-tsung (712-756). The Buddhist trinities that appear on them show a suavity of line, rounded torsos, a feeling for form that are both deeply human and delicately idealized, all of which are characteristic of Indian Gupta art (Mizuno, *Chinese Stone Sculpture*, p. 25).

tle Gupta forms of the same period. Hsüan's metaphysical tendencies, added to the exemplars of iconography provided by the statues brought back by him, could not but favour, at least in a few schools of pious makers of images, the taste that we shall see triumph in caves 6 and 14 at T'ien-lung-shan.

Emperor T'ai-tsung the Great, having quite overcome his initial hostility to Buddhism, gave Hsüan-tsang a most favourable reception. The statues and the texts brought back by the pilgrim were solemnly deposited in one of the Ch'ang-an convents, 'the Monastery of the Great Benedictions' (Hung-fu-ssu), whence they were finally transferred to the 'Convent of the Great Beneficence' (Ta-tz'u-an-ssu), a temple that the emperor had had specially built to this end. It was in the latter retreat that the illustrious traveller and metaphysician was to end his days. He died in 664, after having composed, in addition to the treatise of Buddhist philosophy of which we have already spoken (the *Siddhi*), numerous translations of Sanskrit works, as well as a description of the lands traversed by him in Upper Asia and in India, the *Hsi-yü-chi*, a geographic document of the highest value, to which must further be added the picturesque account of the incidents of his voyage left by his disciples Hui-li and (secondarily) Yen-ts'ung (whose account was published in 688).[14]

Hsüan-ts'ung is far from being the only Chinese pilgrim to have gone to India in search of wisdom. Many were the monks who followed his example and made the pilgrimage to the Buddhist holy land, some, like himself, across central Asia, over the double trail of the Silk Road, others by sea, usually stopping off in Java and in Sumatra, countries that were then virtual advance posts of India, provinces of Outer India.[15] The

[14] French translation by Stanislas Julien (*Histoire de la vie de Hiouen-tsang et de ses voyages dans l'Inde*, Paris, 1853), and our summary, *Sur les traces du Bouddha*.

[15] Cf. E. O. Reischauer, Notes on the T'ang Dynasty Sea Routes, *Harvard Journal of Asiatic Studies*, 1940, p. 253. G. Coedes, *Les Etats hindouisés d'Indochine et d'Indonésie*, Paris, 1948, pp. 136-148.

38. *Horsemen, ink and color on paper, from Tun-huang. T'ang Dynasty. Musée Guimet, Paris.*

39. Kuan-yin, gilt-bronze. Sung Dynasty. Museum of Eastern Art, Oxford, Sir Herbert Ingram Collection.

voyages of all of them have been related by the most illustrious among them after Hsüan-tsang, the monk I-ching.

I-ching (634-713) embarked in 671 at Yang-chou, on the estuary of the Yangtze. He spent eight months in the Buddhist convents of Sumatra (in Srividjaya, present-day Palembang) where he perfected himself in Sanskrit, visited India from 673 to 685, came back to China by sea route in 689, but set out again almost immediately for Sumatra whence he returned for good in 695. From this time forward, established in a convent of Lo-yang, he enjoyed the protection first of the dowager empress Wu Tse-t'ien, then (705) of the emperor Chung-tsung. The account that he has left us of the pilgrimages of his predecessors as well as his own is invaluable for the history of Chinese Buddhism, as also for the history of Sino-Indian relations.[16] Like Hsüan-tsang, I-ching ran a regular official translation bureau, responsible for conveying from Sanskrit into Chinese the main texts of Buddhist philosophy and 'theology'. Empress Wu Tse-t'ien and emperor Chung-tsung took a personal interest in this work and prefaced certain translated texts.[17]

* * *

The favour enjoyed by Buddhism in the T'ang court had a great influence on the history of art.

[16] Chavannes translation: *Mémoire sur les Religieux éminents qui allèrent chercher la loi dans les pays d'Occident*, 1894.

[17] We may note that the favour enjoyed by Buddhism under the government of the terrible Wu Tse-t'ien (who imagined herself to be nothing less than the incarnation of the Bodhisattva Maitreya!), then under the deplorable reign of Chung-tsung, came close to producing an anti-Buddhist reaction upon the accession of the emperor Hsüan-tsung (712). The new sovereign, who was violently hostile to the faction that he had just overthrown, thought for a moment of outlawing Buddhism. But he soon overcame his prejudices, and in 724 bestowed his full favour upon the Ch'an patriarch. Emperor Hsüan-tsung himself inclined rather to Taoism (for which reason the Ch'an spirit was not of a nature to displease him).

24.

Under the reign of the emperor Kao-tsung (650-683), then under the government of his widow, the formidable but pious Wu Tse-t'ien (683-705), the workshops for Buddhist sculpture worked full tilt: for the years around 660 we have a great number of dated statues. The sculptures of the Hsiang-chi-ssu pagoda near Ch'ang-an must be of 681, those of Pao-ch'ing-ssu and of An-ch'ing-ssu, likewise in the Ch'ang-an group and now in the Hayasaki collection, are close to this date (one statue of An-ch'ing-ssu belongs to 703).

The sculpture of the T'ang is particularly well represented at Lung-men; to the T'ang period belong: to the east, caves 1, 5, 6, 7, 8, 9, 10, 11, 12, 16 and 19; northwest, the cave of Ching-shan-ssu (which has been dated 650-660), the cave of Che-yün-tung or Lion Cave (with inscription of 680-681), and the two Wan-fo-tung and Kuei-shih-tung caves; southwest the Great Cave (Ta-tung) and that of Feng-hsien-ssu. It was near Feng-hsien-ssu that the Vairocana Buddha of colossal dimensions was sculpted (15 meters tall, including the base and the halo), with an inscription of 672 that testifies to the piety of Empress Wu Tse-t'ien, the whole being completed in 676. The sculptures of Feng-hsien-ssu itself were begun in 679, likewise by imperial order. Finally, as was stated above, the Pin-yang-tung cave (also at Lung-men), where numerous sculptures date back to the late Wei (about 535-536), received new embellishments under the T'ang (inscriptions extending from 617 to 668, one of which, of 641, was pointed out by Chavannes).

In the T'ien-lung-shan group (central Shansi) the following, despite the absence of dated inscriptions, are attributed to the T'ang period: to the east caves 4, 5, 6, 7, to the west caves 11, 12, 13, 14 and 15, 17, 18, 19, 20 and 21, the whole group being dated by Seiichi Mizuno between 684 and 755.[18]

[18] Mizuno, *Chinese Stone Sculpture*, p. 25. Cf. van Wessem, Een Bodhisattva uit T'ien lung shan, *Maandblad voor beeldende Kunsten*, XI, 3, Amsterdam, 1934.

Reversing the chronological order, we shall begin with the T'ien-lung-shan sandstones, as showing a direct Indian influence. Sirén was able to photograph one of the Bodhisattvas seated on a lotus, which has since been reproduced in all the anthologies.[19] 'The pose is one of remarkable freedom, the legs are separated and the torso turns slightly on the hips. The princely costume is that of the Bodhisattvas of India, with necklace and light scarf over the shoulders'. In cave 14, before the acts of vandalism that have disfigured the site, he was even able to study on the spot two standing Bodhisattvas, remarkable for the sensitivity of their modelling, for their graceful poses—one of them conforming strictly to the Indian *tribhanga*—, for the loving treatment, here too, of the naked torso amid the floating scarves, as well as for the wave-like folds of the *dhoti* clinging to the legs.[20] The decapitated original of the second of these statues is to be found at the present time in a European collection.[21] The seated Bodhisattvas of this same cave 14 have the same charm, like the one that Sirén saw still in place, seated in *lalitāsana*, the right leg down, the other bent on the seat; 'the figure turns slightly in the hips and leans over towards the left side, a movement which brings out the beauty and suppleness of the body'. Here also 'the upper part of it is bare, except for the necklace and the thin scarf which falls in two long curves from the right shoulder. The *dhoti*, which is treated in *draperie mouillée* style, fits closely over the legs and is draped in wavy folds over the throne seat'.[22] Cave 17 likewise contains several Bodhisattvas seated in *lalitāsana*, figures having full forms and free poses, directly inspired by the Indian nude.[23] We may recall how foreign the nude is to Chinese art. Thanks to Buddhism,

[19] Sirén, *Op. cit.*, pl. 488.

[20] *Ibid*, pl. 494 and 496.

[21] *Idem*, La sculpture chinoise à l'exposition de l'Orangerie, *Revue des Arts Asiatiques*, XI, 1, 1937, pl. 2-B.

[22] *Idem, Chinese Sculpture*, pl. 495.

[23] *Ibid*, pl. 498 and 501.

Indian aesthetics, for a brief period, wholly renewed Chinese taste.

Through an unexpected conjuncture this direct importation of the Gupta nude and wet draping resulted in the creation of the equivalent, in a few statues of this group, of Hellenic nudes and draped figures. Such a one is the Lartigue Buddha, whose monastic mantle leaves the chest exposed—a chest worthy of an 'antique', its draping rendered with a sense of rhythm that is wholly Alexandrian.[24] The same classical purity is to be found, with the additional superiority of white marble, in the seated Buddha, legs crossed, clad in a soft 'wet drape' mantle clinging to the expertly modelled body. This statue which was found in Ch'ang-an is today in the Boston Museum.[25] Such statues appeal to our love of plastic beauty, according to the Greek canon. But it must be recognized that the 'Buddhist invasion' here has led us a long way from the true Chinese aesthetic.

No less than the T'ien-lung-shan pieces, however, various Buddhist statues from other regions betray an Indo-Gupta influence. Suffice it to mention the three standing Bodhisattvas leaning to one side—the one, in white marble, in the Boston Museum,[26] the second, likewise in white marble, in the Rockefeller collection, found in Ling-yen-ssu, near Pao-ting, in Hopei,[27] the third in grey limestone from Shensi, in the Freer Gallery in Washington.[28] Similar statues, from the former Grosjean or Yamanaka collections, in grey limestone, very likely have Lungmen as their point of origin.[29] Sinization is more evident in two other standing Bodhisattvas, on which the decoration of strings of jewellery is becoming more and more elaborate, grey

[24] *Ibid*, pl. 504-A.

[25] *Ibid*, pl. 407.

[26] *Ibid*, pl. 375.

[27] *Ibid*, pl. 359. See G. Migeon, Une sculpture chinoise classique, *Revue de l'Art ancien et moderne*, February 1929, p. 57.

[28] Sirén, *Op. cit.*, pl. 377.

[29] *Ibid*, pl. 463, 464.

limestones from Shensi, today in the Philadelphia Museum.[30]
But in these various pieces, even in the last, the elongated elegance of the bodies, their softly rounded forms, the slimness of
their torsos, either naked or readily decipherable beneath the
diagonal scarf of gossamer lightness, beneath the necklaces or,
in certain cases, beneath the long chain of pearls crossed X-wise
at the waist, the transparency of the soft *dhoti* with its wet folds
caressing the legs, the frequent bending of the upper body to
one side with a harmonious jutting of the hip—all are features
which, despite the Sinization of the faces, reveal to us a love
of living forms, a sense of plastic proportions, that are properly
Gupta. Or rather, these elegant, highly adorned Bodhisattvas
recall to us the passage, in India, from the Gupta art of Mathurā
and of Sarnath to Pala art, as we have studied it in the previous
volume of this series.* Aside from this the return to naturalism,
discreet though it still remains, and though it expresses itself
here only through subtle devices, is none the less evident.

The semi-nude in the Indian manner manifests itself also in
the Bodhisattvas of the Pao-ch'ing-ssu bas-reliefs of Ch'ang-an,
now in the Freer Gallery and the Boston Museum.[31] We shall
find the same half-revealed character of the Indian nudes, veiled
by the caress of the light scarves and the *dhotis*, on more than
one Tun-huang painting.[32] Even if (in these as well as in the
Pao-ch'ing-ssu bas-reliefs) the general structure of the bodies
already has lost a good deal of the Indian tropical flexibility,
India still remains discreetly present.

It must be made clear, however, that the T'ang caves of
T'ien-lung-shan and the statues of similar style are somewhat

[30] *Ibid*, pl. 378.
* *L'Inde* (Ars et Historia Collection) (Translator's note).
[31] Sirén, *Op. cit.*, pl. 391-392.
[32] Compare, at the Guimet Museum, the Samantabhadra (P'u-hsien), still
wholly Indian, a Tun-huang painting in the Pelliot collection. See Hackin, Asie
Centrale et Tibet, Mission Pelliot et Bacot, *Bulletin Archéologique du Musée
Guimet*, fasc. 2, 1921, p. 19.

exceptional. T'ang art as a whole springs from a quite different impulse. While, as compared to the Sui style, it shows a greater ease, while the stiffness of the Sui has given way to a more realistic modelling, it is a realism devoid of softness. The modelling of bodies unquestionably shows great progress over previous periods. The true rendering of the human body is no longer a matter of unavowed embarrassment to the religious sculptor. The stiffness of the Sui necks is replaced on the T'ang Bodhisattvas by natural, plump throats, further emphasized by the drawing of three small parallel folds. On the powerful torsos the fabrics are light, the folds simple; they fall naturally. But the attitudes, even of the most compassionate Bodhisattvas, exude strength first and foremost. The dominant impression remains one of dignity, assurance and plenitude. The half-smile of some of the preceding schools has given way to a calm expression of satisfied mastery.

The period of Chinese imperialism in Asia gave birth to a sculpture of 'imperial' spirit.

* * *

A considerable influence in this direction was exerted by the specifically Chinese Buddhist sect of the T'ien-t'ai of which we have already spoken. The T'ien-t'ai doctrine, as we have seen, by a Hegelian process of identity of contraries, reduced all things—nirvana as well as the phenomenal world, Buddhas as well as inferior creatures—to a kind of universal essence and absolute Reality (the *bhūtatathatā*) that constitues the *dharma-kāya* or 'spiritual body' of the Buddhas. The same conceptions gave birth to the 'Tantric' or esoteric sect of Chen-yen-tsung.[33]

---

[33] In Sanskrit, school of the *mantra*, in Japanese *shingon* school. The meaning of the three terms is the same: they refer to 'efficacious words'—that is to say, esoteric formulae having mysterious powers.

The esotericism in question was particularly stimulated by the preaching of three Indian missionaries: Śubhākara-siṁha, who reached Ch'ang-an in 716; Vajrabodhi, who established himself in Lo-yang in 720; and the latter's disciple, Amoghavajra, who arrived at the same time that he did.[34] All three developed the belief in a supreme or primordial Buddha, the ādhi-Buddha *Vairocana* (in Chinese: *P'i-lu-che-na*), a name that evokes a sun of illumination. Now Vairocana (and this is where the T'ien-tai doctrine and the Chen-yen doctrine join) is nothing other than the anthropomorphic manifestation of the *dharmakāya* and the *bhūta-tathatā* that we have just spoken of, in other words he is the manifestation of the 'spiritual body' of all the Buddhas, the manifestation of Absolute Nature or Universal Essence.

'Mahā Vairocana, the Great Illuminator', according to the Japanese philosopher Anesaki, 'is regarded by his disciples as both the all-comprehensive soul and the all-creative life-force of the universe. All beings, divinities, angels, men, animals, are the manifestations of his power. The body and the life of the Great Illuminator can be discerned even in a grain of sand or in a drop of water. Every sound represents his voice. Human speech is but a translation of his cosmic language'. In his eternally serene soul the universe and universal life are contained in the form of a world of Platonic Ideas, the Plane of

[34] Vajrabodhi (in Chinese Chin-kang-chih) (670-741) and Amoghavajra (in Chinese Pu-k'ung) (705-744), when they established themselves in Lo-yang (720), enjoyed the protection of Emperor Hsüan-tsung. The latter was already greatly drawn to Taoist mystical theology and could hardly fail to be attracted also by Vairocanian esotericism. See R. Tajima, *Etudes sur le Mahā-Vairocana-sūtra*, Paris, 1936, p. 23; and Chou Yi-Liang, Tantrism in China, *Harvard Journal of Asiatic Studies*, 1944, pp. 251 and 275. We may recall that the Kōzanji, in Kyoto, has a portrait of Amoghavajra, a painting in colour on silk, which was attributed to the Chinese painter Li Chen (about 800). See Serge Elisseeff, Le portrait en Extrême-Orient, *Etudes d'Orientalisme publiés par le Musée Guimet à la memoire de Raymonde Linossier*, 1932, Vol. I, p. 180.

Ideals which is also the Realm of the Indestructibles, in Sanskrit *vajradhātu*, 'the Diamond element'.[35]

In this esoteric monism, Vairocana thus plays the role of a pantheist god, the soul of souls and of worlds. And it is indeed an impression of this order, an impression of metaphysical grandeur, that is communicated by the giant statue representing the Great Illuminator on the terrace of Feng-hsien-ssu, at Lung-men (672-676). A superhuman, impassive figure, expressing extraordinary dogmatic authority, absolute theological certitude, transcending time and space, dominating the worlds and looking ahead into the distance, beyond the pettiness of humanity, the Vairocana of Lung-men affords a marked contrast to the figures of compassion, such as the primitive Buddhist church might have imagined, which in fact were soon to be portrayed in the art inspired by Sino-Japanese Amidism. It was a combination of the material strength of the T'ang and of the 'diamond' theology of the T'ien-t'ai or of the Chen-yen which led to this cosmic vision.[36]

But here in this same group we come upon some very large figures in relief of Heavenly Kings (*lokapāla*, in Chinese: *t'ien-wang*), which are more directly inspired by the T'ang spirit. The Vairocana had an icy serenity. One of the Heavenly Kings, a Vaiśravaṇa (in Chinese: *To-wen*), is nothing more than a stoutly-armoured T'ang warrior, typical of all the guardian-spirits of this kind, who are soldiers appointed to guard the cosmic 'Four Directions'. The other guardian-king is an athletic figure, astonishingly muscled, with his head three-quarters turned, and his expression threatening to the point of grimace, neck bulging with muscle, body hunched in the posture of combat, and right fist closed and significantly resting on his hip, while his left hand

---

[35] Masaharu Anesaki, *Quelques pages sur l'histoire religieuse du Japon*, Musée Guimet, 1921, p. 44. See also R. Tajima, *Etudes sur le Mahā-Vairocana-sūtra*, pp. 49 ff.

[36] Sirén, *Op. cit.*, pl. 453-454.

40. *Lohan, glazed pottery. Liao-Chin Dynasties (907-1234). British Museum, London.*

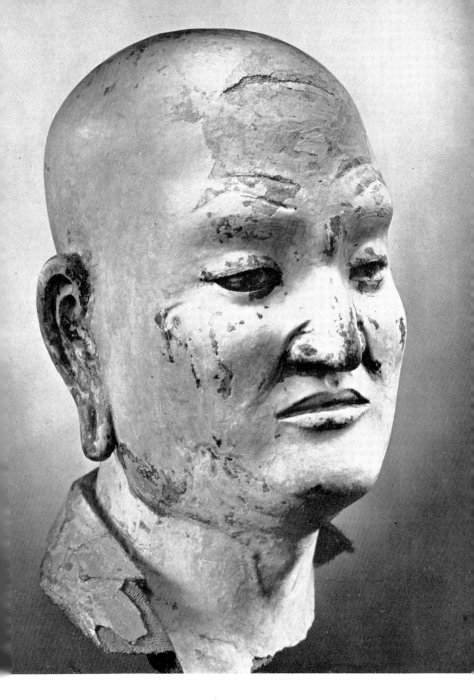

41. *Head of a Lohan, polychromed dry lacquer. Liao-Chin Dynasties (907-1234). Nelson Gallery of Art, Kansas City.*

is raised in an *abhaya-mudrā* that one would not be well-advised to oppose. A good genie, to be sure, but a good genie whom the demons would hesitate to attack; a saint, admittedly, but a saint having all the attributes of a gladiator.[37]

In this same vein should be noted the two wooden statues, 98 centimeters tall, painted brown, green, blue and white, representing *dvārapālas* (genii guarding the gates of a temple), brought back from Tun-huang to the Guimet Museum by the Pelliot Mission.[38] In these, crude realism and the warlike note triumph unrestrainedly. Buddhist art here expresses nothing more than the military propensities of the T'ang. Over-large, ruddy-faced, almost caricatural heads with enormous jaws markedly protruding, athletic build, violent gesticulation, threatening attitude, heavy military trappings with complete armour, leather corselet, breast-plate, back-plate—the picture is complete. We should not forget, in this connection, that we are now in Tun-huang, in an advance post at the extremity of a frontier march, on the edge of a hostile universe, facing the immensity of the deserts and the steppes.

Chinese Buddhism here places itself under the protection of T'ang imperialism. It is but an aspect of the Chinese epos in Central Asia.[39]

* * *

To T'ang Buddhism we owe a number of the most ancient monuments to have been preserved in China: in Ch'ang-an (Sianfu), the Ta-yen-t'a or 'Great Pagoda of the Wild Geese',

[37] *Ibid*, pl. 456, 457.

[38] *Ibid*, pl. 550-552. Hackin, Asie Centrale et Tibet, *Bulletin archéologique du Musée Guimet*, fasc. 2, 1921, p. 11, pl. I.

[39] In addition, for the influence of Tantrism on Chinese Buddhism with its effect on art (especially the terrifying and demoniacal aspect), see Chou Yi-Liang, Tantrism in China, *Harvard Journal of Asiatic Studies*, 1944, pp. 241-332.

25.

a brick pagoda founded in 652 by the pilgrim Hsüan-tsang, and the Hsiao-yen-t'a, another pagoda of 684; in the vicinity of this town, the Hsiang-chi-ssu, a pagoda founded between 681 and 705, and the Hsing-chiao-ssu that marks the site of the sepulchre of Hsüan-tsang (ninth century). These are, as a rule, square towers divided into storeys of decreasing dimensions by overhangs of thin bricks—a pattern that gives the impression, particularly in the case of the Ta-yen-t'a, of a tall, slender pyramid divided into storeys.[40]

At the Court of the T'ang. The Great Period

During the reigns of emperors T'ai-tsung the Great (627-649) and Kao-tsung (650-683), of empress Wu Tse-t'ien (684-705) and of emperor Hsüan-tsung (712-756), the Ch'ang-an court was one of the most brilliant in Asia. The period identified with these princes marked one of the 'golden ages' of Chinese civilization. On its frontiers an epic China was able, for one hundred and thirty years, to subjugate the Turkish hordes, pacify Central Asia, and launch its squadrons beyond the T'ien-shan and the Pamirs as far as Tashkent and the confines of Afghanistan and Kashmir. At the centre, Ch'ang-an was one of the most cultivated and splendid courts that have ever existed, with a galaxy of poets and artists of genius.

The epic predilections of the first T'ang period (618-756) are crystallized in art from the time of the reign of the true founder of the dynasty, T'ai-tsung the Great (627-649), and we find them expressed in the grey limestone bas-reliefs, dated 637, representing the emperor's six warhorses. These reliefs ornamented the vestibule of his mausoleum in Chao-ling, near Li-ch'üan-hsien, in Shensi, and two of them are now in the Philadelphia Museum.[41] The steeds represented are superb creatures of wholly

[40] Sirén, *History of Early Chinese Art*, Vol. IV, *Architecture*, pls. 65, 66, 67.
[41] *Idem, Chinese Sculpture*, pl. 426-427. See Helen Fernald, The Horses of T'ang T'ai-tsung and the Stele of Yu, *Journal of the American Oriental·Society*,

native breed, squatter than the prancing horses of the terra cottas. The treatment is broad, but detail is not overlooked: braided manes, knotted tails, harnesses and saddles are rendered with precision; we sense that the artist was commissioned by a 'horseman' and a soldier. One of the steeds, 'Autumn dew', the faithful companion who bore his master on the reconquest of Honan, is motionless, stiffened with painful effort. He has received, full in the chest, an arrow that his rider is pulling out. This rider, a typical soldier in action, is treated in broad, sharp lines, with the long kaftan and round cap of the T'ang warriors. Another steed, 'Curly', this one shown in a short trot, is likewise wounded by an arrow in the chest and also by three in the croup. Others are in 'flying gallop'. These are reminiscences of T'ang feats of arms that are not without grandeur, if we consider all that they evoke. These sculptures are in effect 'citations' for wounds received on the field of honour bestowed on the mounts of the Chinese conqueror (it was precisely in this way that Rameses II, after the battle of Kadesh, was impelled to 'cite', in his famous inscription, the horses that had drawn his war-chariot). Who ever said that the Chinese was not epically minded? T'ai-tsung the Great wished to sleep his last sleep surrounded by his battle horses, his old companions of a score of combats, in which encounters, as we know, he exposed himself as fully as the least of his foot-soldiers.

The same realism is to be found in the animals sculpted in the round on the tomb of emperor Kao-tsung (died 683), in Ch'ien-chou, near Hsien-yang, in Shensi. We may mention in particular the winged horse or unicorn, unearthed by the Ségalen Mission, a splendid piece of sculpture in its over-all conception (the way the animal holds his head is particularly remarkable) as well as in the perfection of the details (indentations of the

Vol. 55, no. 4, p. 428. Miss Fernald, among other things, raises the question as to whether the two Philadelphia horses belong to the originals commissioned by T'ai-tsung in 637, or whether they are copies made in 1089, under the Sung.

forehead, the way the wing is fastened to the joint of the fore-
limbs, the development of the wings in elegant broad volutes).[42]
In its present mutilation the Chinese Pegasus still remains a work
of pride and nobility. The same may be said of the guardian-
lions, of colossal dimensions, on this same tomb, shown seated,
mouths open in a roar, looking threatening.[43] Alongside these
lions 'in majesty' of the great funerary sculpture should be mentioned several statuettes in small stone sculpture in which the
animal is represented in full movement, like the two T'ang lions
in the Guimet Museum, one in grey limestone, 6 inches tall, the
other in marble, $6\frac{1}{2}$ inches tall, the first rending a sheep, the
second swinging round and growling with a fierce look, both
admirably observed and brought to life.[44]

In taking leave of the great T'ang sculpture we should not
neglect to anticipate the relations of Chinese art with the Indo-
Iranian Buddhist art of the Tarim basin, to which we shall
revert. We shall merely mention here two grey limestone bas-
reliefs from Shensi, $19\frac{1}{2}$ inches and $28\frac{1}{2}$ inches tall respectively, one of them now in the Guimet Museum, the other in
the Boston Museum.[45] The Guimet relief, in particular, should
be noted, with its prince or war-lord on horseback in the middle
register, the musicians who, below, follow him in procession,
and, in the side registers, the figures in the reception and banquet
scenes featuring lords and ladies whose dress (the double turned-
over collar for instance) recalls immediately the princes and
princesses of the mural paintings of Kysil or Kumtura, near

[42] Sirén, *Op. cit.*, pl. 430-B. Ségalen, De Voisins, Lartigue, *Journal Asiatique*,
May-June 1915, p. 485 and fig. 12. Idem, *Mission archéologique, Atlas, I,*
plates IX and X. We may recall that 'the unicorn is an auspicious omen for kings.
It appears only in a time of good government, when power is in the hands of
a sage'.
[43] Ségalen Album, pl. VIII. Sirén, pl. 431-A.
[44] Sirén, pl. 435, B and D.
[45] *Ibid,* pls. 448 and 449. On the Guimet stele (formerly at the Louvre),
a stele $19\frac{1}{2}$ inches by 35 inches, see Migeon, *Art chinois au Musée du Louvre,*
no. 31, plate 19, and Georges Salles, *Arts de la Chine ancienne*, no. 29, p. 28.

Kucha, in the Tarim basin, of which we shall speak further on. What interests us here, as with the six war horses of the tomb of Emperor T'ai-tsung already mentioned, is the influence of the 'T'ang epos' on contemporaneous Chinese art.

* * *

While in the remotest reaches of the Gobi and in the distant Pamir the Chinese squadrons held the Barbarians at bay, the court of Ch'ang-an became the meeting-place of artists and poets.

A great revival now takes place in Chinese literature. Under the Han and at the beginning of the Six Dynasties poetry had not obeyed very fixed laws. Versification was virtually free. Toward the end of the Six Dynasties, however (from about 500), poetry, both in its phonetic and prosodic aspects, in its patterns of tone and of rhyme, began to obey strict rules. This is what is known as 'the new style' (*hsin-t'i*), which was increasingly adopted under the T'ang. Inversely, in prose writing, the T'ang writers abandoned the technique of 'balancing' and the stilted style of the Six Dynasties, returning to the *ku-wen* or 'antique style', that is to say to the direct and discursive manner of the Han prose writers.

For the first part of the T'ang period, in the seventh century, the anthologies record the names of the 'four eminent poets', Wang P'o (647-675), Yang Chiung (died 692), Lu Chao-lin (died before 700) and Lo Pin-wang. The last is equally famous for the courageous manifesto that he drafted against the tyranny of empress Wu Tse-t'ien, as a result of which he was dragged into the catastrophe of the rebels (about 684-686).[46] For this period mention must also be made of Ch'en Tzu-ang (between 661 and about 702) whose poetry returns to the direct and vigorous 'antique style' of the Han period.

[46] See G. Margouliès, *Le Kou-wen*, p. 144.

The reign of Emperor Hsüan-tsung (712-756) witnessed the apogee of Chinese poetry. Hsüan-tsung was himself a poet of talent and has left us subtle, sensitive verses. His favourite, the beautiful Yang Kuei-fei, who like him patronized writers and artists, had her praises sung by the greatest lyric writers of the time.

The most famous poet of this group was Li T'ai-po—or Li Po—(701-762).[47] Presented to the Court in 742 by a Taoist religious, he immediately won the favour of Hsüan-tsung 'in spite of, or perhaps because of, his unconventional manners'. The sovereign invited the poet to sit beside him on the couch of the 'Seven Precious Objects', offered him a cup with his own hand and admitted him to membership in 'the Forest of Brushes', that is to say in the imperial academy. Hsüan-tsung forgave Li T'ai-po everything, even his love of wine. One day when the poet, already slightly drunk, met the emperor, the latter asked him to improvise a song on the beautiful Yang Kuei-fei. This was the poem of the 'flying swallow', which Hsüan-tsung at once accompanied on a jade flute (744). But in the same year Li T'ai-po incurred the displeasure of the favourite and was obliged to leave the court. He took refuge in Shantung, among some Taoist monks (the influence of Taoism is appreciable in his inspiration) and then travelled from province to province. Joining the following

---

[47] See Sung-nien Hsü, *Essai sur Li Po* (preface by Maurice Courant), Peking, 1934. The entire works of Li T'ai-po and of Tu Fu have been translated into French by Sung-nien Hsü, but unfortunately this translation (which we have seen) is unpublished. A part, at least, is to be published in Paris. Among the partial translations of T'ang poets may be mentioned Sung-nien Hsü, Cinquante poèmes chinois, *Annales de l'Institut Franco-Chinois de Lyon*, 1929; Tsen Tsong-ming, *Rêve d'une nuit d'hiver, cent quatrains des T'ang*, Paris, 1927; Lo Ta-kang, *Cent quatrains des T'ang*, Neuchatel, 1942 and 1947; *Idem, Homme d'abord, poète ensuite, présentation de sept poètes chinois* (Li T'ai-po, Tu Fu, Po Chü-i etc.), Neuchatel, 1949; Bruno Belpaire, *Quarante poésies de Li T'ai-po*, Paris-Brussels, 1921. In English translation, Obata Shigeoshi, *The Works of Li Po*, New York, 1922. For the whole of Chinese poetry, the admirable translations of the English Sinologist and poet Arthur Waley, *One Hundred and Seventy Chinese Poems*, London, 1918; *Idem, Chinese Poems*, London, 1946.

of a rebel prince, he incurred the misfortune of a further exile (756-758). He died in 762 while dictating a last poem. (According to legend, on the other hand, he was drowned one night while sailing in a boat in a state of intoxication, trying to embrace the reflection of the moon in the water).

It is interesting to note that Li T'ai-po's family had lived for a long time in Tun-huang, a frontier post on the threshold of Central Asia. Pelliot has even speculated whether he may not have been born in some Chinese garrison, in Suyab, present-day Tokmak, west of Issiq Köl.[48] We are in fact told that one day, at the court of Hsüan-tsung, Li T'ai-po proved to be the only person capable of translating the credentials of a foreign ambassador (in Turkish, 'Tokharian' or east Iranian?). 'It is thus possible that foreign blood may have blended in his veins with that of the Li family. Certain it is that he was strongly affected by foreign influences, and this might explain the affinity of his inspiration with that of Western poets and its disconcerting quality for the Chinese reader'.[49] If this supposition is correct, some of the highly unconventional spirit of the greatest Chinese poet may be owing to Chinese expansion in Central Asia and the 'Far West'.

Odile Kaltenmark, who like Sung-nien Hsü has made a special study of Li T'ai-po, observes for her part that he is the Chinese poet best known to Westerners. 'His poems, relatively uncluttered by learned allusions, are perhaps more translatable than those of most other Chinese poets'. Moreover, 'his favourite themes—the liberating effect of wine, the swift passage of time, friendship—are in no way original; they are those of a great number of other poets. But he handles them with wonderful vividness, originality and mastery of language. Melancholy or joyously carefree by turns, he is able to evoke a landscape, a mood, in a few verses, with an extreme sobriety of means. Other

[48] Pelliot, T'oung Pao, 1922, vol. XXI, p. 236.
[49] Sung-nien Hsü, Anthologie de la poésie chinoise, Paris, 1933, p. 30.

poems have a narrative or even epic character, quite exceptional in Chinese poetry'.[50]

The other great T'ang poet is Tu Fu (712-770), the friend of Li T'ai-po and his rival in fame.[51] Eliminated from the imperial competitions in 735 and again excluded from the court by intrigue in 747, he was reduced to poverty until, in 751, a topical poem finally brought him to the personal attention of the emperor Hsüan-tsung. Barely had he been granted a post, however, when the revolt of 755 (in the course of which the favourite Yang Kuei-fei was put to death) obliged the poet to flee. His fidelity to the legitimist cause at last won him tokens of gratitude from the new emperor, Su-tsung (757). But he had not reached the end of his misfortunes. Being a poor courtier, he was soon deprived of his post (758) and reduced to living in Szechwan, a province whose governor was a friend of his. Old and disillusioned, he sought once more to see his native province of Honan, but died near lake Tung-t'ing before reaching it.

'Tu Fu's poems', Odile Kaltenmark notes, 'do not generally have the brilliant spontaneity of Li T'ai-po's. They are often more erudite, more laborious. But his inspiration is extremely varied and we also find in his work many quatrains, composed toward the end of his life, which are very simple in form, and in which he describes fleeting impressions. A sensitive poet, he felt deeply about the distress which he saw around him'. Thus after having, like his friend Li T'ai-po, described the delights of the court of Ch'ang-an at the time of the triumphs of the beautiful Yang Kuei-fei, he describes the favourite's frightful death, the emperor's flight to Szechwan, and the ruin of the capital ravaged by civil war. He has shown us, too, the sufferings

---

[50] Odile Kaltenmark-Ghequier, *La littérature chinoise*, pp. 71-72. On Li T'ai-po as poet of court life in the time of Emperor Hsüan-tsung and of the favourite Yang Kuei-fei, see A. Waley, *The Poet Li Po*, A.D. 701-762, a paper read before the China Society..., London, 1919.

[51] Florence Ayscough, *Tu Fu, the Autobiography of a Chinese Poet*, London, 1929-1934. By the same author, *Fir-Flower Tablets*, Boston, 1921.

42. *Attributed to Li Ch'eng (c. 940-967): Buddhist Temple Amid Clearing Mountain Peaks. Ink and slight color on silk. Nelson Gallery of Art, Kansas City.*

43. *Tung Yüan: Clear Weather in the Valley.* (*detail*). *Ink and light color on paper. Late tenth century. Museum of Fine Arts, Boston.*

caused among the people by the interminable wars that T'ang
China carried on in the frozen plateaux of Upper Asia or on the
far steppes of the Great West, and, particularly in his opposition
to the militarism of the T'ang, reveals himself as a sharp critic
of the government and of the society of his time. 'Along with
poems that have an academic ring', Odile Kaltenmark concludes,
'there are many that have a realistic and impressionistic turn,
that conjure up scenes experienced in the course of his wander-
ings. More human, less detached in his genius than Li T'ai-po,
Tu Fu exerted a greater influence on later poetry, and particularly
on that of the ninth century'.[52]

Wang Wei (699-759), poet as well as painter, also served
the emperor Hsüan-tsung to whom his heart remained faithful,
even when, in the revolt of 755, he was coerced into following
a usurper. Wang Wei was rewarded by the emperor Su-tsung at
the time of the restoration of 757, but declined the posts that were
offered him (including the governorship of Su-chou) in order
to spend his last days in solitude. It has been said of him that
his poems were landscapes, and his landscapes poems. It seems
indeed—although practically nothing remains to us of his pictorial
work (the powerful waterfall of Chishaku-in, in Kyoto, is obviously only a copy)[53]—that as a landscapist he was particularly
inspired by the Buddhist idealism of the Mahāyāna. Yet while he
was personally a Buddhist, the school of monochrome wash-
drawing in Indian ink, which he is regarded as having founded,
was, in the Sung period when it reached its full development,
to be influenced as much by the mystical monism of the Taoists,
by their ecstasy before the divinity of the Universe, as by the
Buddhist melancholy before the universal evanescence of things.
Wang Wei's poems in fact express this double state of mind.

Meng Hao-jan (689-740), the childhood friend of Wang Wei,
has likewise left us 'poems that are true landscapes'.

[52] O. Kaltenmark-Ghequier, *Op. cit.*, pp. 72-73.
[53] Tajima and Omura, *Masterpieces of Chinese Art*, vol. VIII, plate 8.

26.

The poet Po Chü-i (772-846) belongs to a less brilliant period.[54] The Chinese epos had come to an end. From 756 to 763 the imperial capital of Ch'ang-an was several times sacked. The dynasty had re-established itself there, but China no longer held sway over Upper Asia. Yet the lyrical impetus of the preceding period was not broken. Po Chü-i sought to imitate Tu Fu. But unlike the latter, he filled various administrative posts and was an exemplary official for twenty-five years. A member of the Academy of the 'Forest of Brushes' from 807, he became prefect of Lo-yang. In 834 he resigned in order to retire, as a Buddhist sage, to the hermitage of Mount Hsiang-shan, not far from the Lung-men caves. Around him gathered other scholars and poets who had withdrawn from the world, who with him formed the group of the 'nine old men of Mount Hsiang-shan'. By his own admission (and like most T'ang poets) he found his inspiration both in the Taoist ecstasy of Chuang-tzu and in Buddhist spirituality.[55] Like Tu Fu he composed poems on amorous or epic themes that are still admired, and was a critic of the society of his time. His contemporary, the poet Yüan Chen (779-831), also followed the example of Tu Fu, and likewise described the sufferings of the people under a decadent administration that was leading this brilliant society to its ruin.

To poetry properly speaking must be added poetic prose, as it was practised, for example, by the famous Liu Tsung-yüan (773-819), who in describing his walks through the picturesque landscapes of Hunan has left us true prose poems. Liu Tsung-yüan is another who has, like his follow-poets, left bitter condemnations of the abominable financial policy of the administration, which was causing the depopulation of the countryside.[56]

[54] Arthur Waley, *The Life and Times of Po Chü-I, with translation of 100 New Poems*, London, 1949.

[55] See Sung-Nien Hsü, Po Kiu-yi, *Revue de l'Université de Lyon*, 1930, p. 70.

[56] 'Histoire de l'homme qui attrapait les serpents' (Story of the man who caught snakes). in Margouliès, *Le Kou-wen chinois*, p. 225.

Aside from poetry and poetic prose, the T'ang period witnessed the development of a whole literature of tales—heroic
tales, fantastic tales or love-stories. One of these romances, *The
Bearded Knight*, attributed to Tu Kuang-t'ing (ninth century)
relates the founding of the T'ang dynasty by the young Li
Shih-min, through the devotion of General Li Ching who, moreover, had previously run away with a pretty girl, a love story
thus enhancing the historical romance. Another historical romance, written by Ch'en Hung (also ninth century), deals with
the love of emperor Hsüan-tsung and the beautiful Yang Kuei-
fei, and with the tragic death of the favourite, massacred during
the revolt of 755. Other tales are in the realm of pure fantasy.
One of these, by Li Ch'ao-wei, describes the tribulations of the
daughter of the dragon-king of lake Tung-t'ing, obliged to
herd his sheep (who are really metamorphosed dragons), until
she is saved by the love of a young scholar. As for Shen Chi-
chi's *Dream of the Pillow* (about 780), it is the story of a magic
bolster whereby a Taoist Immortal bestows upon a young man
dreams of the future more beautiful than reality.

* * *

Along with this fantastic vein in which the influence of the
Buddhist or Taoist tales is markedly felt should be mentioned,
in the field of prose, the neo-Confucianist reaction which found
its mouthpiece in Han Yü.

Han Yü (767-824) is considered to be the greatest prose-
writer of the T'ang period. He broke with the 'cadenced prose'
of the previous period in order to achieve greater precision in
the expression of ideas.[57] A militant Confucianist, he composed

---

[57] 'The style that Han Yü brought to perfection, if he did not create it, was
to make possible, under the Sung, the first philosophic works that China produced'
(Odile Kaltenmark, *Littérature chinoise*, p. 77). Cf. Tschen Yinkoh, Han Yü
and the T'ang Novel, *Harvard Journal of Asiatic Studies*, 1936, p. 39.

impassioned pamphlets, of a vigorous eloquence, against Buddhism and against Taoism as well.

Opposing the mystical conception of the *Tao* and of *Te* (the supreme 'Way' and 'Virtue'), as professed by the Taoists, Han Yü comes back to the Confucian interpretation of these ancient notions as being synonymous with *Jen* and *I*, altruism and equity, as taught by Confucius and by Mencius.[58] Going further, he denounces monastic life, whether Buddhist or Taoist, as uncivic and antisocial, depriving the empire of defenders and society of workers, and leading young people to betray their family duties by shutting themselves up in 'the idleness of monasteries'.[59] In 819 Han Yü addressed to Emperor Hsien-tsung an energetic protest because the monarch had gone in person to visit a relic of the Buddha. It was a veritable manifesto of Chinese nationalism, Confucianist conservatism and the anticlericalism of the scholars against the 'foreign religion', above all an indictment, in the name of the State, of monastic life: 'The Buddha was nothing but a Barbarian. He knew nothing of the duties of prince and subject, of father and son'.[60] The emperor, incidentally, took this very badly, and Han Yü's boldness nearly cost him his life. The censor was exiled. By dint of supplications he finally obtained his pardon and was again given an important post at court.

The reaction against Buddhism was in fact increasing. While the emperor Hsien-tsung (806-820) had been personally favourable to the great Indian religion, one of his successors, Wu-tsung (841-846), who was devoted to the Taoists, signed at their instigation in 845 a general edict against Buddhism, ordering the closure of most of the convents (one single convent per town

---

[58] Margouliès, *Le Kou-wen*, p. 177.

[59] *Ibid*, pp. 180-181. Cf. Etienne Balazs, Beiträge zur Wirtschaftsgeschichte der T'ang-Zeit, *Mitteilungen des Seminars für Orientalische Sprachen zu Berlin*, XXXV- XXXVI, 1932-1933, p. 20.

[60] Margouliès, *Op. cit.*, p. 201.

being authorized), wholesale laicizing of monastics, men and women (260,000 were secularized), seizure of the property of the communities by the tax authorities, etc... The clauses of the edict were exceptionally severe and quite rigorously applied. What is particularly regrettable for us is the iconoclastic character that the persecution could hardly fail to assume, orders being given to demolish without delay most of the Buddhist temples and to send the bronze statues to the foundries to be melted down. While it is true that a new emperor, I-tsung (860-873), who favoured Buddhism, soon promulgated a new legislation favourable to the monasteries (861), the acts of vandalism caused by the edict of 845 were none the less, in all too many cases, irreparable.

* * *

From its accession to its fall, the T'ang dynasty in its opulent capital of Ch'ang-an (Hsi-an-fu) presided over a sumptuous flowering of Chinese art. We have spoken above, in connection with the expansion of Buddhism, and in referring to the imperial tombs, of the great stone sculpture of this period. But the 'luxury arts', as we call them today, as well as painting, were no less developed.

The small T'ang bronzes often have a jewel-like perfection. The T'ang mirrors, usually round, sometimes square, often also 'polylobed' in the form of petals, show us in the floral or animal themes of their decoration the naturalist tendency that is basic to T'ang art, but a naturalism that is here dominated by a supreme concern with ornamental elegance. This ornamentation is full of fantasy, a fantasy that at moments casts back to before the Han or the Six Dynasties, recalling the mirrors of the Warring States—with one difference, however, to which we have drawn attention, that in the representation of animal forms T'ang realism remains ever present. The 'vertigo of flight' shown by all these animals is almost the same as that which, on the

Warring States mirrors, swept dragons and clouds. But here, in the representation of leaping beasts, we find that we are faced with the work of true animal-portraitists who miss no detail, and even catch the play of the muscles in spite of the speed that animates all this fauna. At the same time this naturalism, without relinquishing any of its claims, remains faithful to the ornamental aim. The motifs, whether animal or floral, are subordinated to a broad, uncluttered and powerful decorative sense.

It is in this mood that the mirrors are designed: with a floral geometry, the so-called 'flowers of paradise', elegant bouquets prefiguring all subsequent Chinese taste, flower-laden branches and garlands of flowers, scrolls of vines unfurled in delicate arabesques and punctuated by rich grape-clusters. In the midst of these graceful scrolls, in this setting of flowers and vines that rightly reminds us of our Hellenistic art, phoenixes and other wonderful birds, bears, foxes and monkeys, disport themselves, winged horses prance, while stags, horses, lions, panthers, boars, foxes and hares leap freely or pursue one another, all carried along at a 'flying gallop', each and every one (even the lions) treated with a realism that is both broad and precise. Now and again, in the midst of the whirl, we see characteristic T'ang horsemen emerge, armed with bows or lassos, carried along at the same dizzy speed, they too moving at a flying gallop, in pursuit of wild beasts.[61] We may note that, at least in the best specimens of these pieces (in the Sumitomo collection, in the Moriya collection of Kyoto), the décor is spaced out, and there is nothing of the clutter of forms that overloaded the Taoist mirrors of the late Han or of the period of the Six Dynasties.

[61] See, for example, the plates of the great Sumitomo catalogue, *Senoku-seisho...*, part II, *Ancient Mirrors*, plates 125-128, and the abridgment, with the same title, Kyoto, 1934, nos. 67 to 124 (the catologue of mirrors supplied by Umehara). The imperial treasure of the Shōsō-in, at Nara (completed in 756), has several T'ang mirrors that are particularly characteristic (*Catalogue of Exhibition of the Shōsō-in Treasures in the National Museum of Tokyo*, 1949, fig. 53).

The designs of some of these mirrors are enriched by gold or silver inlays that enhance the delicate pattern of interlacings and scrolls.[62] Other T'ang mirrors (or those of Japan, in T'ang style) are inlaid with a delicate mosaic of mother-of-pearl, amber, malachite, black lacquer or translucid lacquer on a red or green background. In addition to this the mother-of-pearl is at times carved. All this polychromy is arranged in motifs of flowers, rosettes, bouquets, garlands and pearls. Exceptionally, in the midst of this mosaic of flowers, a few animals, pigeons, phoenixes, lions or rhinoceros. The whole produces a dazzling decorative effect.[63] In order to appreciate both the luxurious refinement and the 'grand manner' of the T'ang, one must have had the opportunity to admire these polychrome mirrors in the meditative calm of the Shōsō-in, in the Sumitomo collection or the Moriya collection. It matters little that some of them may legitimately be considered as being already 'naturalized Japanese', for the court of Nara, at this period, aimed to be nothing other than an extension of the court of Ch'ang-an.

Several musical instruments of the Shōsō-in, lutes above all, show the same delicate inlays of mother-of-pearl and shell, or else of stained ivory, hartshorn or bamboo, the same magnificent floral ornamentation, flowers and flowerlets arranged in rosettes, flowers strung out as a flourish to elegant scrolls, etc.[64] No less precious, at the Shōsō-in, are the boxes, caskets and luxury furniture for drawing-room games, chessboards inlaid with ivory or hartshorn, with gold and silver flowers and marquetry framing featuring birds, camels, hunting scenes.[65] Likewise on the musical

[62] *Catalogue of the Exhibition of Chinese Art*, London, 1935-1936, in particular nos. 656 (Metropolitan), 663 (British), etc.

[63] *Catalogue of the Shōsō-in (Tōei Shuko)*, 1926, vol. v, nos. 284 and 287. Buhot, *Histoire des arts du Japon*, 1949, I, plate 32, no. 143.

[64] *Catalogue of the Shōsō-in*, vol. I, nos. 34 and 36, and Buhot, plate 33, fig. 144 (A and B).

[65] See for example, for the furniture, the Shōsō-in Catalogue, vol. I, nos. 43-46 (and Buhot, plate 34, figs. 147-148). And for the boxes, *ibid*, vol. III, nos. 145

instruments of the Shōsō-in and on the covers for them, there appear, in mother-of-pearl inlay, now a palmtree with a figure under it mounted on a camel and playing the lute, now a Chinese landscape with river and mountains, plus an elephant bearing four musicians, now a hunting scene with galloping horsemen, footmen carrying the game, etc.[66]

According to Jean Buhot, the Shōsō-in mirrors inlaid with nacre and amber, as well as the musical instruments that are similarly inlaid, are indeed Chinese.[67] This is the 'adornment of life', the 'inimitable life' that Emperor Hsüan-tsung's. entourage led in Ch'ang-an. And it is in such a setting of luxury and refined taste that we must visualize the brilliant descriptions that Li T'ai-po or Tu Fu gives us of the court of Ch'ang-an in the time of the beautiful Yang Kuei-fei. We may add that not only is this or that minute landscape on a musical instrument at the Shōsō-in in every respect specifically Chinese (to the point of being already, by anticipation, almost Ming!), but also that in more than one object T'ang art thus transmitted to Japan shows itself to be penetrated by influences coming from Central Asia and even, through Central Asia (in the Shōsō-in fabrics, particularly), by motifs originating in Sassanid Iran.[68] We shall come upon this same Sassano-Chinese association again in Kysil and in Turfan. It was not without its subsequent effects that Chinese expansion, under the T'ang, had extended beyond the T'ien-shan and the Pamir, and had reached the fringes of the Iranian world.

and 158 (octagonal boxes rimmed with silver, in black lacquered wood, inlaid with mother-of-pearl and amber on red-coloured background.

[66] Catalogue of the Shōsō-in, vol. v, no. 36. Buhot, pl. 34, fig. 144.

[67] *Op. cit.*, p. 124.

[68] Harada, The Interchange of Eastern and Western Cultures as Evidenced in the Shōsō-in Treasures, *Memoirs of the Research Department of the Toyo Bunko*, II, 1939, pp. 55-78 (with 11 very important plates).

44. *Hsü Tao-ning (active c. 1000): Fishing in a Mountain Stream (detail). Ink on silk. Nelson Gallery of Art, Kansas City.*

* * *

If we place them in the setting that we can reconstruct from the luxury furnishings and the musical instruments of the Shōsō-in, and from the verses of Li T'ai-po, we are better able to appreciate the T'ang terra cotta statuettes which, since the Chavannes mission, have been coming out of Chinese territory by the hundred (at times in too great number and without well established proofs of identity).

The T'ang feminine statuettes—musicians, dancers, great ladies or attendants—are well known today in Europe and America, especially since, as has been indicated, numerous imitations have served to popularize the type. But for the question of authenticity there is one sure point of reference, for them, as for the T'ang horses (no less extensively imitated): the figurines discovered by the Aurel Stein mission in the tombs of Astana, near Turfan (dating from the first quarter of the eighth century, the beginning of the reign of Hsüan-tsung). These, as it happens, are pieces whose elegance and freshness of colouring would seem to us to strangely modern if we did not know that they are un-challengeable excavation pieces. Take, for instance, the Astana figurine of a young woman standing, with pale green scarf, saffron-yellow blouse, reddish-brown robe veering toward mauve with brown stripes, a slightly pointed bonnet, her hands hidden under the scarf; or else the amusingly polychrome statuette of a horsewoman in her green and orange costume, with a smart little conical black hat, on her brown horse, dappled on the neck and rump.[69]

[69] Aurel Stein, *Innermost Asia*, vol. III, fig. 99-A. It is interesting to point out that further to the west the Graeco-Buddhist stuccos 'anticipated' the Chinese terra cottas. In Kumtura, near Kucha, for instance, we could point to certain busts of devatas with bare breasts, painted in bright colors. See Le Coq, *Buddhistische Spätantike*, vol. I, plate 25 (and also plates 22, 27, 30) and, in Karashar, small stucco heads that are ethnical types very similar to those of Hadda at the

All the museums of Europe and America (in Paris, the Cernuschi and Guimet Museums) have familiarized us with this
little world of pretty T'ang women, with their delicate grace,
their attitudes that are at times so elegant, their slender lines
(often set off by a flaring of the dress towards the hem), their
long sleeves frequently concealing their hands, their complicated
head-dresses with large uplifted loops.[70]
Because of the lack of controlled excavations, as well as of
a methodical study of fashion under the T'ang, it is impossible
for us at the present moment to sketch even a relative chronology
of these statuettes. Vadime Elisseeff has wondered whether the
feminine figures with 'olive-shaped' faces and plump bodies,
which do in fact seem to correspond to the type of beauty
that the T'ang writers indicate as having been that of the favourite Yang Kuei-fei, should not be considered as contemporary
with Emperor Hsüan-tsung (712-756).[71] Such also is the feminine ideal that we find in the Shōsō-in at Nara on the famous
screen panels known as 'the Six Beauties under the Trees' (under
trees in bloom, six pretty women, alternately standing and seated,
appear, like the statuettes, in ample garments; the garments are
here enhanced by means of feathers glued to the paper, while
the flesh is rendered in delicate pink tones).[72] This ideal of
plumpish beauty is also to be found in the goddess Sri (in Japa-

Guimet Museum (Aurel Stein, *On Ancient Central-Asian Tracks*, fig. 127). All
these influences will be found in the China of the T'ang, in Tun-huang.
   [70] See the abundant reproductions in Hobson, *Catalogue of the Eumorfopoulos
Collection, Ceramics*, VI, London, 1928.
   [71] This is in accordance with the thesis upheld by M. Guillot of the Ecole
du Louvre, on the dating of the Chinese funerary statuettes. *Musées de France*,
October 1949, no. 8.
   [72] Shōsō-in Catalogue, no. 70. Buhot, *Op. cit.*, pl. 30, fig. 133. This theme
of the lady under the tree is also found in Astana in two fragments dated precisely
705-709, or, also in Turfan (Otani mission), in a fragment of about 715. For the
'lady of Astana' and her corsage with its wonderfully fresh tints (deep rose),
see Sirén, *History of Early Chinese Painting*, I, pl. 69, and especially the charming
reproduction in colour of Aurel Stein, *Innermost Asia*, vol. III, pl. CV.

nese: Kichijōten), in a famous painting on canvas of the Yaku-
shiji in Nara, presumed to be of 773, which would make it only
slightly later than Hsüan-tsung's reign.

Apart from the feminine figures, the T'ang period has left
us many terra cotta statuettes representing warriors in whom we
find the same crude realism, the same epic sense as in the 'guardian kings' (*t'ien-wang*), *lokapālas* and *dvārapālas* of the Buddhist sanctuaries. In several of the male figures we observe ethnic
types that are remarkably well observed—Turko-Iranian caravaneers of the Tarim basin, Turko-Mongolian auxiliaries of the
T'ang armies on the outposts of the Gobi.

The epic sense and the gift of realistic animal representation
of the T'ang are given free rein in the terra cottas of horses,
whether alone or with riders. Here again, we can refer only to a
few rare excavation pieces, like the saddled horse from an Astana
tomb (brown coat, dappled on the rump and neck, short knotted
tail, magnificent orange-red saddle with flower pattern, stirrups).[73]
All our museums, all the great collections today have a few specimens of T'ang horses, at rest or impatiently pawing the ground,
snorting or caracoling, rearing or launched upon a flying gallop.
(The Eumorfopoulos collection had a whole stable of them).[74]
In general, the T'ang horse (at least in the terra cottas) is more
robustly muscled than the great steeds of the Han or the Wei,
yet less heavy than the Ming horses.

Innumerable indeed are the copies that have flooded the
market for the past thirty years, and so are the 'improvements'
that the falsifiers have brought to the reproduction of the originals. It is none the less certain that under the T'ang, at least from

[73] *Ibid*, III, pl. 95. Aurel Stein likewise found similar statues of horses in
Karashar. Compare with the horses of the mural paintings of Bezeklik and Idiqut-
chahri (Turfan), reproduced by Grünwedel, *Bericht über archaeologischen Arbeiten
in Idiqutschari*, p. 95, and by Von Le Coq, *Chotscho*, pl. 31.

[74] Eumorfopoulos Collection, Ceramics, Catalogue, vol. I, plates XXVI, XXVII,
XXVIII, XXX.

T'ai-tsung the Great to the catastrophes of the years 751-755, the Chinese had become a 'horseman'. The two dynastic histories of the T'ang tell us of the raids carried out into far Mongolia or Tashkend by the squadrons sent out from Ch'ang-an. The love with which the T'ang claymoulders turned out the statuettes of horses reflects an absorbing interest in these events. From another point of view, we may assume from the establishment of the Chinese protectorate in Turkestan, and from the friendly relations with the princes of the Kabul valley, that there was cross-breeding between the Persian stallions (a variety of what we call Arab horses) and the Chinese native horse. Several of our T'ang horses seem indeed to suggest that there must have been such cross-breeding.

The equestrian figurines are no less numerous. Particularly elegant are the horsewomen, especially the polo players—a sport that had been brought from Sassanid Iran, or more precisely from Khotan, to T'ang China as early as the reign of T'ai-tsung the Great, and that was one of the favourite games of the courtesan Yang Kuei-fei, under Hsüan-tsung.[75] The poems of Li Po or his emulators, for that matter, describe for us the horseback rides of Yang Kuei-fei and the other pretty women of the Court of Hsüan-tsung in the immense parks of Ch'ang-an.

The empire of T'ai-tsung, and of Hsüan-tsung, as we have seen, extended over the immensities of Upper Asia, across the world of the deserts and the steppes. Whence the interest shown by the T'ang modelers in the caravan animal, the camel. It is, after the horse, one of the most frequently reproduced subjects, and it is often rendered with a realism that is almost caricatural.

[75] Berthold Laufer, The Early History of Polo, *Polo, magazine for horsemen*, Vol. VII, no. 5, New York, 1932. Review by Serge Elisseeff in *Revue des Arts Asiatiques*, VIII, i, p. 63.

XII. *Vase. Sung Dynasty. Musée Guimet, Paris.*

* * *

These *ming-ch'i*, as the Chinese call them, that is to say, statuettes intended to honour and accompany the dead, representing human or animal figures, are 'of gray or white earth, often covered with a white slip, and polychromed with pigments applied after baking'. Others of these statuettes, as well as numerous T'ang vases, are 'adorned with lead-glazes, often coloured by means of metallic oxides'. We may note, in this connection, the green (copper), yellow (iron), blue (cobalt), orange red (glazing on red earth), cream-white (glazing on white slip) and pale green (identical composition, plus a little copper oxide in the glaze), all glazes obtained either in monochrome or in mottled effects. The dominant associations are those of green and orange-yellow, secondarily of brown and blue.[76] These colours, both in the statues with polychrome glaze and on cups and vases with the same covering, are without nuance, crude almost, being applied evenly and separated from one another by engraved lines. By way of motifs we often find here the rosettes that we have seen on the inlaid mirrors of the Shōsō-in. This décor is often in relief, 'moulded, stamped or incised', revealing the same love of polychrome inlay in pottery as on the above-mentioned mirrors or the luxury furniture of the Shōsō-in.

True white porcelains likewise make their appearance under the T'ang, which the texts of the period refer to as coming from Hsing-chou, in Hopei, and fragments of which have in fact been found in Samarra (Irak), the capital of the Abbasaid Khalifate

[76] See in particular Hobson, *Catalogue of the Eumorfopoulos Collection*, vol. I, pl. LVIII (T'ang plate with dominant deep blues and dark reds) and vol. VI, pl. XI (T'ang plate and bowl with dominant greens and oranges). We may point out that the three-coloured T'ang pottery featured in the Shōsō-in shows in general the aforementioned colours. In reality the orange and green shades are not altogether identical with the Chinese T'ang. These are 'Japanese T'ang', already slightly differentiated. See *English Catalogue of a Special Exhibition of the Shōsō-in Treasures in the National Museum of Nara*, 1947, p. 17 (text by Jiro Harada).

from 836 to 889, thus providing a precise chronological point of reference.

In the period of the Six Dynasties, as we have seen, the first celadons, in porcellaneous stoneware, the so-called Yüeh ware, had appeared in Chekiang. From the seventh century, under the early T'ang, kilns of these celadons were found in 1936 by the Japanese scholar Manzō Nakao near Yü-yao, on the shores of lake Shang-lin, also in Chekiang.[77] 'They are covered with a bluish grey or grey-green glaze, the ornamentation being usually engraved'. We may note that the Samarra excavations have likewise yielded up some of these same T'ang celadons, which further corroborates the dating.

The fact that T'ang pottery has been found throughout the Abbasid khalifate, not only, as we have seen, in Samarra (Irak), but also in Rayy (Persia) and in Fostat (Egypt), shows how widely the commercial and artistic activity of China extended under the T'ang. The opposite is no less true, and is likewise attested by pottery. A Persian (Sassano-Abbasid) influence and, through Iran, a post-Hellenistic influence, are visible in the form of a great number of vases: 'vases with handles in the form of dragons evoking the Hellenistic amphoras, ewers and lobed cups imitating Sassanid silverware'.[78] We have, it will be remembered, pointed out the same influence (the Iranian influence and the post-Hellenistic influence, transmitted through Iran) on the T'ang mirrors and more generally on Chinese ornamentation of this period as a whole (rosettes, pearled medallions, scrolls, palmettes, vine

---

[77] Cf. Matsudaira, *Oriental Ceramics*, October, 1936. Plumer, *Illustrated London News*, March 13 and 20, 1937. Madeleine David, *Guide du Musée Guimet*, III, 1950, p. 125.

[78] In the Shōsō-in (and also at Uéno Museum and in the Nezu collection) amphoras of this kind, with T'ang dragon-handles, may be seen, showing an Iranian influence. These, however, have glazes with an orange and a green slightly different from the similar Chinese shades. As we indicated, although they are of the same period, they are Japanese T'ang.

leaves, grape clusters). Never was China more 'international', more 'Pan-Asiatic', than under the T'ang.

* * *

T'ang painting is of great importance to us, because it combines traditions that are properly Chinese with Indian influences. We cannot approach it without recalling, here, too, that the conquests of T'ai-tsung the Great and of Hsüan-tsung in Central Asia had placed under Chinese protectorate the caravan oases of the Tarim basin, which by virtue of the phenomenon of Buddhism had become, in the realm of art, a kind of Outer India—indeed, in certain respects, and at the same time, a kind of Outer Iran.

In several of these sites of Central Asia we again find the carving out of cliffs into Buddhist caves (in eastern Turkish: *ming-oï*, 'the thousand cells', freely translated by the Chinese as: caves of the thousand Buddhas), for which the cliff shrines of Bāmiyān, in Afghanistan, had furnished the model. An example is furnished by the Kysil caves, west of Kucha, adorned with famous mural paintings. On these 'frescoes' (as they are improperly called) we observe, from the fifth to eighth century, a continuity of local traditions proving that in this remote corner of the Gobi there existed a true 'Kuchean civilization', possessing an unexpected refinement, an astonishing richness. The albums of the explorer and archaeologist von Le Coq have popularized among us the portraits, from the mural paintings of Kysil and Kumtura, of the elegant noblemen and lovely ladies of Kucha, with their delicately Iranian features. We know these handsome 'knights' in their war regalia, bristling with iron, or in their court costumes that might be taken from a Persian miniature, with their jackets with great turned-over collars, their long swords, their short daggers; the pretty women with elaborate dresses, also showing greater affinity with Iran than with China. As for the

chronology of these paintings, Hackin distinguishes two styles
in Kysil: the first style, between 450 and 650, characterized by a
certain amount of 'modelling', by a discreet colouring (grey, tan,
reddish brown, deep brown and light green), with a preponderance of the Gupta-Indian influence and Iranian contribution;
and a second style (seventh to eighth century), without 'modelling' but with brighter colours (lapis blue, bright green) and a
concern with details of dress that denote a new wave of Iranian-
Sassanid influence.[79] We may add that what we have here is
largely post-Sassanid, resulting from the fact that the last Sassa-
nids, chased out of Persia by the Arabs, had fled in the direction
of the Tarim basin whence, in 670-673, they went to seek asylum
at the court of China.[80]

As we see, the mural paintings as well as the stuccos in
Kysil involve an Indo-Iranian (Sassano-Gupta) 'complex'. We
must not forget, besides, (and this is another of Hackin's discoveries) that this complex was already adumbrated in Buddhist

[79] Hackin, in Réau's *Histoire Universelle des Arts*, 1939, vol. IV, pp. 267-
268, and Ernest Waldschmidt in *Gandhāra, Kutscha, Turfan*, Leipzig, 1925, p. 75.
For the distinction between the two Kysil styles, see the coloured plates of the
albums by von Le Coq, *Die buddhistische Spätantike in Mittelasien*, vols. III and IV,
die Wandmalereien. Waldschmidt assigns to the first Kysil style the 'peacock
cave', the 'navigator's cave', the 'treasure cave' and the 'seahorse cave'; to
the second style 'Maya's cave', the 'musicians' cave', and many portraits of
individual donors. From the ethnic point of view, on the Iranian-tinged character
of this brilliant Kuchean 'chivalry', the reader is referred to von Le Coq's reproductions in his *Bilderatlas zur Kunst und Kulturgeschichte Mittelasiens*, particularly to figs. 5-7 (the painter of the 'painter's cave'), fig. 8 ('cave of the
Sixteen Sword-carriers'), fig. 20 (the king and queen of Kucha) etc. It should be
noted that in Kumtura (about 750) we see, in addition to the Iranian influences,
a Chinese influence that is lacking in Kysil. See von Le Coq, *Peintures chinoises
authentiques de l'époque des T'ang provenant du Turkestan chinois*.

[80] The importance of this long Sassanid 'exile' at the Ch'ang-an court (from
about 670-673) for the history of art has perhaps not been sufficiently dwelt on.
The *T'ang-shu* tells us that under the reign of Hsüan-tsung (712-756) the last
Sassanid pretenders offered to the Court of Ch'ang-an 'fire-coloured embroideries'
(Chavannes, *T'ou-kiue Occidentaux*, p. 173). Now this is precisely the eve of the
'closing' of the Shōsō-in Treasury whose Sassanid or Sassanid-type fabrics are so
remarkable.

45. *Kuo Hsi (c. 1020-1090): Clear Autumn Skies over Mountains and Valleys (detail). Ink on silk. Freer Gallery of Art, Washington.*

Afghanistan, as can be seen from the painted stuccos of Fondu-kistan (seventh and perhaps eighth centuries). It is even obvious that it is the Fondukistan style which, having reached the Tarim basin, is again found on the stuccos of Tumshuk (between Kash-gar and Kucha), brought back by the Pelliot mission.[81]

These various influences persist in the frescoes of Kumtura, southeast of Kysil. Here, however, the Iranian influences, while still represented by elegant 'Tokharian' noblemen, are in slight regression before the Chinese influences.[82] Let us not forget, in this connection, that while the Tarim basin owed its religious and literary culture to Buddhist India, as it owed a part of its material culture to Sassanid Iran, it was a Chinese protectorate during the first part of the period of the T'ang: the kingdom of Kucha (on which Kumtura depended) was subdued by the emperor T'ai-tsung in 647-648, and in 658 Kucha became the seat of the Chi-nese governor of Tarim. The same direct Chinese influences, alongside of Indo-Iranian influences that are already more atten-uated, are observed a little further towards the east, on the Shor-chuk mural paintings, today at the Ermitage Museum of Lenin-grad (incorporating elegant scrolls recalling T'ang jewelry work). We may recall that the kingdom of Karashar, on which Shorchuk depended, was conquered by emperor T'ai-tsung at the same period (campaigns of 644 and 648).

Still further east was situated the kingdom of Turfan, con-quered by emperor T'ai-tsung in 640, which also became the seat of a Chinese governor. Upon Turfan were dependent the rock sanctuaries or open-air structures of Bezeklik and Murtuk. Accor-ding to Hackin, the mural paintings of Bezeklik include an

[81] The Tumshuk stuccos brought back by Pelliot are today at the Guimet Museum, as are also several of the Fondukistan stuccos discovered by Hackin. Their comparison is instructive as showing the progression of styles from Af-ghanistan into Kashgaria.

[82] 'Framed in stylized clouds, *apsaras* represented in full flight, the curve of their long scarves forming a coloured trail : this is a classic motif of the Chinese art of the T'ang' (Hackin, *Loc. cit.*, p. 268).

initial Buddhist period, going back to the beginning of the T'ang, that is to say to a time when the oasis (like those of Karashar and of Kucha) was inhabited by an Indo-European ('Tokharian') population; and a second period, with Manichaean paintings, dating from a period when the Uighur Turks, converted by 763 to Manichaeism, had made themselves masters of Turfan (hence, between 800 and 840).[83] The Bezeklik and Murtuk painting reveals these various influences. We see first of all donors who, by their costumes and their armour, remind us (though inferior in elegance) of the handsome 'Tokharian' knights of Kysil and of Kumtura. But generally speaking, whether we consider the type of the Bodhisattvas, the ascetics, or the demoniacal figures, or the style of the ornamentation (clouds, flowers and rosettes), the dominant influence is that of the art of T'ang China. The character of the figure of the Buddha himself, which for a long time was purely Graeco-Buddhist, has here become Sinicized. The great Buddhist compositions, in Bezeklik as in Murtuk, are directly linked to those of Tun-huang, of which we shall speak further on.[84] A revival of Iranian influence makes itself felt during the first Uighur period, with the Manichaean paintings and miniatures (early ninth century).[85] A Tantric influence had also appeared in Bezeklik (the cupola of temple 3) by the eighth century, perhaps linked to the preaching, in China, by the Indian monks Vajarabodhi and Amoghavajra to which we have called attention above.[86]

---

[83] Hackin, *Recherches Archéologiques en Asie Centrale.*

[84] See Grünwedel, *Bericht...*, pl. IV. Von Le Coq, *Chotscho,* plates 14a, 53, 54.

[85] Von Le Coq, *Spätantike...*, vol. II, *Manichäische Miniaturen,* for example plate 7B.

[86] Regarding the terror-inspiring and, to us, almost demoniacal character of certain Vajrapāni of Idikut-chähri and Bezeklik, see Grünwedel, *Altbuddhistische Kultstätten in Chinesisch-Turkestan,* p. 238. Central Asia, in turning for inspiration both to Tantric Hindu models and to the Chinese sense of caricature, had created the type of the Vajrapāni (Chinese: Chin-kang-shou; Japanese: Kongōshu) and of the very horrific *dvārapāla* and *lokapāla* (Chinese: *t'ien-wang*; Japanese:

This influence could hardly fail to develop in the second Buddhist phase (after 840). After the Uighur occupation (from 800), the 'Tokharian' types among the donors give way to clearly Turkish physiognomies, whether in Buddhist paintings or in Manichaean art.[87] Through this evolution the painting of the Turfan group shows us, generally speaking, a Sino-Iranian complex (with increasingly dominant Chinese influence), even as Kysil showed us an Indo-Iranian complex.

In southern Kashgaria several Buddhist paintings on wood panels, from Dandan-oilik near Khotan (eighth century) show a curious blend of Tantric inspiration and of Persian art (a Sivaized Avalokiteśvara, with three heads, four arms, a blue-tinged body; a Vajrapāṇi with a Sassanid beard, and a no less Iranian green cloak, etc).[88] We may note, too, on these Dandan-oilik panels of painted wood, a camel mounted by a caravaneer, the equivalent of the one from the other side of T'ang China which we noted at the Shōsō-in.[89]

It is in fact through Central Asia that all these diverse influences, set into motion by Buddhism, reached the Far East. Among the mural paintings of Sangim, certain *nakṣatra* figures (feminine moon divinities) in their floating scarves present the most felici-

---

shitennō), which were to be perpetuated by later China and by Japan. One can therefore point with all the more assurance to the link between the Graeco-Buddhist demons (of the Assault of Mara) or damned creatures (prēta) (Hadda and Tarim) and the Chinese devils, inspired by the whole Taoist demonology. With reference to the skeletal damned creatures of Sängim, near Turfan, see von Le Coq, *Chotscho*, pl. 14.

[87] *Idem, Ibid*, plates 30-32, and *Buddhistische Spätantike...*, vol. III, pl. 17. We may note parenthetically how closely these Uighur portraits resemble the portraits, likewise Turkish (Ghaznevid), among the mural paintings recently discovered (1949) by Mr. Daniel Schlumberger in Lashkaribazar, in Afghanistan.

[88] Aurel Stein, *Ancient Khotan*, Vol. II, plates LX and LXI.

[89] *Ibid*, II, plate LIX. Similar representations of caravaneers (here bearded donors, of Turko-Iranian type), followed by their camels and their mules, on Bezeklik mural paintings (Grünwedel, *Altbuddhistische Kultstätten*, p. 274, and *Bericht...*, figs. 155-156). See Shōsō-in catalogue, vol. IV, no. 36, and Buhot, *Arts du Japon*, pl. 34, fig. 144,

tous blend of Indian suppleness, Hellenic elegance and Chinese prettiness.[90] We shall come upon these attractive daughters of the air—*apsaras, nakṣatra,* 'Buddhist fairies' or 'Buddhist angels'—in Tun-huang as well as in the Shōsō-in. Following Jeannine Auboyer's thesis, Toshio Nagahiro's album enables us to retrace their flight from the Bāmiyān mural paintings to those of Kysil, from the reliefs of Yün-kang to the mural paintings of the Hōryūji and the Hokaiji temples.[91]

* * *

We may note further that the Iranian-Chinese complex that we have seen coming into being under the influence of Buddhism in Central Asia, from Kumtura to Turfan, was likewise favoured by two other religions propagated along the caravan trails of the Silk Road: Manichaeism and Nestorian Christianity.

As we know, Manichaeism, a heresy born in Persia in the third century of our era by a syncretism of Mazdaic and Christian conceptions, had in 763 converted the Uighur Turks, then masters of Mongolia, and shortly after (from 800) masters of the Turfan oasis, who remained Manichaeans until about 840. We owe to Manichaeism a part of the Uighur mural paintings of Turfan, as well as the fresh Manichaean miniatures brought back by the von Le Coq mission from the same region, so that these are all works that can logically be dated as belonging to approximately the first forty years of the ninth century. By virtue of their origins the Manichaeans could hardly fail to bring to the frontiers of T'ang China a revival of Iranian influences, which their Turfan paintings indeed confirm. Nestorianism, finally, as we have seen,

[90] Grünwedel, *Bericht...,* pl. XXIV.

[91] Jeannine Auboyer, *Les influences et les réminiscences étrangères au Kondō du Hōryūji,* Paris, Guimet Museum, 1941, p. 100 and plates 44-45. Toshio Nagahiro, *A Study of Hiten or Flying Angels,* Kyoto, 1949.

had been brought to China by Sogdian caravaneers who settled in Ch'ang-an (Sian), where they founded a trade colony governed by an Irano-Syriac clergy (a church was built in this city in 638, and a Syro-Chinese stele 'of Sianfu', inscribed in 781). Nestorian art is represented in Turfan (Shocho) by a very pleasant mural painting featuring either a baptismal scene or, more probably, the celebration of Palm Sunday, a work of broad, refined treatment, both Iranian and Romano-Byzantine in inspiration.[92]

But the Irano-T'ang complex did not stop here. Soviet archaeologists have recently discovered on the upper Jenissei, in the former Kirghiz country of present-day Tannu-Tuva, saddle ornaments, and in particular gold plaques, of the seventh to ninth century, with archers on horseback at a flying gallop, pursuing lions or tigers, of a purely Sassanid treatment; and alongside of these, a silver plaque of T'ang inspiration.[93] Kisselev observes —and this cannot fail to give satisfaction to the historian of the steppes—the connection between these finds and the latest discoveries of the art brought from upper Asia into Hungary by the Avars.[94]

* * *

The culminating point of all these Central-Asiatic influences, with what they contained of Indian traditions or, through Indian Buddhism, of Graeco-Buddhist and Irano-Buddhist traditions, is to be found in Tun-huang. Here, too, we have caves 'of the

---

[92] Von Le Coq, *Die Manichäischen Miniaturen*, vol. II of his *Buddhistische Spätantike*. And also *Idem, Chotscho*, pls. I, 3, 5, 6, etc. On Nestorianism in China, one of the latest comprehensive studies is that of P. Y. Saeki, *The Nestorian Documents and Relics in China*, Tokyo, 1937. On the fresco discovered in Turfan by von Le Coq and apparently representing Palm Sunday in the Nestorian manner, see Von Le Coq, *Chotscho*, pl. 7, and Saeki, *Loc. cit.*, p. 417.

[93] Kisselev, *Histoire ancienne de la Sibérie méridionale*.

[94] Cf. Tibor Horvath, Die avarischen Gräberfelder von Ullö und Kiskoros, *Archaeologia Ungarica*, XIX, Budapest, 1935,

Thousand Buddhas' built in the sides of cliffs in accordance with the traditions of Bamiyan, Kysil and Bezeklik.

Tun-huang was the last frontier post of China proper, facing the desert immensity of the Tarim basin, the point of arrival of caravans coming from the northern trail (via Kucha, Karashar) as well as from the southern trail (Khotan) of the Silk Road. The caves of the Thousand Buddhas are situated 15 kilometers from the city itself. The first were dug out in 366 by the monk Lo-tsun, under the local Tartar dynasty of the Ch'ien-Liang (314-376), in the midst of the Great Invasions. The works of art of this period must have been destroyed in the course of the persecution of 445 ordered, as we have seen, by the Wei king T'o-pa T'ao. Construction was evidently resumed with the pacification of 453. The décor of caves 110 and 111a undoubtedly dates from the last quarter of the fifth century.[95] These were immediately followed by caves 103 and 111, the latter very closely related to the Shih-fo-ssu of Yün-kang, then caves 135 and 120n that can be dated, on the basis of the prevailing late Wei style, about 530-540.[96] According to Sirén's observation, the paintings of cave 120n, a well as of caves 126b and 137b (middle of sixth century) reveal equally the influence of the 'Tokharian' art of Kysil and of Karashar.[97] The art of the T'ang begins with cave 77.

The mural paintings in question are interesting because they show the junction between the Wei steles and the art of Kysil. They are characterized by vast landscapes of a delightful naïveté, with wild animals (antilopes or felines) and horsemen surrounded by tiny mountains, or by Buddhas and Bodhisattvas that are very 'Kuchean' above whom fly *apsaras*, diverse genii and birds amid an unfurling of floating draperies, likewise very 'Central-Asiatic'.[98]

---

[95] Pelliot, *Les grottes du Touen-houang*, pls. CLXXXIX-CXC and CXCI-CXCII.

[96] *Ibid*, pls. CCLXXX-CCLXXXV and CCLVII-CCLXVIII.

[97] *Ibid*, pls. CCLXXIII-CCLXXIV and CCXCVI.

[98] Cf. Eiichi, Matsumoto, Frescoes in the North Wei Style in the Caves of One Thousand Buddhas of Tun-huang, *Kokka*, 1924, no. 400-402. We may recall

The influence of Central Asia in China in the following period under the Pei-Ch'i (550-577) and the Sui (589-618), is corroborated by the presence there of a Khotan painter, Wei-ch'ih Po-chih-na, whose son, Wei-ch'ih I-seng, painted at the court of the first T'ang emperors. The Freer Gallery possesses what may be a late copy of I-seng, a Vaiśravaṇa, which in fact has rather a 'Dandan-oilik' look.[99]

Some idea of the best Buddhist painting of the T'ang period may be obtained from the mural paintings, or as is commonly (though inexactly) said, 'frescoes' of Kondo, in the Hōryūji temple at Nara, whether they be works going back to the first half of the seventh century (?), or to be assigned hypothetically with Jean Buhot to about 690 or, more commonly, to the Wadō period (between 708 and 714).[100] There is discussion also as to whether the authors of these mural paintings were Koreans (?) who had wholly assimilated Chinese art, or a Chinese foreman (and his Japanese pupils?) working after models from Central Asia.[101] Nipponese art critics are not even certain of the identities of the Buddha and Bodhisattva figures represented, except in the case of the Amitābha of 'fresco' 6 (west wall). As for the other central figures, the latest official Japanese catalogues suggest that the main figure of 'fresco' 1 (east wall) might be a Śākyamuni, those of frescoes 9 and 10 (north wall) a Maitreya and a Baichajyaguru respectively, etc.[102] But other specialists propose dif-

that Mr. Matsumoto is the author of the most exhaustive study of the subject (*Tonkō-ga no kenkyū, Recherches sur les peintures de Touen-houang*, Tokyo, 1937).

[99] Sirén, *History of Early Chinese Painting*, I, pl. 20.

[100] Matsumoto favours the Wadō period, early eighth century, in his article, Wall paintings of Hōryūji, *Bulletin of Eastern Art*, no. 13-14, 1941, p. 4.

[101] Jean Buhot (*Arts du Japon*, p. 97): 'The painter, or at least the master in charge of the work, must have been Chinese, a Chinese who had travelled a great deal and learned religious art, if not in India itself, at least at its gates and by contact with Indian artists, perhaps in Central Asia, but perhaps in some other region altogether (along the southern routes, the sea route)'.

[102] *Art Guide of Japan*, vol. I, *Nara, Mie and Wakayama Prefectures*, Institute of Art Researches, Tokyo, 1943, p. 222 (with plan).

ferent identifications, not only for the seated central figures but
for the standing Bodhisattves who surround each of these.[103]
What is certain—whatever the divinities represented may be
and whatever may have been the nationality of the artist—is
that we here have before us the complex that we have seen in
formation in Central Asia. The Amitābha of 'fresco' 6, with the
dark red monastic mantle, has a Gandharian draping, such as
was transmitted by Tarim art. On the other hand the seated
Buddhas of 'frescoes' 1 and 9 are draped Chinese-fashion—or
more precisely, as Jeannine Auboyer notes, in the fashion of Tun-
huang, and beyond Tun-huang, of Turfan art.[104] As for the numerous Indian motifs (for example the thrones or the lotuses on
which the Buddhas are seated), the treatment recalls Central Asia
(Bezeklik by way of Tun-huang). As for the standing Bodhisattvas who surround the seated Buddhas, certain details of their
costume (the belt with double hanging loop) are purely Indian
(not Chinese), but are also found at Tun-huang. Other details of
ornament on the Bodhisattvas (the long chains worn crosswise)
were not found in India and come from Bezeklik. As for the flying
genii of the Hōryūji—here feminine deities plunging from the
upper air—they are related to the similar figures of the T'ang
paradises, which are in turn derived from Indian models transmitted through Central Asia.[105]

What constitutes the superiority of the mural paintings of
the Hōryūji as compared to the models of Central Asia and Tun-
huang is the art with which these diverse elements are now combined. 'The figures' says Sirén, 'are powerful, the tall Bodhi-

[103] J. Auboyer, Les influences..., pp. 3-6; and Buhot, Arts du Japon, I,
pp. 95-96.
[104] We may note too (with respect to Greek influence) analogies with Miran,
even though Miran is much earlier. See Nobuo Kumagi, Miran and Hōryūji,
Buddhist Art, IV, 1949.
[105] J. Auboyer, Op. cit., pp. 100-103. In Tun-huang wonderful flying genii
are to be seen on a fresco in cave 77 (seventh century). See Pelliot, Les grottes
de Touen-houang, pl. CLVI.

46. *Ma Yüan (active c. 1190-1230): Bare Willows and Distant Mountains. Ink and color on silk. Museum of Fine Arts, Boston.*

47. Left: *Liang Kʻai: Li Po. Ink on paper. Thirteenth century. Cultural Properties Protection Commission, Tokyo.* Right: *Liang Kʻai: The Sixth Patriarch Tearing up the Sūtras. Ink on paper. Thirteenth century. National Museum, Tokyo.*

sattvas appear still, in spite of their highly decorated skirt-like 'dhoti', quite manly; and there is an air of stateliness and refinement about all these divine beings, which carries inspiration... the firm, yet highly sensitive drawing is still plainly distinguished'. While so many paintings, even in Tun-huang, are but the work of pious craftsmen, amalgamating Indian contributions and permanent Chinese elements as best they can, at the Hōryūji we admire a balanced and harmonious synthesis, which has culminated in a great new art.[106]

In China itself the Buddhist painting of the T'ang is mainly represented by the mural and banner paintings of Tun-huang. For the mural paintings Pelliot laid out the following main chronological points of reference: to the seventh century belong caves 77 and 104; to the eighth, caves 146, 70, 140, 31, 34; to the end of the eighth, cave 120 G; to the ninth century, cave 52; to the second quarter of the tenth century, cave 74.[107] Among the banners or fragments of banners of Tun-huang brought back by Pelliot to the Guimet Museum, we may note, by way of dates, a Kāśyapa of 729; the great paradise of Avalokiteśvara, dated 981; and the judgment of souls (with a view to the determination of reincarnations) by Kṣitigarbha (Ti-Tsang), dated 983.[108] As for the dated paintings on silk, brought back by Aurel Stein from Tun-huang to the British Museum or to Delhi, they can be situated between 864 and 983. As we see, these banners represent works distributed throughout the whole T'ang period and into the period of the Five Dynasties (907-960) and even beyond the accession (960) of the Sung dynasty.

A number of mural paintings at Tun-huang recall the delightful simplicity of subject and the unity of composition of those

[106] Conclusions by Matsumoto, Wall Paintings of Horyuji Temple, *Bulletin of Eastern Art*, Tokyo, no. 13-14, 1941, p. 6.

[107] Pelliot quoted by Auboyer, *Op. cit.*, p. 12.

[108] Hackin, *Guide-catalogue du Musée Guimet, collections bouddhiques*, 1923, pp. 39-47.

of the Hōryūji temple, for example the group of Amitābha surrounded by Bodhisattvas and monks of cave 146 (eighth century).[109] But presently, as Sirén observes, there appears an overcrowding of figures and motifs, a juxtaposition of secondary scenes, landscapes and architecture, in which artistic considerations become secondary to religious teaching and to the need for edification. This overcrowding, in fact, had already appeared in cave 104 (which is of the seventh century), where a whole procession of celestial beings surrounds Amitābha, not to mention the paradise placed above and the jātaka that line the sides.[110] In the eighth century (perhaps in the beginning of the eighth), a 'fresco' of cave 70 accentuates this tendency with a central group, isolated by architectural features, sitting in state on a platform with balustrades and steps, while above and on the sides are numerous episodic scenes.[111] Increasingly therefore (as in the theatrical representations of our medieval 'mysteries') we have the impression of buildings seen in vertical cross-section, forming 'scaffoldings', with 'compartments' and lateral strips which, incidentally, can be used to present not only landscapes but also heavens or hells.

It is, for that matter, in Tun-huang that we must seek the most authentic T'ang landscapes, like the one that covers the left partition, on the right side, of cave 70, a vast panorama with a foreground composed of buildings, a walled town, then, piling up vertically, mountain roads on which horsemen and pedestrians travel.[112] On the right-hand partition, on the left side of the same cave 70, we see an episode of the 'war of the relics' with two rows of T'ang warriors in the foreground, brist-

---

[109] Pelliot, *Les grottes de Touen-houang*, pls. CCCXVIII-CCCXIX.

[110] *Ibid*, pl. CLXXXVII.

[111] *Ibid*, plates CXVIII to CXXV. Sirén, *History of Early Chinese Painting*, I, p. 48. On the technically unjustifiable but generally adopted use of the word *fresco* for the Asiatic mural paintings (since the process used in Asia differs from the specifically *a fresco* method), see Auboyer, *Les influences...*, p. 18.

[112] Pelliot, *Op. cit.*, pl. CXX.

ling with iron weapons and on the point of grappling; at a distance the Indian city of Kuśinagara represented as a fortified city in the Chinese manner, and in the background a landscape of shrubbery and mountains.[113] As on the preceding partition wall, what we have here is a bird's eye view landscape, treated in an austere manner but with a good deal of power, and one which despite the vertical piling-up of planes and episodes manages successfully to convey a 'feeling of space'.[114]

Dedicated though they are to Buddhist art, the mural paintings and banners of Tun-huang are not devoid of the epic quality characteristic of the T'ang period. In cave 17B (seventh century), we see a donor surrounded by a squadron of horsemen caracoling in several files, standards waving in the wind, and some galloping at full speed.[115] The perfect understanding of the anatomy of the horse, not to mention the movement that sweeps the whole cavalcade, gives us an idea of what military painting under the T'ang may have been like, in the period of the painter Han Kan, who about 750 declared to emperor Hsüan-tsung, 'The horses of your Majesty's stables are my only masters'.[116] As for the warrior types that we have encountered in these mural paintings,

---

[113] *Ibid*, pl. CXXIV.

[114] Sirén, *Op. cit.*, p. 48. We may recall a guitar (*biwa*) of the Shōsō-in treasure, belonging to the T'ang period, with inlay of rosewood, which has as background for a hunting scene (horsemen at a gallop fighting a tiger) the peaks of mountains piercing a sea of clouds. Within the dimensions of a T'ang miniature we here already have an immense landscape of distances in the manner of the Sung (*English Catalogue of a Special Exhibition of the Shōsō-in Treasures...*, fig. 30).

[115] Pelliot, *Op. cit.*, plates XLIV-XLIX. We should also remember copies of Tun-huang 'frescoes' representing horsemen and hunting scenes of the Wei period (fifth century) or of the T'ang period (seventh century) and the Five Dynasties (tenth century), copies that were featured in September 1947 at the exhibition of the Chinese painter Ou Sogene at the Musée Galliera (*Catalogue*, p. 13, no. 67).

[116] To Han Kan (about 720-780) has been attributed a scroll in the Freer Gallery (horses brought in tribute by men from Upper Asia)—in all likelihood belonging to a later date—and a small ink painting on paper, representing one of Emperor Hsüan-tsung's steeds. This painting is now in the Percival David collection.

even better examples are to be found in the paintings on silk brought from Tun-huang either to the Guimet Museum by the Pelliot mission, or to the British Museum or Delhi by the Aurel Stein mission. We may mention a fragment on paper at the Guimet Museum, representing a high dignitary on horseback, followed by a mounted lancer, which again bears witness to the probable character of T'ang military painting.[117] Likewise, at the Guimet and at the British Museum, two paintings on silk, both representing Vaiśravaṇa (the *lokapāla* or guardian king of the North in Indian mythology), featured as a formidable T'ang warrior, with dazzling armour and adornment done in golds, reds, blues and greens.[118] Buddhism, under the influence of the T'ang conquerors, was swept by an epic inspiration.

Thanks also to the Tun-huang paintings on silk (Guimet, British Museum and Delhi) we have excellent portraits of men and women donors in full T'ang or Five Dynasties dress. The lovely ladies thus represented in court attire, often all rose-patterned brocade, with their elaborate piled-up and flower-adorned head-dresses, give us a better insight into the ideal of feminine beauty and into the changes in fashion from the eighth to the tenth century than any amount of dubious terra cottas.[119]

With regard to the Tun-huang paintings dating from the first half of the eigth, century onwards, Sirén observes that the manner in which the celestial hierarchies and the episodes are architecturally compartmentalized, as in the 'paradises' of Amitābha, Avalokiteśvara, Bhaiṣajya and other Buddhist divinities, is evidence of a tendency towards order and clarity combined with a

[117] Sirén, *History of Early Chinese Painting*, I, pl. 32.
[118] Odette Monod-Bruhl, *Guide-catalogue du Musée Guimet*, 1939, p. 127. Aurel Stein, *On Central Asian Tracks*, pl. 100. Also: Stein, *Serindia*, IV, 72, 73, 84, and Pelliot, *Op. cit.*, pls. CVI (cave 61) and CLXXIII (cave 83-B).
[119] Pelliot, *Op. cit.*, cave 74 (end of tenth century), pls. CXXXIII-CXXXV; caves 117-119, pls. CCIV, CCXIII, CCXLIV. Also, on the Musée Guimet banners, the men and women donors of several paradises of Avalokiteśvara or of Kṣitigarbha (dated 943, 981 or 983).

minuteness of detail which is not without a certain dryness. Sirén recalls the fact that from 763 the Tibetans occupied Tun-huang on several occasions, and that one particular tribe related to them, the Hsi-hsia, or Tangut, was to conquer and keep it throughout the eleventh and twelfth centuries.[120] The Swedish archaeologist wonders, confronted with the manifestation of these tendencies in cave 120G (end of eighth century) and in cave 139A (beginning of ninth) whether we are not here witnessing the beginnings of Tibetan (or Nepalo-Tibetan) art, as we shall in fact see it develop autonomously some eight centuries later.[121] There is indeed something of Pala-Sena art (of Northeast India)—an art subsequently more and more stereotyped as it passed through Nepal and Tibet—in the wonderful Avalokiteśvara with forty arms, a painting on silk brought to the British Museum by Aurel Stein, which belongs, in fact, to the ninth century.[122] Through the muted vibration of the golds, pinks, violets, greens and faded reds, the Bodhisattva with half-naked body—a frankly Bengali or Nepalese nakedness—combines Buddhist suavity with the cosmic majesty of a Hindu *deva*; above, small Bodhisattvas, likewise with a delightful treatment of the nude and similarly *Pala*; below, divinities that could be Sivaites; to the left, an elegant Chinese figure; to the right, a Hindu ascetic, as we shall see them in the Tibetan banners of the Bacot collection. In sum, pure enchantment, but an enchantment that prefigures the Indo-Tibetan painting of some eight centuries later.

Sirén, after Bachofer, points out the affinities (particularly in the costumes of donors) between the Uighur paintings of Turfan and certain paintings of caves 52 and 74, in Tun-huang.[123] Cave 52, as we have seen, does in fact belong to the ninth century;

---

[120] The Hsi-Hsia kingdom in Kansu (capital Ning-hsia), 1001-1227.

[121] Sirén, *History of Early Chinese Painting*, I, p. 50.

[122] Aurel Stein, *Serindia*, vol. IV, pl. 64. Reproduction, also in colour, in Springer, *Kunstgeschichte*, vol. VI, by Curt Glaser, Stella Kramrisch, Kühnel, etc., *Die Aussereuropäische Kunst*, pl. VII (pp. 360-361).

[123] Pelliot, *Op. cit.*, plates LXXXVIII and CXXXIV-CXXXV.

cave 74, to the second quarter of the tenth; at this period the Uighur were temporarily masters of Tun-huang as they were of Turfan.[124]

Despite the fact that several of these are of great interest, one sometimes regrets that the Tun-huang paintings were for the most part merely the work of 'honest and pious craftsmen'. Other mural paintings, visited by Langdon Warner in the cave of Wan-fo-hsia, a three-days' march from Tun-huang, seem to be of higher quality. These are likewise Buddhist works, representing a *mandala* of Vairocana, a *pien-hsiang* of Maitreya, etc. Warner emphasizes the splendour of these mural paintings which, he tells us, are the work of true artists.[125] But it is not certain that these are paintings of the ninth century, as he at first thought. They may be rather works of the tenth century (period of the Five Dynasties) or may even date from the period when the Tun-huang March, like all Kansu, was a part of the Tangut or Hsi-Hsia kingdom, founded in this region by a tribe having Tibetan affinities, half Sinicized (1001-1227).

* * *

The Tun-huang mural paintings or paintings on fabric are the work of anonymous painters who are, as we must recognize, in most cases pious hagiographers rather than real masters. Masters nevertheless did exist and Chinese documents have not only transmitted their names to us but have also enlightened us as to the nature of their talent.[126] On the other hand, we can scarcely boast of knowing many authentic works by them.[127] Among the

[124] See also Eiichi Matsumoto, Li Sheng-tien, king of Khotan (938) and the Thousand Buddhas Caves at Tun-huang, *Kokka*, no. 140, 1925.

[125] Langdon Warner, *Buddhist Wall-Paintings. A Study of a Ninth-century Grotto at Wan Fo Hsia*, Harvard, 1938.

[126] L. Bachofer, Chinese Landscape Painting in the VIIIth Century, *Burlington Magazine*, Nov. 1935.

[127] The best reproductions of the masterpieces of Chinese painting are to be found in: *Tōyō Bujutsu Taikwan*, or *Masterpieces Selected from the Fine Arts*

great T'ang painters must be mentioned Yen Li-pen (died in 673) who lived at the court of emperors T'ai-tsung the Great and Kao-tsung and after whom the Boston Museum has at least copies (portraits of emperors and of scholars, psychologically powerful and solidly composed).[128] The following period produced the painter Li Ssu-hsün (651-716), who belonged to the imperial family of the T'ang, and his son Li Chao-tao who lived at the court of emperor Hsüan-tsung. The Freer Gallery has a landscape that may be the copy of a work by Li Ssu-hsün. It is, in any case, a landscape 'in which' according to Sirén, 'heaven and earth meet like the white clouds and the green mountains, and the sun paints a golden lining round every form'. We may observe that this is a landscape of pure enchantment recalling (except that here it is a work of talent) the visions of space hinted at in the background of the Buddhist paradises of the same period. So too the 'summer palace' attributed to Li Chao-tao, at the Boston Museum, presents with the brush of a real artist the same airy constructions and rearing mountain backgrounds that the honest craftsmen of Tun-huang had let us glimpse.[129] We may add that, through their love of colour, Yen Li-pen, Li Ssu-hsün and Li Chao-tao likewise have affinities with the art of Tun-huang.

Wu Tao-tzu (died about 760), regarded by all his contemporaries as a painter of genius and undoubtedly one of the greatest artists of the period of Hsüan-tsung, frequently sought his inspir-

---

of the Far East, vols. VIII-XII, Tokyo, 1910. Sirén, History of Early Chinese Painting. William Cohn, Chinese Painting, London, 1948.

[128] See, on behalf of the authenticity of the scroll of the Thirteen Emperors, K. Tomita's arguments in Sirén, loc. cit., I, pp. 57-58. K. Tomita's articles on the Chinese paintings of the Boston Museum have appeared in the Bulletin of the Museum of Fine Arts, nos. 155 (1928), 174 (1931), 177 (1932). On the portraits attributed to Yen Li-pen, see also Serge Elisseeff, Notes sur le portrait en Extrême-Orient, in Mélanges Linossier, vol, I, pl. 175, Musée Guimet, 1932.

[129] See Jeannine Auboyer, L'influence chinoise sur le paysage dans la peinture de l'Orient et dans la sculpture de l'Insulinde, Revue des Arts Asiatiques, IX, 4, pp. 228 ff.

ation in Buddhist subjects. The famous Kuan-yin seated in *lilāsana* on a rock on the seashore, at the Daitokuji Temple in Kyoto, was for a time attributed to him. Three kakemonos at the Tōfukuji, likewise in Kyoto, have also been attributed to him, representing respectively Śākyamuni, Mañjuśrī and Samantabhadra, although these paintings are actually Yüan. Such attributions, while they may reveal themselves to be ill-founded, nevertheless give one an idea, it may be, of the painter's subjects and manner.

Wang Wei (699-759) of whom we have spoken as a poet, was no less famous as a painter. We have seen that he too was inspired by Buddhism. Some Japanese or Chinese collections claim to have copies (or at least copies of copies) of his 'Clearing after Snowfall on the Hills by the River', and the Chishakuin, in Kyoto, presents under his name a cascade reproduced in all the anthologies but which, according to the best Japanese art critics, is certainly only a copy. Actually, in the absence of authentic pictorial works, we can form an idea of Wang Wei's feeling for nature as well as of his conception of landscape, on the basis of his poems. Did not the great Sung scholar Su T'ung-po say of him, 'In reading his poems, I discover in them a painting; in contemplating his paintings, I hear in them a poem'? The Sung artists, in fact, loved the old T'ang master because they tended to see in him (erroneously, most certainly) the inventor of the monochrome landscape (with Indian ink). But such assertions, even when proved wrong, none the less indicate the trend of Wang Wei, a trend towards broad impressionist landscapes, which later (in the Sung period) were to be executed in wash, in contrast to the still prevailing polychromy of the T'ang period. It is this difference that the geographically inadequate terms of 'School of the North' (polychrome school, placed under the name of Wu Tao-tzu) and 'School of the South' (monochrome school, under the name of Wang Wei) were intended to indicate.

48. *Kuan-yin, wood with traces of color. Eleventh century. British Museum, London.*

49. *Kuan-yin, wood. Yüan Dynasty, thirteenth century. Nelson Gallery of Art, Kansas City.*

CHAPTER FIVE

THE SUNG PERIOD

Fall of the T'ang. The Five Dynasties

Towards the end of T'ang rule, Chinese society was shaken by a grave economic crisis. Since the military disasters in Turkestan and in Yunnan that had marked the year 751, and especially since the terrible revolt of An-Lu-shan (755) and the civil war that followed (755-762), taxes, statute labour and military service had become so oppressive that people thought only of ways of evading their obligations.[1] In order to escape the levy by taking advantage of the immunity enjoyed by religious foundation, peasants would offer themselves to Buddhist convents as Church serfs, while sons of notables became monks. The resulting increase in mortmain property was one of the causes of the drastic secularization edict of 845 of which we have spoken.[2] In any case, the peasants were often reduced to selling up their holdings and to hiring themselves out as agricultural labourers to the nearest big landowner, on whom they became wholly dependent—if not literally as slaves, at least as agricultural labourers at the mercy

---

[1] The number of taxable families fell from 9,069,154 in 754 to 2,900,000 in 764. Cf. C. P. Fitzgerald, The Consequence of the Rebellion of An Lu-shan upon the population of the T'ang Dynasty, *Philobiblion*, Sept. 1947.
[2] Balazs, Beiträge zur Wirstschaftsgeschichte der T'ang-Zeit, *Mitteilungen des Seminars für orientalische Sprachen zu Berlin*, XXXV-XXXVI, 1932-1933, p. 20.

of their 'lord', that is to say, virtually as serfs. The disappearance of small property, hence of the class of really free peasants, was so swift that by the end of the eighth century, according to the writer Lu Chih (754-824), the families of landowners represented no more than 4 to 5 per cent of the total population.[3]

At the same time the monetary situation had become unhealthy. There was a shortage of currency and of copper coins. In order to meet the needs of trade, 'flying currency', that is to say paper money, had appeared, in the form of 'deposit tokens' which facilitated transactions.[4] But trade itself underwent grave perturbations when on successive occasions the Silk Road was cut by bands of Tibetans, while the Arab-Persian warehouses of Canton were pillaged by the peasant uprising of 879. The State on several occasions had recourse to issues which were considered counterfeit, upon which attempts real devaluation followed.[5]

Out of the wretchedness of the ruined peasants sprang terrible peasant revolts, such as the one headed by Huang Ch'ao, a disgruntled intellectual who organized insurgent bands (875) on the borders of Shantung, Hopei and Honan, and pillaged the great port of Fu Chou (878), then, as we have just said, that of Canton (879), and finally even the imperial capitals of Lo-yang and Ch'ang-an themselves (880-881).

The house of the T'ang could hardly survive this blow. In 907 it was deposed by a roving adventurer, and in its place five ephemeral dynasties succeeded one another in North China, with K'ai-feng as capital (907-959), while the south was divided among several provincial ruling houses.[6] Opposing the emperor of K'ai feng, there were thus independent kings in Nanking, Hangchow,

[3] Maspero, *Etudes Historiques*, Musée Guimet, 1950, p. 175.

[4] Balazs, *loc. cit.*, p. 37.

[5] *Ibid.*, pp. 30 ff.

[6] On the Turkish tribe of the Sha-t'o that founded one of the 'Five Dynasties' in North China—the ephemeral dynasty of the Hou-T'ang (923-936), with K'ai-feng as capital—see W. Eberhard, Some Cultural Traits of the Sha-t'o Turks, *Oriental Art*, I, 2, p. 50.

Canton, Szechwan, etc., for about half a century. Certain of these provincial courts (those of Nanking and Hangchow in particular) had, as we shall see, a real importance in the realm of art.

* * *

In the realm of art, the period of the Five Dynasties (907-959), a period of transition between the T'ang and the Sung, is one that cannot be neglected.

We may note first of all the sculptures on the tomb of a local prince of Szechwan, Wang Chien, who reigned over this province from 907 to 918. Situated at Ch'in-t'ai, in the suburbs of Chengtu, this tomb contains a statue in the round of Wang Chien himself, a realistic portrait with heavy eyebrows, hollow eyes and large ears, in which the rugged personality of the adventurer turned sovereign prince comes to life. Also in the round, there are statues of warriors, with armour and helmets variously decorated. Finally, in high relief, there are women musicians and dancers with round faces (in the T'ang style), of which the details of costume are of particular value, since the monument is dated.[7]

The period of the Five Dynasties is no less interesting from the point of view of Chinese painting.

The influence of the mystical Buddhism of the Ch'an sect expressed itself at this time, through the painters Kuan Hsiu (832-912) and Shih-K'o (tenth century), in powerful portraits of *arhats* or Buddhist saints, represented as old men of strange and almost disquieting intellectuality, or in figures of patriarchs with fiery eyes in the manner of the Bodhidharma (Ta-mo).[8] The painting

---

[7] Cheng Te-K'un, The Royal Tomb of Wang Chien, *Sinologica*, II, i (With plates).

[8] Cf. Carol Baumann, A Few Psychological Aspects of Ch'an Buddhism, *Artibus Asiae*, VIII, 2-4, p. 216. Also the study by Serge Elisseeff, Le Portrait en Extrême-Orient, *Mélanges Linossier*, Musée Guimet, 1932. We may recall that the intensity of the eyes in *Ch'an* painting is related to old animist conceptions.

of flowers and birds, subjects that were to undergo such development in subsequent art, was established by the Szechwanese Huang
Ch'üan, who flourished at the provincial court of Chengtu about
920-950, and by his emulator Hsü Hsi, a painter at the provincial
court of Nanking. The court of the kings of Nanking (937-
975) likewise attracted the painters Wang Ch'i-han and Chou
Wen-chü, both of whom had a predilection for. pleasant scenes
with pretty women and children. The art that then developed in
this provincial kingdom, in its tendency toward 'prettiness' and
perhaps finickiness, foreshadows certain aspects of Ming taste.
Hu Kuei, on the other hand, in whose manner the Boston Museum
has two fine Tartar horsemen, recalls the T'ang military paintings.
He was himself a Tartar, of the horde of the Ch'i-tan or Khitai,
then holding sway over Peking.

The painting of the Five Dynasties also created the monochrome landscape, with wash technique (using Indian ink), which
the Sung period was to develop to its apogee. As we shall see, this
new manner, in contrast to the love of colour of the T'ang period,
was influenced by the philosophical conceptions of Ch'an
Buddhism.

The masters of landscape (in Chinese: *shan-shui*, 'mountains
and waters')—of landscape thus conceived—are, for the period
of the Five Dynasties, Ching Hao, Kuan T'ung and Li Ch'eng,
all three of whom lived in North China (which proves that wash-
drawing is not necessarily a 'Southern School' as has been claimed). The paintings attributed to these three artists (Freer Gallery
and Boston Museum) have, for that matter, a powerful and

In the Chinese tradition it was by 'opening the eyes' of a portrait that the artist
'animated' (in the most literal sense of the word) the being represented. The
classically quoted example is that of the painter Chang Seng-yu (sixth century)
who, after having painted some dragons, 'opened' their eyes in this way: the
dragons, immediately coming to life, leaped from the painting and flew skyward,
not without reducing the whole building to cinders. Moreover, the funerary
tablets, the 'perpetual tablets' at least, were 'dotted', that is, decorated with dots
representing the eye and thus conferring life upon them.

almost rough technique ('sculptural' rendering of the mountains) which forms a transition, in the evolution of the landscape, between the crudeness of the T'ang and the flowing grace of the Sung.

Another transition painting, if this is really an original of the Five Dynasties, is the silk scroll in the Peking Museum, 'Stag and Does beneath the Red Maples of Autumn', which was one of the revelations of the Burlington House Exhibition in 1935. The elegance, the nobility, the pride of this herd remind us of the genius of the T'ang masters of animal representation. The shimmer of the autumn colours on the maple leaves ranging from green to reddish brown through shades of pink and grey is also an echo of the love of colour that characterized the T'ang painters, but the softening of the tints is a harbinger of more sophisticated tastes. The 'melancholy of autumn landscapes' that they convey already suggests the great Sung masters. How quiveringly sensitive is this revelation of the 'secrets of the forest'! 'A herd of brown deer sheltering in a forest of maples with their luxuriant green leaves turning to autumnal red, is startled by the approach of man. An antlered stag, full of power and virility, stands in an attitude of wariness, taut and quivering as a drawn bow, about to give the signal of alarm. The hinds, shy, appealing, delicate-footed, regard us with a look of mingled fear and reproach in their startled eyes. Nowhere is the disturber of the woodland peace disclosed...' [9]

The Five Dynasties had two centres of ceramic production. In the north, in K'ai-feng, the annalists tell us, emperor Shih-tsung (954-959) of the Hou-Chou dynasty ordered from his potters a porcelain 'blue as the sky, bright as a mirror, thin as paper and having the resonance of a musical stone'. In the South, the celadons of porcellaneous stoneware, the so-called Yüeh ware from

[9] Sir Percival David, Chinese Exhibition (1935), *Revue des Arts Asiatiques*, IX, 4, p. 175. Cf. Sirén, *History of Early Chinese Painting*, I, pl. 64. *Catalogue of the Exhibition of Chinese Art*, No. 755.

Chekiang, a specialty that, as we saw, was created in the T'ang period, now became the *pi-se yao*, a pottery reserved for the kings of Wu Yüeh of the Ch'ien family, a provincial dynasty which governed Chekiang, with Hangchow as its capital, from 907 to 978.[10]

We may note, to conclude, that the provincial dynasties of the South, at the beginning of the tenth century, were also outstanding in architecture. We owe to them the charming stone pagoda of the Ch'i-hsia-ssu, near Nanking.[11] But in 'imperial' China, the China of the North, emperor Shih-tsung of the Hou-Chou dynasty promulgated in 955 a severe edict against Buddhist monasticism (imposing restrictions on entry into monasteries, and ordering the closing of monasteries and even the destruction of a great number of pagodas etc.) Fortunately for Buddhism, the house of the Hou-Chou was deposed five years later by the great dynasty of the Sung.

The Period of the Sung and the Confucianist Reaction

In 960 there came to the throne in North China, in K'ai-feng, a great national dynasty, that of the Sung, which in a few years restored the unity of China by putting an end to the provincial kingdoms that had divided the South.

Sung rule (960-1276) is divided into two periods: the first, from 960 to 1126, in which the Sung reigned over all China (except for the Peking region and Kansu), with K'ai-feng as their capital; the second, from 1127 to 1276, when the Sung, having lost North China to the Tartars, reigned only over South China, with Hangchow as their capital.

Even when its territories still included nearly all China proper, the Sung dynasty, renouncing external conquests, did not have

[10] On the difference between the pottery of the North and the pottery of the South throughout Chinese history, see Koyama, La Céramique chinoise, style du Sud et style du Nord, *Bijutsu Kenkyū*, 4, CLVII, pp. 1-28.

[11] Sirén, *History of Early Chinese Art*, IV, *Architecture*, pl. 87.

the interest in the outside world that was characteristic of the
T'ang period. Apart from this, the penetration of Islam into
Kashgar since around the year 1000 and, from about the same
date, the conquests of the Moslems in India, and finally the
progressive disappearance of Buddhism in the latter country, were
all upheavals that were to cut off the Chinese from the Indian
world and cause them to fall back on their own civilization.

It thus came about that the Sung epoch, throughout both periods, was an age of Confucianist reaction. However, the preaching of Buddhism had now been continuous for several centuries, a long enough time for it to have become assimilated,
to become Chinese. Thus the codification of Chinese thought
which triumphant Confucianism now proceeded to shape into its
final form was actually, although perhaps without conscious in-
tent, a true syncretism of Buddhist, Taoist and Confucian
thought.[12]

The Sung scholars, triumphing in this return to Confucianism,
were nevertheless determined to base their doctrine on a critical
and relatively objective interpretation of the canonical texts. Thus
the great scholar Ou-yang Hsiu (1007-1072) undertook to 'expur-
gate from the commentaries on the classics all interpretations of
a philosophic-religious character drawn from the *wei-shu* of the
Han. He raised doubts as to the authenticity of the traditional
commentary of the *Shih-ching*, thereby inaugurating a more critical attitude with regard to the canonicals'. Likewise the famous
philosopher and historian Chu Hsi (1130-1200) and with him
numerous scholars 'began to suspect the "ancient text" of the
Shu-ching, which is in fact a falsified text. Chu Hsi also eliminated

[12] There was, however, no persecution of the Buddhist cult under the Sung.
It was then that the famous T'ieh-t'a pagoda (or 'iron' pagoda, because of its red
brick), which dates from 963-967, was built. Cf. Sirén, *History of Early Chinese
Art*, IV, *Architecture*, pl. 73). And towards the end of the dynasty we likewise
have the erection in Ch'üan-chou (Fukien)—which is the great port of Zayton,
admired by Marco Polo and Odoric de Pordenone—of the two large octagonal
stone pagodas, with inscriptions of 1228 and 1247 (Sirén, *Ibid.*, pl. 84. Cf. G.
Ecke and P. Demiéville, *The Twin Pagodas of Zayton*, Harvard, 1935).

the preface of the *Shih-ching* from his edition of this classic, because he did not consider it authentic. He devoted himself to setting forth clearly the general meaning of the passages studied, without however neglecting the philological point of view'.[13] In short we see here, in the study of texts, the birth of a critical instinct comparable to that of our first humanists.

There can be little doubt that this medieval criticism of texts led to conclusions that modern criticism would refute. Such was the case with the scholar Fan Chung-yen (989-1052) who was of the opinion 'that the *I-ching* expressed the ideas of Confucius, whereas the *Ch'un-ch'iu* represented his practical teaching'. But the main concern was to rationalize the Confucian tradition, and it is this state of mind that is interesting. Moreover, in conformity with the spirit of ancient Confucianism, the Neo-Confucianism that was thus being elaborated remained dedicated to wholly civic and social ends. 'It was in the *Ch'un-ch'iu* that Sun Fo (about 1050) discovered the secrets of the prosperity of States, and Ou-yang Hsiu a solid basis for civic morality.'

Indeed these scholars, henceforth closely linked with government, from the highest ministerial functions in the immediate entourage of the sovereign, to provincial administration, brought to the reading of the classics and to the commentaries which they compiled for them, a realistic and positive, not to say positivist spirit. Men of the library, undeniably, but at the same time experienced in practical affairs, the great Sung scholars were almost all, in one way or another, intellectuals who were, as we say today, 'committed'.

Such a one was the reformer Wang An-shih (1021-1086). In 1075 he promulgated by imperial edict a decision concerning the three canonical books, the *Shih-ching*, the *Shu-ching* and the *Chou-li*, to the effect that the only authorized commentaries would be those that he himself had composed under the suggestive title of 'New Meaning of the Three Classics' (*San-ching hsin-i*). In

¹³ O. Kaltenmark, *Littérature chinoise*, p. 83.

50. *Wang Meng (died 1385): Landscape (details). Ink and color on paper. Freer Gallery of Art, Washington.*

51. *Ni Tsan* *(1301–1374): Landscape, dated 1362 (detail). Ink on paper. Freer Gallery of Art, Washington.*

the same spirit, he eliminated from the examinations the purely literary tests and replaced them by practical subjects (law, political economy). The planned economy which he introduced was, in fact, the practical application of the social theories of traditional Confucianism. Before him, other Sung ministers had already organized a public welfare system and adumbrated what we would call a social security programme. Wang An-shih pushed social insurance and planned economy to the point of a veritable state socialism (crop loans, price control, law of maximum profit, etc.) [14] A minister from 1069 to 1074 and again from 1075 to 1085, he was able, with the support of emperor Shen-tsung, to apply his reform programme, but was finally forced to relinquish power before the opposition of the conservatives.

The chiefs of the conservative party were also scholars: Ouyang Hsiu, already mentioned (1007-1072), Ssu-ma Kuang (1019-1086) and Su Tung-p'o (1036-1101). Hostile to Wang An-shih's state socialism (in particular as regards crop loans), they were by no means opposed to the laws on social aid, which were then unanimously accepted.

Ssu-ma Kuang gave to neo-Confucianist traditionalism a majestic foundation in composing his monumental *Historical Mirror (Tzu-chih t'ung-chien)*, completed in 1084, the first manual of Chinese history to be obtained by compiling the successive dynastic histories; a work, moreover, in the Confucian manner which, despite a remarkable topo-chronological precision, is consistently concerned with civic education and moral enlightenment, as the very title announces, proclaiming that it has been composed 'in order to help govern'.[15]

Sung thought is characterized by the founding of a powerful

---

[14] H. R. Williamson, *Wang An-shih, a Chinese Statesman and Educationalist of the Sung Dynasty*, London, 1935-1937.—Tcheou Hoan, *Le prêt sur la récolte et Wang Ngan-che*, Paris, 1930.

[15] See Robert Des Rotours, *Le traité des examens*, pp. 74-81.—We may recall that Ssu-ma Kuang's compilation covers the period from 403 B.C. to 959 A.D., the eve of the accession of the Sung.

philosophical school, of a strictly Confucianist description, but one which, having assimilated the metaphysical conceptions of Taoism and Buddhism, brought to the ancient Confucian 'positivism' what it still lacked: a fully-fledged philosophical system. As has been said—although the comparison is somewhat strained—it is Auguste Comte 'crowned' by Herbert Spencer's *First Principles*.

As a precursor of this great movement, mention should first be made of the exegetist and mathematician Shao Yung (1011-1077). Strongly imbued with Taoism and Buddhism, Shao Yung, taking the commentary on the *I-ching* as the basis of his teaching, sought to discover in the heart (*hsin*), that is to say in the absolute self, the equivalent of Buddha-hood as also of the *tao* or, as he expressed it, the Supreme Ultimate (*t'ai-chi*). 'Always quoting Confucius, he thought like Lao-tzu'. But the synthesis of the three doctrines was not yet complete in his case, since its various elements could still be distinguished.[16] It was left to a contemporary of Shao Yung, Chou Tun-i, to present a neo-Confucianist syncretism which had absorbed Buddhist and Taoist metaphysics to such a degree that the suspicions of the scholars would no longer be awakened.[17]

Chou Tun-i (1017-1073) did in fact fully develop the concept of the 'Supreme Ultimate' (*T'ai-chi*), the primary principle of all things, the cause and the purpose of the evolution of the universe. Like all Neo-Confucianists, he went back to a very ancient concept, borrowed from primitive cosmogony, which enabled him to invoke the authority of the *I-ching*. In reality, as we have seen in connection with Shao Yung, the supreme principle thus conceived could appear as such only to thinkers already familiar with the Taoist concept of the Absolute (the *Tao* according to Chuang-tzu), as with the concept of 'Absolute Nature' or im-

---

[16] Maspero, *Les religions chinois*, p. 106.
[17] Fung Yu-Lan, Rise of Neo-Confucianism and its Borrowings from Buddhism and Taoism, *Harvard Journal of Asiatic Studies*, April, 1942.

manent Essence of the universe (*bhūta tathatā*) according to the Buddhism of the T'ien-t'ai.

The system in question was developed by the two brothers Ch'eng Hao (1032-1085) and Ch'eng I (1033-1107). It was immortalized by Chu Hsi (1130-1200).[18]

Chu Hsi was active, and showed equal mastery, in three fields: in philosophy, in the criticism of canonical texts or Confucian exegesis, and in historical synthesis.

As a thinker, Chu Hsi has given us the philosophical *Summa* of his time. At the origin of things he places Non-Being (*Wu-chi*), in reality universal potentiality, since it is from this that the First Principle (*T'ai-chi*) emerges and frees itself—the universal Substance, in other words, in its still undifferentiated plenitude. Similar to the *Tao* of the Neo-Taoists, or to the supreme *Brahman* of Hindu thought, the T'ai-chi, in differentiating itself, gives rise to and, up to a certain point, temporarily becomes the world of matter as well as the world of spirit. These two worlds both proceed from universal Energy (*ch'i*), which is nothing other than the universal urge of the *T'ai-chi*, a cosmic urge, a vital urge, soul of souls and of worlds. It is difficult to avoid noting how close such concepts are to Indian metaphysics, in this case to Brahmanic philosophy, already propagated in China (in the T'ang period) by Buddhism, even when Buddhism was fighting it. What seems at first sight more specifically Chinese is the importance given by Chu Hsi to the combined laws of nature (*li*) that dictate this whole evolution, 'necessary' laws which, through a mechanistic determinism deriving from the intermeshing of cause and effect, free absolute being from universal potentiality, and then oblige it to emit its Energy and to regulate the flow of

---

[18] Le Gall, *Le philosophe Tchou Hi*, Shanghai, 1894. J. Percy Bruce, *Chu Hsi and his Masters, an Introduction to the Chu Hsi and the Sung School of Chinese Philosophy*, London, 1923. J. P. Bruce, *The Philosophy of Human Nature by Chu Hsi*, London, 1922. Fung Yu-Lan, Philosophy of Chu Hsi, *Harvard Journal of Asiatic Studies*, April, 1942. W. E. Hocking, Chu Hsi's Theory of Knowledge, *ibid*, p. 109.

this Energy in accordance with an evolutionary process, which, in its passage from the homogeneous to the heterogeneous, is both logical and inevitable, and which causes the worlds and the creatures that inhabit them to appear in sequence, one after the other. Such phases of evolution and of creation, however, by virtue of the same determinism, are succeeded by periods of involution and of regression, of return from the heterogeneous to the homogeneous, which bring things back to the primordial indeterminate. Periods of creation and periods of destruction thus succeed one another mechanically through time eternal.

A Chinese philosopher friend of ours has pointed out to us that Chu Hsi had thus anticipated the quite modern conception according to which the cosmos 'breathes' with a gigantic rhythm, through phases of 'universe in expansion' and of 'universe in contraction', from the primordial atom to the galaxies, from the galaxies back again to the Abbé Lemaître's and Paul Couderc's single atom. What we observe, in any case, is that this rhythm of cosmic breathing is first and foremost an Indian conception, a Brahmanic concept, linked to the periodic sleeping and awaking of Viṣṇu.[19]

Chu Hsi's system could never have become the official system of the School of Scholars (*Ju-chiao*), the very codification of Neo-Confucianism, if it had not shown that the entire traditional code of ethics could be deduced from these first principles, if it had not established unshakably on these scientific foundations the very bases of society. In point of fact, the rigorous determinism that he developed enabled him, in social and individual

---

[19] Compare the theory of 'creation, conservation and dissolution of the world' in the Hindu Vedanta (Oltramare, *Théosophie brahmanique*, Musée Guimet, 1906, pp. 181 ff.) and the similar theory in Chu Hsi (trans. Le Gall, pp. 99 ff.) The 'bridge' is provided by the Buddhist treatise *Abbhidharma kośa śastra* by Vasubandhu, a Sanskrit text widely distributed in China, which, in order to combat the Hindu thesis, expounds it in obliging detail. (René Grousset, *Les philosophies indiennes*, I, p. 174). May we recall that the *Abbhidharma kośa śastra* had been translated into Chinese (under the title *A-p'i-ta-mo chiu-she shih lun*) by Paramārtha (died 569) and by Hsüan-tsang (died 664).

ethics, to arrive at the equivalent of our Kantian categorical imperative. He holds that the moral law, for each one of us, is but the emanation of the laws of nature and our participation in these laws. Universal determinism imperatively determines our submission to the laws of the civic State and to virtue. It is an application, on a grandiose scale, of the ancient Confucian conception of the harmony between 'earth' and 'heaven', with its identification of the cosmic and the moral orders.

We need not be astonished if Chinese thought felt itself at home in Chu Hsi's system; if, despite the unconscious borrowing that he may have made from what Neo-Confucianist thought had assimilated of Taoism and of Indianity, he was considered the very incarnation of Neo-Confucianism. He had transformed the most ancient 'Confucian' conceptions into a complete philosophical system, thus deservedly being regarded in future centuries as the incarnation of Chinese thought, even as Aristotle was regarded by the men of the Middle Ages as the incarnation of Greek thought, and as Saint Thomas is still in our eyes the incarnation of mediaeval thought.

In the realm of exegesis, Chu Hsi, as we have seen, rejected the traditional preface of the *Shih-ching* from his edition of the classics because he considered it (and rightly so) to be a falsification. Apart from this, it was he who combined the 'Analects of Confucius' (the *Lun-yü*) 'The Great Learning' (*Ta-hsüeh*), 'The Doctrine of the Mean' (*Chung-yung*) and 'The Book of Mencius' (*Meng-tzu*) to form the collection known as the 'Four Books' (*Ssu Shu*), which became thenceforward the definitive basis for all official teaching.

Finally Chu Hsi revised and abridged Ssu-ma Kuang's historical compilation by writing, in 59 chapters, the *T'ung-chien kang-mu*, a manual of Chinese history dated 1172, the main part of which covers the period between 403 B.C. and 959 A.D.[20] This

---

[20] The period previous to 403 was added by a disciple of Chu Hsi.

is the work of historical synthesis that served so long, from Mailla to Wieger, as a basis for our studies.

* * *

Several of the philosophers and statesmen whom we have named above were also writers of talent. Ou-yang Hsiu and Su Tung-p'o are regarded as the best prose-writers of the period. Ou-yang Hsiu (1007-1072), in collaboration with Sung Ch'i, wrote the 'New History of the T'ang' (*Hsin T'ang shu*), which was completed in 1060 and immediately printed. He has also left us in prose 'some essays on landscapes that are very appealing'.[21] Apart from his impressionist descriptions in prose, the anthologies always include his verses, both those in the style of the old T'ang poetry (*shih*) and those in the new style (*tz'u*) which became popular with the Sung and which were poems written to be sung to music for which the author composed the melody as well as the words.[22] In verse as in prose, Ou-yang Hsiu's descriptions of scenery recall the painting of the same period.

Su Tung-p'o, also known by the name of Su Shih (1036-1101), who was, and still is, regarded as an authority on art history and art criticism,[23] has also left us picturesque descriptive essays. All the anthologies include the account of his two excursions to the 'Red Cliff', a famous piece of scenery on the banks of the Yangtze in Hupei, or his journey to the Mountain of the Stone Bell on the shores of Lake Po-yang.[24] Su Tung-p'o's

[21] See in Margouliès, *Le Kou-wen*, pp. 257 ff., and by the same, *Anthologie de la littérature chinoise*, p. 363, various translations of the poetic prose of Ou-yang Hsiu, relating travel impressions, full of picturesqueness and sensitivity ('Story of the Cottage of the Drunken Old Man', 'Sounds of autumn', etc.).

[22] See Feng Shu-lan, *La technique et l'histoire du ts'eu*, Paris, 1935.

[23] See Sirén, *History of Early Chinese Painting*, I, pp. 112, 116 etc.

[24] Translations in Margouliès, *Le Kou-wen*, p. 292, and *Anthologie de la littérature chinoise*, p. 385. See also Lin Yu-tang, *The Gay Genius. The Life and Times of Su Tung-p'o*, London, 1948. Le Gros Clark, *Selections from the Works*

verses have the same sources of inspiration. He is an archeologist as well as a poet, and no one has evoked the melancholy of ruins more movingly:

South of the old town, ten leagues beyond the walls,
The murmur of a spring can be heard between the rocks by the road.
In the distance stands a temple. You must dismount from your horse to get a better view.
If you proceed to the foot of the temple, you discover the spring.
The earth is fertile; the grasses and the trees are startlingly green.
The old thujas grow thick, casting a blue shade...
... Here men have fought for centuries.
The whole population has left for other parts, the old battlements have been levelled.
The autumn grasses spread their greenness that blankets the empty walls.
All is abolished, there remain only the vestiges of the past.
All is peaceful and silent in the mountains and on the river.
I have come here, I have climbed up to see, I have sighed.
My white hairs have been reflected for a moment in the pure spring.
The birds sing, the men have left, the gates of the temple are closed.
Only the moon of the mountains ever strays here, solitary.[25]

Painting under the Sung

We noted that during the period of the Five Dynasties land-scape painting (literally 'mountains and waters', *shan-shui*), had seen the introduction of monochrome painting or wash-drawing

---

of *Su Tung-p'o*, London, 1931; and *The Prose Poetry of Su Tung-p'o*, Shanghai, 1935. Teng Ku, Su Tung-p'o als Kunstkritiker, *Ostasiatische Zeitschrift*, VIII, 1932, p. 104.
[25] Margouliès, *Anthologie*, p. 376.

in Indian ink.* But it was the Sung masters who immortalized this genre. For the idealized painting that they were to practise, wash constituted the most adequate mode of expression. 'The tones of Indian ink, skilfully varied, merging into or contrasting with the spaces left blank, brought out the essential planes of the landscape; the mist which the painters knew how to make use of so adroitly, conferred upon the scenes painted a magic detached from everything material'.[26]

In order fully to understand the technique of these wash-drawings we must remember the unchanging rules of Chinese perspective. The best description of it remains that of Raphael Petrucci: 'Chinese perspective... was evolved in an age when the method of superimposing different registers to indicate different planes was still being practised in bas-reliefs. The succession of planes, one above the other, when codified, led to a system totally different from our monocular perspective. It resulted in a perspective as seen from a height. No account is taken of the habitual height of the eye in relation to the picture. The line of the horizon is placed very high, parallel lines, instead of joining at the horizon, remain parallel, and the different planes range one above the other in such a way that the eye embraces a vast space...'—a panoramic space, so to say—. 'To this linear perspective is added moreover an atmospheric perspective. Having elected from a very early time to paint in monochrome, Chinese painters were led by the nature of this medium to seek to express atmospheric perspective by means of tone values and harmony of shading instead of by colour. Thus they were familiar with chiaroscuro before the European painters. Wang Wei established the principles of atmospheric perspective in the eighth century. He explains how tints are graded, how the increasing layers of air deprive distant objects of their true colouring, substituting a bluish tinge, and how forms become indis-

---

* Indian ink, in French: *encre de Chine* (translator's note).
[26] Serge Elisseeff, *Histoire universelle de l'art* (Réau), Vol. IV, p. 337.

52. Above: *Chao Méng-fu (1245-1322): A Sheep and a Goat. Ink on paper. Freer Gallery of Art, Washington.* Below: *Chao Yung (born 1289): Horse and Groom in a Red Coat. Ink and color on paper. Freer Gallery of Art, Washington.*

tinct in proportion as their distance from the observer increases'.[27] Indian ink readily lent itself to these conceptions. Diluted with water in varying proportions according to the relative importance of the planes and in places applied with 'cloud-like' reserves, it enabled the painter to give full value to the mists and impalpable vapours which, when interposed between the foreground and the distances, invested these with mystery and dream-like suggestiveness.

The landscape thus conceived reflected the influence of the mystical idealism that the Buddhist sect of the Ch'an had propagated since the T'ang.

We have spoken of the origins of this sect, the name of which is simply the Chinese transcription of Sanskrit *dhyāna*, 'meditation', 'contemplation', and whose doctrine was supposed to have first been preached after the first quarter of the sixth century by the Indian missionary Bodhidharma (in Chinese: Ta-mo). It was not, however, until a century later, in the time of its sixth patriarch, Hui-neng (637-713, patriarch in 675), that its doctrines were finally formulated. According to Suzuki, Hui-neng must in fact be considered to be the real founder of Ch'an Buddhism, both because of his doctrine of intuition (the apprehending in ourselves of our own 'true nature', which will reveal itself to be a 'Buddha-nature') and because of his method (the 'abrupt' or 'instantaneous' teaching—in Sanskrit: *yugapad*, in Chinese: *tun-chiao*), a doctrine and a method, Suzuki observes, that are purely Chinese.[28] It is indeed difficult not to see in them unconscious reminiscences of Taoism.

Even though emperor Chung-tsung (705-710) extended his favour to Hui-Neng, the T'ang period was of too realistic a character for Ch'an to have exerted much influence. It was a time when, as we have seen, other forms of Buddhism prevailed. In

[27] Raphael Petrucci, *Chinese Painters*, translated by Frances Seaver, New York, 1920, pp. 29, 30.

[28] Suzuki, *Essays in Zen Buddhism*, First Series, in the Collected Series, London, 1950, pp. 216-226.

the Sung art coteries, on the other hand, Ch'an mysticism found a favourable setting and was to make its influence felt to the full.[29] Where, if not here, might one expect to find a better understanding of the pure dhyānic doctrine—the doctrine according to which 'Buddha-hood', that is to say the spiritual essence of things, is the same in everything, is inherent in man as in animal, in the tree as in the rock? (We are familiar with the way in which, in Zen gardens, devotions were made to the 'personality' of every rock that forms a part of the miniature yet vast landscape).[30] Where, if not here, might one expect to find a better appreciation of the dhyānic affirmation that it is the voice of Illumination that speaks to us in the dialogue of birds, in the roar of torrents, in the moaning of the wind in the pine-groves?

Like the Ch'an contemplatives, the Sung painters were to spend much time 'meditating on nature'. They were to 'lay bare its spirit' and it was 'the spirit of nature' that they were to reveal to us. They were to recreate nature for us, not in an artificial and academic manner, to be sure, but so to speak metaphysically, after having purified it of its materiality (whence the abandonment of colour) by removing almost every concrete feature and retaining nothing but its hidden spirituality and its pure essence.

Landscape thus conceived truly became, as Serge Elisseeff notes, the expression of a soul-state, of a mood (*chi-yün*) induced by the composition itself, and also, according to the Sanskrit formula, the expression of a mystical communion (*samādhi*). It became a 'subjective landscape'.[31] Because he abolishes time and number the dhyanist, as Arthur Waley remarks, has at one stroke reduced the universe to unity, the landscape to unanimity.

[29] See Carol Baumann, A few psychological aspects of Ch'an Buddhism, *Artibus Asiae*, VIII, 2-4, p. 216.
[30] See in particular Tsuyoshi Tamura, *Jardins japonais*, Tokyo, 1939, pp. 27 & 45.
[31] Chou Ling, *La sagesse chinoise*, Paris, 1946, p. 44.

The concrete once dissociated from it, the universe ceases to be anything other than the universal soul.[32] Inspired by these conceptions, Sung wash-drawing was to transpose nature (to use the Buddhist formulas once more) on the 'plane of ideals' (*dharmadhātu*), to the state of all-ideality (*Cittamātra, vjiañamātra*). The visions of space in which the Sung masters were to delight were such as to express the sentiment, both Ch'an and Taoist, that things are but ideality, that all the apparent concrete is but an 'assemblage of mists'. Cloud, haze, mist—mist above all—is in Buddhism as in Taoism the very image of universal impermanence and insubstantiality. (The concept of impermanence, in the texts of both religions, is evoked in every line).[33] Behind the interposed mists that separate the various planes in the Sung wash-drawings, the mountains themselves float as if they had no real existence. All concreteness becomes dissolved, to reveal, in the very heart of the universal void of Buddhism (*śūnyatā*) which lies behind the moving veil of 'this world of dew', a glimpse of the ancient *tao* of Chuang-tzu, which is identical with the supreme *t'ai-chi* of the Chu Hsi school: the essence of the cosmos, the ultimate reality.[34]

[32] Arthur Waley, *Zen Buddhism in its Relation to Art*, pp. 21 and 24.

[33] See for example among many texts the *Dharma-samuccaya (Compendium de la Loi bouddhique)*.

[34] It is strange to note that the metaphysical flight over the realm of nature to which the Sung landscape painters of dhyanic or Ch'an inspiration invite us furnishes us real 'aircraft views' of the face of the earth, a universe perceived or half-made-out from beyond the clouds. Compare in this respect the landscapes of the last 'Sung painter', alive at the present time, the old Japanese master Taikan whose exhibition in Tokyo in 1949 we had the privilege of admiring, and certain albums of views taken from aircraft, for example that of Afred Curry (*A travers les nuages*) or that of Chombart de Lauwe, *Découverte aérienne du monde*, Paris, 1948. The analogy is often striking... On the Chinese equivalents of our perspective and on 'the Chinese eye', see in particular: Raphael Petrucci, *Philosophie de la nature dans l'art d'Extrême-Orient*, Paris, 1911. *Idem*, in his monumental translation of the *Kiai tseu yuan houa tchouan* or *Encyclopédie de la peinture chinoise*, Paris, 1912. Wang Wei (attributed to), *Révélation des secrets de la peinture*, trans. Serge Elisseeff in *Revue des Arts Asiatiques*, Dec. 1927. Otto Fischer, *Chinesische Landschaftsmalerei*, Munich, 1923. Ludwig Bachofer,

It would, however, be excessive to see in such aesthetic conceptions the influence of Ch'an Buddhism alone. The great cosmic dream of the Taoists was along the same line, and so was *Ju-chiao* monism. Like the metaphysics of Chu Hsi, the Sung wash-drawing expressed in its own manner the fusion of the most ancient Chinese traditions with the Buddhist contributions, which had by this time become assimilated as an integral part of Chinese aesthetics as well as of Chinese philosophy.

* * *

In the early years of the Sung dynasty we find three good landscapists attracting attention at the court of K'ai-feng: Hsü Tao-ning, Tung Yüan (a Buddhist monk who had come in 975 from Nanking to K'ai-feng) and Fan Kuan (born about the middle of the tenth century, died after 1026). Under the name of Tung Yüan the Boston Museum owns an admirable fragment called 'A Clear Day in the Valley', an impressionistic panorama, remarkably well balanced. 'We travel—first in a ferry across the broad river', writes Sirén, 'then along the road that winds among the trees on the promontory, and finally on the mountain path which leads up to the temple, faintly visible at the bottom of the misty gorge. The peaceful grandeur of the whole scenery is brought out with rare force and concentration; it impresses us as a symphonic composition, or an epic description of the great mountains and waters... The mist and the water form, so to say, the bridge to the infinite... But the big masses of mountains and

---

'Die Raumdarstellung in der chinesischen Malerei, *Münchner Jahrbücher der Bildende Kunst*, 1931. B. March, Linear Perspective in Chinese Painting, *Eastern Art*, III, Philadelphia, 1931. A. Waley, *An Introduction to the History of Chinese Painting*, London, 1923. Chiang Yee, *The Chinese Eye*, London, 1935. S. Kanahara, *Studies in the Theory of Painting in Ancient China*, Tokyo, 1924. O. Sirén, *The Chinese on the Art of Painting*, Peking, 1936. Okumura Ikura, La montagne dans les peintures chinoises, in the review *Yurinasu*, Tokyo, 1939. George Rowley, *The Principles of Chinese Painting*, Princeton University, 1948.

XVI. *Vase, famille verte. Ch'ing Dynasty, 1622-1772. Musée Guimet, Paris.*

the clusters of the dark trees are painted with a firm and resolute brush which gives to every detail its full volume'.[35]

As for Fan Kuan, he abandoned the lessons of the learned in order to attend solely the school of the hills and forests, to 'study the soul of the mountain'. Over his name the Boston Museum shows two wash-drawings in the form of fans (or 'screens'), 'Trees and Rocks' and 'Snow on the River-bank', of a penetratingly poetic quality. The second of these, a small painting 10 inches wide, nevertheless conveys an intense impression, with its snow-covered heights, its bare and twisted trees and 'the moisty winter air', as Sirén says, 'from which the contours of the distant mountains barely emerge'. The other 'fan' is again a winter landscape with huge trees that have 'bare trunks with big roots that penetrate amidst the snow-covered rocks', a work of 'uncommonly bold and large design' no matter from whose hand it may have come (it does not seem to be by the same painter as the previous one).[36]

To the following generation belongs Kuo Hsi (about 1020-1090). He was born in Honan. His contemporaries praised in him a powerful and original feeling for nature: his mountains, we are told, coiled like clouds, like serpents. His rocks were crouched like tigers ready to leap, or else had the look of demoniacal heads. His bare trees stretched or twisted their branches like the claws of beasts of prey. Among the works that can be attributed to him, on the basis of such testimony, with least improbability, is the scroll in the Freer Gallery called 'Autumn Day in the Valley of the Yellow River'. Here again we have a vast panorama with enormous mossy rocks standing up like 'menhirs', and bare, knotted trees like weird monsters.[37]

[35] Sirén, *Chinese Paintings in American Collections*, Annales du Musée Guimet, Bibliothèque d'Art, Nouvelle Série, 2 vols., Paris, Brussels, 1928, Vol. I, pls. 22-24. *Idem, History of Early Chinese Painting*, Vol. I, pp. 133-134, pls. 94-96.
[36] *Idem, Chinese Paintings in American Collections*, Vol. I, pls. 12 and 17. *Early History of Chinese Painting*, I, pl. 100.
[37] *Idem, Chinese Paintings in American Collections*, Vol. I, pls. 27-29.

While Kuo Hsi's paintings have nearly all been lost, his son has collected his remarks on art. This is a text entitled 'Great Message of the Forests and Rivers' (*Lin ch'üan kao-chih*), introduced by a 'Commentary on mountains and rivers', that is to say on landscape painting (Shan-shui hsün).[38] The deep sources of Sung sensibility, of Sung impressionism, are here directly revealed to us as this master of the brush passes on to us the secrets gained from long experience. The interest of such a text lies in the fact that its precision of technical detail, its indications as to how a thing is done, by no means detract from the aesthetic sensibility it conveys. The virtuoso who teaches his pupils the practice of his craft, those methods whereby representations of mountains and waters, trees and clouds, may be given their full value, remains a poet in ecstasy before the clouds and trees, the waters and the mountains. Herein lies the difference between this kind of 'artist's notebook' and the treatises on painting of the Ming or Ch'ing periods, the difference between Sung spontaneity and later academicism. *Sung art is a living art.* Kuo Hsi himself proclaims it: 'Water (in a painting) which does not flow and murmur may be called dead water. Clouds which are not alive may be called frozen clouds'. He ridicules, in the work of a contemporary painter, 'mountains, on which one cannot distinguish the clear from the dark parts' and which have no 'mist or shade'. 'Mountains without mist and cloud', he proclaims, 'are like a spring without flowers and grass'. Unwearyingly, he repeats to us that 'water is a thing alive', and that the mountain is like a human being.

Not of least interest is the kind of picturesque geography, with precise details, that he gives us as he recounts his travels

[38] Translation in Sirén, *History of Early Chinese Painting*, II, pp. 14-22. Also see A. Waley, *An Introduction to the History of Chinese Painting*, pp. 189-194. And a more recent translation, *Kuo Hsi, An Essay on Landscape Painting (Lin ch'üan kao-chih)*, translated by Shio Sakanishi, London, 1935. See also Soper, Some Technical Terms in the Early Literature of Chinese Painting, *Harvard Journal of Asiatic Studies*, 1948, p. 163.

through the various Chinese provinces and his visits to famous sites.

Kuo Hsi's fundamental idea, Sirén observes, the idea of the intimate communion between the artist and the very soul of nature, animates and explains all Sung painting. His sense of space and of atmospheric perspective, too, was to inspire most of the landscape painters of this great period. Even more than the mountains and waters, space is a living thing for the Sung painters. It is all life and all spirituality. In nearly all the Sung paintings it remains the principal subject. Space is here a presence.

But what varied talents there are in this galaxy! Mi Fei (1051-1107) for example, had his own manner. Enormous mossy rocks standing up like menhirs and roughly sketched, or corners of forests submerged in cotton-wool mists. It is exemplified by a scroll in the Peking Museum: in the foreground a group of pine trees; on the horizon a great crested wave of peaks, half seen through the mist and drowning all the intermediate space.[39] A scroll in the Freer Gallery has the same character: a forest river in the foreground; further off, the crests of rounded mountain peaks, separated by trails of mist rising from the valleys.[40] By contrast, Chao Ta-nien, a lord of the imperial family of the Sung (circa 1080-1100), works in a minute style. His name is mentioned in connection with a round fan called 'The Pavilion under the Willows' today in the Boston Museum, a little masterpiece in which the wash-drawing has the finish of a miniature: on the bend of a creek, at the foot of a hill the summit of which

[39] Sirén, History of Early Chinese Painting, II, pl. 5.
[40] Idem, Chinese Paintings in American Collections, I, pl. 26. History of Early Chinese Painting, II, pl. 6. We know that Mi Fei went to study the landscapes of the region of Kweilin, in Kwangsi. See the photographs of the vicinity of Kweilin compared to the painter's works, in Okumura, Les montagnes dans la peinture chinoise, in the review Yurinasu, Tokyo, 1935, pp. 531-539. On the karst limestone character of the Kwangsi mountains, see Cressey, Asia Lands and Peoples, New York, 1944, p. 138. On the personality and very original character of Mi Fei, cf. Percival David, The Chinese Exhibition, Revue des Arts Asiatiques, IX, 4, Dec. 1935, p. 173.

is blurred, a house screened by a weeping willow with branches from which the leaves have partly fallen; atmospheric values rendered with a delicate touch.[41]

The painter Li Lung-mien (1040-1106), from the province of Anhwei, a friend of the reformist minister Wang An-shih, excelled in the most varied genres, from Buddhist or Taoist scenes to landscapes. As Sirén justly remarks, however, he seems perhaps to have brought to religious subjects less spirituality than intellectuality, and to landscape less lyrical feeling than intellectual grasp. Admirable in intellectuality, in lucidity, in delicacy are the few rare works that critics are still inclined to attribute to him. In particular may be noted, in the Freer Gallery, an 'imaginary landscape, peopled with fairies and immortals', a dream vision, with its unreal palace, standing surrounded by peaks so abrupt, so phantasmagoric that they might be structures of clouds, with the mannered elegance of the clump of pinetrees that crowns the foreground, with the peaceful, almost childish delicacy of the river that winds between calm banks, guarded by a weeping willow.[42] Also in the Freer Gallery there is an 'Imperial Summer Palace', or rather a succession of palaces and courts, which is typical of 'architectural painting', treated here, in the drawing of the pavilions and the 'thousand columns', with the refined elegance of backgrounds in Florentine paintings of the Quattrocento.[43] Not without reason did Victor Goloubew compare Li Lung-mien's technique to that of Botticelli's drawings.[44]

Among the figures that were at one time attributed to Li Lung-mien we may note, in the Kuroda Naganari collection, the

[41] Sirén, *History of Early Chinese Painting*, II, pl. 13. See also in Tajima and Omura, *Masterpieces...*, VIII, pls. 26-27, other wash-drawings in connection with which the name of Chao Ta-nien is mentioned (Akaboshi Tetsuma and Hara Tomitaro collections).

[42] Sirén, *Chinese Paintings in American Collections*, I, pls. 30-31; Idem, *History of Early Chinese Painting*, II, pl. 28.

[43] Idem, *American Collections*, I, pls. 32-33. *History of... Painting*, II, pl. 29.

[44] V. Goloubew, Li Long-mien, *Gazette des Beaux-Arts*, April 1914, p. 277.

53. *Hsia Chʻang (1388-1470): The Serene Bank of the Hsiang River (details). Ink on paper. Nelson Gallery of Art, Kansas City.*

Buddhist 'faithful' (*upasāka*) Vimalakīrti (Chinese: Wei-mo-ch'i) an erroneous attribution, undoubtedly, but the figure of the holy man and saint is one of amazing psychological penetration and of luminous intellectuality.[45]

* * *

The Sung emperor Hui-tsung (1101-1126) is one of the most interesting figures in Chinese history. A supporter, in politics, of Wang An-shih's reformism, in religious matters he proved to be strongly drawn to Taoist mysticism.

Taoism was then in the process of turning into a kind of theism, with a supreme divinity, 'the Jade August One' (*Yü-huang*) or 'August Pure One' (jade being a symbol of purity), an Absolute conceived as a transcendant and personal god.[46] One of Hui-tsung's predecessors, emperor Chen-tsung (998-1022), had in 1012 already proclaimed the existence of the August Pure One, 'Great Celestial Sovereign, Supreme Author of Heaven and of physical laws, of Good and of the Way'. In 1113 the August Pure One in person manifested himself before emperor Hui-tsung. The latter then undertook to carry out in favour of his celestial visitor a real syncretism of the Three Religions, a syncretism in which the new transcendant Taoist god found himself identified with the ancient Sovereign from On High of the Confucians, while the Buddhas, Bodhisattvas and *arhats* of Buddhism were invited to become incorporated in the pantheon thus fused.[47]

Besides being a mystic, Hui-tsung was an aesthete, an ar-

[45] Tajima and Omura, *Masterpieces Selected from the Fine Arts of the Far East*, vol. VIII, Tokyo, 1910, pl. XXV.

[46] H. Y. Feng, The Origin of Yu Houang, *Harvard Journal of Asiatic Studies*, 1936, p. 242.

[47] In 1119 Hui-tsung went so far as to contemplate granting the property of the Buddhist communities to the Taoists and obliging the Buddhist priests to choose between secularization and entering a Taoist monastery. These measures had been suggested to him by a renegade, Lin Ling-su, a former Buddhist novice who had gone over to Taoism.

33.

chaeologist, and an enthusiastic collector. He brought together in his palace of K'ai-feng a veritable museum of painting, of which we still have the catalogue. He felt at home only among the members of the T'u Hua Yüan academy who, clad in violet garments, adorned with insignia of gold and jade, obtaining the 'golden Girdle' as supreme recompense for an immortal master-piece, held familiar discussions with their imperial colleague on whatever questions of art were uppermost in their minds.[48] Hui-tsung, according to his contemporaries, was himself a painter of talent. Many works are attributed to him, in particular paintings of birds (ducks, falcons, etc.) One that can be attributed to the imperial brush with a maximum of plausibility is the 'Quail and Narcissus' of the Marquis Asano collection, in Odawara, a paint-ing that is in fact extraordinarily forceful in its technique.[49] There are two other paintings in Japanese collections that used to be attributed to emperor Hui-tsung—paintings on silk (ad-mirable, in any case, whoever may have been the painter): at the Konchi-in, in Kyoto, a poet seated at the foot of a cedar tree, on a mountain-side, contemplating an immense expanse of distances and mists traversed, at the extreme limit of visibility, by a flight of birds; at the Daitokuji, a standing figure, similarly contemplating, at early dawn, the far reaches of a landscape of rocks and mists.[50]

* * *

While the imperial court of the Sung, in K'ai-feng, reigned over nearly the whole of China, Peking had since 936 fallen into the hands of a people of Tartar race, having Mongolian affinities, the Ch'i-tan, or Khitaï (in Chinese: the Liao), a people originally

---

[48] Cf. Arthur Waley, *Introduction to the Study of Chinese Painting*, pp. 177-178. Wenley, Note on the So-called Sung Academy of Painting, *Harvard Journal of Asiatic Studies*, 1941, p. 269.

[49] Sirén, *History of Early Chinese Painting*, II, pl. 21.

[50] Tajima and Omura, *Masterpieces...*, VIII, pls. 28 and 30.

from southern Manchuria (country of Liao-yang), as well as from the eastern portion of Inner Mongolia.[51]

These Ch'i-tan were on the whole 'good Barbarians', in the sense that they proved to be relatively peace-loving and became Sinicized rather rapidly. We have seen that one of the painters of the Six Dynasties, Hu Kuei, was a Ch'i-tan, which perhaps explains his love of painting horses (cf. the Tartar horsemen of the Boston Museum). In the Ch'i-tan kingdom itself there developed a local school, revealed to us by the eleventh century funerary reliefs and paintings found at several sites in southern Manchuria, in particular at Shih-chü-tzu (east of Liao-yang), An-shan (southwest of Liao-yang) and Luan-feng (40 kilometers from An-shan);[52] also in Inner Mongolia, at War-manha in the Barin district, where one of the Ch'i-tan royal residences was situated.[53]

The mural paintings at War-manha adorning the tomb of the Ch'i-tan king Yeh-lü Tsung-chen, *alias* Hsing-tsung (1031-1055), are very beautiful; they have been studied by the Torii mission, and copies are kept at the University of Kyoto.[54] Special note should be made of a herd of stags, does and fawns in a landscape of wooded hills, and also a river with wild ducks and swans, all rendered with remarkable vividness and elegance.[55] Such a work is not unworthy of the famous Five Dynasties painting on silk in the Peking Museum representing an identical

[51] K. Wittfogel and Feng Chia-Sheng, *History of Chinese Society. Liao (907-1125)*, Transactions of the American Philosophical Society, Philadelphia, March 1949.

[52] Ryuzo Torii, *Sculptured Stone Tombs of the Liao Dynasty*, Harvard-Yenching Institute, 1942.

[53] *Idem*, On the Wall Paintings of the Liao Dynasty, *Kokka*, XLIX, 9-12, Tokyo, 1931.

[54] War-manha (the modern name) is 20 *li* northwest of Tsaghan-khoton, in present-day Jehol. See Ryuzo Torii, *Illustrations of Archaeology*, vol. III, preface, Tokyo, 1936. Wittfogel and Feng Chia-Sheng, *Op. cit.*, p. 132, note 62.

[55] Ryuzo Torii, *Illustrations*, pl. 208. Wittfogel and Feng Chia-Sheng, Fig. I (frontispiece). Good reproductions, too, in Tamuro Jitsuzo, The Murals of Ch'ing-lung, *Bijutsu Kenkyū*, CLIII, 2.

subject.[56] Again at the tomb of Hsing-tsung, at War-manha, we may note portraits of Ch'itan lords or of Chinese high officials in the service of the Ch'i-tan kings, firm compositions, showing psychological insight which is both sober and realistic.[57] It is interesting to note that what we have here is less a branch of Sung art than a survival of the T'ang. These portraits of War-manha seem indeed to form the transition between the last portraits of donors at Tun-huang (those of the years 980)—which are also 'posthumous T'ang'—and the later Korean funerary portraits in the manner of late Ming.[58]

It is quite possible, as we have also seen, that the mural paintings discovered by Langdon Warner in Wan-fo-hsia, near Tun-huang, and first dated by him as ninth century, may have to be brought up to the period of the Sung and the Ch'i-tan, perhaps even to the domination of the Hsi-Hsia or Tangut in Kansu (1001-1227).

The Ch'i-tan, in their domain on the south-Manchurian borders as well as in Peking, were thus in process of Sinization, when the Sung emperor Hui-tsung, in order to recover Peking, manoeuvred other Barbarians into invading them. These were originally from North Manchuria and of Tungus stock (hence ancestors of the Manchus),—the Ju-chen, since known in Chinese by the name of the Chin ('gold' dynasty). The Chin occupied Peking (1122), but kept it for themselves, and, turning their arms against the Sung empire, next seized the imperial capital, K'ai-feng, where they captured the emperor Hui-tsung (1126). All north China fell into the hands of the Chin. The Sung empire fell back into South China, with Hangchow, in Chekiang, as its new capital.

In North China, which was subject to them for a century,

[56] *Catalogue of the International Exhibition of Chinese Art*, 1935-1936, London, fig. 755.

[57] Wittfogel and Feng Chia-Sheng, *loc. cit.*, p. 229.

[58] *Musée Cernuschi, Exposition d'art coréen*, 1946, p. 20.

the Chin, as later their great-nephews the Manchu, set up strong military colonies.[59] Perhaps this proto-Manchu population influx in the region of Peking and the Yellow River basin in the twelfth century had, as we shall see later, a certain influence on art.

* * *

The Sung empire, henceforth restricted to South China (1127-1276), very rapidly recovered its prosperity. Hangchow, the new imperial capital, built on one of the most picturesque sites in the Far East and celebrated as such by the greatest Chinese poets, was also admired by our Marco Polo and by the blessed Odoric de Pordenone who both, we distinctly feel, looked upon this Citadel of the Waters, this city of lakes and bridges, as a Far-eastern Venice.[60]

Dispersed for a brief period by the invasion of the Chin, the Academy of Fine Arts at K'ai-feng was re-established in Hang-chow around a constellation of talented painters. Among those of the first generation, in the reign of emperor Kao-tsung (1127-1162), we shall mention Chao Po-chü and Chiang Ts'an. Attached to the former name is a handscroll in the Boston Museum on which a vast panorama of mountains is the setting for historical episodes; the subject is most skilfully treated, the procession of small figures having the finish of a miniature—a manner that we find in Japanese art in the Kamakura period. Under the name of Chiang Ts'an, the Metropolitan Museum, New York, displays another panorama known as 'The Hundred Oxen', equally clever and even a little facile.

In the following period, during the last quarter of the twelfth century, Hangchow produced the greatest Chinese land-scapists of all time. First of all, the Ma family. Labelled with

[59] Cf. *Harvard Journal of Asiatic Studies*, 1938, p. 194 (according to Mikami Tsuguo).
[60] Marco Polo, Chap. CLI. Odoric de Pordenone (French adaptation by René Grousset and Henriette Demoulin-Bernard), Chap. XXI, p. 53.

the name of one of the first Ma, Ma K'uei (*circa* 1150-1224), the Magoshi Kyōhei collection in Tokyo has a fan representing a boat on a lake at nightfall: 'a projecting stone, a few reeds, a boat with two men, and the faint silhouette of mountain tops in the misty background... It is one of those exquisitely simple compositions where the painter with the greatest economy of means has suggested something beyond definition—a reflection of infinity...' [61]

Ma Yüan, brother of the former, who worked around 1190-1224, is even greater. His themes and his manner not only inspired later Chinese art but also the Japanese school of the Kano: villas in winter beneath pinetrees or bamboos, groups of stray cypress or cedars on some abrupt rock, effects of mist drowning the November plains, solitary trees twisted by the wind in a denuded landscape...

Among the works most plausibly attributed to Ma Yüan may be mentioned the one in the Count Tanaka Mitsuoki collection, in Tokyo: 'A philosopher (accompanied by his servant) seated at a stone table under a huge pine, which grows along the side of the composition and sends out a branch diagonally across the narrow field';[62] also the moonlight scene in the Kuroda collection: 'an overhanging cliff... from which a gnarled pine reaches out like a giant arm under the moon. The old man who sits on the terrace turns slightly towards the background gazing at the moon, a small circular orb which in its loneliness serves to accentuate the wide, empty space'.[63] Likewise a painting in the Peking Museum which Sirén notes: 'Two large pines are growing on the terrace, bending diagonally and spreading their angular branches far over the empty space beyond. At the opposite end of the picture rises a straight vertical rock; the middle section between

[61] Sirén, *History of Early Chinese Painting*, II, p. 78, pl. 54.

[62] Sirén, *History of Early Chinese Painting*, II, p. 79. Tajima and Omura, *Masterpieces*, VIII, pl. 43.

[63] Sirén, *Op. cit.*, II, pp. 79, 80, pl. 55. Tajima and Omura, *Op. cit.*, VIII, pl. 44.

these lofty side-wings is quite blank—bare silk—something unde-
fined and unlimited'. Or else the Landscape in the Rain of the
Iwasaki collection: 'Steep towering mountains fill the middle
part of the background... The wind is shaking the trees that
bend over the promontory where a boat is moored; a man with a
large paper umbrella is hastening along the the mountain path towards the houses, which lie half hidden in the mist at the foot
of a precipice. The design is centralized, but towards the right
side it floats out into misty space where all forms disappear'.[64]
On a smaller scale the Boston Museum has a 'Landscape in
Early Spring', an album leaf in the form of a fan, of remarkable
delicacy: 'A mountain range in the background; at its foot a
village hidden in the mist. A stretch of water spanned by a bridge,
and closest to the foreground two old willows with slender
plumy branches, quivering like tendrils... There is a breath of
morning wind touching the tops of the willows; the mist is slowly
dissolving—otherwise no movement, no sound. The spring is still
hesitating'.[65]

The most remarkable example of Ma Yüan's manner is perhaps the one to be found in the Baron Mitsui collection: a solitary
fisherman in his boat, on a lake in winter, holding his rod. The
boat is lost in the middle of the lake with no bank visible;
nothing but the motionless water and the man attentive to his
task. One of the most poignant works of painting of all time.[66]

Ma Lin, son of Ma Yüan, continued the tradition that his

[64] Sirén, *Op. cit.*, II, p. 81. Tajima and Omura, *Op. cit.*, VIII, pl. 42. Otto
Fischer, *Kunst Indiens, Chinas und Japans*, pl. 499.
[65] Sirén, *Op. cit.*, II, p. 81, pl. 57. William Cohn, *Chinese Painting*, London
(Phaidon Press), 1948. pl. 90.
[66] 'The flat-bottomed sampan is just large enough to carry the man who
sits in its stern, bent over the angling rod. Some faint wavy lines along its side
indicate the water. That is all. The rest of the picture is emptiness—a silent grey
tone as of evening mist. Motives like this may still be observed on the West Lake
in Hangchow, but seldom, if ever, did an artist grasp so much of their significance
in so few strokes of the brush'. Sirén, *Op. cit.*, II, p. 82, pl. 59. Tajima and
Omura, *Op. cit.*, VIII, pl. 46.

father had initiated. The Nezu collection in Tokyo has an admirable 'Evening Landscape' by him, with a seal of 1254. 'The cliffs at the shore emerge only in part from the dense mist, and the swallows that circle over the water carry the imagination far into the limitless expanse'.[67]

Hsia Kuei (about 1180-1234), rival of the Ma, belonged to the order of the 'golden girdle' under emperor Ning-tsung. A certain number of paintings are still attributed to him. Among these is the autumn squall in the mountain, a wash-drawing on paper in the Kawasaki Shōzō collection, in Kobe, a romantic landscape in which the violence of the elements bends the trees and tosses their branches about, blowing their leaves towards the torrent.[68] There is a marked difference between the sharp drawing of the Ma (every pine-needle stands out) and the fluent, ink-splash technique of Hsia Kuei. Another example of Hsia Kuei's manner is the summer landscape, a wash-drawing on silk, in the Iwasaki Koyata collection in Tokyo. It is a water scene, showing a bay or river with a boat moored behind a point of land. On the right, a few water grasses, a few trees indicated by ink dots. Half seen in the background, above the mist, a horizon of mountains. There is absolute mastery of technique, an impression of immensity in the expanse of water, and the sweep of the distant chain of mountains. Water and light are blended, in contrast to the ink strokes and dots of the foreground.[69] It is interesting to compare such works by Hsia Kuei with certain Japanese landscapes by Sesshu, as we were invited to do in Odawara, at the Marquis Asano's residence.[70]

Mention should also be made of a handscroll in a similar

[67] Sirén, *Op. cit.*, II, p. 83, pl. 62.

[68] Tajima and Omura, *Op. cit.*, VIII, pl. 55. Sirén. *Op. cit.*, pl. 67.

[69] *Ibid*, pl. 56. William Cohn, *Op. cit.*, pl. 93. And, likewise attributed to Hsia Kuei, the hand-scroll of the 'Ten Thousand *Li* of the Long River', *ibid*, pls. 94-96.

[70] See also Robert Paine, Hsia Kuei and Motonobu, *Revue des Arts Asiatiques*, IX, 1935, p. 154.

54. Ch'iu Ying (active c. 1522-1560): Saying Farewell at Hsün-yang.
(detail). Color on paper. Nelson Gallery of Art, Kansas City.

雪屑胃凌晨月更枝
乱盖偃奇岫喋老夫記
真亡廈全珠站牙金世

55. Above: *Wên Chêng-ming* (1470-1559): *Cypress and Weathered Rocks. Ink on paper. Nelson Gallery of Art, Kansas City.* Below: *Ch'ên Tao-fu* (1483-1544): *Lotus* (detail). *Color on paper. Nelson Gallery of Art, Kansas City.*

manner in the Akaboshi Tetsuma collection in Tokyo, representing a river viewed from a height upstream, with its windings and the singing, bright flow of its waters, while under a tree on a hummock a traveller is seated, taking in the cool freshness of the landscape.[71] In contrast to these impressions of water and light, certain scrolls in the Mayeda Toshimoto collection display romantic trees with prodigious personalities, trees that struggle and dominate with their twists, their angularities and their gnarled humps, and their branches that are gestures of appeal or of menace.[72] This eerie play of dark masses, shaken by wild storms, entirely dispels the impression of airiness, the sense of limitless space, conveyed by previous Sung masters.

Let us note also that while Hsia Kuei excelled in panoramas, he was also skilled in composing small pictures of compelling intimacy, like the often reproduced winter landscape of the Shimitsu collection, Kyoto: shiveringly clustered in the depths of a valley surrounded by lines of snowy mountains, on the edge of an indistinct body of water, between two tall bare trees whose twigs stand out black against the white background, a few snow-covered huts.[73] An equally penetrating sense of melancholy is conveyed by a similar fan, in the Boston Museum, evoking impressions of autumn, attributed to the painter Liu Sung-nien (*circa* 1170-1230).[74]

Apart from these artists gravitating round the imperial academy, Hangchow in the Sung period produced several painters of genius inspired by the contemplative Buddhism of the Ch'an school. Most of them led a monastic life in the hermitages of this sect on the heights west of Hangchow, between the West

---

[71] Tajima and Omura, *Op. cit.*, VIII, pl. 59.

[72] *Ibid*, pls. 62-64.

[73] E. Grosse, *Le lavis en Extrême-Orient*, pl. 10.

[74] 'A rocky promontory with old maples around a pavilion in the foreground; wide expanse of water dissolving into the mist, and on the opposite side, some projecting rocks with leafy trees and bamboos bending in the wind'. Sirén, *History of Early Chinese Painting*, II, p. 89, pl. 70.

Lake (Hsi-hu) and the mountains of the Chekiang interior. Such a one was Liang K'ai who, after having been decorated with the 'golden girdle' of the imperial academy about 1202-1204, retired to a monastery.

Liang K'ai is a virtuoso of the brush, which he manipulates with an imaginative sense and an airy nonchalance that are breathtaking. Such qualities were of the very kind to be fostered by the Ch'an doctrine, the nature of which, with its stress on 'the spontaneous act' and the irrational, was frankly non-conformist and 'surrealist', so that its converts were not without that secret delight in scandalizing ordinary people experienced by those who feel themselves to be above the ordinary. The disciple of Ch'an, the dhyānist, was encouraged not to hesitate to push metaphysical freedom to the point of expressing it in actions that the profane would regard as sheer eccentricity. One has only to read, in this connection, the biographies of the Fathers of the *dhyāna*.[75] Such is in fact the spirit that animates the portraits attributed to Liang K'ai's brush—portraits of Buddhist saints (the *arhat* of the Abé collection; in the Matsudaira collection, the patriarch Hui-neng gleefully tearing up a *sūtra*, a Buddhist sacred text), or portraits of Chinese poets (the Su T'ung-po in the same Matsudaira collection).[76]

Liang K'ai's masterpiece is a picture of Śākyamuni as an ascetic, standing leaning on his stick near a stream, in a strange landscape of steep mountains (in the Count Sakai Tadamichi collection, Tokyo). The Blessed One is represented at the moment when, after a period of terrible mortifications, he is on his way to the Bodhi Tree where he will receive the Illumination that is to save the world. The intensity of thought, the violence of his meditation, are expressed with a kind of bitter spirituality in this

[75] See Suzuki, *Essays in Zen Buddhism*, First Series, in the Collected Series, London, 1950, pp. 174-226, and Second Series, pp. 212 ff. Also Waley, *Zen Buddhism in relation to art*, London, 1922, p. 22.

[76] Sirén, *History of Early Chinese Painting*, pls. 77 and 78. On Liang K'ai, see Otto Kümmel, in *Ostantische Zeitschift*, 1929, p. 206.

hirsute, almost savage face. This inner violence, as much as the wind that blows through the mountain gorge, animates the strange folds of the sparse garment and has its counterpart in the convulsed roots of a bare tree-trunk, in some twisted branches, and in the scrub that bends towards the ascetic or crawls at his feet like some weird beast.[77]

We come, finally, to the greatest of all these painters, Mu-ch'i. Mu-ch'i, according to tradition, came (about 1215?) from Southwest China to settle near Hangchow in a Ch'an monastery or hermitage situated on the shores of the West Lake (Hsi-hu). His production is presumed to have been at its peak about 1250-1270.[78] Towards the end of the Sung dynasty he incurred the displeasure of the public authorities, was disgraced and fled to Szechwan. Upon the accession of the Yüan he returned to Hangchow and it was then that he finally became a Ch'an monk.[79] If the paintings that are attached to his name are really by him, we are indebted to him for superhuman visions of fabulous animals as well as of divine beings. How powerful, for example, is the evocation of the she-monkey at the Daitokuji in Kyoto, clutching her little one in her arms, perched with him on a knotty branch suspended in the void, at the top of a pine-tree; for the presence of the two shivering—and so human!—creatures transports us at once to the crest of the forests, above easily-imagined immensities, above a world that may be full of terror.[80] At the Daitokuji too, we come upon the most prodigious dragon that the Chinese imagination has ever given birth to.[81] The monster, with its awesome muzzle, long crustacean's tentacles, demon's horns and fiery eyes whose gaze has the lambent gleam of lightning, is revealed to us in the *chiaroscuro* of a storm-cloud.

[77] Tajima and Omura, *Op. cit.*, Vol. IX, pl. 70.
[78] On Mu-ch'i, see Waley, *Zen Buddhism...*, p. 22.
[79] Taro Kotakane, Some Materials Newly Discovered on the Life of Mu-ch'i, *Bulletin of Eastern Art*, Tokyo, no. 21, 1941, p. 16.
[80] Tajima and Omura, *Op. cit.*, vol. IX, pl. 85. Sirén, *Op. cit.*, II, pl. 81.
[81] Tajima and Omura, *Op. cit.*, vol. IX, pl. 90.

All the indeterminate menace of the unknowable seems to be concentrated in this bestial yet divine mask. This, however, is a wholly western interpretation, for we know that in the Chinese view the dragon symbolizes divine power, the spiritual urge. Physical strength—animality—is represented, in a diptych with the dragon, by a tiger of equal power.

It is not devoid of interest to note that the Ch'an artist here dedicated his genius to magnifying the most ancient Chinese conceptions, those of the old pre-Confucian mythologies inherited by Taoism. The fact is that unwittingly the Ch'an had assimilated the spirit of Taoism. It was like a 'Buddhist Taoism'. Indeed, one of the most famous paintings of the Iwasaki collection reminds us of some page or other in the book of Chuang-tzu.[82] Unforgettable is the impression made by the Ch'an ascetic absorbed in ecstasy on a rocky ledge overhanging the void, at whose feet float mists that seem to support him. A fearful serpent winds round his waist, resting a menacing head on the saint's knees, seeking to fascinate him with the livid flash of its stare. But the saint is totally unconcerned, and it is the silent power of his mental concentration, the force of the dhyānic ecstasy, that master the serpent. The face of the ascetic, both fierce and ecstatic, terrible and illuminated by a transcendent gentleness, expresses a matchless grandeur.

But Mu-ch'i, intensely Ch'an as he here shows himself, also embraces another form of Buddhism, the religion of tenderness incarnated in Avalokiteśvara and Amitābha.

The Bodhisattva Avalokiteśvara, who represents a kind of Buddhist Providence, was in the process of undergoing, with the assumption of the features of Kuan-yin-with-the-white-garments (*Po-i Kuan-yin*), a feminine incarnation.[83] And it is

---

[82] Tajima and Omura, *Op. cit.*, vol. IX, pls. 87-88. Sirén, *Op. cit.*, vol. II, pl. 82. The Ch'an ascetic of this painting was formerly designated as the *arhat* Vanavāsin.

[83] We may recall, with Maspero, that the type of the Kuan-yin with white garments is linked to the apparitions and miracles that occurred on the island

in fact the goddess Kuan-yin whom Mu-ch'i immortalizes for us in the famous painting of the Daitokuji in Kyoto, a white and majestic figure with a meditative expression, both gentle and grave, seated on a rock, at the foot of a sheer mountain wall, with a river or lake at her feet and water vapours floating around her.[84]

Mu-ch'i's ambition seems indeed to have been nothing less than to embrace all nature—nature conceived in the Ch'an manner (in the manner also of the T'ien-t'ai), as expressing the very soul of the cosmos. Although we still lack positive proof of this, Mu-ch'i is traditionally considered to be the author of two scrolls having as their subject 'the eight landscapes of the Hsiao and the Hsiang', rivers that flow into lake Tung-t'ing. These paintings are today scattered among various Japanese collections.[85] Of the first scroll (the smaller one) there are four fragments: 'The Autumn Moon', in the Tokugawa collection; 'Night Rain' in the Baron Masuda collection; 'Evening Bells' in the Count Masuda collection; 'Evening of Snow' in the Suenobu collection. Of the large scroll four other fragments remain: 'The Return of the Boats on Lake Tung-t'ing', in the Matsudaira collection; 'Evening Bells', formerly in the Tokugawa collection, now in the Mayeda collection; 'Sunset on a Fishing Village', in the Nezu collection; 'Wild Geese Alighting', formerly in the Matsudaira collection, now in the Ishino collection.[86] The most famous of

of P'u-t'o (an island of the Chu-san archipelago, off Chekiang). The goddess had appeared there as early as 847; in 858 the Japanese monk Egaku, as a result of a fresh miracle, had founded a temple there to Kuan-yin, and in 916 a great monastery had been built to house a statue of Kuan-yin, the work of the monk Chi-chung. Several Kuan-yins-with-white-garments are mentioned among the works of the painters of the Five Dynasties.

[84] Tajima and Omura, *Op. cit.*, vol. IX, pl. 84. Sirén. *Op. cit.*, vol. II, pl. 80.

[85] Yukio Yashiro, On the Eight Scenic Views of Hsiao-Hsiang by Mu-ch'i, *Bulletin of Eastern Art*, No. 21, Tokyo, 1941.

[86] For the names of the present owners and for the grouping of the paintings we here rely on Mr. Yashiro (article quoted above), supplementing Dr. Sirén. Mr. Yashiro's valuable article reproduces six of the eight paintings.

these views is the one in the Matsudaira collection, the return of the fishing boats at evening on the lake. The boats can barely be made out. The whole landscape is composed of water, of mist-laden air, of space, of indistinct distances. On the horizon mountains progressively vanish in the mist. In the left foreground a fishing village, its outlines blurred, is half hidden between a clump of trees and the shore, so completely are man and his works here swallowed up in immensity. 'The rest of the picture', says Sirén, 'is free expanse; there is no foreground, no background, simply open space. The only support that the eye can find here are two small sailing boats which are more felt than seen'.[87]

Of all the landscapists, Mu-ch'i was the greatest visionary. Sirén sums this up when he says: 'He painted landscapes which are simply fragments of the universe, formulae for his visionary ideas of unlimited space and soundless harmony'.

In the T'ang period the portrait, insofar as the Sino-Japanese texts enable us to reconstruct it, had been conceived as an attempt to 'transmit the spirit' (ch'uan-shen) of the model, roughly to bring out the essential character, to capture the individuality of the subject (in particular by the drawing of the lines of the mouth), while sacrificing all secondary details. To this end, as Serge Elisseeff has well shown, portraitists did not hesitate to 'represent the various parts of the face at different moments, but these moments were so closely related that the whole remained harmonious'. This manner—the ch'uan-shen—was to exert a lasting influence on later Japanese portrait-painting, but in China in the Sung period, under the influences of Ch'an Buddhism, we see Chinese portraits more concerned with details, or more exactly 'with a better rendering of the whole by giving more details'. It was at this point that two new treatments appeared: 'The portrait in which the model is represented fully,

[87] Sirén, Op. cit., II, p. 102, pl. 83. Tajima and Omura, Op. cit., IX, pl. 94. William Cohn, Chinese Painting, pl. 107.

usually seated, and the bust portrait (*ting-hsiang*) which was created by the Ch'an monks'. Of this order are the portraits of *arhat* or *lo-han*, treated 'diagonally', with the subject shown at an angle, foreshortened—a 'romantic' composition of very powerful effect.[88]

* * *

The influence of Ch'an teaching likewise made itself felt in the painting of flowers. The imperial academy, first in K'ai-feng, then in Hangchow, had specialized in 'an ornamental and minutely naturalistic kind of flower painting' with a predilection for peonies, hibiscus and lotus. The Ch'an painters aimed to express 'the life and spiritual significance of flowers rather than their outward beauty'. Their favourite themes were plum blossoms—'messengers of spring'—vines, orchids and narcissus.[89] A whole literature was even developed around these motifs. In his treatise on the philosophy of the flowering plum tree (*Hua kuang mei p'u*) the monk Chung Jen (late eleventh century) went so far as to see in this theme the representation of the universe itself. As for the bamboo, by its rectitude, its upward thrust, the inner emptiness of its hollow stems, it symbolized the whole Buddhist ideal. To devote oneself to the painting of the bamboo was an ascetic exercise paving the way to a state of spirituality.

* * *

We may note that the mysticism of the Sung period, whether Ch'an or Taoist, did not confine itself to philosophic speculation and to art. About 1133, a Buddhist priest of Soochow, named Mao Tzu-yüan, founded the society of the White Lotus (*Pai-lien*

[88] Serge Elisseeff, Notes sur le portrait en Extrême-Orient, *Etudes d'orientalisme publiées par le Musée Guimet à la mémoire de Raymonde Linossier*, vol. I, pp. 169-202 (Paris, 1933).

[89] Sirén, *History of Early Chinese Painting*, vol. II, p. 109.

chiao). This was a secret society, not to be confused with the former sect of the same name (*Pai-lien tsung*), founded, we may remember, about the year 400.[90] The first Lotus sect had restricted itself to the religious field. The eminent leaders who had headed it—Tan-luan (died about 600) under the Sui, Tao-ch'ao (died about 645) under the T'ang—had been pure mystics, and it was in the light of this that the T'ang emperor Kao-tsung (650-683) had given his full favour to Amidism. The new society, on the other hand, as founded by 'the Master of the Lotus' Mao Tzu-yüan, at once evinced tendencies that were so clearly political and subversive that the government banished Mao. We know, moreover, that 'the Master of the Lotus' had little use for official Buddhism. Once outlawed, the Society of the White Lotus went underground. It was to reappear periodically and it was associations claiming to stem from it or from similar groups that subsequently were to foment the insurrection of 1351 (which in a brief space of time brought about the downfall of the Mongol dynasty) that were to shake the throne of the Ming (1622), stir up the revolt against the Manchu emperor Ch'ien-lung (1793) and come close to carrying out the assassination of emperor Chia-ch'ing (1813). This corrosive activity of the secret societies from the Sung to the Manchus, this persistence of revolutionary agitation throughout the centuries, are facts that must not be forgotten if we wish to understand the hidden springs of Chinese history.

It is worth calling attention to the appearance of this movement during the Sung period.

No less interesting to note, under the heading of the age of the Sung, is the Buddhist-Taoist complex revealed by such esoteric social manifestations as the *Pai-lien chiao*. The origin of this secret society seems by its very name—the White Lotus—to be Amidist, and the revolt of 1351 that was to stem from it was carried out in the name of Buddhist messianism: the insurgents

[90] Cf. Wieger, *Histoire des croyances*, 1917, p. 643. *Idem, Textes historiques*, vol. II, pp. 1718, 1734. B. Favre, *Les sociétés secrètes en Chine*, Paris, 1933, p. 80.

昔文湖州有暮靄橫看宗
思陵題識寒首觀其筆力
不在郭熙之下於樹間寫叢
竹乃自其師謝中流出之不
可以筆墨畦徑觀如方文廣
儔之筆力不能似郭天錫行
文出希求畫倩竹遠山惜乎
得湖州此㦯咸哀若拙林鄰野
縱意塞廣抹㮙可以寫一時三
趙姑塞廣文之雅意云
黃鶴山中人王蒙
歲次甲辰九月謁漢音
軍翁先生於白長安寓齋
海虞 王翬

56. *Wang Hui (1632-1717): Bamboo Grove and Distant Mountains. Ink on paper. Cleveland Museum of Art, John L. Severance Collection.*

山水有清音得
者只心是寒泉
激石恨冷々語心耳
何日我携琴田釣
風雲變念之所彌
懷春風吹月起
清湘大滌子畔心州
忠老呈
山先生博笑

57. *Tao-chi* (*1630-1707*): *Landscape. Color on paper. Museum of Fine Arts, Boston.*

of 1351 were 'adventists' who awaited the coming of the Bodhisattva Maitreya. A great number of magic practices, fumiga-
tions, etc., however, stem from Taoism, and one of the later
off shoots of the White Lotus was to be the brotherhood of the
'Eight Trigrams' (*Pa-kua*) in the seventeenth century, obviously
originating from Taoism.[91]

The Buddhist-Taoist admixture in which the Taoist spirit
predominated amid late Mahāyāna, Amidism and Maitreyanism,
the imperceptible invasion of Buddhist brains by Taoist conceptions, these represent—like the painting of Hangchow and for
the same reasons—one of the characteristic features of the Sung
period.

* * *

The sculpture of the Sung period is represented in great part
by a Buddhist statuary due less to the Chinese dynasty of that
name than to the Tartar dynasties that ruled the North, the
Ch'i-tan and especially the Chin, whose capital was Peking—the
former from 936 to 1122, the latter from 1122 to 1215. The Chin
in particular strongly marked this sculpture with their stamp.
There was certainly among these Tartar occupants, now that
they were becoming Sinicized, a meritorious desire, a willingness
to restore the Buddhist sanctuaries that had been destroyed by
the invasions. In this respect the Chin period represents a kind
of Renaissance in the field of religious sculpture, but a renaissance
that immediately turns to the baroque, to borrow Sirén's term,
in its statues of marble (originating in large part in Hopei) or
of polychrome-painted wood.

The Kuan-yins, which constitute the main theme of this statuary, enlighten us as to the iconographic transformation that
this divinity was then undergoing. Whether standing or in the
attitude of *maharajalila* (or 'royal ease'), in which the right arm

[91] B. Favre, *Op. cit.*, p. 99.

35.

rests on the lifted right knee while the left leg hangs down to reach the ground, the former Bodhisattva, in his various ritual poses, is in process of becoming a goddess, and the goddess is a beauty of imposing stance and full, voluptuous form which shows through the arrangement of scarves, a plump, developed torso and a belly with generous curves,—a bejewelled and rather ripe 'prima donna' with the majestic indolence of a sultana.[92] This is an aesthetic conception similar to that which is revealed to us by the mural paintings of the same region under the Tartar dynasties.

Particularly striking is the Tartar continuity maintained around Peking throughout the Sung period, both under the Ch'i-tan and under the Chin. Alongside the intellectual, idealistic and impressionist art of the Sung, an entirely different spirit reigned in the art of the two Tartar dynasties, a spirit that harked back to the lush sculpture and the pompous mural paintings of late T'ang. A contrast in aesthetic conceptions, this, that discloses racial dissimilarities. We must remember that under three successive dynasties (Ch'i-tan, then Chin, then Mongols), Peking remained Tartar from 936 to 1368. The history of art cannot but bear the trace of this occupation of four hundred and thirty-two years.

However this may be, the Buddhist piety of these Tartar dynasties is quite remarkable and contrasts with the difficulties that Buddhism always came up against, under purely Chinese dynasties, from official Confucianism as well as from Taoism.[93]

[92] Cf. Sirén, Chinese Sculptures of the Sung, Liao and Chin Dynasties, B.M.F.E.A. 14, pp. 45-64. Idem, A Chinese Temple and its Plastic Decoration of the Twelfth Century, Etudes d'orientalisme publiées par le Musée Guimet..., Paris, 1932, pp. 499-505 (sculptures of the temple Tsia-hua-yin ssu near Ta-t'ung, in Shansi, built in 1037 under the Ch'i-tan, burned in 1119 and rebuilt in 1140 under the Chin king Ho-lo-ma). See Hugo Münsterberg, Zum Problem der weiblichen Kuan-yin, Artibus Asiae, IX, 1946, p. 316.

[93] We know, for example, that the Ch'i-tan king Yelü Hung-chi, alias Tao-tsung (1055-1101) copied religious texts on the Bodhisattvas in gold ink with his own hand.

The consideration shown by the Tartar dynasties for the great Indian religion manifested itself particularly in the field of architecture. From the Ch'i-tan or Liao period we might mention the elegant octagonal brick pagoda of Ting-chou (Hopei) dated 1001-1053,[94] as well as the no less elegant Nan-t'a pagoda in Fang-shan-hsien (also in Hopei), dated 1117;[95] and from the Chin period the famous thirteen-story pagoda of Pai-ma-ssu (the White Horse Pagoda), near Lo-yang, rebuilt in 1175,[96] as well as the Ch'ing-ta pagoda of the Lin-chi-ssu at Cheng-ting, dated 1185.[97]

Finally, it was the Chin rulers—thus justifying their name of 'Gold' kings—who first made their Forbidden City, in Peking, one of the wonders of Asia.[98] While nothing remains of this creation of theirs, destroyed in 1215 by Gengis-khan, the Mongols themselves—the 'Yüan'—in the reign of Kublai, and later the Ming, in the reign of Yung-lo, seem merely to have carried on their programme.

We must likewise go back to the Chin period in North China (1125-1234) for the origin of the style of the Buddhist and Taoist mural paintings from southern Shansi that continued into the Yüan period, in particular the paintings of the Kuang-sheng-ssu near Chao-ch'eng, and of the Hsing-hua-ssu near P'ing-yang that are now in the museums of Toronto, Philadelphia and Kansas City.[99] These are for the most part heavenly processions, well ordered, solemn, even pompous, but rather cold and not to be

[94] Sirén, *History of Early Chinese Art*, vol. IV, *Architecture*, pl. 78.

[95] *Idem, ibid*, pl. 76.

[96] *Idem, ibid*, pl. 69.

[97] *Idem, ibid*, pl. 80.

[98] See G. N. Kates, A New Date for the Origins of the Forbidden City, *Harvard Journal of Asiatic Studies*, 1942, p. 180.

[99] Cf. Helen Fernald, *Museum Journal*, University of Pennsylvania, Philadelphia, Sept. 1926 and June 1928. W. C. White, Chinese Temple Frescoes, *Royal Ontario Museum*, no. 12, 1937. *Idem, Chinese Temple Frescoes, a Study of Three Wall-Paintings of the Thirteenth Century*, Toronto, 1940. Laurence Sickman, Notes on Later Chinese Buddhist Art, *Parnassus*, XI, 4, p. 13.

compared with the 'primitives' of Tunhuang. They present great stylistic analogies with wood sculptures of the end of Chin period, dated 1195.[100]

Two great Taoist 'frescoes', found in Shansi and now in the Toronto Museum, representing stellar or terrestrial divinities (the Lord of the Great Bear or of the Small Bear, the Seven Stars, the Emperor of Heaven, the Empress of Earth, the gods of the Five Planets, etc.) are probably of the twelfth century. Other mural paintings of the P'ing-yang region may date from 1238 (?), that is to say from a period when the Mongols had replaced the Chin as masters of Shansi, but still followed the tradition of their predecessors.

* * *

Foreign influences make themselves felt at about the same period in the textile arts. T'ang China had manufactured silk tapestries, included under the general denomination of *chih-ch'eng* or *chin* (brocades) which we know well from the examples in the Shōsō-in at Nara. But it is not until Sung times that the term *k'o-ssu* appears. Its etymology must, it seems, be sought in the Persian word *qazz*, which designates silks in general. We know, in fact, that the Uighur, a Turkish people then established in the northeast of present-day Sinkiang, in Turfan, Karashar and Kucha, manufactured multicoloured silk rugs ('in five colours') which were probably influenced by the Iranian technique and must in turn have influenced the *k'o-ssu* of the Northern Sung, in the K'ai-feng period.[101]

We should not forget, moreover, that in the following period, from 1134 to 1211, we see established in Eastern Turkestan a

[100] W. C. White, *Op. cit.*, pp. 42-45, fig. 8.

[101] Schuyler Cammann, Origin of Chinese k'o-ssu Tapestry, *Artibus Asiae*, XI, p. 90. Cf. Jean Pierre Dubosc, Contribution à l'étude des tapisseries d'époque Song, *ibid*, p. 73. Bernard Vuilleumier, Exposition des tapisseries et tapis de la Chine (VIIe-XIXe siècles), Musée des Gobelins, April-May, 1936,

branch of the Ch'i-tan or Khitaï, the *Kara-Khitaï* as they were called, who after being chased out of Peking by the Chin had gone and founded an unexpected empire in the basins of the Ili and Chou rivers in Kashgaria.[102] There can be no doubt that this people, who at the very gates of the Iranian world had remained Buddhist and Chinese in culture, helped to maintain those relations between Iran and China to which the history of the *k'o-ssu* bears witness. We may note, during the same period and certainly with the Kara-Khitaï as intermediaries, the inverse influence that Sung China exerted on Persian pottery. Thus among the bowls of the late twelfth century or the first twenty years of the thirteenth discovered since 1945 in Gurgan (Khorassan), we find real Persian imitations, in milky white, snow white, etc., of the *ju, kuan*, celadons and other specialties of Sung ceramics.[103] The fact that the town of Gurgan, which had until then been an integral part of the empire of the Khwarezm-shahs, was destroyed by Gengis-khan's Mongols in 1220, furnishes us with indubitable proof of the artistic exchanges between the shahs of Khwarezm, of Persian culture, and their immediate neighbours the Kara-Khitaï, of Chinese culture.

* * *

The Pottery of the Sung

Sung pottery 'is rightly considered the most beautiful and the most perfect of all time'. 'Advances in technique, and the rigorous selection of pastes and glazes, then made it possible to create wares with thick, smooth glazes in many subdued tints. These are in the main highly vitrified stonewares or translucent

---

[102] On the Kara-Khitaï, see K. A. Wittfogel and Feng Chia-Sheng, *History of Chinese Society Liao*, pp. 619-674.

[103] René Grousset, L'exposition iranienne du Musée Cernuschi, *Oriental Art*, 1948, p. 110. Mehdi Bahrami, *Gurgan Faiences*, Cairo, 1949, p. 41.

porcelains'. Moreover, 'the forms differ from those of the T'ang by their simplicity. The contour of the T'ang vases, interrupted at the neck and at the base, give way to continuous and harmonious curves'.[104]

The main categories of Sung pottery are the following: [105]

1. *Ju.* The pottery so named is presumed to have been manufactured about 1100-1126 in the imperial palace of K'ai-feng by potters of the town of Ju Chou, likewise in Ho-nan. These pieces are remarkable for their thick glaze, especially in lavender-blue or bluish grey, sometimes slate blue, greenish blue or slate grey.[106]

2. *Kuan.* That is to say 'official' ware, manufactured first in K'ai-feng, then, after the Chin invasion of 1127, withdrawn to Hangchow, where the imperial potters established themselves chiefly in the Ch'ü-tan, the 'Altar of Heaven', quarter, of this city. This pottery is often very thin, the glaze generally crackled, in greenish grey, bluish, grey, bluish grey, slate grey, dove grey, pinkish grey, light iron-grey and lavender blue tints. *Kuan* pieces are very difficult to distinguish from the *ko,* of similar hues and likewise crackled. At first sight, in an exhibition—that of Burlington House (1935) and that of the Orangerie (1937) for example—the *kuan* crackling might at times seem to form a looser 'cobweb', and the *ko* crackling a closer mesh; the bluish

[104] Guimet Museum, fascicule III, *Céramique chinoise. Guide abrégé de la Collection Grandidier,* 1950 (by Madeleine David), p. 126.

[105] The basic works on Chinese pottery in general, and Sung in particular, are still those of : Hobson, *Chinese Pottery and Porcelain,* 2 vol., 1915. Hetherington, *Early Ceramic Wares of China,* 1922; Hobson, *Catalogue of the Eumorfopoulos Collection, Ceramic,* vols. II and III, 1926; *Idem, Catalogue of the Collection of Sir Percival David,* 1934; Georges Salles, *Arts de la Chine ancienne,* Musée de l'Orangerie, 1937 (*céramique* par Michel Calmann, pp. 97-223); Madeleine David, *Musée Guimet, Guide, III, Céramique chinoise,* 1950; Sherman Lee, Sung Ceramics in the Light of Recent Japanese Research, *Artibus Asiae,* XI, 1948, p. 165; Koyama, *The Story of Old Chinese Ceramics;* Sir Herbert Ingram, New Approach to the Early Chinese Ceramics, *Oriental Art,* 1948, p. 17.

[106] Examples of colour in Hobson, *Catalogue of the Eumorfopoulos Collection,* vol. II, pls. 5, 8, 11.

shades would seem to predominate in the *kuan*, the pale greys in the *ko*. Actually, these are but first impressions, and the exceptions to any such criteria would be likely quickly to invalidate them.[107]

3. *Ting*. This pottery was manufactured in the kilns of Ting-yao, the site of which was recently identified by Koyama near the village of Chien-tz'u-ts'un in the district of Ting-hsien, central Hopei.[108] 'The most perfect *ting* have a white body of fine, close grain, often translucent; they are coated with an ivory white glaze that at times forms droplets on the outside of the bowls and cups. The base is generally glazed; the upper rim, which is bare, is often concealed by a metal ring. The colour ranges from *pai-ting* (ivory white) to *fen-ting* (floury white) and *t'u-ting* (earth white)'.[109] Alternatively, the glazes may be described as ivory, cream, light bistre, beige-white, white-bistre, beige, and chamois. Ornamentation is generally incised. Michel Calmann, a specialist well qualified to pronounce judgment, regards *ting* as 'the best ceramic ware of any country and of any time'.[110]

Ting may be compared with the so-called Chü-lu-hsien ware, which has a thick creamy white glaze. Chü-lu-hsien, a locality situated in the south of Hopei, was destroyed by a flood in 1108.[111]

In 1127, because of the Chin invasion, the *ting* potters fell back to Chi-chou in Kiangsi. In these *tings* of Kiangsi, dating from the Hangchow Sung, the incised décor is often replaced by moulded designs.

[107] Examples of *kuan* and *ko, idem, ibid*, vol. ii, pls. 16, 19, 20.
[108] Koyama, Discovery of the Ruins of Tingyao, *Bulletin of Eastern Art*, No. 23-24, Tokyo, 1941.
[109] M. David, *Op. cit.*, p. 128. Examples in Hobson, *Eumorfopoulos Catalogue*, vol. iii, pls. 31, 33, etc.
[110] G. Salles, *Arts...*, p. 175.
[111] But perhaps the so-called Chü-lu-hsien pieces came from the Tzu-chou kilns about which we shall presently have something to say.

4. *Ying-ch'ing*, or 'cloudy blue', called 'light-coloured group' by Michel Calmann. These pieces are related to the *ting*, but have a more vitrified glaze with a high gloss. They were manufactured at Ching-te-chen (Kiangsi) and at Te-hua (Fukien). Exported *ying-ch'ing* has been found at places ranging from Korea to Fostat, in Egypt. The glaze is pale blue, bluish, bluish white, grey-blue, cream, etc., often with flower designs.

5. Celadons (Chinese: *ch'ing-tz'u*; Japanese: *sei-ji*). The old celadons 'of Yüeh', in Chekiang, of which we have already spoken in connection with the Five Dynasties, continued to be improved under the Sung, and gave rise, outside of China, to the Korean celadons (which have their own characteristic hues, ranging from blue-grey to apple-green, but with a predominance of greys with a very soft glaze.[112] But the finest celadons came from the workshops of Lung-ch'üan (in southwestern Chekiang). 'The Lung-ch'üan pieces can be distinguished from those of Yüeh by their fresher tint of green. The thick, smooth glaze ranges from olive green to bright green'.[113] Certain particularly fine pieces are known by the name *kinuta*, a Japanese term which indicates their superior quality.[114] There was a considerable export of Lung-ch'üan celadons to Japan, Indochina, Irak, etc.

Tradition has singled out two potters, brothers, of the Chang family, as being the outstanding masters of Lung-ch'üan. 'The "younger-brother", which in Chinese is *ti*, worked in the local tradition. The "elder-brother", which in Chinese is *ko*, is supposed to have specialized in producing crackled ware: hence the name of *ko* for this category of pieces'.[115] As we have seen, these

---

[112] George J. Lee, On the Relations of the Early Korai Celadons to the Chinese Ware of Yüeh, *Bulletin of Far Eastern Ceramic*, Nov. 1948, pp. 20-25. *Musée Cernuschi. Exposition d'Art Coréen* (1946). *Notes sur l'histoire de l'art de la Corée*, by Madeleine David, p. 19. Langdon Warner, Korai Celadons in America, *Eastern Art*, II, 1930.

[113] Madeleine David, *Guide du Musée Guimet*, III, p. 129.

[114] Examples in Hobson, *Eumorfopoulos Catalogue*, vol. II, pls. 29, 31.

[115] Michel Calmann, *Catalogue de l'Orangerie*, 1937, p. 141.

58. *Chu Ta (1626-c. 1705): Landscape after Kuo Chung-shu. Ink on paper. Cleveland Museum of Art, John L. Severance Collection.*

ko crackled wares, with glazes that are slate, blue-tinged grey, green-hued, olive grey, green-grey, water-green, etc., are difficult to distinguish from the *kuan* crackled ware. Like the latter, they show extreme delicacy of workmanship.

There were also celadon workshops in North China at the time when those of Lung-ch'üan were active. One of these was discovered in 1931 at Ju-hsien (Honan) by the Japanese professor Harada. These Northern celadons have a glaze, verging on olive-green, which is darker than those of Lung-ch'üan.[116] Their colour somewhat relates them to the Korean celadons which veer towards grey.

6. *Chün.* This ware derives its name from the Chün-chou workshops, to the southwest of K'ai-feng (Honan). The colours range from pale blue or lavender blue to tourquoise shades, with red or purple, violet or aubergine splashes. Hence the appellation 'moonlight'.[117]

7. *Chien.* This pottery takes its name from the locality of Chien-ning, in the north of Fukien, according to an identification of the site suggested by J. S. Plumer.[118] It is 'coated with a thick brown glaze, with golden or silvery *hare's fur* or *partridge feather* glints. The rim is fitted with a metal ring'. The 'hare's fur' glaze is often known by its Japanese name *temmoku* (in Chinese: *t'u-mao*).[119]

8. *Tz'u-chou.* A ceramic ware so called from the city of the same name, in Hopei. Its decoration is extremely varied. The standard pieces have a décor of flowers or leaf-scrolls, painted in black or brown clay on white slip and under a transparent glaze. The painted designs are sometimes replaced by

---

[116] Examples in Hobson, *Op. cit.*, vol. II, pls. 49, 51.

[117] *Ibid*, vol. III, pls. 2, 9, etc. Cf. George Lee, Numbered Chün Ware, *Transactions of the Oriental Ceramic Society*, 1945-1946.

[118] J. M. Plumer, in *Illustrated London News*, October 26, 1935. *Idem*, Note on the Chien yao (Temmoku), *Ostasiatische Zeitschrift*, N.F. XI (XXI), 1935, p. 193.

[119] Example in Hobson, *Op. cit.*, vol. II, pls. 55 ff.

incised or carved motifs. Some monumental vases in the Guimet Museum have a dark brown glaze, which picks out floral designs carved before firing and left in relief on the slip-covered body. The Tz'u-chou manufacture seems in fact to form a link between the ceramic art of the T'ang and that of the Ming'.[120]

But this is exceptional. Mrs. Daisy Lion-Goldschmidt has shown how 'foreign to the true genius of China' T'ang pottery remained, with 'its clashing yellows and greens, its almost crude incised décor, its bold unexpected forms which seem so alien...' The Sung pottery, on the other hand, rightly appears to her to be 'the most authentic language of the Chinese soul': 'The celadons with their shaded greens, the finely engraved white waves, the *chün* with its purple splotches, the small black bowls with thick spotted glaze in hare's fur or partridge feather finish are outstanding by virtue of the smoothness of the material, its lustre and gloss that delight not only the eye but also the touch... They represent a summit of achievement in which are expressed the civilized refinement, sensibility, and purity of taste of a race for whom sobriety is the supreme luxury'.[121]

[120] M. David, *Guide du Musée Guimet*, III, p. 132. — Examples in Hobson, *Op. cit.*, vol. III, pls. 46, 49, 56, etc.

[121] Daisy Lion-Goldschmidt, Au Musée Guimet, *Revue de Paris*, Sept. 1950, p. 162.

CHAPTER SIX

FROM THE MONGOLS TO THE MANCHUS

The Yüan

It took the Mongols some seventy years to conquer China. It was in 1205 that Genghiz Khan began his warlike activities, first directed against the provincial kingdom that had been founded in Kansu about the year one thousand by the Tibetan tribe of the Tangut or Hsi-hsia. In 1215 he captured Peking from the Chin, of proto-Manchu race. In 1233 his son and successor Ogodai seized the last Chin capital, K'ai-feng (in Honan). Then in 1276 Kublai, Genghiz-Khan's grandson, (who had mounted the Mongol throne in 1260) seized the capital of the Sung Chinese empire the great city of Hangchow (in Chekiang). By 1270 he had succeeded in reducing the last centres of resistance around Canton. All China was now his. From this point on, in his capital of Peking, he was a legitimate Chinese emperor (1276-1294) and his dynasty, the Yüan dynasty, was to assume its rank in the official annals as a sequel to some nineteen native dynasties (1276-1368).

While the Tartars looked upon him as a Mongolian Grand Khan, Kublai was determined to become, for the Chinese, an authentic Son of Heaven. I have dealt elsewhere with his role in world history in these twin capacities.[1] What he did for the

---

[1] René Grousset, *Figures de proue*, p. 285,

reconstruction of China, after seventy years of war, is related in the *Yüan-shih*, the dynastic history (not compiled until after the fall of the dynasty), as well as by Marco Polo. Let us not forget (and Marco Polo is there to remind us) that it was Kublai who made Peking one of the most beautiful cities of Asia.[2] Owing to him, there was no break in the continuity of Chinese civilization. The Tartar origin of the Yüan did, however, have an indirect influence on literature and art. As Odile Kaltenmark observes, 'the existence of a court free of certain cultural prejudices enabled certain literary tendencies to develop freely'. The theatre, 'a genre which up to that time had been considered too vulgar for scholars to devote themselves to it openly', was at last permitted to flourish officially. Born of age-old song-and-dance entertainments, the drama at this period included a part that was sung—sung by an actor who fulfilled the same role as the ancient Greek chorus—and roles (nine in number at this time) which were declaimed. Several Yüan dramas (in particular some of the plays of Wang Shih-fu) are still famous. The themes are often taken from popular historical tales, and are treated with great pathos: e.g., the surrender of a beauty of Han times to a Hun chief, the love affair and misfortunes of the T'ang emperor Hsüan-tsung and the beautiful Yang Kuei-fei, etc.[3]

Emperor Kublai and his descendants (as subsequent Confucianist historians did not fail to point out in harsh disapproval) proved to be extremely pious Buddhists. The Yüan period accordingly witnessed a continuation of the tradition of Buddhist painting that had such brilliant flowering under the Sung of Hangchow. The Ch'an monk Yen-hui who worked under Kublai (he was still painting in 1312), left portraits of Buddhist saints (*arhat*—in Chinese, *lo-han*).[4] Attributed to him are certain figures with a strong flavour of 'mystical humour', such as the hermits

[2] Bretschneider, *Recherches archéologiques sur Pékin*, pp. 42-63.
[3] Cf. Tsiang Un-kai, *K'ouen K'iu, le théâtre chinois ancien*, Paris, 1932.
[4] Iwasaki collection (Tokyo), Murayama collection (Osaka), etc.

Te-kuai and Ha-ma in the Chion-in collection, Kyoto, the former, in the manner of the Taoist magicians, emitting a small genie with his breath, the latter sitting in a thicket, holding flowers in one hand, his eyes full of dreaminess and magic power, his toad 'familiar' clinging to his shoulder and lovingly caressing his hair.[5] Also, in the Kawasaki Shōzō collection, Kobe, the hermits Han Shan and Shih-te laughing, full of monastic malice.[6]

For the Yüan period we may note also four good landscapists: Huang Kung-wang who was still painting in 1348, at the age of eighty; Wu Chen (1280-1354); Wang Meng (died in 1385); and Ni Tsan (1301-1374), the first three being from Chekiang, the fourth from Kiangsu, regions that had been the very home of Sung painting in the Hangchow period.[7] Their landscapes, or the copies that are attributed to them, do indeed form a transition between the art of the Sung and that of the early Ming.

The Yüan conquerors brought back into Chinese painting the epic strain that had characterized the T'ang: portraits of warriors (often amounting to studies of racial types, particularly of authentic Tartars), portraits of horses, hunting scenes. It should be noted that the T'ang tradition in this respect had never been lost, and this (as we have seen in the discussion of the Ch'i-tan frescoes) was outstandingly the case in the North where Tartar dynasties had reigned uninterruptedly in Peking since 936. It was, however, a true Chinese—Chao Meng-fu (1254-1322)—a prince of the Sung imperial family itself, who had gone over to Kublai, who best represents this tendency.[8]

The paintings of horses attributed to Chao Meng-fu are in-

[5] Sirén, *History of Early Chinese Painting*, vol. II, pl. 89. Tajima and Omura, *Op. cit.*, vol. IX, pls. 114-117.

[6] *Ibid.*, IX, pls. 118-119.

[7] Wu Ti-fen, *Le développement de la peinture de paysage en Chine à l'époque Yuan*, Paris, 1932.

[8] Cf. Raphael Petrucci, Tchao Mong-fou, *Revue de l'art ancien et moderne*, Sept. 1913, pp. 173, 184. On Chao Meng-fu and his friend the painter Ch'ien Hsüan (who broke with him rather than rally to the Mongols), cf. Percival David, Chinese Exhibition, *Revue des Arts Asiatiques*. Dec. 1935, p. 175.

numerable, or rather there is hardly a painting of horses that is not attributed to him. We reproduce here only some scenes from the famous handscroll in the Henri Rivière collection, representing a band of Mongol horsemen at the halt, a horseman readjusting the girths of his horse after bringing down an antelope, another horseman pursuing a runaway horse with a lasso, etc. One could scarcely hope for more precise historical documents than these portraits, drawn from life, of the cavalry of the 'World Conquerors'.

Also attributed to the Yüan period are a number of Buddhist and Taoist murals found in temples situated in southern Shansi (and northern Honan), in close continuity with the 'frescoes' of the same region attributed to the end of the Chin period. Laurence Sickman, curator of the Kansas City Museum, has made a special study of these, and distinguishes two manners, used concurrently: 'One, known as "scudding clouds and running water" ' (closely-folded, agitated drapery and floating scarves, rendered in painting by numerous black lines), and the 'iron wire' style in which the folds are simpler. The Buddhist personages represented are characterized by full, round faces with double chins, and plump hands with short fingers.[9] (It will be noticed how closely this type follows that of the carved wood Kuan-yins of the preceding period, the Chin). The Buddhas 'wear a sort of jacket, with a round collar ending in volutes, the jackets are bound in below the breast with a sash tied in a bow...'. The wide sleeves end in a series of very complicated S-folds. The Bodhisatvas are 'nude to the waist, wearing heavy necklaces and with a scarf crossing the breast from the left shoulder'. The colours are thick and opaque. The white flesh tones of the female figures contrast with the reddish tones of the masculine nude. Clouds fill the background. The prevailing colours are red and green, with constant use of an emerald green combined with blue.

[9] Cf. Laurence Sickman, Notes on the later Chinese Buddhist art, *Parnassus*, XI, 4, 1939.

Sickman calls particular attention to certain Taoist mural paintings decorating the Ming ying wang tien of the Kuang-sheng-ssu temple (also in southern Shansi), which are presumed to have been executed between 1319 and 1326.[10] His reproductions show animated scenes with actors and musicians in either Chinese or Mongol costume: human or supernatural beings, including demons, in a rather cluttered landscape with a stream straddled by a bridge, pines and weeping willows, mountain-peaks and mist; the genie Ming Ying Wang, a divinity of the mountains and streams of the region, is seated in majesty, and, despite his T'ang costume, already resembles a Ming portrait; beside him stand his mandarin advisers, who remind us of the later lay donors of Tun-huang; and there are other processions of genii and of military attendants, with a few attractive feminine figures among them, and in the distance a cavalcade escorting relics, in the usual landscape of trees, rocks and clouds; around a laden table is a group of beautiful women in full court attire, bearing flowers, vases, flasks etc.; and in another festive scene are fierce warriors who serve to remind us of the military proclivities of the Mongol court.

The museums of Toronto and Kansas City are today the most important centres for the study of these mural paintings, the former having acquired some of those from Hsing-hua-ssu near Ping-yang, and the second those of Kuang-sheng ssu in the same region. Particularly admirable is a Maitreya paradise in Toronto (Maitreya between Mañjuśri and Avalokiteśvara with two assistants, two monks and two *apsaras*); we next come upon the historical scene of the tonsuring of the emperor Liang Wu-ti, the entry into a convent of Queen Hu of the Wei T'o-pa, etc.[11] American and Canadian specialists have assigned some of these

[10] *Idem*, Wall paintings of the Yüan period in Kuang-Shêng-Ssu, Shansi, *Revue des Arts Asiatiques*, XI, 2, 1937, p. 53.
[11] W. C. White, *Chinese temple frescoes of the XIIIth century*, Toronto, p. 122.

mural paintings to the year 1238, that is to say, to the beginning
of the Yüan period, which would explain the continuity with
the Chin style. On the other hand, the present labels of the Toronto Museum bring forward the date of the great 'fresco' of
the Hsing-hua-ssu to a later Yüan period (inscription of 1298).[12]

* * *

    The ceramic art of the Yüan continues that of the Sung. Shu
Fu Yao is the only Yüan official ware. The ateliers of Lung-ch'üan
continue to manufacture celadons. The 'moonlight' Chün wares
also appear to have enjoyed great favour at this time, and those
who like them less than the other Sung creations see in this fact
the somewhat facile predilection of the conquerors for a genre
more immediately accessible than the celadons, the *ting*, and the
crackled wares.

    To the Yüan period is attributed the introduction of a cobalt
blue, called 'Mohammedan blue' (*hui-ch'ing*) because it was supposed to have originated in Iran. There can be no doubt that
Mongol 'pan-Asianism' had established a direct contact between
Persian civilization and that of China. Two branches of the Genghiz-khan family now reigned, one in China (the house of Kublai,
1260 or 1276-1368), the other in Persia (the house of Hulagu,
brother of Kublai, 1256-1335). Relations between the two related
courts remained excellent to the very end, and exchanges of luxury
gifts between them were constant. The consequences of this
interpenetration in the realm of art has perhaps not yet been
sufficiently studied.

[12] The inscription bears the date 'year *wu-hsü of the Great Yüan*', a cyclical
date recurring every sixty years (i.e. 1238, if it can be considered that the Yüan,
as such, were then reigning in Shansi, as they certainly were in 1298).

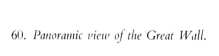

60. *Panoramic view of the Great Wall.*

The Ming

In the middle of the fourteenth century South China began to rise up against the Mongols.[13] The agitation originated among the secret societies of the White Lotus (*Pai-lien chiao*) and the White Cloud (*Pai-yün*), with their esoteric and millenarian doctrines. The Mongol administration had on various occasions outlawed the White Lotus (e.g. in 1308, 1322). The latter carried on its activity underground, and in 1351 its chief, Han Shan-t'ung, gave the signal for revolt by having his followers adopt a red turban as a rallying sign. He announced the coming of the *Millennium*, which would be manifested by the descent upon earth of the Buddhist Messiah, the Bodhisattva Maitreya (Mi-lo-fo).[14] His doctrine, a mixture of Mahayanic esotericism and Taoist sorcery, stirred up the masses. But the prophet lacked a gift of leadership, and was defeated by the Mongols, and it was the leader of another band of rebels, the future emperor Hung-wu, who benefited by the uprising. Hung-wu had no mystical leanings, but he was a remarkably skilful politician who, after having seized Nanking (1356), progressively drove the Mongols from the rest of China, and in 1368 completed the liberation of the territory by taking Peking from the last descendant of Genghiz Khan and of Kublai. He then founded the dynasty of the Ming, destined to reign over the Chinese empire from 1368 to 1644.

The greatest Ming sovereign, after Hung-wu (1368-1398), was his second son Yung-lo (1403-1424). The first two Ming emperors had retained Nanking, the city whence the movement of national liberation had sprung, as their capital. In 1409 Yung-

---

[13] On the financial errors that had shaken the prestige of the Mongols, particularly in South China (reckless issuing of paper money, inflation, devaluation of 'promissory notes', etc.), see H. Franke, *Geld und Wirtschaft in China unter der Mongolen-Herrschaft...* Leipzig, 1949.

[14] B. Favre, *Les sociétés secrètes en Chine*, p. 82.

lo moved the capital to Peking. It was he who conceived the plan and began the building of the 'Imperial City' (*Huang-ch'eng*), and within it, of the 'Forbidden Purple City' (*Tzu-chin-ch'eng*), with their ensemble of buildings, porticoes, terraces, gardens and stretches of water—a plan that was all the more remarkable since its aesthetic aspect had to harmonize with very strict astronomical and geomantic considerations.[15] Outside the Imperial City, and southeast of the Chinese City, Yung-lo built the Altar of Heaven (*T'ien-shen-t'an*), a circular temple resting on three marble terraces which remains one of the masterpieces of Chinese architecture (1420). One of the succeeding Ming emperors, Chia-ching (1522-1556), built other peripheral monuments, in particular the Altar of Agriculture (*Hsien-nung-t'an*) and, to the northeast, the Altar of Earth (*Ti-t'an*). To Chia-ching we also owe several monuments in the Imperial City, such as the Lamaistic Temple (*Ta-kao-tien*).

North of Peking, the tombs of the Ming, with their triumphal approach lined with great statues of dignitaries or animals (all marked, alas, by the decadence of sculpture under the Ming), begin chronologically with the tomb of Yung-lo, which has remained 'the Great Tomb' (*Ch'ang-ling*) and of which the ensemble—gateways, temple, altar—is the work of emperor Hsüan-te (1426-1435).

* * *

The first Ming, and in particular emperors Hung-wu and Yung-lo, took upon themselves the task of effecting a complete restoration of traditional values. To this end, looking back of course to before the Mongols, and even beyond the Sung (since the Sung, in 1127, had allowed the Tartars to occupy North China and Chinese unity to be broken), they decided to take as their models the T'ang, who before them had been the last sovereigns

---

[15] J. Bredon-Lauru, *Peking, Historical Description*, Shanghai, 1931, p. 81.

of a united China. The *Code of the Ming*, promulgated in 1373 by emperor Hung-wu, accordingly imitated the *Code of the T'ang*.[16] For the recruiting of administrative staff they reestablished the system of examinations that the Mongols had in general allowed to lapse.[17] Emperor Yung-lo tried to revive the traditions of T'ang imperialism by means of expeditions into Upper Mongolia and to Vietnam, and even by naval ventures in the Indian Ocean. But his successors did not imitate him, and immediately after Yung-lo's death (1424), the Ming virtually abandoned all military and naval expansion.

In the realm of art, however, the 'Restoration' style favoured by Ming conservatism exerted an undeniable influence. The Ming bronze vases sought, with a great deal of application and erudition if not, alas, of intelligence and vigour, to imitate the various styles of the archaic bronzes. And undeniably, as we shall presently see, Ming painting continues in its monochrome landscapes the tradition of the Sung wash-drawings, often with a great deal of talent. But at the same time (and this is the essential fact of Ming art) the love of colour reappears in a whole category of paintings. This would seem to represent a resurrection of T'ang polychromy, as manifested in the Tun-huang banners and in the marquetry of the luxury goods in the Shōsō-in. The T'ang love of colour, as well as of 'prettiness', seems in fact to have Spanned the Sung in order to give zest to the decorative surroundings of life in the age of the Ming. The same holds good for pottery, where the chorus of colours that we witnessed under the T'ang reappears under the Ming to replace the severe monochromy of the Sung aesthetes. But here, too, we should perhaps remember that during the whole Yüan period (1276-1368), as a result of the Mongol domination common to the two countries,

[16] Cf. Pelliot, Le droit chinois, *Bulletin de l'Ecole Française d'Extrême-Orient*, IX, pp. 132 ff.; Escarra, *Le droit chinois*, Paris, 1936, p. 99.
[17] *Idem, Ibid.*, p. 353. On the recruitment of the 'mandarinate' by means of competitive examinations, refer again to Robert des Rotours, *Traité des examens*, Paris, 1932.

the China of the Kublai Grand Khans had remained in close relationship with the Persia of the Hulagid *ilkhans*, and that in ceramics as in the miniature, Iran is the kingdom of colour. The extinction of the Mongol dynasty in Persia in 1335 and the expulsion of the Mongols from China in 1368 might have brought an end to these relations; such was not the case. The Ming continued to maintain close diplomatic and commercial contacts with the new masters of Iran, first Timurid, then Safavid. Thus the artistic consequences of 'Mongol pan-Asianism' were able to survive: namely, the defeat of Sung monochromy by Persian polychromy.

* * *

The art of Ming times is especially remarkable for its ceramics.[18] Under the Ming, pottery even became associated with architecture.[19] The founder of the dynasty, Hung-wu, decided in 1394 to replace wood by brick in the new structures. Thus he had erected in Nanking a pagoda of green and yellow bricks, unfortunately destroyed in 1854. The first Ming also launched an imperial factory in Ching-te-chen, a city situated in the northeast of Kiangsi and already known for its ceramics under the Sung, indeed even from the time of the Han.

The main categories of Ming ceramics are the following:

1. *San-ts'ai* or 'three-colours', namely green (from copper), yellow (from iron) and aubergine-violet (from manganese). But there are variations, and under Chia-ching (1522-1566) the 'three colours' may include green, yellow, aubergine, turquoise and a deep blue (derived from cobalt).

---

[18] Cf. Hobson, *Wares of the Ming Dynasty*, London, 1923; *Idem, Eumorfopoulos Catalogue*, vol. IV, London, 1927; Madeleine David and Daisy Lion-Goldschmidt, *Guide du Musée Guimet, III, Céramique chinoise*, 1950 which we here follow; A. D. Brankston, *Early Ming Wares of Chingtechen*, Peking, 1938.

[19] In what is to follow I shall conform to general usage, which instead of the names of the emperors of the Ming and Ch'ing dynasties substitutes the designation of their 'period of rule' (*nien-hao*).

XVII. *Plate, famille rose. Ch'ing Dynasty, 1736-1796. Musée Guimet, Paris.*

2. *Monochromes.* Ching-te-chen manufactured series of monochromes that were iron-red, a lustrous black (from cobalt and manganese), cobalt blue or violet. The finest date from Chia-ching. In Chekiang and elsewhere celadons continued to be produced, though in truth they are inferior to those of the Sung, and these were exported everywhere (to Persia, Egypt, Istanbul) through Ming commercial and diplomatic channels. Special mention must be made of the white porcelains of Te-hua, in Fukien, which were to achieve such great perfection under the following (Ch'ing) dynasty, in particular in the eighteenth century. We must note, too, under the Ming, the white wares of Ching-te-chen, with thick glaze of 'bacon-fat' appearance. For emperor Yung-lo small bowls were manufactured in this porcelain, pared down to the 'bodyless' (*t'o-t'ai*) fineness of egg-shells.

3. *Blue and white porcelain,* manufactured mainly at Ching-te-chen. For this product a cobalt mineral was imported from Iran on a number of occasions, especially under Yung-lo (1403-1424) and Hsüan-te (1426-1435), and for this reason it is called 'Mohammedan blue' (*hui-ch'ing*). The blue décor on white may also have been inspired by Persian ceramics. We must note that in certain periods, in particular in the Ch'eng-hua period (1465-1487), the import of Mohammedan blue appears to have been interrupted, forcing potters to make do with a local blue which was softer and greyish. Mohammedan blue reappeared in the Ch'eng-te period (1506-1521), mixed in varying proportions with the Chinese blue. Under Chia-ching (1522-1566) blue and white had a great vogue, employing a 'deep, often violet-tinged blue which formed a magnificent contrast with the white porcelain'. Under the emperor Wan-li (1573-1619), although the Mohammedan blue and even the kaolin had become rare, we still have, along with dull and greyish blues, those of a fine deep purplish tint. Apart from this, a technique of underglaze red distinguishes the Hsüan-te (1426-1435) and Ch'eng-hua (1465-1487) periods, but seems to have lapsed in the sixteenth century,

to be revived again under the following dynasty, in the K'ang-hsi period (1662-1722).

The technique of underglaze blue in association with brilliantly-coloured enamels (green, yellow, red), had developed under the reign of Ch'eng-hua (1465-1487). This play of colours is outstanding in the 'painting in contrasting tints' (*tou-ts'ai*), 'an opposition between pale blue underglaze and brilliant green, yellow and red enamels'. It triumphs particularly in the 'Five Colour' pieces (*wu-ts'ai*) (turquoise blue, red, green, yellow, aubergine, etc.) which appear under Chia-ching (1522-1566) and continue under Wan-li (1573-1619).[20]

The contrast between Sung and Ming ceramics is striking. The former developed into a kind of spiritualization of matter, and if it appeals to our senses it is a wholly philosophical sensuality. With the Ming, Chinese ceramics loses something of this idealism. It descends from heaven to earth, but we must hasten to add that the garden in which it 'lands' remains one of the most marvellous that the imagination of the centuries has created.

Mrs. Daisy Lion, who under the direction of Mr. Georges Salles and in collaboration with Miss Madeleine David carried out the new arrangement of these wares in the Grandidier Collection at the Guimet Museum, has clearly brought out the impression experienced by the visitor in passing from the Sung show-cases to those of the Ming: 'The colour harmonies are first limited to a narrow gamut, blues that range from turquoise to indigo, somewhat acid greens, yellows and violets. It is all rather loud, and certainly bold enough. The large hall in which these wares are exhibited is filled, as it were, with the sound of violence, with a tremendous chorus; the forms are majestic, assured, imposing. But this is only a stage; at the next turn there is recreated the calming atmosphere of the time of the Sung

---

[20] M. David and Daisy Lion, *Guide du Musée Guimet*, III, pp. 133 ff., which we here quote briefly and which should be consulted for fuller details. For the Ming shades, see the colour-plates in Hobson, *Eumorfopoulos Collection*, vol. IV.

with monochromes in a warm red, crackled glazes that amaze contemporary potters, and the incomparable *Blanc-de-Chine*, never equalled elsewhere. It is a place of calm, of fullness, of purity. Further on we come upon one of the greatest glories of the Grandidier collection. The *Blue-and-White* wares are displayed in a vast bright room in which their astonishing symphony produces a startling effect. Beneath their apparent uniformity, the diversity quickly becomes apparent: a lively variety of forms, a variety of pastes, now dense, now translucent, an endless variety of designs and lastly a variety in colour scale that ranges from a delicate, silvery blue to the deep, purplish blue of the sixteenth century, and concludes with the radiant sapphire of the seventeenth'.[21]

* * *

Ming painting admittedly did not produce geniuses of exceptional stature like those of the Sung period, but it did bequeath to us many works that by themselves alone would do honour to any period. These are commonly classified into four groups.[22]

1. In the beginning of the fifteenth century, Ming painters were still under the influence of the Yüan style. Among them may be mentioned the emperor Hsüan-te (1398-1435), and two painters of bamboos (we have seen how highly honoured this theme is in China for its philosophic symbolism): Wang Fu (1362-1416) and his pupil, Hsia Ch'ang (1388-1470).

2. The 'Wu' group, (i.e. the group of Wu-men, the former name of Suchow, in Kiangsu, near the mouth of the Yangtze). The founder of the school was Shen Chou (1427-1509), who was

[21] Daisy Lyon, Au Musée Guimet, p. 162.
[22] Sirén, *A History of Later Chinese Painting*, London, 1938, (and the review by Jean Buhot in *Revue des Arts Asiatiques*, XII, 2-3, pp. 129-130); J.-P. Dubosc, *Exhibition of Chinese Painters of Ming and Ch'ing Dynasties*, New York, 1949; E. H. von Tscharner, *Grosse chinesische Maler der Ming und Ts'ing Dynastien und chinesische Volkskunst*, Zurich, 1950; J.-P. Dubosc, A New Approach to Chinese Painting, *Oriental Art*, III, 2.

a native of this region, an artist with a truly original talent, who in many respects revitalized the art of landscape-painting.[23] His pupil, Wen Cheng-ming (1470-1559), also born near Suchow, is nearly as well known as a poet as he is as a landscapist. T'ang Yin (1470-1523) painted Buddhist subjects as well as landscapes. Wen Po-jen (1502-1575), the nephew of Wen Cheng-ming, continued his tradition.

3. The school of Chekiang. In this group attention may be called to Wu Wei (1459-1508), who in particular has left paintings of piled-up mountains in mist; Hsü Wei (1521-1593), painter and poet; Lan Ying (about 1578-1660) and Ting Yün-peng, who painted between 1585 and 1625.

4. The group formed around Tung Ch'i-chang (1555-1636), a native of Kiangsu, who was the last great Ming painter.

As we see, the majority of these masters—those of the last three groups—even if they came to live in Peking, were natives either of the region of the mouth of the Yangtze, or of the province of Chekiang, which so many Sung artists had made famous. But although there is continuity from the Sung to the Ming, it would be unjust to see mere imitation in this. 'On the contrary, what strikes us' as Jean Buhot notes, 'is the extreme vitality of this art that does not content itself, as is too often believed, with exploiting old formulae, but always seeks novelty in composition, in technique, even in mannerism. What novelty, what freshness there is in this intimate genre!'

Special mention must be made of the Ming funerary portraits which are often distinguished by the sober realism of their drawing, the sharpness of psychological insight, the force of character communicated. At their best they may be called the Clouets, Holbeins and almost the Franz Halses of the Far East.

Academic interest in art under the Ming produced art theoreticians, art critics and art historians of real merit. We may

---

[23] Tomita and Chiu Kai-ming, An Album of Landscape and Poems by Shen Chou, *Bulletin of the Museum of Fine Arts*, Boston, Oct. 1948.

61. *The Temple of Heaven, Peking. 1420 A. D.*

mention Mo Shih-lung, who painted between 1567 and 1582 and left us the treatise on painting *Hua shuo*.[24] Another treatise on painting is the *Chieh tzu yüan hua-chuan* ('Manual of the Mustard-Seed Garden'), the basic material of which is the work of Li Ch'ang-heng (also called Li Liu-fang) a scholar and land-scapist of the late sixteenth and early seventeenth centuries. The book was re-edited and prefaced in the Manchu period, at the end of the seventeenth century, by the art critic Li Yü and the landscapist Wang An-chieh. The first part of this work appeared in 1679, the second in 1701.[25]

It was towards the end of the Ming period that the Chinese print reached its peak.

Like printing itself, the print in China grew out of the taking of rubbings from engraved stones. Then, in the T'ang period, had come xylography, the use of wood blocks, for the printing not only of edifying texts (generally Buddhist), but also of Buddhist images. From Tun-huang, the Pelliot and Aurel Stein missions brought back to Paris (Guimet Museum and Bibliothèque Nationale) and to the British Museum, wood-cuts representing the *lokapāla* of the North, Vaiśravaṇa, dated 947, a paradise of Avalokiteśvara, likewise of the tenth century, etc.[26] (The Pelliot mission also brought back from Kucha a small 8th century wood-block used in printing the image of the Buddha). The Pelliot wood-cuts of Tun-huang are in black on white, but sometimes enhanced by hand-colouring. Among 'lay' prints, the Bibliothèque Nationale owns the reproduction of a Sung album, published in 1261, representing 'the life of a flower', engraved after the painter Sung Po-jen. Under the Yüan the print developed a considerable technical maturity, as can be seen from an illustrated edition of the *Kuan-yin Sūtra* dated 1331. Under the Ming, as we have

---

[24] Translation by Victoria Contag in *Ostasiatische Zeitschrift*, 1933.

[25] Translation by R. Petrucci, *Encyclopédie de la peinture chinoise*, Paris, 1918.

[26] Vandier-Nicolas, *Estampes*, in Salles, *Arts de la Chine ancienne*, p. 70, pl. XIX; Hambis, Manuscrits et peintures de Touen-Houang, Mission Pelliot, 1906-1909, *Catalogue de l'Exposition du Musée Guimet*, Oct. 1947.

said, the print enjoyed great favour. As in so many paintings and porcelains, its theme is generally that of 'birds and flowers'. At the beginning of the sixteenth century the region of Nanking and of Suchow was an important centre. Here were published, after the drawings of T'ang Yin (1466-1524), several albums of engravings printed in red, yellow, blue and green without black outlines. The Wan Li period (1573-1619) was one of great refinement, both for prints and for porcelain.[27]

The tradition of the Chin and Yüan mural paintings was also maintained under the Ming, especially in the province of Shansi and the adjoining districts. The famous 'frescoes' of the Eumorfopoulos collection, which were attributed to the Yüan by W. C. White, have been brought forward to the Ming period by Pelliot.[28] One of these, representing three large Bodhisattvas, comes from Ch'ing-liang ssu (near Hsing-t'ang-hsien, in Hopei), a temple built in 1188, rebuilt in 1424, and restored in 1466-1468. The frescoes in question are accordingly attributed by Pelliot to the fifteenth century. We may note that the gilt plaster ornaments in relief with which they are adorned is a feature that had first appeared under the Yüan. The temple of Fan-hai ssu, in the northwest suburbs of Peking, built in 1440, was likewise decorated with Buddhist frescoes ('The Western Paradise', Kuan-yin, etc.) in the Ming style, with ornamentation in gilt plaster.[29]

[27] Vandier-Nicolas, Op. cit.; Marian Densmore, Essai pour servir à l'étude de la gravure chinoise, Revue des Arts Asiatiques, XI, i, pp. 13 ff. (with illustrations).

[28] Cf. L. Binyon, Catalogue Eumorfopoulos. Frescoes. Pelliot, Les fresques de la collection Eumorfopoulos et les fresques de Touen houang, Revue des Arts Asiatiques, V, 1928, p. 43. As we have seen, the term fresco is used here by extension, for the technique of the mural painting of Central Asia and the Far East differs from the true a fresco process.

[29] Angela Latham, Illustrated London News, Feb. 27, 1937, pp. 357-359.

* * *

It is in the Ming period that ivory statuettes first make their appearance in the history of art.

Regarding the craftsmen of the Ming of the K'ang-hsi era, Maurice Paléologue has made the remark that none have since then ever understood better 'how ivory should be worked in such a way as to give full value to its texture at once veined and glossy, and bestow a soft charm and a mellow glow on what might be called its skin'. We may add that the Ming and K'ang-hsi ivories are noteworthy for the happy simplicity and purity of their lines, having none of the tiresome virtuosity and *tours de force* found in the nineteenth century 'curio'.

We here witness once again a phenomenon well known in the history of art—a 'transposition of genres'. In the field of ceramics, the Ming figurines (we need only compare them in the show-cases in our museums) are far from equalling the T'ang terra cottas. On the other hand, those 'Chinese tanagras', which had been absent since the tenth century, here reappear in the best feminine statuettes of the Ming or K'ang-hsi ivories. The styles of dress have changed, the charm of the attitudes remains the same. Perhaps the lightness of the terra cotta lent more 'springiness' to the T'ang dancing girls, but the richness of the ivory, with its warm tones, like flesh illuminated by an inner sun, confers upon the figures carved out of this material a voluptuous appeal.

Moreover, the Ming and Ch'ing ivories succeeded, better perhaps than any other material, in portraying the popular pantheon, which by then was definitively fixed. They have provided us with excellent specimens of the various canonical attitudes of Kuan-yin, the former Bodhisattva Avalokiteśvara, who by now had become a 'madonna': Kuan-yin sitting in state, with or without attendants, Kuan-yin in the posture of 'royal ease', etc. By virtue of the very slightness of their dimensions and the limitations of the material, these ivories avoid the turgidity of the large Kuan-yin of the Ming, and even of the Sung, periods. A type dear to the popular imagination and often found both in ivory and in porcelain (*blanc-de-chine*) is that of the 'Kuan-yin giver of children' (*Sung-tzu Kuan-yin*), also called the 'Kuan-yin with white garments' (*Pai-i Kuan-yin*), whose chance similarity of attitude to that of our own Virgin-and-Child has often been remarked upon. In the same category is the Taoist counterpart of Kuan-yin, the 'Princess of the Mottled Clouds' (Pi-hsia yüan-chün) who likewise grants progeny to hitherto barren families. No less interesting from the iconographic point of view are the ivory statuettes of Taoist genii: the 'Eight Immortals' (*hsien*); and the three Gods of Happiness—literally the 'Three Stars' (*San Hsing*), for these supernatural beings, represented on earth in the guise of wise old men, have their heavenly correspondence with three stars, namely the Star of Happiness (*Fu-hsing*), the Star of Official Dignities (*Lu-hsing*)—for this is a land of mandarins, of a 'transcendent', pantheonized mandarinate—and the Star of Longevity (*Shou-hsing*). On many of the ivories in our possession these kindly old men with their flowing beards and protuberant craniums—made deliberately droll, yet without detracting from their dignity—gaze upon us with smiling good-nature, indeed with a somewhat mocking benevolence: the epitome, in fact, of Chinese humour.[30]

* * *

Ming literature enjoys little critical favour today. 'In many respects', Odile Kaltermark writes, 'it is marked by conventionality and lack of imagination. The Confucianist scholar class, which seemed to have ceased to be anything but a decadent bourgeoisie, perpetuated and aggravated an absurd system of examin-

[30] See Maspero, René Grousset and Lucien Lion, *Les ivoires religieux et médicaux chinois*, Paris, 1939; Maspero, Mythologie de la Chine moderne, in *Mythologie Asiatique Illustré* by P.-L. Couchoud, 1928, pp. 227-362; *Idem*, Les dieux taoïstes. Comment on communique avec eux, Académie des Inscriptions, séance publique ann. elle du 19 novembre 1937.

ations that merely encouraged its inertia'. The period never-theless produced one original philosopher, Wang Yang-ming (1472-1528 or 1473-1529).[31]

Wang Yang-ming sought to react against the mechanistic determinism of Chu Hsi, or at least to correct it, through Men-cius's theory on the goodness innate in the heart of man. Chu Hsi, for that matter, admitted that the moral conscience represents our participation in the laws of the universe or, as he said, in the 'Heavenly Norm' (*T'ien-li*). Wang Yang-ming concludes that the objective study of the universe is less important to us than intuition, through which we communicate with the essence of things. He discovers in intuitive knowledge the release of uni-versal spontaneity, the source of metaphysical freedom. Certain present-day Chinese writers see in it a kind of 'Bergsonism' in reaction against the cult of science ('à la Herbert Spencer') of the school of Chu Hsi. In reality the doctrine of intuition de-veloped by Wang Yang-ming unwittingly bore traces of the Buddhist conceptions of the Ch'an school.

In the literary field proper the Ming period achieved distinc-tion in the theatre and in the novel. The Yüan theatre had kept something of its original character of popular entertainment. The more refined Ming theatre (*Ch'uan ch'i*) became a pastime for the great. Several Ming plays—'the Guitar' (*P'i-p'a chi*) composed by Kao Ming about 1367, 'the Pavilion of Peonies' (*Mu tan t'ing*), by T'ang Hsien-tsu (1550-1611), works full of romantic adventures,—can still be read with interest. The same is true of several Ming novels, among which must first be men-tioned historical novels like the *San-kuo-chih yen-i*, a fictionalized history of the Three Kingdoms, full of action, and with the characters of heroes and villains often powerfully drawn, which occasionally achieves an epic feeling.[32] The author, a certain Lo

[31] F. Henke, *The Philosophy of Wang Yang-ming*, Chicago, 1916; Wang Tch'ang-tche, *La philosophie morale de Wang Yang-ming*, Shanghai, 1936.
[32] Ou Itai, *Le roman chinois*, Paris, 1933, p. 59.

Pen whose dates can be placed only very approximately between 1330 and 1400, is considered by Sung-nien Hsü as having manifested democratic tendencies amid the highly conservative society of the Ming.[33] Another historical novel, but at the same time having a considerable element of fantasy, is the story of the 'Voyage to the West' (i.e. India) of the pilgrim Hsüan-tsang (*Hsi-yu-chi*), which is attributed to Wu Ch'eng-en (very approximately between 1510 and 1580).[34] As Odile Kaltenmark observes, the fanciful predominates here to such an extent that the atmosphere is as much Taoist as it is Buddhist. The hero becomes, not so much Hsüan-tsang as his ally, the extraordinary Monkey King Sun Wu-k'ung who is endowed with magic powers and accomplishes prodigious exploits in the earthly and heavenly worlds. We find here, along with a delight in the fanciful, a considerable ingredient of humour.[35] Another novel, the *Feng-shen yen-i* or 'novel of the investiture of the gods', has gods, genii and demons intervening to bring about the downfall of the dynasty of the Shang-Yin and the accession of the house of Chou.[36]

Other novels have a quite different character, as exemplified by the *Chin-P'ing-mei* ('the flowers of *mei* in a golden vase'), erroneously attributed to the poet Wang Shih-cheng (1526-1590), typical of the realistic novel of manners, and somewhat ribald.[37]

[33] Sung-Nien Hsü, *Anthologie de la littérature chinoise*, p. 61.

[34] Cf. Ou Itai, *Op. cit.*, pp. 31-40.

[35] Wu Che'ng-en, *Monkey*, translated by A. Waley, London, 1945; and *Monkeys Pilgerfahrt*, German translation by Georgette Boner and Maria Nils, Zurich, 1947.

[36] Ou Itai, *Op. cit.*, p. 41.

[37] *Idem*, p. 79.

The Ch'ing

In 1644 the Manchus took advantage of a serious insurrection that had broken out in China to seize Peking.[38] Almost without striking a blow, they made themselves masters of the immense empire and founded a new and final imperial dynasty, the Ch'ing dynasty (1644-1912). Like the Mongol emperors four centuries before, the Manchu emperors were eager to assume, in the eyes of their Chinese subjects, their role as Sons of Heaven. The two greatest among them, K'ang-hsi (1662-1722) and Ch'ien-lung (1736-1796), were brilliantly successful in this. Both performed a Chinese imperial task in restoring the Peking palaces.[39] The Forbidden City had been pillaged and in part burned down during the 1644 revolt that had occasioned the Manchu intervention. K'ang-hsi restored not only the palaces of the Forbidden Purple City (*Tzu-chin-ch'eng*), but also the monuments of the other districts, such as the Lamaistic temple of *Chan-t'an-ssu*. On the outskirts, the Temple of Heaven (*T'ien-t'an*) and the Temple of Agriculture (*Hsien-nung-t'an*) were likewise restored by Ch'ien-lung. K'ang-hsi and Ch'ien-lung thus showed themselves to be the true heirs and faithful trustees of the ideas of the Ming emperor Yung-lo. In Inner Mongolia K'ang-hsi in 1703 erected the summer palace of Jehol, which was later further embellished by Ch'ien-lung.[40]

Their reigns and that of the intervening emperor Yung-cheng (1723-1735) are also of great importance in the history of ceramics.[41]

[38] Cf. Frantz Michael, *The Origin of Manchu Rule in China: Frontier and Bureaucracy as Interacting Forces in Chinese Empire*, Baltimore, 1942.

[39] See Sirén, *Les palais impériaux de Pékin*; Idem, *Gardens of China*, New York, 1949-1950.

[40] See Tadashi Sekino, *Summer Palace and Lama Temples in Jehol*, Tokyo, 1935.

[41] See particularly Hobson, *Catalogue of the Eumorfopoulos Collection, Ceramic*, vol. v; J. P. van Goidsenhoven, *La Céramique chinoise sous les Ts'ing*,

* * *

The ceramic art of the K'ang-hsi period (1662-1722) is particularly noteworthy for its copper-red monochromes, with their rich, so-called *sang-de-bœuf* hues. Among K'ang-hsi monochromes are also white wares of excellent quality. A new use of cobalt blue produced 'mottled' and 'powdered' blues. K'ang-hsi porcelain is likewise remarkable for 'the range of yellows derived from iron, as well as from ochre, brown ochre, sienna and burnt umber (Nanking yellow and café-au-lait)'.[42]

K'ang-hsi 'blue and white' is one of the glories of the reign (blue painted underglaze on a white background, and fired at a high temperature). 'The blue here is a local cobalt, refined and purified to the famous sapphire tone of unequalled brilliance'. The 'Five Colours' (*Wu-ts'ai*) of the K'ang-hsi period, used in designs of flowers and animals, marks the transition between the similar Ming pieces and the *famille verte* characteristic of the new reign.

The K'ang-hsi use of enamels represents the culmination of a long process. Under the Sung we had seen red, yellow and green. At the end of the Ming there had been added a few touches of bright turquoise blue. But 'the genre reached its full development only in the K'ang-hsi period, in dazzling pieces in which coral red and green predominate, heightened here and there by light touches of yellow and pale violet'.[43]

K'ang-hsi porcelain is marked above all by the triumph of the *famille verte*, 'with its infinite gradation of colour and attractive diversity of pictorial design'.[44] Madeleine David and

Brussels, 1936. And Madeleine David, *Guide du Musée Guimet*, III, *Céramique chinoise*, which we follow here.

[42] *Ibid.*, p. 153.

[43] *Ibid.*, p. 154.

[44] In this connection we would call attention, in particular, among the pieces of the Grandidier collection at the Guimet Museum (show-case no. 47), to the famous *vase with the thousand stags*, 'a magnificent example of this technique in which the whole gamut of the greens is used'.

62. *Ju Peon: Horses. Ink on paper. Twentieth century. Musée Cernuschi, Paris.*

63. *Fu Pao-shih: Landscape. Ink and color on paper. Twentieth century. Musée Cernuschi, Paris.*

Daisy Lion, who have furnished us with the best short introduction to the subject, point out in this connection that the *famille verte* 'differs from the "Five Colour" wares in the substitution of an opaque purplish blue enamel for underglaze blue, and in the frequent use of a dark green enamel shading into black'. To imitate the 'Three.Colours' of the Ming, *famille verte* enamels were also used on biscuit-ware, predominantly in green and yellow. 'This is the classic period in porcelain, when the skill and experience of the potter reached their full development during the reign of the great scholar and art-lover K'ang-hsi... Its most perfect expression is perhaps in the large vases of the so-called *famille noire*: the vigour of the colours, the majesty of the forms reach a peak at which art cannot remain for any length of time'.[45]

During the Yung-cheng period (1723-1735) the *famille verte* was superseded by the *famille rose* 'in which a pink enamel of western origin, somewhat purple in tint, predominated'.

The reign of Ch'ien-lung (1736-1796) is the last great period of Chinese ceramics. The career of the *famille rose* attains its climax in the 'harlequin' style, and then gives way to the *mille fleurs* (veritable 'pictures on porcelain')—a last burst of splendour before the onset of decadence.

In a process of development begun under the Ming, continued under K'ang-hsi and reaching its culmination under Ch'ien-lung, we have witnessed a remarkable transposition of genres: the art of the painter—of 'birds and flowers', landscape, etc.—has been transferred to ceramic decoration.

In monochrome-glazed wares the Ch'ien-lung period has also to its credit some use of red enamels (*rouge de fer*, coral, tomato), turquoise blues and amethyst violets, as well as black often accompanied by enamels of the *famille rose*; and in addition some tours-de-force which, while representing the summit of technical

[45] Daisy Lion, Au Musée Guimet, p. 163.

39.

skill, also betray the drying-up of inspiration that is a forerunner of an abrupt fall from eminence.

* * *

Ch'ing painting of the seventeenth and eighteenth centuries can boast several painters of talent.[46] One prominent school of landscapists is that which included Wang Shih-min (1592-1680), Wang Yüan-ch'i (1642-1715), Wang Hui (1632-1717), Huang Ting (1660-1730) and Fang Shih-shu (1692-1751), all past masters of firm, sure drawing, full of skill and delicacy; while among the individualists were the monk Pa-ta Shan-jen (approx. 1626-1705), K'un-ts'an (painted between 1650 and 1675), the monk Shih-t'ao (approx. 1630-1707), and Kung-hsien, the Nanking master (painted between 1656 and 1682). Somewhat apart from these are the provincial painters of Anhui, such as Hung-jen (died 1663), or of Yang-chou, like Chin Nung (1687-1764).

The life of Shih-t'ao (also known as Tao-chi), one of whose most powerfully constructed landscapes was acquired by the Guimet Museum in 1951, was strongly determined by fate. As a descendant of the Ming house, he was unable to accept the Manchu domination and became a Ch'an monk. He wrote a treatise on painting, the *Hua yü lu*, in which he proclaims his own fierce independence in the face of official academicism.

Prints continued to be esteemed in the early part of the Ch'ing dynasty. It was, as we saw, in 1679 that the first edition of the *Manual of the Mustard-seed Garden*, with its numerous plates, was published. The best colour prints belong to this period (end of the seventeenth and first half of the eighteenth century). 'They represent flowers, baskets or bowls of fruit, landscapes, and sometimes subjects with figures of a more popular character. Their technique is complex and ingenious, their range of colour very

---

[46] *Catalogue of the Exhibition 'Great Chinese Painters of the Ming and Ch'ing Dynasties'*, New York, March-April 1949.

varied: yellows, orange, browns, greens of several hues, reds, pinks and blues; sometimes the engravers further enrich it by superimposing different colours one on another'.[47] In the former Curtis and Vever collections in Paris were prints of the K'ang-hsi and Yung-cheng periods showing a remarkably delicate treatment of bird and flower themes.[48]

In another volume in the present series we shall have occasion to speak of the western influence in the Far East, both in connection with the porcelains of the India Company and with the painting of Father Castiglione.

Modern Times

Among the Confucian scholars of the seventeenth and eighteenth centuries were a few substantial thinkers who pursued research in an already scientific spirit. Such a one was Ku Yen-wu (1613-1682), who reproached Wang Yang-ming's intuitionist philosophy for having, under the influence of Ch'an mysticism, turned Chinese thought away from all that was constructive in Chu Hsi's ideas. Ku Yen-wu undertook to bring the mind back into the path of positive knowledge. Along these lines he wrote, in particular, a historical, ethnographical and economic geography. Other scholars, like the exegetist Hui Tung (1697-1758), going even beyond the interpretation of the Sung and finding their point of reference in the Han, undertook a rigorous criticism of the canonical texts. The philologist and mathematician Tai Chen (1723-1777) built on these foundations, which we should call positivist, a separate system that he opposed even to that of Chu Hsi. In historical criticism, Ts'ui Shu (1740-1818) did not

---

[47] Vandier-Nicolas in Salles, *Arts de la Chine ancienne*, pp. 73-74.
[48] Good reproductions in Densmore, *Op. cit.*, and in Vandier-Nicolas, *loc. cit.*, plates XX-XXI; Cf. Dubosc, Images imprimées et gouaches populaires chinoises, Catalogue of the Exhibition *Chinesische Malerei der Ming und Ts'ing Dynastien*, Zurich, 1950,

hesitate to demonstrate that the most venerated traditions regarding Chinese origins were all cluttered with folk legends.

Launched upon this path, textual criticism led inevitably to the publications of the Cantonese K'ang Yu-wei (1858-1927), who considered the texts incorporated in the Confucian canon in the period of the second Han (the so-called *ku-wen*) as no less apocryphal than the subsequent additions. In a sensational manifesto on 'Confucius as Reformer' (1897), K'ang Yu-wei presented the Sage as the very incarnation of the social reformer as conceived by the younger generation. For western ideas, made available by a galaxy of translators, were inevitably finding their way into the intellectual world. Among such translators must be mentioned Yen Fu (1852-1921) who translated into Chinese the works of the English positivist and evolutionist school, and Lin Shu (1852-1924) who translated a whole library of English, French and Russian social novels.[49]

While the spontaneous workings of the Chinese mind, further stimulated by the invasion of western ideas, were shaking thousand-year-old conservatism, the Manchu dynasty, incapable of defending China against the West, was 'losing face' in the eyes of the Chinese people. The first Chinese national reaction against the bankruptcy of the 'foreign dynasty' had been the revolt of the T'ai-p'ing who had remained masters of Nanking for eleven years (1853-1864). They had failed by reason of the poverty of their ideology—an illuminism, a millenarianism that was a hodge-podge of all the reveries of the neo-Amidic or neo-Taoist sects (White Lotus, White Cloud, etc.), mixed up with strangely interpreted Biblical conceptions.[50]

[49] See E. R. Hughes, *The Invasion of China by the Western World*, London, 1937.
[50] The T'ai-p'ing of the years 1850-1864, as later the Boxers (*Ch'üan-fei*) of 1900, are modern instances of the many occasions throughout Chinese history when secret societies have headed popular movements, from the time of the Red Eyebrows (*Che-mei*) in 18 A.D. and the Yellow Turbans (*Huang-chin*) in 184. The intervening centuries also witnessed the agitations fomented by the association

In foreign policy disasters followed one upon another. After the humiliation of the Opium war (1842) came the capture of Peking by the Anglo-French (1860), then the defeats of the Sino-Japanese war (1894-1895) which were a prelude to the new occupation of Peking by foreign armies (1900). K'ang Yu-wei, the scholar of whom we have spoken as having undertaken the modernization of Confucianism, in the same spirit had the idea of saving the monarchy by converting it to reformism. He was seconded in this undertaking by his disciple, the historian Liang Ch'i-ch'ao (1873-1929), who proposed as models of regenerated, modernized and prosperous monarchies the Russia of Peter the Great and the Japan of Meiji; and as an example not to be followed, that of the immobile and decrepit Ottoman empire. Unexpectedly, these lessons were heeded by the young emperor Kuang-hsü, who in 1898 called K'ang Yu-wei and Liang Ch'i-chao into his councils. There followed the 'Hundred Days', which were marked by a series of hasty imperial edicts, intended to modernize the old empire at one stroke by a thoroughgoing application of K'ang Yu-wei's reformist programme.

We know that the Dowager Empress Tzu-hsi, who adhered to the ideas of the most retrograde Manchu party, brought this endeavour to an abrupt end. K'ang Yu-wei and Liang Ch'i-ch'ao barely had time to take refuge in Japan where the latter, abandoning his dream of a modernized monarchy, passed over to republican ideas. As for K'ang Yu-wei, he was to go even further, since in 1913 he was to expound, as the doctrine of the 'Great Concord' (*Ta-t'ung*), a communist-tinged interpretation of Confucianism.

To replace an abortive reformism there arose the radicalism of Sun Yat-sen. This cantonese intellectual (1866-1925) who had studied medicine and political economy in Honolulu and in

known as the *Ko-lao-hui*, the Triad (*San-ho-hui*), and the associations of the White Lotus (*Pai-lien-chiao*) and of the White Cloud (*Pai-yün*), etc. See Favre, *Les sociétés secrètes en Chine*, Paris, 1933.

Hong-kong, was a son of Overseas China, with a cultural background as much Anglo-Saxon as it was Chinese, and a follower of the Christian Church. His doctrine, 'Triple Demism', that is to say the Three Principles of Democracy (*San min chu i*), consisted of, 1. nationalism (expulsion of the Manchus, government of China by the Chinese); 2. democracy (government of the people by the people, and in the interim by its most enlightened guides, the members of the nationalist party or *Kuo-min-tang*); 3. a state socialism, not yet Marxist, it seems, but with a whole network of social laws.

It was on this programme that the followers of Sun Yat-sen, having brought about the revolt of a part of the army, unleashed the revolution of the winter of 1911-1912 that deposed the Manchu dynasty and proclaimed the republic. As we know, a viceroy of the old regime, the too-clever Yüan Shih-k'ai, was able to manipulate the revolution to his own advantage and while holding the title of president of the republic set up a dictatorship (1912-1916). He succumbed in 1916 before the double revolt of the other military chiefs in the North and of the republican party in the South. But China then fell into a state of military anarchy similar to that which a study of history shows us to have obtained during the period of the Great Crumbling (316-589) and the time of the Five Dynasties (907-959).

Nevertheless, in the midst of the worst anarchy, the intellectual movement pursued its course.[51] Two university men, Ch'en Tu-hsiu and Hu Shih, were appealing as early as in 1916 for a radical reform of teaching and of literature. They were successful in having the written language (*wen-li*) in the schools replaced by the spoken language (that of Peking), the 'clear language' (*pai-hua*), which in turn became the written language and was henceforth taught as the national language in all the provinces (1920). It was in the spoken language that Hu Shih, preaching

[51] Cf. Hu Shih, *The Chinese Renaissance*, 1934,

by example, had published his *History of Chinese Philosophy* in 1919.

Sun Yat-sen, who died in 1925, was succeeded at the head of the Kuo-min-tang by a southern general, Chiang Kai-shek, who from Canton had marched north against the northern generals, driving them out of Nanking (1927) and Peking (1928), thus, at least officially—and with Nanking as his capital—reestablishing the unity of China. For twenty years, from 1928 to 1948, Chiang Kai-shek, surrounded by the polysynody of the Kuo-min-tang, governed official China, if one except the Japanese invasion and occupation in the eastern provinces (1937-1945) and the Communist uprisings at the most diverse points.

For the communist party (*Kung-ch'an-tang*) was gaining ground. After having for a brief time (1927-1933) set up a soviet republic in the southern province of Kiangsi, the communists, moving to the other end of China, re-formed in the extreme north of Shensi, in Yennan. They now had at their head an energetic soldier, of Marxist training. Mao Tse-tung, who in Yennan organized a disciplined army. At the head of the communist-minded intellectuals was the writer and archaelogist Kuo Mo-jo who soon exerted a considerable influence over university circles.[52] We know that in the face of the incapacity of the Kuo-min-tang to reform itself the armies of Mao Tse-tung, after having established a central communist government in Peking—which thus once again became the capital—were able to drive Chiang Kai-shek out of Nanking and occupy all China (1949).

[52] Kuo Mo-Jo is the author, among other works, of *Chung-kuo ku tai shi nien chiou*, Research on the History of Chinese Antiquity, Shanghai, 1931, and of volumes on the inscriptions of the Yin and Chou bronzes, *Liang Chou chin wen tz'u ta hsi k'ao shih,*—and *Yin Chou ch'ing t'ung ch'i ming wen yen chiu*, Peking, 1931, 1935.

* * *

In the realm of Chinese art the last thirty years have witnessed a considerable revival.[53]

In 1919 a lover of French art, Ts'ai Yüan-p'ei, founded the Academy of Fine Arts of Peking, and a team of new talents formed around Hsü Ta-tsang. The 1933 exhibition was in itself a revelation, with the works of innovators (in other respects faithful to the traditional Chinese genius) like Wang I-ching (born in 1869), Fan Yüeh-yü (born in 1870), Chang Ta-ch'ien (born in 1889) and Chen Shu-jen (born in 1884).

A very great painter, the son of Hsü Ta-tsang, the master Jupéon (Hsü Pei-wong), born in 1894 (and who worked in Paris from 1921 to 1926) is in the very front rank among creative talents. His familiarity with Montparnasse has deprived him of none of his original spontaneity. Probably no one has more surely realized the East-West synthesis. In his Indian-ink wash drawings in which, in the words of Mr. Shu Ling, 'the design and the ink become one', in which 'the art of Jupéon, in all its sobriety and power, renders the whole essence in a few violently flung lines', the present president of the Chinese Academy of Fine Arts conjures up unbroken stallions, wild mares, who whinny, snort and cavort before our eyes, or—without ever departing from the frankest naturalism—he shows us, in the heat of action, monstrous buffalos holding demoniacal snakes at bay. His art reveals a freedom, a spontaneity, a passion worthy of the greatest. One has the illusion of witnessing, as seized by the most modern

[53] See Mr. Shu Ling's magnificent album, *La peinture chinoise contemporaine*, Paris, 1949; Jupeon and Salles, *Catalogue de l'Exposition de peinture chinoise, art chinois contemporain*, May-June, 1935; Vadime Elisseeff, *Catalogue de l'exposition de peintres chinois au Musée Cernuschi*, Paris, June 1946; Association France-Chine, *Exposition des artistes chinois en France* (at the Ecole des Beaux-Arts), Catalogue by Shu Ling, October 1946; *Exposition des peintures d'Ou Sogène au Musée Galliera*, Paris, 1947; Lu Cha-kwan, *Catalogue de l'Exposition de peintures chinoises au Musée Municipal d'Art Moderne*, Paris, November-December 1948.

64. *Wu Tso-jen: Yacks. Ink on paper. Twentieth century.*

brush, the galloping of stallions glimpsed by Chuang-tzu through swirling clouds of dust, the buffaloes, bestial and at the same time divine, of the ancient Ch'an painting.[54]

Fu Pao-shih, also 'a fiercely lyrical landscapist', revolutionizes and revives the most classical Sung themes while stripping them of all banality: as in the reverie of the sage letting his boat drift, in a broad and luminous water landscape, with the slow meanderings of a river circling the vertical cliff of a promontory.

Lien Fong-mien, born in 1906, who worked in Montparnasse in 1918, is 'a landscapist using violent colours juxtaposed with incisive art'—a fauvist of Far Asia.

Ting Yen-yung (born in 1903) revives what would have been considered screen subjects not long ago—blades of grass, insects and frogs—'picking them off' with a few touches—a few spots—quick, spare, witty.

So too Ch'i Pai-shih (1859-1948), with his rats and his chicks, has reminded us, even in his ripe old age, that humour—a Buddhist humour full of tenderness for creatures and for things—remains one of the permanent elements of the Chinese genius.

The Szechwanese Chang Ta-ch'ien (born in 1889) ranges from the painting of flowers (e.g. the giant lotuses of his last exhibition in the Cernuschi Museum) to austere defiles in the gorges of the Yangtze.

Among the 'young' we must mention Wu Tso-jen ('Ou Sogène') who has brought back from the steppes of the Kokonor and the high plateaux of Tibet immense visions of desert spaces, endless expanses of snow across which tea caravans plod, windand stretch away, in which herds of yaks are swallowed up, from which at times two monstrous yaks loom forth to engage in a duel to the death on the edge of a precipice. Ch'ao Wu-chi, whose poignant 'cemetery' we exhibited at the Cernuschi Museum (1946) is a Chinese Raoul Dufy. We also call attention to our

[54] Cf. Suzuki, *The Ten Ox-Herding Pictures* (paintings of buffalos by the Sung Dhyanist painter Kuo-an Shih-yüan), Kyoto, 1948.

40.

friends Lü Sha-kuan, former curator of the Hangchow Museum, Shu Ling, president of the Chinese artists of Paris, Zao Wu-ki, Mrs. Pan Yü-lin and Mrs. Fan Chun-pi, all of whom show a very sure and refined talent.

With Louis Hambis we want also to point to the revival of Chinese ceramics, which he had an opportunity to study at the last Peking salons (the vases, for example, of the master potter Yeh Lin-chih).[55] Finally, in the person of Hua T'ieh-yu, China has a very great sculptor, whose powerful group 'Mother and children under a bombardment' was recently shown at the Cernuschi Museum.

It is to be noted that, like Wu Tso-jen, Chang Ta-ch'en and Pan Shun-ching have gone to Tun-huang to capture in the frescoes of the Wei and the T'ang the secret of the old medieval schools. Thus the most modern China—a China that is so close to us through its affinities with Montparnasse—links up with the traditions of the most distant past...

Through all political changes, eternal China continues.

Musée Cernuschi, March 30, 1951.

[55] Louis Hambis, Où en est l'art chinois? Le dernier salon de Pékin, in the weekly, *Arts*, May 6, 1949.

CHRONOLOGY OF CHINESE DYNASTIES

CHINESE PROTOHISTORY

Ch'i-chia-p'ing pottery	*circa* 2500-2200 (pre-Hsia period), according to Andersson; *circa* 1400-1300 (Shang period), according to G. D. Wu.
Yang-shao I pottery	*circa* 2200-1900 (pre-Hsia period and early Hsia), according to Andersson; *circa* 1700 (Hsia), according to G. D. Wu.
Yang-shao II pottery	*circa* 1900-1700 (Hsia period), according to Andersson; *circa* 1200 (Shang period), according to G. D. Wu.
Pan-shan pottery	Middle Yang-shao period, *circa* 1900, according to Andersson (time of the Hsia); Late Shang, *circa* 1300-1000, according to G. D. Wu.
Ma-ch'ang pottery	*circa* 1700-1300 (Hsia and early Shang), according to Andersson; *circa* 1000 (early Western Chou), according to G. D. Wu.
Hsin-tien pottery	*circa* 1300-1000 (second part and end of Shang period), according to Andersson; *circa* 700 (early Eastern Chou), according to G. D. Wu.

CHINESE DYNASTIES

Hsia (North China) . . . . 1989(?)-1523(?)

Shang (North China) . . . . 1523(?)-1028
(after 1300 assuming the name of *Yin* dynasty)

Chou (North China) 1027-256
Chronologically divided into:

    1. *Western Chou* (centre in Shensi) 1027-771
    2. *Eastern Chou* (centre in Honan) 770-256

Period of *Spring and Autumn Annals (Ch'un-ch'iu)* . . 772-481
Period of *Warring States (Chan-kuo)* 481-221

Ch'in (North China unified and racially alien kingdoms of
South China subjugated) 2210-207

Han (reign extending over whole of China) . . . . . . 206 B.C.-220 A.D.
Chronologically divided into:

    1. *Early Han (Ch'ien-Han)* or *Western Han (Hsi-
Han)* (capital Ch'ang-an, or Hsi-an-fu) . . . . 206 B.C.-8 A.D.
Wang Mang usurpation . . . . 9 A.D-22 A.D.
    2. *Later Han (Hou-Han)* or *Eastern Han (Tung-
Han)* (capital Lo-yang) 25-220

The *Three Kingdoms* split China as follows:

    1. *Han of Szechwan (Shu-Han)* 221-263
    2. *Wei* (North China) 220-265
    3. *Wu* (South China—Nanking) 221-280

Chin (Ssu-ma family), reigning until 316 over all China . . 265-(420)
Losing North China to the Tartars in 316, the Chin fell
back on South China. This dynasty therefore chronologically divided into:

    1. *Western Chin* (capital Lo-yang), holding sway
over all China 280-316
    2. *Eastern Chin* (capital Nanking), pushed back by
the Tartar invasions to South China 317-420

Period of division between the North and the South or
Nan-Pei-ch'ao: the North being occupied by the
Tartars, the South having become the refuge of the
Chinese national Empire 317-589
This period corresponds *practically* to what is called the
Six Dynasties (Liu-tai), although the latter expres-
sion covers the entire span 220-589.
During the *Na-Pei-ch'ao*, the following five imperial
dynasties succeeded one another *in the South* (capital
Nanking):

    1. *Eastern Chin* (above-mentioned) 317-420
    2. *Sung* of the Liu family (*Liu-Sung*) 420-479
    3. and 4. *Ch'i*, 479-501, and *Liang* 502-556
    5. *Ch'en* 557-588

A great number of successive Tartar dynasties in the
North, including:
— Several hordes of *Hiung-nu* (Huns) *Chao* . . . 316-352
— Several hordes of *Hsien-pei* (proto-Mongols), led
by the *Mu-jung* clan 349-407
— The Tartar king *Fu Chien* 357-385

— The *Tabghach* (in Chinese, *T'o-pa*), of Turkish
race, also called kings of *Wei*, who successively
annexed the other Tartar kingdoms of North
China, thus unifying them. This is the dynasty
of the *Northern Wei (Pei-Wei)* that within a
short time reigned over all Northern China . .   398-534
This dynasty in 534 divided into:

1. *Eastern Wei (Tung-Wei)* in Northeast China,
around Honan   534-550
2. *Western Wei (Hsi Wei)* in Northwest China,
around Shensi   534-557

succeeded by the following, respectively:

1. in the Northeast (Honan, etc.) the *Pei-Ch'i* . .   550-577
2. in the Northwest (Shensi, etc.) the *Pei-Chou* .   557-581

Sui, from 581 in the North;

from 589 in the whole of China, which it unified by
annexing the southern empire of Nanking. The Sui
capital is Ch'ang-an (Hsi-an-fu)   589-618

T'ang (capital Ch'ang-an or Hsi-an-fu), reigning over all
China   618-907
Period of the *Five Dynasties (Wu-tai)* in the North only
(capital K'ai-feng), namely:

1. Hou-Liang   907-923
2. Hou-T'ang   923-936
3. Hou-Chin   936-946
4. Hou-Han   947-950
5. Hou-Chou   951-959

In the South during this time, various provincial dynas-
ties, among which may be mentioned:
— *Wu-T'ang*, then *Nan-T'ang* in Nanking . . .   902-975
— *Wu-Yueh* in Chekiang (Hangchow)   907-978
— *Nan-Han* in Canton   907-965

Sung   960-1276
The Sung dynasty chronologically divided into:

1. Northern *Sung (Pei-Sung)*, capital K'ai-feng,
reigning practically over all China, which they
had reunified   960-1127
2. *Southern Sung (Nan-Sung)*, reduced by the Tartar
invasion (of the Chin) to South China (capital
Hangchow)   1127-1276
(or 1279)

In the Far North, in Peking, the *Ch'i-tan* or *Chitat* (in
Chinese, *Liao*) of Mongol race   936-1122

In Kansu, the *Hsi-Hsia* or Tangut, of Tibetan race
(capital Ning-hsia)   1001-1227
In all North China (except Kansu) the *Djurchet* (in Chinese, *Chin*), of Tongus (Manchu) race, capitals
Peking (1122), then K'ai-feng (1214)   1127-1234
The *Mongols* descending from Genghiz Khan (in Chinese, the Yüan dynasty), masters of all China . .   1276-1368
The accession of the Yüan dynasty can be dated from
1260, when its founder Kublai, grandson of Genghiz
Khan, mounted the Mongol throne in conquered
North China; or from 1276, when Kublai in Hangchow captured the last officially consecrated Sung
emperor; or from 1279-1280, when Kublai put to
death the last Sung pretenders in the Cantonese region. The Yüan capital is Peking.

The *Ming* dynasty, reigned over the whole of China
(capital Nanking from 1356, then Peking from
1409)   1368-1644

Manchu, or *Ch'ing*, likewise masters of all China (capital
Peking)   1644-1912

Chinese Republic   1912
(capital Peking from 1912, then Nanking from
1928, and again Peking from 1949).

INDEX

abhaya-mudrā, see gesture
ādhi-Buddha 191
agriculture, sedentary 4
'aircraft views' and landscape painting 251n.
alchemy 123
altars, Buddhist 158, 173; of Heaven, Agriculture, Earth, in Peking 290
Amidism 140, 143, 163, 172, 192, 272-3
Amitābha (A-mi-t'o) 136, 137, 140, 143, 156, 163, 166, 268; paintings of 223, 224, 226, 228
Amitāyus (Wu-liang-shou) 140
Amoghavajra, Buddhist missionary 191, 218
An Lu-shan, leader of revolt (T'ang) 233
An Shih-kao, first translator of Buddhist scriptures 140, 142
An-yang, art of 11-30
Ancestor worship 13, 34, 58, 59, 91
'animal art' of the steppes 30, 37n., 40, 44, 47, 52, 102; route of transmission of 152 (See also Ordos art)
animal representation, on bronzes 17-25, 26-30, 32, 33, 37n., 38, 52, 84; on lacquer 82; on Han reliefs 87, 90, 93; in statuettes 94, 95, 96, 98, 105, 128, 129, 211; on pottery 6, 105, 106; on murals 133; on steles 164; on mirrors 205-6
apsaras 158, 167, 168, 173, 182, 217n., 220, 222, 287
architecture 238, 275, 290, 292
arhat (lo-han), Buddhist saints 150, 166; portraits of 235, 268n., 271, 284
Asanga, Buddhist metaphysician 183

Astana, tombs of 209, 210n., 211
Avalokiteśvara (Kuan-yin) 136, 137, 156, 163; transformation of into Kuan-yin 268; paintings of 219, 225, 228, 229, 287; wood-cut of 297
Avars 164n., 221

Baichajyaguru 223
bamboo, the painting of 271, 295
'Bamboo Annals, The' 4n.
Bāmiyān 149n., 150, 215
'Barbary Road', the 151-2
bas-reliefs, see reliefs
battle scenes, on Han reliefs 90
bells *(chung)* 33, 37, 39
belt buckles 100, 101
Bezeklik 211n., 217-18, 224
Bhaiṣajya, painting of 228
bhūtatathāta 190, 191, 243
birds 20, 38, 44, 45, 93, 222, 258
'birds and flowers' in painting 236; in prints 298, 307; on porcelain 305
blanc-de-Chine porcelain 295, 300
Blue-and-white porcelain 293, 295, 304
Bodhidharma 146, 147, 235
Bodhisattvas 134, 135, 136, 137, 141; statues of 155, 156, 157, 158, 159, 160, 161, 166, 167, 168, 174, 175, 187, 188, 189, 190; paintings of 218, 222, 223, 224, 226, 229, 286, 298 (See also under Avalokiteśvara, Kṣitigarbha, Maitreya, Mañjuśrī, Samantabhadra, Vajrapāṇi)
Bodhisri, Buddhist missionary 172
Boxers (Ch'üan-fei) 308n.
bronze: chariot ornaments 24, 42; cultures 10, 11; harness adornments 24,

48; technique, transmission of to China 11, 12, 13; technique, regional schools in 74; vases and vessels: Shang 6-8, 13, 14, 15-23, 26-30; Yin-Chou transitional 31-2; Middle Chou 32-4; 'Huai' or 'Warring States' style 36-40, 43-52, 68, 80; Han 84-6, 103; Ming 291. Weapons 24-5, 29, 30, 42, 47, 48
Buddhabhadra, Buddhist missionary 146
Buddhas 134, 135, 136, 137, 141, 142, 190; statues of 150, 154, 155, 158, 159, 161, 162, 165, 168, 173, 188; paintings of 182, 222, 223, 224, 286 (See also under Amitābha, Śākyamuni, Vairocana)
Buddhism: and 'Silk Road' 78; as a religion of salvation 120, 137, 166; transformation of into a new religion 134, 137, 138; propagation of 135, 138, 140, 141-8; and Taoism 141-4, 156, 274; Chinese 148; and Confucianism 144, 180, 204, 274; antipathy to and prohibitions against 149, 170, 180, 181, 204-5, 238; furthering of and favour towards 149, 170, 184, 185, 273, 284; Chinese, history of 185; disappearance of in India 239; Tantric 190 (See also Amidism, Ch'an, T'ien-t'ai, White Lotus)
Buddhist apologetics 142, 143, 144; — art 134, 141, 149-151, 153-162, 164-9, 172-5, 182, 183, 186-190, 192-4, 215-220, 222-230, 286, 287, 298; — caves 149-151, 153, 157, 159, 161, 165, 166, 168, 172, 181, 182, 186, 215-16, 221-2, 225-230; — iconography 134, 135, 136, 156, 184; — scriptures 179, 180, 181, 183; — scriptures, translation of 140, 141, 145, 146, 148, 184, 185
Buddhistic communities 78, 139, 140; admittance of to China in Taoist disguise 142

camels 128, 129, 207, 208, 212, 219
caves, see Buddhist caves
celadons (ch'ing-tz'u) 127-8, 280-1, 288, 293
Chang Chiao and Chang Lu, founders of Taoist church 111

Chang Fei, Three Kingdoms hero 115
Chang Seng-yu, Six Dynasties painter 236n.
Chang Ta-chien, present-day painter 312, 313
ceramics, see pottery
Ch'an Buddhism, beginnings of 146-7; and Taoism 147, 249; and art 162, 235, 236, 249-51, 265-8, 284, 306; and Wang Yang-ming 301, 307
Ch'ang-an, Han capital 69, 114; a centre of Buddhism 145, 146; Sui capital 170; T'ang capital 180, 184, 186, 193, 200, 202, 205, 212, 234; Sogdian trade colony at 221
Chao Meng-fu, Yüan painter 285-6
Chao Po-chü, Sung painter 261
Chao Ta-nien, Sung painter 255
Ch'ao Wu-chi, present-day painter 313
chen-jen, 'True Man', Taoist term used by early translators for arhat 142
Chen Shu-jen, modern painter 312
Chen-yen-tsung, Tantric Buddhist sect 190-2
Ch'en Hung, writer of romances 203
Ch'en Tu-hsiu, promoter of language reform 310
Ch'en Tzu-ang, T'ang poet 197
Ch'eng Hao and Ch'eng I, Sung philosophers 243
Ch'i Pai-shih, present-day painter 313
Ch'i-tan (Khitai) Tartars, founders of Liao dynasty 236, 258-261, 273, 274
chia, type of bronze vase 15, 16, 27
Chia-ch'ing, Ch'ing emperor 272, 290, 292
Chiang Kai-shek 311
Chiang Ts'an, Sung painter 261
ch'iang, halberd 24, 26
Chieh-tzu yüan hua-chuan, 'Manual of the Mustard-seed Garden' 297
chien ware (pottery) 281
Chien-an poetry 113, 114
Ch'ien Han Shu, 'History of Early Han' 80
Ch'ien Hsüan, Yüan painter 285n.
Ch'ien-lung, Ch'ing emperor 272, 303
chih, type of bronze vase 28
Chih Ch'ien, translated life of Śākyamuni 142
Chih-i, founder of the T'ien-t'ai sect 148, 171

41.